Contemporary Political Theory

CONTEMPORARY POLITICAL THEORY

Andrew Shorten

macmillan
international
HIGHER EDUCATION

RED GLOBE
PRESS

First published 2016 by
RED GLOBE PRESS

Red Globe Press in the UK is an imprint of Springer Nature Limited,
registered in England, company number 785998, of 4 Crinan Street,
London, N1 9XW.

Red Globe Press® is a registered trademark in the United States,
the United Kingdom, Europe and other countries.

ISBN 978–1–137–29914–7   ISBN 978–1–137–29916–1 (eBook)

This book is printed on paper suitable for recycling and made from fully
managed and sustained forest sources. Logging, pulping and manufacturing
processes are expected to conform to the environmental regulations
of the country of origin.

A catalogue record for this book is available from the British Library.

A catalog record for this book is available from the Library of Congress.

For Catherine

Contents

List of Tables/Boxes

Tables

Boxes

Acknowledgements

The most difficult parts of this book were written whilst I was a Visiting Fellow in the Institute of Philosophy at the University of London. I would like to thank the members of the Institute for their hospitality, and especially Shahrar Ali. From the University of Limerick, I would like to thank my colleagues in the Department of Politics and Public Administration for temporarily relieving me of teaching duties, and also the Faculty of Arts, Humanities and Social Sciences, who provided additional teaching relief to allow me to bring the project to a close. I would also like to thank the multiple cohorts of students at Limerick who have unwittingly sat through different variations of the material contained in this book. Their bafflement, enthusiasm and constructive engagement alike helped me to see what worked, what didn't, and what needed more work.

One of the aims of this book is to help students to realise that they can do political theory for themselves. For myself, I was extremely fortunate to first encounter the discipline as a pupil at what was then South Wolds Comprehensive School. It is regrettable that too few schoolchildren in the English-speaking world are exposed to philosophy in general, and especially political theory. I am glad for being one of the lucky few. Later, I was also fortunate enough to learn from three different but equally vibrant groups of political theorists and philosophers, initially as an undergraduate at the University of York, then as a graduate student at the University of Manchester, and later as a postdoctoral fellow at University College London. Each of these institutions, and many of the people I encountered in them, made lasting impressions on what I take political theory to be and what I think political theorists ought to try to do. As such, they shaped this book in more ways than I am probably aware of, and I would like to record my gratitude to them.

I would also like to thank Richard Shorten, who read a complete draft of the book at short notice, and provided some very helpful feedback. The three anonymous referees from Palgrave did an admirably thorough job and also helped save me from some unnecessary blunders. Moreover, they restored my confidence as I began work on the final draft, for which I am extremely grateful. Stephen Kennedy and, later, Lloyd Langman, were an invaluable source of advice at various stages in the project, especially at the beginning and the end.

Finally, I would also like to thank Catherine O'Mullane, to whom the book is dedicated. She has patiently tolerated frequent absences, both short- and long-term, and taken up the slack on many other fronts. She has also been a consistent source of kindness, support and care, as well as an excellent judge of when enough writing has been done for the day. I do not know if I would have completed the book without her, but I am sure that writing it would have been a less pleasant experience.

1
Introduction

What is political theory?

Political theory describes an activity rather than a body of knowledge – it is something we 'do' rather than something we 'know about', and we do political theory whenever we reason and argue about important political questions. This book aims to help you to become better at these activities by introducing you to some of the most important arguments to have been proposed by political theorists writing today and in the recent past, focussing mostly on work that has been produced in the last three decades. Exploring how these authors develop their theories and probe those of their rivals will help you to better understand what is at stake in political argument and what you yourself think about important issues. Moreover, it will also help you to make arguments for yourself and to evaluate those you come across in ordinary political life.

At its most basic, political theory involves asking and trying to answer questions about how we ought to live together. Thus, for example, you are doing political theory when you ask about how to design taxation systems or environmental policies, or whether we ought to modify the electoral system or constitution. You are also doing political theory when you ask more challenging questions, such as whether you always have a duty to obey the law, or whether the citizens of wealthy states ought to be doing more to alleviate global poverty. Often, professional political theorists address these questions by asking different ones, which are more abstract and less familiar, such as questions about the nature and value of things like democracy, equality, freedom, justice and rights. Although these questions are less frequently the subject of heated discussions in pubs or at the dinner table, they are just as important for people who care about politics and ideas.

This book aims to give you an overview of contemporary political theory, equipping you to explore the field for yourself and to engage with the arguments of political theorists. As will become clear, contemporary political theorists have addressed a very wide range of questions, topics and issues. We will focus on two of their main preoccupations, both of which concern how we ought to arrange our societies. The first of these has to do with the possibilities and challenges of democratic community, and it will be our focus throughout Chapters 2–6. Political theorists have addressed this not only by thinking carefully about the nature and practice of democracy itself, but also by thinking about how political representatives ought to act, about the ways in which political communities might be bound together, about the challenges of accommodating diversity and disagreement, and about democracy's complex relationships with power and domination. The second major preoccupation of contemporary political theorists has to do with the concepts of freedom, equality, justice and rights, and how they relate to one another. Although these are values that nearly everybody supports, there is not much agreement about what exactly they consist in or about how they ought to be realised. As we shall see in Chapters 7–10, considerable portions of contemporary political theory have been devoted to trying to elucidate a compelling theory of each of these concepts, to mapping their various relations, and to criticising the attempts of others to do the same.

In the remainder of this introduction we will briefly examine the recent history of the discipline of political theory, discuss some of the methods and tools used by its practitioners, and set out the plan for the remaining chapters. Before doing anything else, however, it will be helpful to set out more carefully what I understand political theory to be. Political theory is an activity in which we try to figure out how we ought to arrange our collective affairs. Like other branches of philosophy, it proceeds by making arguments, and these arguments are evaluated according to the standards of reason. It is distinguished from other parts of philosophy by its subject matter – politics. Exactly what qualifies as 'political' is a deeply contested matter. Certainly, the activities of governments and the institutions of states count, as arguably do things like the organisation of the family, personal relationships and the construction of identities. Meanwhile, some people think that politics is present wherever there is power, and since power is ubiquitous to social life then nearly everything should be up for scrutiny by political theorists. In this book I do not intentionally exclude anything from the domain of 'the political'. However, many of the authors we will examine endorse much narrower conceptions, and most of the topics we shall cover concern the values and concepts that have been traditionally associated with political life.

We can get a clearer sense of the subject domain of political theory by considering some of the questions that political theorists address. Historically, the most important of these concerned the nature and justification of political rule, also understood to include the extent of legitimate government. This was the primary concern of the classical political theorists, who included Thomas Hobbes and John Locke in the seventeenth century, and Jean-Jacques Rousseau, David Hume and Immanuel Kant in the eighteenth century. With the development of capitalism and the emergence of institutions of representative government, political theorists began to develop new interests and agendas. In particular, they more frequently came to ask about the distribution of important social goods, including political power as well as money and opportunities. For example, during the eighteenth century early feminists like Mary Wollstonecraft questioned the exclusion of women from civil and political rights, whilst in the eighteenth and nineteenth centuries utilitarian political theorists like Jeremy Bentham, John Stuart Mill and Henry Sidgwick argued forcefully that it was the business of government to improve the well-being of ordinary people.

As we shall see in this book, contemporary political theorists have extended this repertoire considerably. For example, they have developed intricate and sophisticated theories about democracy, community, freedom, equality and justice. Moreover, they have confronted difficult questions about the possibility of establishing legitimate political institutions amongst people who disagree deeply about religion and ethics, and they have drawn attention to complex machinations of power and to the covert forms of domination sustained by contemporary social formations. The methods they have used to do these things vary considerably. Sometimes they use theories in a critical manner, in order to bring particular forms of oppression or injustice to the forefront of our attentions. In other cases they proceed by proposing, developing and criticising principles that can be used to evaluate or govern our social institutions and collective lives.

A distinctive feature of contemporary political theory is its normative orientation, which means that it is concerned with how the world ought to be, rather than how it actually is. In this respect it is distinguished from political science, which aims to explain how politics works, and whose practitioners are often suspicious of what they regard as the moralising tendencies of political theorists. We shall return to the relationship between political science and political theory shortly. Another distinction is sometimes drawn between political philosophy and political theory. Sometimes people mark this by saying that political philosophy is what people employed in philosophy departments do, and political theory is what people employed in departments of politics or political science do (Barry, 1981). This is probably about as accurate a line as can be drawn. In any case, there is nothing that political philosophers do that does not also qualify as political theory, whilst there is quite a lot that political theorists do that arguably does not qualify as political philosophy. Hence, although I will treat this pair as synonyms in this book, unless it would be distracting to do otherwise I will favour the term political theory.

The description of political theory that I have just given excludes many important branches of scholarly inquiry that are pursued by political theorists. These include the study of the history of political thought, the analysis and comparison of political ideologies, the explanation of the emergence and development of political ideas, and attempts to trace the influence of political ideas on actual politics, amongst other things. All of these areas of study are important, both in terms of grasping the ideational components of political life and in terms of explaining how we have arrived at our current predicament. However, these various projects only indirectly address the normative issues that are at the heart of this book, and for that reason I will not consider them in depth here.

The recent history of political theory

This book aims to familiarise you with some of the most significant disagreements amongst contemporary political theorists. Although we will focus on writings from the last three decades, often we will need to go back further, because many current debates continue to be influenced by earlier authors and texts. For example, contemporary theories of representation, which we shall examine in Chapter 4, are informed by concepts and categories developed by Hanna Pitkin in her *The Concept of Representation*, published in 1967. Similarly, as discussed in Chapter 5, an important reference point for contemporary democratic theorists is Joseph Schumpeter's *Capitalism, Socialism and Democracy*, originally published in 1942. Meanwhile, contemporary discussions of power, which are examined in Chapter 6, have been conducted under the shadow of the 'community power' debates, which took place during the 1950s and 1960s. Likewise, as we shall see in Chapter 7, current debates about freedom still take place within terms that Isaiah Berlin set out during his inaugural lecture at the University of Oxford, which was delivered in 1958. Finally, and perhaps most importantly, large chunks of contemporary political theory owe a significant debt to the work of John Rawls, and especially his *A Theory of Justice*, which was first published in 1971.

In order to situate the various debates that are the primary subject matter of this book, it will be helpful to begin by sketching out some of the most important trends amongst political theorists working during the second half of the twentieth century, and this is what I aim to do here. Selecting a starting point for this kind of a survey is to some extent an arbitrary decision. We will start with Peter Laslett's famous declaration of 1956 that '[f]or the moment anyway, political philosophy is dead' (1956, p. vii). This statement is symbolically significant because it marks a relatively fallow phase in the development of political theory, which as we shall see, was to persist until the 1970s.

In at least one sense, Laslett's claim was clearly an exaggeration, since numerous important contributions to political theory had been published in the preceding years. Amongst many others, these included Friedrich Hayek's *Road to Serfdom* (in 1944), Karl Popper's two-volume *The Open Society and Its Enemies* (in 1945), Theodor Adorno and Max Horkheimer's *Dialectic of Enlightenment* (in 1947) and Hannah Arendt's *The Origins of Totalitarianism* (in 1951). Moreover, in the years immediately following Laslett's declaration, Arendt was to publish her *The Human Condition* (in 1958), Berlin gave his famous lecture (also in 1958) and Stanley Benn and Richard Peters published their *Social Principles and the Democratic State* (in 1959). Further, Rawls had begun to publish important papers that were to become part of his *A Theory of Justice*, which from the current vantage point is the most important recent contribution to the discipline.

So why, then, did Laslett declare political philosophy to be dead? The main reason he gave was that it had been 'killed' by 'logical positivism', which had 'called into question the logical status of all ethical statements' and raised the question 'of whether political philosophy is possible at all' (Laslett, 1956, p. ix). Logical positivism was a philosophical doctrine that came to prominence in the 1920s and 1930s. According to this view, statements about values were best seen as expressing emotions, or conveying an imprecise sentiment of approval or disapproval. The logical positivists suspected that since much of what passed for political theory could neither be verified empirically nor proven by logical reasoning alone, it contained little of scientific or philosophical value. The influence of these ideas on the profession of philosophy was profound, and they led to the dispersal of a distinctively modest view about the discipline's central purpose, which was to explicate the meaning of concepts through linguistic analysis. As this approach took hold, it began to seem as if it were simply 'a mistake to suppose that the true business of moral, social and political philosophy can ever be to provide us with reasoned defences of particular ideals or practices' (Skinner, 1985, p. 4). Beyond the realm of philosophy, other developments in political science also contributed to political theory's relative torpor, such as the emergence of behaviouralism and rational choice theory, as well as the aspiration to develop a dispassionate, value-free and scientific approach to the study of politics and society.

Perhaps logical positivism and the emergence of modern empirical political science succeeded in deflating some of the ambitions of political theorists. However, they did not kill them off entirely, and two important strands of political theory continued to develop during this period, albeit largely in isolation from one another. The first of these emerged from the 'community power' debates, which had divided 'elitists' and 'pluralists' working in political science and sociology departments in the United States. Elitists believed that dominant political institutions had been captured by an elite, who used their control to advance the interests of the wealthy. On the opposite side, pluralists believed that power was dispersed rather than concentrated, and that different groups in society were able to influence political decisions. As we shall see in Chapter 6, radical critics of pluralism – such as Peter Bachrach and Morton Baratz (1962, 1963), as well as Stephen Lukes (2005) – believed that this view was mistaken because of shortcomings in its understanding of power, and they instead developed more complex two- and three-dimensional views.

The 'community power' debates also influenced debates about democracy, since the pluralist view was aligned with the 'competitive' theory of democracy, which had already been developed by the economist Joseph Schumpeter and which we will explore in Chapter 5. Amongst other things, this theory was relaxed about political apathy, and understood democracy to be nothing more than a 'method' for selecting governments. Again, this theory was criticised by radical political theorists, such as Carole Pateman (1970) and C. B. Macpherson (1973, 1977), whose arguments we will also explore in Chapter 5 and who argued that voter apathy reflected a failure of existing democratic systems. To rehabilitate democratic life, they argued for a more active model of democracy, which was as much concerned with associational life and workplace decision making as with elections and political parties. The underlying concerns of the participatory democrats were also to influence other subsequent developments in political theory, such as the communitarian critique of liberalism, which emerged during the 1980s, theories of agonistic pluralism, which emerged during the 1990s, and republican theories of freedom, which were recovered during the 1990s. We shall examine each of these in Chapters 2, 3 and 7 respectively.

The second strand of political theory during this period remained at least partially within the confines of the logical positivist revolution, since it identified the analysis of political concepts as the central activity of political theory. This ambition was reflected in the title of probably the best known logical positivist work on political philosophy, T. D. Weldon's *The Vocabulary of Politics*, published in 1953. On Weldon's account, the task of the political theorist was to eliminate unnecessary confusions by clarifying the meanings of basic political terms. As we have seen, logical positivists believed that trying to do more than this took political philosophers beyond the domain of philosophy proper, and was therefore to be avoided. Although later political theorists often rejected this austere account of the scope of their profession, they retained Weldon's emphasis on conceptual analysis, and the 1950s and 1960s saw the publication of important works on the concepts of freedom (Berlin, 2002), equality (Williams, 1962), democracy (Wollheim, 1962), rights (Hart, 1961, 1984) and representation (Pitkin, 1967).

It was from within this second strand of political theory that the most important development in twentieth-century political theory took place, namely the emergence of systematic and ambitious theorising about the concept of justice. At the centre of these developments was John Rawls's *A Theory of Justice* (1999a). Rawls held a much more ambitious view about the role of political philosophy than the one implied by logical positivism, which in a later work he described as 'the defence of reasonable faith in the possibility of a just constitutional regime' (1996, p. 172). The conception of a just society that Rawls developed sought to reconcile the values of freedom and equality. Freedom was to be honoured by ensuring that each person has as much of it as possible, and equality was to be vindicated by guaranteeing genuine equality of opportunity and by seriously restricting the range of permissible economic inequalities.

The details of Rawls's theory of justice as fairness are examined in Chapter 9. For the moment, we should note four points about its influence on subsequent political theory. First, that influence was immense. For example, in a not untypical formulation, Richard Arneson credits Rawls with having 'single-handedly revived Anglo-American political philosophy' (2006, p. 45). Second, Rawls widened the scope of political theory by demonstrating that 'grand' political theory was possible, in the tradition of Hobbes, Locke, Rousseau, Kant, Mill and Sidgwick. In doing so, he contributed to overcoming the restrictive vision that had been imposed by logical positivism. Third, Rawls helped to establish liberalism, and especially liberal egalitarianism, as the dominant mode of political theory. Whilst late nineteenth- and early twentieth-century moral and political philosophers generally took utilitarianism as their starting point, subsequent generations of political theorists were to be defined by the attitude they took towards liberalism, and especially towards Rawls's own theory. Fourth, he put the concept of distributive justice at the centre of political theory. As we shall see in Chapter 9, some 'realist' political theorists have recently complained about the tendency of contemporary political theorists to equate political theory with theorising about justice. Whatever we make of objections like these, the emergence of this predicament reflects Rawls's enduring influence on the discipline.

Rawls's theory attracted intense controversy, and the terms of much subsequent political theory were defined by disagreements that were inspired by his work. Three of these supply much of the subject matter for Chapters 8–10. First are disputes about the substance of justice, and Rawls was criticised from both the left and the right. Whilst right-wing libertarians appealed to a principle of self-ownership to criticise redistributive taxation and the welfare state, left-wing egalitarians and socialists argued that Rawls's theory did not take equality seriously enough, and suggested alternative and more demanding theories of distributive and social equality. Second are disagreements about the subject matter of justice, which Rawls had identified as being how the major institutions of a society distribute resources. Whilst feminists, communitarians and socialists all objected to Rawls's focus on institutions, some egalitarians also objected to his emphasis on resources, suggesting that we should be more interested in how other things are distributed, such as human well-being or people's effective opportunities. Third are disagreements about the scope of justice, and especially about whether principles of justice should only apply within the confines of an existing political community. In a later work, called *The Law of Peoples* (1999b), Rawls outlined a 'realistically utopian' vision of international society, in which wealthy states have only very limited obligations to improve the circumstances of the global poor. This was subsequently criticised by cosmopolitans, who argued that the logic of his earlier argument demanded the global application of his principles of justice.

Rawls's work also inspired another cluster of disagreements that were to dominate political theory during the 1980s. These were the liberal-communitarian debates, which ranged over a number of topics and involved a lengthy cast of participants, including liberals like Rawls, Ronald Dworkin, Joseph Raz and Richard Rorty, and communitarians like Alasdair MacIntyre, Michael Sandel, Charles Taylor and Michael Walzer. At its most basic, liberalism describes the view that people should be treated as both free and equal. A liberal society treats people as equals by equipping them with the same set of rights, and it respects their freedom by allowing them to pursue their own freely chosen ends. Communitarians registered two objections against this view. First, they said that liberalism neglected the many different forms of communal solidarity that are to be found in the real world, since it treats individuals as strangers to one another and because it underestimates the extent to which individuals are 'constituted' by their societies and social memberships. During the 1990s, as we shall see in Chapter 2, some liberals responded to this by reviving earlier liberal nationalist theories, or by developing new theories of constitutional patriotism. Meanwhile, some multiculturalists developed a twist on the communitarian critique, drawing attention to the significance of cultural memberships for minorities. The second communitarian critique said that liberalism could only be justified by appealing to controversial assumptions that are not universally shared, such as the significance of choosing one's own plan of life. Whilst liberals continue to disagree about the force of this objection, Rawls attempted to answer this challenge in his second major work – *Political Liberalism* (1996) – which we shall examine in Chapter 3. Here he addressed the problem of formulating shared political principles in a society characterised by 'reasonable pluralism', in which people disagree about the ultimate ends of human life and about the purposes of political association. Rawls was optimistic about the prospects of reaching an 'overlapping consensus' about terms and values of social co-operation. Meanwhile, his critics suggested that his optimism was unjustified and that the pursuit of consensus was too costly, either because it conceded too much to illiberal and inegalitarian worldviews, or because it required an unacceptably restrictive mode of political discussion.

Although much political theory since the 1970s was inspired by Rawls's contribution, there are some other strands of work that developed in a relatively independent manner. One of the most important of these was the 'deliberative turn' in democratic theory, which took hold during the 1990s (Dryzek, 2000). As we have seen, an earlier generation of participatory democratic theorists had criticised the then dominant theories of competitive democracy for being insufficiently attentive to political participation. Like them, a new wave of deliberative democrats also criticised the identification of democracy with elections and voting. Moreover, they drew attention to the significance of deliberation and developed an intricate theory of democracy that equated it with a procedure in which citizens exchange arguments with one another about how to arrange their common affairs. Perhaps optimistically, these theorists believe that if citizens talk and listen to one another, they are more likely to overcome their prejudices and biases, and to make better and more informed decisions. As we shall see in Chapter 5, critics of deliberative democracy have questioned the feasibility, as well as the attractiveness, of this theory.

Another important trend in recent political theory has been an increased emphasis on sexual, cultural and gender identities. In some cases, this reflects a response on the part of political theorists to more worldly considerations. For example, as explained in Chapters 2 and 3, political theorists began to ask questions about the accommodation of religious, cultural and national minorities in the wake of real-world challenges to the ideal of a homogeneous nation-state. Similarly, as noted in Chapter 4, debates about the political representation of women and minorities took shape after calls for all-women shortlists and special representation rights for cultural groups had become a familiar feature of the political landscape. In other cases, theoretical developments in one domain influenced the ways in which other topics were addressed. This can be seen most clearly in the case of feminism. For example, the idea that inequality is perpetuated in familial and domestic life was eventually to have a significant impact on theories of justice and equality, as we shall see in Chapters 8 and 9. Similarly, feminist analyses of gender, subordination and oppression were to greatly shape developments in the understandings of power, domination and freedom, as explained in Chapters 6 and 7.

Whilst most contemporary political theory continues to utilise the tools and approaches of mainstream 'analytic' or 'Anglo-American' political theory, this paradigm has been consistently challenged by postmodernist and poststructuralist theorists, as we shall see in Chapters 3, 4 and 6. One of the most significant features of this approach is the attention that it gives to the complexities of the multiple operations of power. For example, according to Michel Foucault, whose work is examined in Chapter 6, power is less about repressing people or issuing commands, and more about producing identities and ways of living. The implications of this approach for many questions in political theory remain unclear, and many political theorists are deeply sceptical about it (Taylor, 1985; Habermas, 1990). However, as explained in Chapters 3 and 4, poststructuralism has had a significant impact on how some political theorists think about difference, democracy and representation.

Finally, perhaps the most significant trend of political theory in the last decade has been the increased attention given over to global issues. Earlier political theorists had generally envisaged political theory as a domestic enterprise, with only limited applications to international society. Likewise, they often engaged in local debates, amongst scholars writing in their own languages and usually from their own societies. The various debates about human rights, triggered by the post-1945 reforms in international society, were an important exception to this, which we shall examine in Chapter 10. More recently, political theorists have begun to more seriously confront the challenges of globalisation. For example, they have begun to ask difficult questions about the possibilities of global society and global democracy – discussed in Chapters 2–5 – and about the obligations of the global rich to the global poor – as we shall see in Chapters 7–9. Moreover, as explained in Chapter 6, North American and European political theorists have begun to look beyond the confines of their own traditions by engaging more seriously with the writings of non-Western philosophers and political theorists.

Some useful tools, methods and distinctions

In this book, we are mostly concerned with exploring some of the answers that political theorists have given to two different kinds of questions. First are questions about concepts, which usually take the form 'What is such-and-such?'. For example, in the subsequent chapters we will compare some of the different answers that contemporary political theorists have given to questions such as 'What is political community?', 'What is democracy?', 'What is representation?', 'What is power?', and so forth. Second are normative questions, which concern how the world ought to be. Often political theorists answer these by attempting to identify the principles and values that we should use to evaluate our social and political affairs. Because conceptual analysis and normative reasoning are two of the most important approaches used by contemporary political theorists, this section will explore some of the tools and methods that political theorists use to do them.

Conceptual questions are fundamental to political theory, since if we are to make sense of the political views of other people, we need to understand what they intend. Indeed, unless we do this there is a real danger that we will end up talking past one another. Sometimes political concepts play a clear and relatively unambiguous role in political debate. For example, whilst market capitalists are generally 'for' freedom, many religious fundamentalists are 'against' it, and whilst the political left is generally 'for' equality, the political right is typically 'against' it. However, often things are not as simple as they seem. For example, many on the political right are not opposed to equality *per se*, only to an interpretation of it that requires the redistribution of property or wealth. In another – perhaps weaker or more formal – sense, they are 'for' equality, since they mostly believe that citizens should have an equal right to vote and should be treated as equals before the law. Moreover, as we shall see in Chapter 7, political theorists from both left- and right-wing traditions – including egalitarian socialists and market capitalists – are 'for' freedom, but generally mean quite different things by it. Likewise, although nearly everyone favours justice and democracy, they disagree deeply about what these things require.

One reason why some political concepts are so confusing might be because they are 'essentially contested' (Gallie, 1956). To describe a concept as 'essentially contested' means something stronger than observing that it is the subject of fierce disagreement. Rather, this term of art aims to capture the sense in which disagreements about some concepts are unresolvable, because the concepts themselves are 'permanently and essentially subject to revision and question' (Hampshire, 1965, p. 230). Amongst other things, this means that the criteria governing the application of an essentially contested concept are not agreed upon, and that disputes about their proper use cannot be settled rationally by appealing to facts, language or logic. For example, consider democracy. To say that this concept is contested in the simple sense is to say that people disagree about what it is. This is certainly true, since as we shall see in Chapter 5, some people believe that democracy is really about voting for candidates and political parties whilst others say that it involves citizens directly participating in self-government. Meanwhile, to say that democracy is *essentially* contested is to add the claim that this disagreement cannot be rationally resolved – that we can never have adequate grounds for saying that one or the other vision is closer to the 'true' ideal of democracy. If democracy really is essentially contested, then although adherents of different definitions might learn something by arguing with one another, they cannot resolve their disagreements by appealing to an uncontroversial and overarching definition or principle.

Essentially contested concepts are not unique to political theory. For example, art might qualify as one, as might religion and science. However, essentially contested concepts are arguably a pervasive feature of the subject domain of political theory. Indeed, a case can be made for saying that each of the nine concepts that we focus on in this book is essentially contested. This is a controversial claim, and as we shall see, many political theorists reject it (for example, as explained in Chapter 6, some political theorists argue that power cannot qualify as an essentially contested concept, since they deny that it is an evaluative concept).

One reason why some people worry about describing concepts like liberty, justice or democracy as essentially contested is that doing so might license an 'anything goes' attitude, in which all possible definitions of contested concepts are thought to be equally plausible. This possibility can be resisted if we keep in mind an important distinction between 'concepts' and 'conceptions', which was introduced by legal philosopher H. L. A. Hart (1961). Hart noticed that people can disagree about something whilst agreeing about what it is that they are talking about. For instance, people who disagree about whether democracy is mainly about voting or mainly about participation nevertheless agree that democracy is definitely not about the configuration of the planets. Thus, despite their disagreements they share a general sense of what democracy is. Hart labelled the general structure that underlies disagreements like these the 'concept', and contrasted it with the different 'conceptions' that people endorse. For example, as we shall see in Chapters 8 and 9, political theorists endorse a variety of different conceptions of justice, sometimes favouring and sometimes opposing redistributive taxation. Notwithstanding this, they mostly agree about the 'concept' of justice, which is about giving people what they are due. Their disagreements are, in a sense, secondary, since they concern how to fill the basic concept out. Thus, equipped with Hart's distinction, we can say that people who disagree about things like justice, democracy, power, freedom and rights endorse different 'conceptions' of the same 'concepts'. Importantly, the distinction between concepts and conceptions does not depend on a concept being essentially contested, since it might turn out to be the case that one or another of the suggested conceptions is rationally preferable to all of the others.

Much contemporary political theory is normative in orientation. A normative theory is concerned with values, and normative principles specify how the world ought to be. For example, 'from each according to his abilities, to each according to his needs' is a normative principle that aims to explain how work and resources should be distributed. Similarly, 'people should obey democratic laws' is a normative principle that aims to explain the limits and justification of political obligation. Political theorists develop normative theories and principles for different reasons. Sometimes, they want to understand how different political values fit together, such as whether freedom and equality are in conflict with one another, or if justice requires upholding rights. Sometimes they want to evaluate actual policies, actions, practices or institutions, for instance by developing principles that can be used to measure the extent to which reality conforms to an ideal. Sometimes they want to make recommendations about what should be done, for instance by suggesting proposals of their own, or by critically evaluating the proposals suggested by others.

When political theorists engage in normative theorising, they are trying to describe how things ought to be, rather than how they actually are. Normative theories are therefore unlike the explanatory theories developed and used by political scientists. Those theories aim to explain the causal relations between different phenomena, such as class membership and voting behaviour, or poverty and political radicalism. Most political scientists are involved in a descriptive enterprise, since they aim to describe the world of politics and to explain how it actually operates in a value-neutral way, without allowing their own prejudices and biases to contaminate their research. Meanwhile, most political theorists are engaged in normative enterprises, and their theories directly address values themselves. For instance, when normative political theorists think about democracy and justice, they are usually only indirectly interested in how democratic procedures actually operate, or in how wealth and opportunities are currently distributed. For them, the main goal is to figure out how democratic procedures *should* operate, and how wealth and opportunities *should* be distributed.

The precise relationship between facts and values in political theory has recently become a source of contention. Whilst some political theorists believe that normative principles, such as principles of justice, are timeless and fact-free (e.g. Cohen, 2008), others believe that they depend on both general facts about human beings and specific facts about particular groups of people (e.g. Miller, 2013). One reason for thinking that political principles depend on facts is because of a concern about feasibility. For instance, recall the principle 'from each according to his ability, to each according to his needs'. Critics of this principle allege that it is impossibly demanding, since it requires some people to work harder than others without offering them anything more in return. As a result, these critics reject the principle on the basis of a factual claim about human psychology. In turn, a supporter of the principle might respond by disputing the factual claim at hand, for instance by arguing that human beings are capable of making altruistic sacrifices for one another. Notice, however, that this reply assumes that facts are relevant to determining the plausibility of normative principles. Against this, advocates of the fact-free view say that the truth of normative principles stands independently of all facts (Cohen, 2008). On this view, facts are relevant for the activities of political theorists only in the limited sense that they help us to know how principles might be applied, and they do not tell us whether the principles themselves are the right ones.

Political theorists have no privileged status when it comes to making normative statements, which are a ubiquitous feature of public life. For example, politicians often make normative claims during political campaigns, such as when they say that a particular manifesto pledge will further the cause of social justice or deepen the quality of democracy. Likewise, political activists, bloggers and newspaper columnists often make normative statements when they criticise the actions or policies of their government. Notwithstanding this, a training in political theory might improve someone's ability to evaluate normative statements, and in this respect political theory can potentially make three important contributions to real politics (Swift and White, 2008). First, it can help to clarify the principles and values invoked by politicians and others. For example, political theorists can set out arguments in support of or against them, they can draw attention to their implications and complexities, and they can demonstrate the ways in which some values and principles conflict with others. Second, political theory can also draw attention to implicit normative premises that politicians themselves may be prone to glossing over. For instance, discussions of the taxation system often take it for granted that adjustments to it should not compromise economic growth. This is a normative claim, about the priority of economic growth, which must be recognised as such in order for it to be evaluated. Third, political theory can also draw attention to alternative normative possibilities that are neglected by prominent political actors. For example, taxation systems might be designed with other goals in mind, such as promoting individual dignity or well-being, or reducing material inequality, or fostering a democratic community.

So far, we have seen that political theorists are especially interested in the normative aspects of politics, as well as the concepts that we refer to during political arguments. Some people, however, think that addressing normative questions is a fruitless exercise, since normative theories cannot be tested with the same degree of reliability as explanatory theories. For example, suppose that a political scientist thinks that citizens are less likely to vote for incumbent governments during a recession. This theory can be tested against the factual evidence, and it should be discarded if the facts disprove it, or at least modified so that it sits comfortably with them. Meanwhile, normative theories and principles cannot be falsified by the same procedure. For instance, suppose that a political theorist thinks that 'people should obey democratic laws'. Although the theorist might go out and ask people whether they believe this principle is true, this would only reveal the extent to which the principle is endorsed, and would tell us nothing (or at least very little) about the truth of the principle itself.

Political theorists have responded to this kind of scepticism in a number of ways, and here I will just mention one strategy, suggested by John Rawls. He starts from the observation that we have some considered judgements in which we are justifiably confident. For example, he thinks that our judgements about the injustice of religious intolerance and racial discrimination have been reached after careful consideration, and are unlikely to be the products of self-interest or ignorance (Rawls, 1999a, pp. 17–18). This suggests that just as scientists can test their theories against facts, political theorists can test their theories against judgements like these. Considered judgements are like fixed points, and in most cases it makes sense to modify or reject a theory if it yields results that are at odds with them. However, they are fixed points only in a provisional sense, since a distinctive feature of normative theories is that awareness of them might prompt us to revise our judgements (Rawls, 1999a, p. 49). For example, careful consideration of equality of opportunity might cause someone to alter their beliefs about what services should be provided for people with disabilities. In cases like these, it might be better to modify our judgements if they are at odds with the theory. According to Rawls, this is what political theorists should do. Specifically, they should move back and forth between their judgements and theories until the two are in a state of 'reflective equilibrium' with one another. A theorist achieves this when their judgements about particular cases are consistent with their general convictions, and when both of these are consistent with their philosophical views.

The structure of this book

This book will introduce you to the major puzzles, debates and approaches found in contemporary political theory. Each chapter summarises recent developments on a topic, describing the main problems, positions and protagonists, and introducing the most important arguments and texts. Although the chapters are organised thematically, we will focus on evaluating arguments, and we shall do so by addressing substantive disagreements that divide contemporary political theorists. Hopefully, this will enable you to form a sense of the relevant intellectual terrain without compromising on the complexity of the issues. In addition, throughout the book we will explore the implications of theoretical controversies by examining real-world examples.

In order to familiarise you with contemporary debates, it will be necessary to frame them against their appropriate intellectual backdrops. Consequently, the first half of each chapter will describe some of the different theories and approaches that have been taken to a particular topic. These are referred to as 'rival perspectives', and in the course of the book we will cover some of the most important views that have been canvassed by contemporary political theorists. Thus, when taken as a whole, these will give an indication of the breadth of contemporary political theory.

Although the book proceeds by comparing different perspectives, these are much less important than the arguments themselves. Whilst some of these perspectives represent distinctive traditions in political thought – such as liberalism, utilitarianism and republicanism – in many cases they are simply convenient labels for gathering together a cluster of related views and arguments. The advantage of arranging material in this way is that it helps to map out the relevant intellectual space, especially by drawing attention to some of the major fissures and tensions. However, the drawback is that it could give rise to the misleading impression that each perspective is an intellectually cohesive tradition that can be clearly separated from its rivals. As we shall see, this is rarely true. Not only are there important disagreements within most of the perspectives, but there are also significant commonalities across them. Furthermore, the depth of the disagreements between the different views varies considerably. Whilst some of the rivalries that we shall consider are more like sibling rivalries, or disagreements amongst friends, others are much deeper, and reflect fundamental disagreements about how to think about politics.

As will become clear, the different perspectives that we shall consider are connected to one another in complex ways. Sometimes this is because a particular perspective is relevant to more than one topic. For example, the liberal theory of community, which we will examine in Chapter 2, appears in another guise in Chapter 3, as a theory of pluralism. In other cases, it is because a particular political theorist, or group of political theorists, is associated with more than one perspective. For example, John Rawls is responsible for one of the theories of justice examined in Chapter 9 and for one of the theories of pluralism examined in Chapter 3. Likewise, the communitarians Charles Taylor and Michael Sandel, discussed in Chapter 2, also endorse a positive conception of liberty, which we shall examine in Chapter 7. Finally, perspectives in different chapters are also connected because they share intellectual affinities. For example, the theory of constitutive representation (Chapter 4) resembles the constitutive theory of power (Chapter 6) and also shares important features with the agonistic theory of pluralism (Chapter 3). Similarly, some multiculturalists and difference theorists (Chapter 2) also favour the descriptive theory of representation (Chapter 4) and have influenced theories of social equality (Chapter 9).

After setting out the various rival perspectives, the second half of each chapter will be dedicated to exploring some 'key debates'. Some of these will concern pressing issues of political morality, which we will address by comparing the answers of different rival perspectives. Others concern important theoretical divisions, and exploring them will help to illustrate why advocates of one view prefer their approach to another. Meanwhile, some of the key debates will focus narrowly on a single rival perspective. In some cases the key debate will reveal how and why proponents of the same rival perspective disagree about how best to formulate their position, and in others it will explore important criticisms that a particular theory has attracted. Because students of political theory often find it difficult to draw the connections between abstract theories and real-world politics, there will also be a number of 'discussion boxes' dispersed throughout the text, to enable you to explore some of the implications of the theoretical material under discussion.

Finally, each chapter concludes by considering some of the 'future challenges' that political theorists are likely to face. In many cases, these have arisen as a result of political theory's recent global turn. For example, in Chapter 4 we will explore how political theorists have begun to respond to the challenge of making international institutions more representative, whilst Chapters 2, 3 and 5 explore some different facets of the challenge of establishing democratic community in a deeply divided world. In other cases, these 'future challenges' reflect new areas of inquiry that are likely to set the agenda for political theorists in the years to come. For example, in Chapter 6 we will explore the prospects and challenges faced by calls for a comparative form of political theory, whilst in Chapter 9 we will consider some of the recent realist challenges to political moralism.

Political theory is an intellectually dynamic field and any attempt to give an overview of the current state of play is likely to face two different kinds of objection. First, some people will feel that important views have been neglected, or that their favoured views have not been given due prominence. Second, others may worry that important issues have been glossed over too quickly, and that they merit more detailed discussion. Both of these are undoubtedly true of *Contemporary Political Theory*. However, although this book aims to acquaint you with some of the most significant disagreements amongst contemporary political theorists, it does not aspire to offer a comprehensive snapshot of political theory as it currently stands. Instead, I hope to inspire you to further inquiry, to equip you to navigate the contemporary literature for yourself, and to enable you to engage independently with substantive issues in political theory, including those which fall beyond the scope of this work.

2

Political Community

Introduction

There are many different kinds of human association, such as households, families, companies, universities, trade unions, religious congregations and friendship groups. We explore political communities in this chapter, which are distinguished from these other associations by two things. First, they are more encompassing, since they establish the terms under which other associations regulate their affairs. Aristotle, for example, described the political community as the 'highest' community that 'embraces all the rest' (Aristotle, 1996, p. 11). Second, they are self-governing, in the sense that the community itself gives shape to its laws and is not controlled by an external authority. Increasingly, this has come to mean that political communities should be democratic communities, which means that members should – in principle at least – be given an equal say over how their common affairs are conducted. In Chapters 3 and 4 we will look at how a political community might realise the ideal of democracy, whilst Chapters 6–9 will explore some other important values that contemporary political communities have sought to honour. Meanwhile, in this chapter we will focus on the question of what it is that makes a political community a *community*.

According to one very general account, communities are forms of social friendship that dispose us to 'show special concern and loyalty to people with whom we share things' (Yack, 2012, p. 4). In the case of political communities, this definition leaves a number of issues open, such as what it is that members are supposed to share in common and what forms of concern and loyalty they are supposed to exhibit towards one another. In the first half of this chapter we will explore five rival perspectives, each of which supplies different answers to these questions, and which are summarised in Table 2.1. In the second half of the chapter we will compare these perspectives by exploring some important contemporary controversies about political membership.

As Table 2.1 illustrates, the wide range of views contemporary political theorists have endorsed about political community are connected to other disagreements they have about culture, democracy and human nature. In addition to these disagreements about what things are really like, political theorists also disagree about how things should be, and these normative disagreements also shape how different authors make sense of the ideal of political community. For example, the *liberal* theory of political community contains a moral thesis which says that members should share a moral concern for one another as free and equal citizens. Although this is a demanding ideal, liberalism does not require that citizens have much else in common with one another. Against this, *communitarians* argue that political community must be based on social bonds that are stronger or deeper than liberalism requires. For example, one communitarian has argued that ties of language, culture and history should bind members together to produce a 'collective consciousness' and a 'world of common meanings' (Walzer, 1983, p. 28). Meanwhile, *liberal nationalists* also criticise the conventional liberal theory of political community for being too thin, arguing that a shared national identity is a prerequisite for democracy and social justice. In turn, and against liberal nationalism and communitarianism, *constitutional patriots* favour a 'post-national' form of political identity in which members share common political values but not necessarily a common national identity. Finally, *multiculturalists* and *difference theorists* have developed a radical critique of traditional theories of political community, arguing against the 'homogenising' tendencies they associate with the other theories considered in this chapter.

These different theories about the *ideal* of political community have important implications for how we think about citizenship or political membership. Thus, in the second half of the chapter we will begin by looking at what the rights and duties of citizenship should be, focussing in particular on the question of whether these should be the same for everyone or if minority groups might be entitled to additional group-specific rights. In the developed world, controversies about minority rights have often arisen alongside other controversies relating to immigration, integration and citizenship acquisition. Consequently, we will also explore how the different theories of political community can provide different frameworks to address these issues. As should become clear, an important question in the immigration debate is whether immigration threatens democracy,

Table 2.1 Summary of rival perspectives on political community

	Liberalism	Communitarianism	Liberal Nationalism	Constitutional Patriotism	Multiculturalism / Difference Theory
What connects members to one another	Moral concern for one another as free and equal citizens	Shared understandings and common meanings, typically based on a shared history, culture or worldview	Shared nationality, based on a common history, language and/or culture	Shared commitment to democratic values and human rights	Members need not share a common culture, history, worldview, language or value system
Individuals and their communities	Individuals are 'prior to' their political communities.	Individuals are 'constituted' by their communities, including their political communities	Individuals are at least partially 'constituted' by their national communities, to which they have strong ties of affection	Individuals are 'prior to' their communities but ideally should have robust patriotic ties	Individuals are strongly attached to their cultural groups and/or traditions, and may have multiple and complex identities and/or affiliations
Disagreement about values	Value pluralism (within 'reasonable' limits) is a permanent and welcome feature of modern social life	Different political communities embody different worldviews; value pluralism potentially threatens the integrity of a political community	Value pluralism may be a welcome characteristic of political community but it must be compatible with a cohesive national culture	Agreement about fundamental political values is a prerequisite for a flourishing democracy	Different cultural groups may possess incompatible value systems and it may be unfair to 'impose' unfamiliar values on cultural groups
Cultural differences	Cultural differences are mostly irrelevant to political community	Cultural diversity can undermine political community if it jeopardises common projects or the shared moral life of society	Cultural pluralism is potentially threatening to democracy and political stability	Cultural differences are mostly irrelevant to political community, provided that worldviews are compatible with basic constitutional principles, such as equal respect	Cultural differences can be a source of socio-economic disadvantage; cultural traditions should be accommodated

Table 2.1 (Continued)

	Liberalism	Communitarianism	Liberal Nationalism	Constitutional Patriotism	Multiculturalism / Difference Theory
State neutrality and the promotion of values and culture	Accepts neutrality and rejects promoting particular conceptions of the good	Rejects neutrality and favours a 'politics of the common good'	Broadly accepts neutrality but also favours promoting national cultures	Broadly accepts neutrality but strongly opposes worldviews that are incompatible with basic constitutional principles, such as equal respect	Sceptical about the possibility and desirability of neutrality; opposes promoting a single national culture and favours preserving vulnerable cultures
Immigration	Opposes 'illiberal' restrictions on entry and exit	Communities are entitled to set their own terms of entry	New citizens are expected to integrate into the national culture	New citizens are expected to endorse constitutional values	Integration should be a two-way process; immigrants may be entitled to special supports
Democracy	Democracy requires some degree of solidarity and civic virtue	Democracy requires strong ties of loyalty and/or affection	Democracy requires a shared nationality	Democracy requires agreement about democratic values	Minority and/or oppressed groups may require special representation rights

and we will explore how the different theories of political community supply us with different ways of thinking about necessary conditions for democratic self-government. Finally, to conclude the chapter, we will examine some future challenges that the ideal of political community is likely to face in light of the ongoing transformations associated with the phenomenon of globalisation.

Rival perspectives

Liberalism

Many liberals are sceptical about the 'community-talk' that is now a familiar part of political rhetoric. One reason for this is that liberalism is an individualistic doctrine which places a premium on individual freedom and rights. Consequently, its adherents often worry that promoting a strong sense of communal identification could stifle freedom and individuality. As it has been developed by political theorists such as John Rawls, Ronald Dworkin and Charles Larmore, the liberal ideal of political community does not require that members share in a single comprehensive way of life, speak the same language, or even be sentimentally attached to one another. Rather, what matters is that members recognise one another as people to whom they owe a duty of justification, because of the moral concern they share for one another as free and equal citizens. The reservations of these liberals may be something of a historical aberration. For example, the 'new' liberals of the early twentieth century, like T. H. Green, L. T. Hobhouse and John A. Hobson, were positively enthusiastic about community, and many of the 'classical' liberals of the nineteenth century, such as John Stuart Mill, looked favourably on the cause of national self-determination. However, these sympathies are found less frequently in recent liberal writings, with the notable exception of the liberal nationalists, who we will consider later.

To make sense of how liberals understand political community, three background features of liberalism itself need to be set out. First is the *assumption of pluralism*, which is the expectation that the political culture of a society governed by liberal institutions will be 'marked by a diversity of opposing and irreconcilable religious, philosophical and moral doctrines' (Rawls, 1996, pp. 3–4). As we shall see in Chapter 3, liberals expect citizens to disagree about the ultimate ends and purposes of human life – for instance about what morality requires of us and about which plans and projects are worthwhile or meaningful. Moreover, they believe that this kind of pluralism will be a persistent feature of social life, and that convergence around a single religious, philosophical or moral doctrine cannot be sustained without oppression.

Second is the *requirement of public justification*, which follows from a distinctive understanding of political legitimacy. As we shall see in Chapter 3, liberals tend to argue that the coercive exercise of power is legitimate if and only if it can be justified to those who are subject to it. Characteristically, proponents of this view argue that members of a society are treated with proper respect only when the institutions and laws governing them can be justified in terms that they can accept. This is because being subject to institutions and laws that can only be justified by reasons which one rejects, or cannot make sense of, fails to respect one's status as an equal citizen. As one leading contemporary liberal puts it:

> [E]xercise of political power is fully proper only when it is exercised in accordance with a constitution the essentials of which all citizens as free and equal may reasonably be expected to endorse in light of principles and ideals acceptable to their common human reason. (Rawls, 1996, p. 217)

Importantly, the requirement of public justification does not go so far as to require that all institutions and laws are *in fact* endorsed by all citizens. Rather, it requires that coercive power be justified by reasons that are *in principle* acceptable to all (and for this reason, it is sometimes described as a form of 'hypothetical consent').

The third relevant feature is the *requirement of neutrality*. In its most basic form, this means that the liberal state should be neutral amongst the different religious, philosophical or moral views endorsed by its members. Because all citizens are to be treated with respect, and because pluralism is a permanent feature of social life, the purpose of laws and institutions is to provide fair background conditions against which individuals are able to pursue their own plans and projects, in accordance with their own beliefs about the good life. In particular, liberals object to using laws and institutions to promote particular views about the purposes of human life (such as, for example, religious views).

Combining these three features delivers a demanding ideal of political community, which many contemporary societies do not live up to. For example, consider a society that upholds a blasphemy law on the grounds of majority preference, and where the majority make no effort to justify their preference in terms that could be accepted by the minority. Such a society does not uphold the liberal ideal of community, since the majority have failed to recognise at least some of their fellow citizens as people to whom they owe a duty of justification.

Communitarianism

Since the 1980s, a number of communitarian political theorists – such as Alasdair MacIntyre, Charles Taylor, Michael Walzer and Michael Sandel – have developed a broad and multifaceted critique of liberalism, covering a wide range of methodological and philosophical issues (for an overview, see Mulhall and Swift, 1996). At the heart of their project is the idea that liberal individualism, and in particular the conception of personhood associated with it, neglects the profound significance of social ties as well as the ways in which people's identities are con-stituted by their unchosen memberships. According to communitarians, our par-ticular cultural and national memberships profoundly shape our identities, goals and the ways in which we understand the world. Because liberals set aside these particular characteristics, and instead focus on universal ones all people share (such as our capacity to think rationally or make choices), they end up with an ideal of community that communitarians think to be unappealing and incoherent.

Let us start with the first of these objections – that liberal community is unappealing. Communitarians diagnose an unhealthy individualism in modern society, and blame this on the pervasive influence of liberal ideas. According to them, liberalism – with its emphasis on individual rights and freedoms – puts the individual before the community (Taylor, 1985). As a consequence, a liberal political order will tend to create selfish and atomised people, preoccupied with their own private interests, and incapable of appreciating and acting for the common good. Liberalism, on this view, has disrupted the deep and natural ties of community, replacing them with a shallow egoism, and some liberal responses to this criticism are discussed in Box 2.1. One point worth noting is that if the communitarians are right, and our societies are now irredeemably fragmented as a consequence of the pernicious influence of liberal ideas, then this might actually be an argument for liberalism (Walzer, 2004, pp. 145–6). If we are doomed to live

BOX 2.1   NEUTRALITY AND THE COMMON GOOD

Communitarians and liberals disagree about the doctrine of neutrality. This doctrine requires the state to adopt no particular view about the ends of life, to neither reward nor penalise particular ways of life, and to refrain from adopting policies for the purpose of supporting favoured national, cultural and linguistic identities. For its liberal proponents, a neutral state will deliver a fair framework within which different ways of life can attempt to flourish and is not biased against traditional or collective ways of life (Kymlicka, 1989b). Meanwhile, communitarians say that neutrality neglects the common good and is unfair, since it puts some group identities and collective projects at a disadvantage. Moreover, they say that it neglects the ways in which politics is a communal project, in which people together seek to realise their shared goals and ideals. In response, liberals argue that their ideal of community is a moral ideal, in which members acknowledge one another as free and equal citizens. They think that this supports a distinctively liberal understanding of the common good, which is realised when members are jointly committed to sustaining just institutions that respect the freedom and equality of all (Mason, 2000, p. 68).

Is liberal neutrality unfairly biased against some ways of life? Is the liberal ideal of the common good adequate?

in a society of strangers, then what better political theory than liberalism – with its commitment to freedom, justice and rights – to cope with such a society!

The second communitarian objection is that the liberal ideal of community is incoherent because it rests on an implausible conception of the person. Communitarians believe that liberals underestimate the deep and enduring significances of our loyalties, social ties and inherited identities, and consequently endorse an unrealistic conception of the person that neglects the complex ways in which we are embedded in, and even constituted by, our communities. The basis of this objection is that liberals insist that individuals must be free to alter their beliefs and practices, and that they not be constrained by tradition, law or social pressure. However, communitarians think that this ideal conjures up an image of a person who is, in some sense, detached from their beliefs and practices, which Michael Sandel captures by saying that liberals are committed to a peculiar vision of an 'unencumbered self'. A self is 'unencumbered' when it has no roles, commitments or projects that are 'so essential that turning away from [them] would call into the question the person I am' (Sandel, 1984, p. 86). Not only would an 'unencumbered self' lack character and moral depth, since these things depend on an awareness of the ways in which we are shaped by our histories and cultures, but it also goes against our deepest self-understandings, because it rests on a mistaken understanding of how we relate to our beliefs and practices.

According to communitarians, the practices that give meaning to our lives are *social* practices, which are not fully our own creations but are instead complex products drawing on the histories and cultures into which we are born and socialised. For example, the choice to pursue a career in the theatre will be given its meaning by the ways in which the dramatic arts are understood within a particular culture. Taking socialisation seriously means that we should recognise that our choices are not made in a vacuum, but are based on options that are given meaning to us by our linguistic, cultural and communal heritages. On the communitarian account, liberals neglect this complexity, and in doing so unwittingly commit themselves to an implausible conception of personhood. This aspect of the communitarian critique gives rise to an important disagreement about the relationship between politics and community. On the one hand, liberals emphasise the importance of equipping individuals to question their social roles, and want to provide them with the opportunity and resources to 'step back' and critically evaluate their beliefs and practices. On the other hand, communitarians think that liberal individualism neglects the social character of freedom, and instead want to commit the state to promoting a politics of the common good.

Liberal nationalism

Liberals and communitarians disagree about the doctrine of state neutrality. Whilst the liberal state is agnostic about the content of its members' beliefs and practices (provided that they are not harmful to others), communitarians favour using political power to support collective goals or a vision of the common good (such as nourishing a distinctive way of life). Since the 1990s, a number of liberal nationalist political theorists – such as Margaret Canovan, David Miller, Wayne Norman and Yael Tamir – have carved out a new position that reaches across this divide. Like the earlier wave of communitarians, liberal nationalists were reacting against what they perceived to be shortcomings within orthodox liberalism. However, theirs is a more sympathetic critique, which aims to retain the basic features of the liberal worldview. Although this theory comes in many different forms, liberal nationalists advance two basic claims.

The first of these is that liberalism is compatible with some of the practices and principles associated with nationalism, including nation-building and compatriot priority. Nation-building refers to promoting a sense of shared nationality throughout the polity, for instance by teaching the national history and literature in schools, by subsidising distinctive cultural traditions and practices, by supporting the national language, and by encouraging the celebration of national holidays (Norman, 2006, pp. 33–53). The practice of nation-building is controversial as it potentially conflicts with the liberal commitment to neutrality. Meanwhile, compatriot priority is the principle that, under certain circumstances, the needs and interests of compatriots override those of foreigners (Miller, 2007, pp. 23–50). This principle underlines a number of familiar features of contemporary politics, such as border controls and decisions about spending on foreign aid. However, compatriot priority is controversial as it potentially conflicts with the liberal commitment to treating all people with equal concern and respect.

The second basic claim of liberal nationalism is that liberal politics and institutions depend upon members sharing a common national culture. This claim is much stronger than the first one, since it says that not only are liberals permitted to promote national cultures or prioritise the interests of compatriots, but also that liberals must do these things. At its most basic, the argument is that if we want to have welfare states or vibrant democracies, then we will need the kind of solidarity that shared nationality fosters. Margaret Canovan (1996), for example, compares the nation to a battery. This metaphor suggests a conception of the nation as a repository of loyalty, trust and belonging that the state can draw upon when it needs to mobilise its citizens. Liberal nationalists worry that if a state lacks this battery, then it will be unable to convince its members to make compromises with, or sacrifices for, one another. On this view, orthodox liberals have been too squeamish about the passions of political loyalty and belonging, since despite their intensity, these things are necessary if democratic community is to flourish.

This part of the liberal nationalist argument invokes a set of controversial hypotheses. For example, liberal nationalists believe that we are more likely to accept unwelcome democratic decisions when they are made by co-nationals, that we are happier to pay taxes for the benefit of our co-nationals, and that we are more willing to participate in democratic life if we share that life with members of our own national group. If these hypotheses are true, then liberals should take heed of communitarian concerns about the importance of social ties. In particular, they should be committed to both promoting a sense of shared nationality throughout the polity and to ensuring that political boundaries coincide with national ones. Even more controversially, as we shall see, liberal nationalists also favour using migration controls to ensure that national cultures retain their character and integrity. Meanwhile, critics of liberal nationalism point out that multination states – such as Canada, Belgium and Switzerland – also seem to be capable of motivating their citizens to make sacrifices for one another, thus casting doubt on some core liberal nationalist assumptions. Furthermore, even if nations do often perform an important function in supporting liberal democratic institutions, critics worry that unleashing the unpredictable and often destructive forces associated with nationalism might be too great a risk to take.

Constitutional patriotism

Liberal nationalism was a controversial addition to both the liberal tradition and to the theory of political community. Some critics deny that liberalism and nationalism are compatible, others reject liberal nationalist claims about the significance of nationhood, and still others think that nationalism is too explosive a phenomenon to legitimise. Interestingly, some of the underlying preoccupations of the liberal nationalists have also emerged in the writings of an avowedly anti-nationalist group of political theorists, who have developed a theory known as constitutional patriotism. Initially, this theory emerged as part of an attempt to work out an acceptable form of collective identification for a post-national Germany (where it is known as *Verfassungspatriotismus*). More recently, it has also been used to explain the kind of political identity that a more closely integrated European Union might take in the future. Although an early version of the position was developed by political scientist Dolf Sternberger, its contemporary prominence is largely owed to the writings of philosopher Jürgen Habermas and his followers, including Jan-Werner Müller, Attracta Ingram and Anna Stilz.

Like the liberal nationalists and their communitarian predecessors, constitutional patriots are concerned about the fragmentary tendencies of modern complex societies and emphasise the importance of political loyalty and membership. However, instead of appealing to the unifying force of shared nationality, constitutional patriots want to 'uncouple' nation and state, and believe that post-national political allegiance should be based on a shared civic loyalty to the principles and practices of a democratic community. By connecting political membership to abstract and universal principles, constitutional patriots point to a form of political community that does not depend on the exclusionary ties of shared history, ethnicity or culture. Thus, whilst liberal nationalists push liberalism in a particularistic and communitarian direction, constitutional patriots emphasise its universalistic and cosmopolitan aspects.

The central claim of constitutional patriotism is that a post-national political identity should be based on the 'recognition of democratic values and human rights as these are contextualised in a particular constitutional tradition' (Ingram, 1996, p. 2). This means that political attachment should be focussed on the values that are reflected in a democratic constitution, such as fairness, democracy, equal dignity and freedom. Importantly, constitutional patriots do not think that political loyalty should be directed at the constitution itself, since the contestation of particular constitutional provisions is a symptom of a reflective citizenry and a vigorous political community. What matters is that citizens share a basic moral framework within which they can resolve political disputes, and it is the absence of such a framework that threatens political community. The contrast with liberal nationalism here is worth noting. For constitutional patriots, political community is jeopardised when substantial numbers of citizens reject fundamental democratic norms and procedures. Meanwhile, for nationalists, political community is at risk when citizens are not united by ties of common nationality.

Three major lines of argument have been advanced against constitutional patriotism. First is the 'civil religion' objection, which says that constitutional patriotism risks turning the political community into 'a kind of confessional state' (Canovan, 2000, p. 420). Why should this be so? Constitutional patriots think that political community should be arranged around shared political principles. If those principles are rejected by some citizens, such as members of orthodox and traditional religious communities, then constitutional patriots worry that political community will not be viable. Consequently, efforts must be made to inculcate the necessary principles amongst citizens, for instance by teaching them in schools and promoting them in public culture. But according to critics, this kind of manipulation is incompatible with the principle of freedom of conscience. Meanwhile, constitutional patriots respond to this by pointing out that the dispositions which they wish to cultivate do not include unquestioning obedience. Recall, constitutional patriots do not want citizens to venerate the constitution itself or its founding fathers. Rather, they want to encourage a more self-critical and reflective political community, orientated around basic democratic freedoms.

A second objection is that constitutional patriotism is unrealistic. Communitarians and nationalists point out that real political communities have much more in common with their models than with those of the constitutional patriots, and that this is because patriotic attachments to political ideas and values are too weak to sustain the strong ties of membership that political community depends upon. Bernard Yack, for example, suggests that even if attachment to constitutional principles is now a necessary condition for political loyalty, it is not a sufficient one. To illustrate this, he points out that '[n]o matter how much residents of the United States might sympathise with the political principles favoured by most French or Canadian citizens, it would not occur to them to think of themselves as French or Canadian' (Yack, 2012, p. 28). On his account, real political community is always based on ties that are less rational and voluntary than those emphasised by constitutional patriots. For example, despite the influence of constitutional patriotism in German political and cultural life, when the opportunity for reunification arose, shared nationality proved to be far more important to East and West Germans than their attachments to (often quite different) political principles.

Finally, a third objection is that because constitutional patriotism appeals to universal political ideas and values, it cannot explain what binds people to their own political communities. For example, liberal nationalist David Miller makes the following argument:

> A constitution usually contains a statement of principles and a delineation of the institutions that will enact them. The principles themselves are likely to be general in form, more or less the common currency of liberal democracies. Subscribing to them marks you out as a liberal rather than a fascist or an anarchist, but it does not provide the kind of identity that nationality provides. In particular, it does not explain why the boundaries of the political community should fall here rather than there. (Miller, 1995, p. 163)

If Miller is right, then constitutional patriotism can supplement but cannot replace nationalism within the theory of political community. This is because it cannot tell us 'who' and 'where' the political community is, but only 'how' political community should be done. Meanwhile, Jan-Werner Müller has suggested that although constitutional patriotism 'has to rely on existing political units' and 'is not a free standing theory of political boundary-formation' (Müller, 2007, p. 48), it can address objections such as Miller's by characterising political allegiance in terms of attachment to a particular 'constitutional culture' (Müller, 2007, p. 59). On this reading, membership is about endorsing universal political principles *within* your own particular cultural and historical setting. Thus, the task of patriotic citizens is to 'sustain and re-work particular constitutional cultures which are trying to express universal norms of justice and fairness in specific contexts' (Müller, 2007, pp. 59–60).

Multiculturalism and difference theory

Despite their disagreements, both liberal nationalists and constitutional patriots base their theories of political community on what members are said to share in common, whether that is national culture or political principles. Meanwhile, recent writings on diversity have suggested that this emphasis on uniformity could exacerbate the marginalisation, exclusion and oppression of minority communities. In a number of different ways, multiculturalists like Will Kymlicka and Bhikhu Parekh, and difference theorists such as Iris Marion Young, have objected to the 'one-size-fits-all' assumption that underlies orthodox models of political community, arguing that it threatens diversity and reinforces underlying structures of privilege and oppression.

Multiculturalists and difference theorists are especially concerned about the tendency of contemporary political communities to reinforce homogeneity. Things that are homogeneous are of the same kind, and a culturally homogeneous political community is one in which all members share the same culture. Multiculturalists worry that if left unchecked, liberal democracies could exert pressure on minorities to assimilate into the majority culture (for instance, speaking its language, adopting its customs and losing their distinctiveness). To resist these dynamics, they favour measures to protect and promote linguistic, cultural and religious diversity. For example, and in common with many communitarians and liberal nationalists, multiculturalists have been especially concerned with the situation of minority nations, such as the Basques, Welsh and Québécois. The practices and languages of such groups are often jeopardised as a result of their proximity to dominant majority cultures, and multiculturalists favour 'self-government' rights to allow these groups to protect their distinctiveness. Multiculturalists also worry about other cultural minorities, including indigenous peoples and religious minorities, for whom they favour extending a range of accommodations such as exemptions from generally applicable laws, so as to enable groups to preserve their traditional ways of life. For instance, Amish communities in the United States sought to remove their children from compulsory schooling at a younger than usual age, whilst Ultra-Orthodox Jews in Israel have been granted exemptions from compulsory military service.

In addition to cultural minorities, difference theorists are also concerned about the prospects of other marginalised or oppressed groups, such as women, LGBT people and the disabled. Like multiculturalists, they have drawn attention to the various ways in which economic success and political influence are often positively correlated with membership in the dominant social group. For example, the composition of legislatures and executive boardrooms often favours historically privileged groups. In response, difference theorists and multiculturalists argue for a range of targeted and special rights – such as quotas and affirmative action policies – to ensure that all members of society have an equal chance to flourish (Young, 1989; Kymlicka, 1995).

Multiculturalists and difference theorists agree that orthodox theories of political community are flawed. However, they do not endorse a single positive ideal. For example, multiculturalists disagree amongst themselves about whether to prioritise protecting vulnerable cultural identities from wider societal pressures or to encourage individuals to engage with different cultural traditions. Whilst some multiculturalists are 'border guarders' (Yack, 2002) and endorse a 'protective' form of multiculturalism (Goodin, 2006, p. 289), according to which minority rights are required to protect cultural minorities from majority-favouring policies, others celebrate 'border crossing' (Yack, 2002) and endorse 'polyglot' (Goodin, 2006) or 'hodgepodge' (Joppke and Lukes, 1999) visions of multiculturalism, according to which people's lives go better when they engage with new traditions and embrace cultural complexity and change.

Protective multiculturalism points towards a view of political community as a 'mosaic', in which each distinctive cultural group is given the opportunity to flourish separately and on its own terms (Joppke and Lukes, 1999, p. 11). This vision has had a modest influence on public policy and is reflected in occasional proposals to reconfigure the political community as a 'community of communities'. However, it has also attracted fierce criticism, including from political theorists. Some believe that mosaic multiculturalism more closely resembles international society than a single political community, and for that reason will lack stability and coherence (Walzer, 1997). Meanwhile, as we shall see in Chapter 3, others worry that a 'community of communities' could worsen the position of vulnerable group members, leaving women, religious dissenters and other 'internal minorities' open to exploitation and oppression within their groups (Green, 1994; Okin, 1998).

The rival 'hodgepodge' or 'polyglot' vision of a multicultural society rejects the ideas that people need their cultures to be preserved and that this should be done by insulating them from external pressures. For example, the cosmopolitan political theorist Jeremy Waldron argues that people do not need 'immersion in the secure framework of a single culture to which, in some deep sense, they belong' (Waldron, 2000, p. 228). Instead of a quilt stitched together from different pieces of fabric, advocates of this view set out an exhilarating vision of society in which cultures intermingle, both amongst groups and within individuals. According to them, because individuals are boundlessly creative they should relish the opportunity to create their identities from heterogeneous source materials and 'the really great virtue of multiculturalism is that it provides a broad smorgasbord of mix-and-match options from which to choose' (Goodin, 2006, p. 295). There are two noteworthy features of this vision of political community. First, it rejects the rather static view of culture implied by mosaic multiculturalism, with its discrete cultural groups separated by carefully guarded borders, and instead implies that cultural identities are dynamic and that boundaries between them are in a constant state of flux. Second, it also implies that individual lives are lived more fully and authentically when individuals embrace cultural complexity and change. However, aside from undercutting the case for mosaic multiculturalism, its concrete implications are unclear. As

Joppke and Lukes observe, it is 'in the first instance, an aesthetic phenomenon, expressed in world music, fashion, literature and cuisine' and as such does not have clear implications for 'the imperatives of political organisation and state policy' (1999, p. 11).

Key debates

What should the rights and duties of citizenship be?

A citizen is a full member of a political community, and as such is entitled to certain rights and is expected to uphold certain duties. These rights and duties vary considerably. For instance, some (but not all) political communities provide their members with a right to a subsidised university tuition, and some (but not all) impose a duty to carry out a period of national service. The rules governing which members of society are eligible for citizenship also vary by jurisdiction, and these have generally become less exclusionary during recent centuries, for instance as women and the working classes have been incorporated as full members. In the next key debate we will take up some difficult normative questions about the conditions under which immigrants should be entitled to acquire citizenship. Here, we will focus on three other normative disagreements about citizenship: what rights should citizens hold, what duties should be associated with citizenship, and should those rights and duties be identical for all members?

Most contemporary political theorists agree about the basic rights of citizenship, such as those guaranteeing important civil and political liberties (for instance, the freedoms of expression, conscience and association, and the rights to vote and take part in politics). However, left- and right-wing political theorists disagree about whether citizenship rights should also include social or welfare rights, such as rights to healthcare or an education. Perhaps the most far reaching proposals of this kind involve allocating to each citizen a 'stakeholder grant' or a 'basic income', and these schemes are discussed in Box 2.2. As we shall see in Chapter 9, right-wing libertarians object to social or welfare rights on the grounds that they will undermine freedom and violate other rights (such as property rights). Importantly, this disagreement cuts across the different theories of political community we have discussed and, for example, left-leaning liberals and communitarians find common cause against their right-wing opponents.

Different theories of political community agree about many of the duties of citizenship, such as the duties to obey legitimate laws, to pay one's fair share of taxes and to tolerate the lawful behaviour of fellow citizens. Similarly, they also agree that citizens have duties to deliberate responsibly about politics and the law. However, they supply different accounts about *how* citizens should uphold these deliberative duties. For instance, the liberal duty of justification requires that citizens should refrain from offering certain kinds of reasons in political discourse.

BOX 2.2 CITIZENSHIP AND ECONOMIC RIGHTS

In most democracies, citizens now hold more rights than their ancestors did. For instance, citizens now generally have not only the rights to a fair trial, to vote and to stand for office, but also rights to education and healthcare (Marshall, 1992). Some contemporary political theorists want to extend these rights further, arguing that citizens should be granted a right to a 'basic income' or a 'stakeholder's grant'. A basic income is a regular payment 'paid by a political community to all its members on an individual basis, without means test or work requirement' (Van Parijs, 2004, p. 8). One initiative that partially reflects this goal is the Alaska Permanent Fund, which is based on investments from mineral sales and royalties, and pays out an annual divided to all children and adults who have been resident in Alaska for at least one year (with the exception of those convicted of a felony). Meanwhile, a 'stakeholder grant' is a single lump-sum, paid to all adults upon reaching the age of maturity. Proponents argue that these schemes would strengthen political community, improve the bargaining position of workers (by protecting them from having to take on exploitative or alienating work), and allow less well-off members of society to invest in business or educational opportunities. However, critics argue that they would incentivise 'free-riding' on the part of those who choose not to work and involve allocating wasteful subsidies to already wealthy members of society.

Should citizens be granted a basic income?

Because political power is the joint property of all, virtuous liberal citizens engaging in political debate will trade in 'public reasons', which are intelligible or accessible to everyone. Thus, they will not support their favoured outcomes or policies by referring to controversial religious or moral views, which their compatriots might reasonably reject. Meanwhile, communitarians are sceptical about the demand that citizens should bracket off their deepest beliefs when deliberating about politics and the law. For them, the liberal duty of justification relies on the kind of detachment that is characteristic of the 'unencumbered self'. Instead, communitarians favour a more 'contextual' form of political deliberation, in which citizens jointly seek to find collective answers to collective problems by investigating and reflecting on their shared culture and values. By drawing a connection between the common good and the collective identity of the political community, communitarians emphasise the ways in which participation in politics can benefit and even enrich citizens. As Sandel puts it, 'when politics goes well, we can know a good in common that we cannot know alone' (1998, p. 183).

Although different theories of political community disagree about *what* the rights and duties of citizenship should be, most agree that these rights and duties should be identical for each member. Indeed, for many political theorists, the 'sameness' of citizenship is particularly important, as it expresses the equality of citizens and furthers the goal of political unity. However, some political theorists challenge this 'unitary' conception of citizenship, and instead argue for a 'group-differentiated' conception, in which the rights and duties of citizenship are tailored to the needs, interests or identities of particular groups. For example, liberal nationalists and multiculturalists have pressed the case in favour of special rights for national minorities, including rights to protect their national languages and rights of national self-determination. Similarly, multiculturalists and difference theorists have argued for special representation rights (for instance, favouring affirmative action or positive discrimination in universities and legislatures) and for rights to protect the distinctive interests of particular groups (for instance, favouring land rights for Aboriginal peoples).

One of the most radical claims associated with the case for differentiated citizenship is that the traditional unitary conception of citizenship actually undermines equality, properly understood. Difference theorist Iris Marion Young (1989) makes three arguments to this effect. First, she argues that because the traditional model of democratic deliberation is orientated around a politics of the common good, it tends to privilege dominant interests, squeezing out the preferences and needs of marginalised or weaker groups. Second, she argues that the traditional model of citizenship is stifling, because 'the idea that citizenship is the same for all translated in practice to the requirement that all citizens be the same' (Young, 1989, p. 254). Third, she points out that the unitary model of citizenship has often been accompanied by unjust forms of exclusion. For example, the historical exclusion of women from citizenship was supported by a belief that they were swayed by passions and not reason, whilst until the nineteenth century the poor were excluded for allegedly being too motivated by their immediate needs.

When are immigrants entitled to become full members of society?

As we have seen, political theorists disagree about the rights and duties of citizenship, and about whether those rights and duties should be the same for all. Perhaps more importantly, they also disagree about how membership itself should be allocated. Political membership is one of the most important goods in the modern world, as citizenship status inevitably has a serious impact on the availability of opportunities and resources (and therefore, on a person's life prospects). Some critics of global inequality identify current citizenship practices as a major obstacle to a fairer global order, in one case characterising citizenship in Western liberal democracies as 'the modern equivalent of feudal class privilege – an inherited status that greatly enhances one's life chances' (Carens, 2013, p. 226). Two disagreements about immigration and citizenship are especially significant, and we shall take each of these in turn. First, liberals and communitarians have outlined contrasting views about the *admission* of immigrants. Second, liberal nationalists, constitutional patriots and multiculturalists have each set out different views about the *integration* of immigrants.

According to communitarian Michael Walzer, political communities are 'communities of character' containing 'men and women with some special commitment to one another and some special sense of their common life' (1983, p. 62). Like other communitarians, Walzer thinks that communities are *constitutive* of individual identity. Each political community has a unique and intergenerational 'collective consciousness' that supplies its members with a 'world of common meanings' (1983, p. 28), and this shapes their plans and projects as well as their sense of who they are. Because political communities need shared understandings, they have the 'right to protect their members' shared sense of what they are about' (1983, p. 50), and this means that current members are entitled 'to decide freely on their future associates' (1983, p. 41):

> The right to choose an admissions policy ... is not merely a matter of acting in the world, exercising sovereignty, and pursuing national interests. At stake is the shape of the community that acts in the world, exercises sovereignty, and so on. Admission and exclusion are at the core of communal independence. They suggest the deepest meaning of self-determination. (Walzer, 1983, p. 62)

Thus, on Walzer's account, political communities must be entitled to set their own admissions policies. If they could not control their borders in this way, then their very way of life could be put in jeopardy.

The contrast between communitarianism and orthodox theories of liberalism is striking. The communitarian theory of political community supports immigration restrictions if the members of a political community believe that newcomers will threaten their universe of shared understandings and common meanings. Ultimately, the admissions criteria adopted by a communitarian state will depend on how inclusionary or exclusionary its members' self-understanding is. Importantly, this is a matter that the community must decide for itself, and communitarian citizens must always have the final say on who is (and is not) to be admitted. Meanwhile, because the liberal state is neutral about matters of identity, it cannot discriminate amongst potential immigrants on the grounds that are – in principle – available to the communitarian state. Indeed, some liberals – such as Joseph Carens (1987, 1992) and Michael Dummett (2001) – suggest that liberals should be committed to dismantling border controls. For these proponents of 'open borders', current restrictions on migration unfairly limit the freedom of movement of non-members, as well as their opportunities. Furthermore, and as discussed in Box 2.3, current restrictions concerning the acquisition of citizenship potentially leave some people – such as stateless persons, refugees and precarious migrants – with few and perhaps no effective rights.

BOX 2.3 STATELESS PERSONS, REFUGEES AND PRECARIOUS MIGRANTS

The calamity of the rightless is not that they are deprived of life, liberty, and the pursuit of happiness, or of equality before the law and freedom of opinion – formulas which were designed to solve problems *within* given communities – but that they no longer belong to any community whatsoever. Their plight is not that they are not equal before the law, but that no law exists for them. (Arendt, 2004, p. 375)

According to Hannah Arendt, people without effective citizenship – such as stateless persons, refugees and precarious migrants – lack a legal personality, or 'the right to have rights', and this is tantamount to 'expulsion from humanity' (Arendt, 2004, pp. 376–7). Stateless people typically reside in their country of birth, and may either be *de jure* stateless (because they lack citizenship status) or *de facto* stateless (because their state is unwilling to uphold their rights of citizenship). Some people are stateless as a consequence of discrimination (such as some of the Nubian people in Kenya) whilst others become stateless following secession (such as the Biharis in Bangladesh). Meanwhile, refugees are people who have fled their country of nationality as a result of persecution, either individually or as a group. Although refugees are entitled to various rights and protections under international law, their ability to access these rights and protections is often insecure. Finally, precarious migrants reside in states where they do not have citizenship status and where they lack a right to remain. Unlike the stateless they may have a citizenship status, and unlike refugees they may not fear persecution if they were to return to their country of origin. However, they lack the effective ability to appeal to their current state to protect their rights, and will often be vulnerable to the threat of deportation. All three groups suffer comparable disadvantages, for instance often living at society's margins, lacking democratic voice and being subject to threats of violence.

How might the situations of stateless persons, refugees and precarious migrants be improved? Who is responsible for doing so?

Suppose that an immigrant has crossed the first hurdle and gained legal access to the territory of a political community. What can the political community legitimately expect of them? Can it demand that they 'integrate'? And if so, what form should this integration take? According to liberal nationalist David Miller (2008), host societies should expect immigrants to absorb some aspects of the national culture, since the modern democratic welfare state depends on its members sharing a cultural identity. On this account host societies should strongly incentivise the acculturation of immigrants, for instance by making full membership conditional on demonstrating familiarity with the national language, culture and history. Thus, he looks favourably on citizenship tests as a means of assimilating immigrants into the national culture. Meanwhile, constitutional patriots argue against cultural assimilation and instead advocate a more 'political' form of integration (Habermas, 1998; Müller, 2007, pp. 85–92;

Stilz, 2009, pp. 169–72). For them, what really matters is that immigrants 'assent to the principles of the constitution' (Habermas, 1998, p. 228). Thus, if aspiring citizens are required to pass tests, these should focus strictly on political values and institutions. However, critics of this view doubt that political integration in practice will differ significantly from cultural assimilation, since political values and institutions will frequently be shaped by the character of the dominant national culture (for example, using its language, paying special attention to its history, reflecting its customs and so on).

Multicultural approaches to immigrant integration have a different emphasis, because they insist that immigrant integration should be a two-way process. For example, Will Kymlicka (2001, p. 162) accepts some key liberal nationalist claims, such as the idea that immigrants should be expected to become competent in the official language and learn about the history and culture of the host society. However, he also stresses the importance of ensuring that the terms of integration are fair. This means that immigrants should be supplied with transitional supports, such as translation services and special welfare provisions, and that society's major institutions respond fairly to the new forms of diversity in their midst, for instance by recognising minority religious holidays, subsidising minority cultural festivals and revising their dress codes to accommodate the religious beliefs of immigrants. Another and more demanding multicultural approach is discussed in Box 2.4.

What kinds of political community best nourish democracy?

Many theories of political community agree that supporting democracy is a legitimate aim of integration policy. However, because these different theories

BOX 2.4   MULTICULTURALISM AND BELONGING

Multiculturalist Bhikhu Parekh proposes that we replace talk of assimilation and integration with an ideal of an inclusive and egalitarian political community in which old and new citizens can feel equally at home. For Parekh, the aim of multicultural belonging should be to cultivate 'a broadly shared feeling among the citizens that they form part of the same community, belong together, share common interests ... and wish to live together in peace for the foreseeable future' (2008, p. 87). Conceivably, achieving this feeling amongst all members may require demanding adaptations on the part of immigrants and host society alike. This is because 'immigrants cannot belong to a society unless it is prepared to welcome them, and conversely it cannot make them its own unless they wish to belong to it, with all that entails' (2008, p. 87).

What might multicultural belonging require? Is it a feasible and desirable goal?

have different views about what kinds of community sustain democracy, they also disagree about what form an integration policy should take. In this section we will look more closely at the question of what qualities citizens must exhibit if their political community is to be democratic. First, we will examine the significance of democratic solidarity and civic virtue for democratic community. Second, we will compare the views of communitarians, liberal nationalists and constitutional patriots about how democratic solidarity and civic virtue are to be sustained. Third, we will explore the challenges of establishing democratic political communities amongst people with different cultural backgrounds.

The idea of democratic solidarity has been stressed by authors from a range of theoretical perspectives. For instance, one liberal argues that democratic politics 'presupposes citizens who can think of themselves as contributing to a common discourse about their shared institutions' (Barry, 2001a, p. 300). On this account, democracy requires that citizens are capable of adopting a 'we-perspective' orientated towards the common good, since without a sense of solidarity citizens may find it difficult to trust one another, to co-operate in the pursuit of shared ends, or to deliberate responsibly about matters of mutual concern. Moreover, democratic citizens must arguably be united by bonds of solidarity if they are to conceive of the laws that bind them as being 'their' laws. If they cannot think of themselves as being joint authors of the rules to which they are subject, then citizens may come to think of laws as unwelcome and external constraints on their freedom.

Because democracies need public-spirited citizens who are willing to volunteer their time to participate in politics, and who are inclined to exercise their democratic duties responsibly, some political theorists argue that solidarity must be accompanied by a range of other 'civic' virtues (Macedo, 1990; Galston, 1991; Callan, 1997). One of these is civility, which describes both a kind of conduct and a form of deliberation. Civil citizens refrain from abusing one another in political speech and defend their political preferences in terms that their fellow citizens can understand. Another is tolerance, which refers to a stable disposition to refrain from impeding the practices of others despite disapproving of them. Tolerant citizens do not interfere with one another's lawful practices and have a 'live and let live' attitude. A final disposition emphasised by these theorists is fraternity, which describes a willingness to further the common good ahead of one's private ends. Fraternal citizens are not purely self-interested, are willing to make sacrifices for one another, and take seriously the concerns and interests of their fellow citizens.

Communitarians have criticised liberalism's theory of political community for being unable to explain what nourishes the ties of loyalty and affection that democratic solidarity and civic virtue require. On their account, liberalism's commitment to individualism and the 'unencumbered self' means that its proponents cannot appreciate the extent to which meaningful citizenship depends upon deep and unchosen feelings of identification and community. A characteristically communitarian account of the relationship between democracy and community can be found in this passage from Charles Taylor:

> The societies we are striving to create – free, democratic, willing to some degree to share equally – require strong identification on the part of their citizens... A citizen democracy can only work if most of its members are convinced that their political society is a common venture of considerable moment and believe it to be of such vital importance that they participate in the ways they must to keep it functioning as a democracy. Such participation requires not only a commitment to the common project, but also a special sense of bonding among the people working together. (Taylor, 1996, pp. 119–20)

For Taylor and the other communitarians, the 'us' that democracy requires must be grounded on a 'special sense of bonding'. Without such a sense, political communities will be less likely to cultivate a sense of trust and unity, making them vulnerable to factionalism and inhospitable to civic virtue. On this account, democracy depends upon strong feelings of membership that dispose citizens to take one another's interests and concerns seriously, and these feelings are typically rooted in shared membership of an intergenerational cultural community.

Communitarians challenge liberals to explain what motivates citizens to exhibit democratic solidarity and civic virtue. This gauntlet was taken up by the next generation of liberal nationalist political theorists, who agreed with the communitarians about the importance of shared identity for motivating solidarity and civic virtue. Importantly, these authors argued that only a shared *national* identity can motivate the required dispositions and attitudes of good citizenship, and concluded that liberal democracy presupposes the cultural nation. David Miller summarises this argument as follows:

> [T]o the extent that we aspire to a form of democracy in which all citizens are at some level involved in discussion of public issues, we must look to the conditions under which citizens can respect one another's good faith in searching for grounds of agreement. Among large aggregates of people, only a common nationality can provide the sense of solidarity that makes this possible. Sharing a national identity does not, of course, mean holding similar political views; but it does mean being committed to finding terms under which fellow-nationals can agree to live together. (Miller, 1995, p. 98)

Miller's argument, in short, is that democratic solidarity and civic virtue depend upon feelings of belonging, and these feelings are nourished by the common identity supplied by a shared nationality. By contrast, if citizens are not united by a common national identity, then they will not trust one another, and they will not be committed to finding mutually acceptable terms of co-operation. Thus, according to Miller, in the absence of a common national identity 'politics at best takes the form of group bargaining and compromise and at worst degenerates into a struggle for domination' (Miller, 1995, p. 92).

As we noted earlier, a potential challenge to the liberal nationalist thesis is the existence of multinational and multilingual democracies, such as Switzerland, Belgium and Canada. Miller deals with these cases during a discussion of nineteenth-century liberal John Stuart Mill. Like the modern liberal nationalists, Mill believed that 'free institutions are next to impossible in a country made up of different nationalities' (quoted in Miller, 1995, p. 98). This is because Mill believed that national divisions are likely to undermine co-operation and instead promote division and petty resentments. However, according to Miller, 'Mill was well aware that a common sentiment of nationality could co-exist with linguistic and other cultural differences' (Miller, 1995, p. 98). In another passage, Miller himself seems to endorse and extend this view, arguing that 'Belgium, Canada, and Switzerland work as they do partly because they are *not* simply multinational, but have cultivated common national identities alongside communal ones' (Miller, 1995, p. 96). Miller's claim then is that multinational democracy is possible *if* the wider political community cultivates either a common national identity or a common sentiment of nationality. Thus, multinational democracy is possible when there is a sufficiently strong overarching national unity.

A rival view about the relationship between community and democracy can be found in the writings of constitutional patriots, who argue that the seemingly powerful relationship between democracy and nationhood is an historical contingency. Jürgen Habermas captures this by saying that 'the nation-state established only temporarily the close link between the *ethnos* and the *demos*' (Habermas, quoted in Lacroix, 2002, p. 946). On this reading, although the ethnic or national community (the 'ethnos') often does provide the basis for the political community (the 'demos'), the connection between the two is not as close or persistent as communitarians and liberal nationalists suggest. Moreover, according to Habermas, alternative sources of civic solidarity are more appropriate for complex and post-national political communities. In particular, he thinks that we should strive to promote forms of solidarity that coalesce around the shared practices of democratic citizenship and a shared commitment to universal values. For some constitutional patriots (e.g. Lacroix, 2002; Müller, 2007), breaking the connection between 'ethnos' and 'demos' opens the door to the possibility of a future European Union that is based around a form of constitutional patriotism. However, as Box 2.5 indicates, the democratic challenge faced by the EU is complicated by the fact that it is not only multinational but also multilingual.

If both constitutional patriots and liberal nationalists agree that solidarity is important, what exactly distinguishes the two positions? Although constitutional patriots often characterise their theory in terms of allegiance to universal

BOX 2.5 LANGUAGE AND DEMOCRACY IN THE EUROPEAN UNION

According to Brian Barry 'for democratic politics to work, the citizens must be able to communicate with one another, and have access to the same forums of political debate' (1991, p. 178). Because the European Union recognises 24 official languages, and many more are spoken within its borders, some critics are sceptical about whether it can ever be democratic. This scepticism has been supported by some political theorists, who point out that democracy across different language groups is difficult because people are often only comfortable discussing political questions in their first language. For instance, Will Kymlicka proposes that 'the more the political debate takes place in the vernacular, the greater the participation' (Kymlicka, 2001, p. 214). One solution to Europe's language problem is to promote English as a European *lingua franca*; that is to say, as a language to be used widely for communication amongst people with different mother tongues. For instance, Philippe Van Parijs argues that greater adoption of English within Europe will create 'a transnational demos' and will enable 'not only the rich and powerful, but also the poor and powerless to communicate, debate, network, cooperate, lobby, demonstrate effectively across borders' (Van Parijs, 2011, p. 31). A different solution is to carve Europe up into regions where linguistic competences overlap, so as to take advantage of the passive bilingualism that already exists. For instance, Peter Kraus identifies a 'converging multilingualism' in the European public sphere, and envisages 'the emergence of a Latin, a Scandinavian, a Teutonic and an Atlantic network' (Kraus, 2008, pp. 177–8). Kraus's solution falls short of a single European-wide demos but instead aims to promote greater democratic engagement across nation-state boundaries.

Can Europe's language problem be solved?

democratic principles, they also emphasise that the practice of democracy is always rooted in a particular historical and social context. Patriotic citizens themselves are not attached to abstract democratic values but to 'how we do democracy here'. According to critics, this particularist mode of allegiance makes constitutional patriotism look very similar to liberal nationalism. Against this view, Anna Stilz (2009, p. 167) identifies three features that seem to distinguish the two theories. First, constitutional patriots emphasise that political identities are open to ongoing democratic revision whilst liberal nationalists tend to treat national cultures as fixed and static. Second, constitutional patriots favour a shared allegiance to a 'thin' political culture rather than a 'thick' national culture whilst liberal nationalists maintain that such a distinction is spurious. Third, constitutional patriots believe that 'our values' carry force for us because they are ultimately rooted in universal political principles, whilst liberal nationalists believe that the force of 'our values' has ultimately to do with them being 'ours'.

Recent political experiences – including shifting patterns of migration and the intensification of claims made by sub-state ethno-cultural minorities – have combined to unsettle the assumption that the political community can be orientated around a single shared identity. This raises the question of whether people from different cultural backgrounds can establish a genuinely democratic political community. Constitutional patriots and some liberals (though not liberal nationalists) solve this problem by insisting on a strict separation of culture and politics. On this approach, cultural differences are depoliticised and rendered secondary to a shared political identity around which citizens can unite. If this identity is to sustain civic virtue and democratic solidarity, then all members of society must be capable of regarding it as being in some sense 'theirs'. However, multiculturalists and difference theorists have suggested that this may be difficult to achieve, since immigrants and other minorities often do not experience the political community as a relationship amongst equals. One reason for this is that ostensibly neutral political institutions are often perceived by minorities to be laden with cultural biases and therefore alienating. For instance, the political identity of a community will typically reflect the dominant national identity, and minority practices and perspectives are often stigmatised as strange, deviant or 'other'.

Moreover, multiculturalists and difference theorists worry that if society is characterised by relationships of privilege and oppression, then the strategy of depoliticising cultural differences may actually frustrate equality. As part of an alternative and inclusive approach that aims at 'equalizing the ability of oppressed groups to speak and be heard' (Young, 1990, p. 189), Iris Marion Young has argued in support of special democratic rights for marginalised minorities. These might include guaranteeing the representation of minorities in legislatures, funding interest groups to campaign on behalf of minority issues, and allocating minority groups 'veto rights' to block policies that directly affect them. In each case, the strategy is to promote the inclusion of marginalised groups within the democratic community by politicising group identities and memberships. In addition to counterbalancing the exclusion of minority groups, this approach may also help to broaden the self-understanding of a political community.

Young's theory of inclusive democracy has attracted a great deal of controversy, to which we will return in Chapter 4. For the moment, let us note one point in its favour and one reason for scepticism. On the positive side of the ledger, Young's approach offers a way to satisfy the demands for 'recognition' that are often made by minority groups. As we shall see in Chapter 8, political theorists such as Axel Honneth (1995, 2007), Nancy Fraser (1997, 2008) and Charles Taylor (1994) have argued that the failure to recognise the distinctive identities of minority cultures can impose a real harm on members. For example, according to Taylor, adequate recognition is a 'vital human need', and 'nonrecognition' or 'misrecognition' can be oppressive, 'saddling people with a crippling self-hatred' (Taylor, 1994, p. 25). A potential advantage of Young's approach is that the formal and institutional recognition of cultural minorities will allow previously marginalised groups to organise themselves and to express political demands on their own terms. Not only might this counter the threat of invisibility but it might also support democratic solidarity by fostering a sense of belonging amongst minorities. Meanwhile, against Young, it has been argued that her approach may promote division by encouraging groups to focus on their differences. In particular, since only oppressed groups are entitled to special rights, Young's approach might encourage a grievance politics, turning groups against one another and fossilising divisions.

Future challenges

In this chapter we have seen that different theories of political community supply rival explanations about what members are supposed to share in common and what should connect them together. Underlying these differences are deep and fundamental philosophical disagreements about human nature and about the significance of culture, which have also fed into persistent disputes amongst political theorists about the proper role of the state and the doctrine of state neutrality, about the extent to which political communities should accommodate value pluralism and cultural differences, and about the circumstances that make democracy possible. As we have seen, these disagreements are reflected in complex contemporary disputes about immigration and the integration of minorities.

In recent years political theorists have begun to recognise that the phenomenon of globalisation poses new challenges for political community, and they have begun to ask difficult questions about the future prospects of democratic political community. 'Pessimists' have suggested that the increasing influence of multinational corporations and global, supra- and transnational institutions – such as the United Nations, the World Bank, the International Monetary Fund, and the African and European Unions – mean that the very possibility of democratic self-rule is being jeopardised by forces beyond traditional state borders. On this view, the capacity of a single nation-state to determine its own fate can no longer be taken for granted in a world of complex interdependencies. Meanwhile, 'optimists' have suggested that these changing political conditions open up new possibilities for global political community and transnational democratic engagement. We will conclude this chapter by looking at two 'optimistic' proposals and the challenges they raise for traditional theories of political community.

First, cosmopolitans such as Andrew Linklater and David Held (Held, 1995, 2010; Held and Archibugi, 1995; Linklater, 1998; Held and Koenig-Archibugi,

2003) acknowledge that the changing political landscape has radically altered the conditions for democratic citizenship. For them, people have a right to shape the world in which they live, and the world in which people live today has been profoundly influenced by global practices and institutions. Consequently, they argue that we need to think of citizens as part of a global community and not simply as members of a particular nation-state. In particular, they believe that we need to democratise transnational institutions and decision making procedures by increasing the opportunities for people to influence the institutional arrangements that directly affect them. For instance, cosmopolitans favour greater use of cross-border referenda, making international organisations more accountable, and the creation of new sites for transnational democratic activity. Ultimately, cosmopolitan democrats aim to extend the traditional logic of state-centred democracy to the new circumstances of a globalised political order and to bring global legal, economic and political frameworks under the ambit of popular control. For instance, according to Held this can be achieved by combining a complex scheme of 'multi-layered' democratic governance with global legal institutions.

A second, and perhaps more modest, approach has been suggested by John Dryzek (2006, 2010), who argues that the cosmopolitan model is too optimistic about the prospects of democratising international organisations and practices. Dryzek instead favours a model of 'transnational discursive democracy' that focuses on strengthening informal mechanisms of international democratic deliberation. What really matters on Dryzek's approach is that transnational civil society has the opportunity to contest the *discourses* that shape the institutions of global governance. Thus, instead of bringing the new administrative and technocratic institutions of the global order directly under popular control, as Held urges, Dryzek wants to democratise the discourses that underlie and influence these institutions. For example, the discourses of market liberalism, globalisation, realism, sustainable development and human rights have all played important roles in constructing the current global order. On Dryzek's approach, the best prospects for global democracy have to do with opening up spaces in which those discourses can be subjected to popular contestation.

In Chapters 3 and 4 we will explore more fully the prospects for realising global democracy. For now, let us note that both cosmopolitan and transnational democracy will require broadening how we think about the political community, and this is something that many advocates of the rival perspectives discussed in this chapter are sceptical about. For instance, constitutional patriots like Habermas (2006) doubt that the kinds of solidarity which support democracy are achievable at the global level. Liberal nationalists like Miller make a similar claim, arguing that democratic politics requires conditions that are currently absent on the global stage, such as a 'public who speak the same language … are exposed to the same mass media, form parties and other political associations, and so forth' (Miller, 2007, p. 26). Furthermore, and as we have seen already, multiculturalists such as Kymlicka and communitarians such as Taylor also connect the possibility of meaningful democratic citizenship to shared membership in relatively small, bounded and homogeneous groups. For all of these political theorists, global democracy will inevitably be a pale imitation of real political community, since cosmopolitan citizens will not be bound together by the kinds of ties that sustain democracy as a common project.

Moreover, even liberals – who typically endorse the 'thinnest' theories of political community – have expressed doubts about the democratic credentials of global democracy. John Rawls, for instance, suggests that a world government would have to be despotic if it were to prevent different groups within it from asserting their freedom and autonomy (Rawls, 1999b, p. 36). He thinks that a unified global political community would be torn between tyranny and instability, and that it would compromise cultural diversity and fail to respect the attachments that people have to their own societies. This follows from an idea shared by many liberals, communitarians, liberal nationalists and constitutional patriots, namely that:

> [I]t is surely a good for individuals and associations to be attached to their particular culture and to take part in its common and civic life. In this way belonging to a particular political society, and being at home in its civic and social world, gains full expression and fulfilment. This is no small thing. It argues for preserving significant room for the idea of a people's self-determination. (Rawls, 1999b, p. 111)

Consequently, finding ways to democratise global institutions without compromising the values of political community will be an important challenge for political theorists in the coming years.

3

Pluralism

- INTRODUCTION
- RIVAL PERSPECTIVES
  Political liberalism • *Modus vivendi* • Agonism
- KEY DEBATES
  How should society respond to cultural diversity? • Is political liberalism fair to
  religious believers? • Can pluralism and equality be reconciled?
- FUTURE CHALLENGES

Introduction

The fact that people disagree fundamentally about morality, religion and the
good life is a defining and intractable feature of modern social life. It also raises
a number of difficult normative questions for political theorists. For instance,
can citizens who favour conflicting ethical, political and religious ideologies
agree about fundamental political values? Can a broadly secular society treat
religious believers as equals, and *vice versa*? And how should a society respond
to individuals and groups who are profoundly sceptical about, or even hostile
to, its basic values? In this chapter we will explore three different ways in which
contemporary political theorists have responded to questions like these.

Political theorists use the word pluralism in a different way to political
scientists. In political science, pluralism describes a political system in which
power is dispersed amongst a number of actors or institutions (thus, for instance,
pluralist states are typically contrasted with states dominated by elites). This
application of the term can be both descriptive (for instance, when categorising
different political systems) and normative (for instance, when recommending
a programme of political reform). Meanwhile, for political theorists pluralism
generally refers to 'value pluralism', which is a contested philosophical view
about the nature of value. Value pluralism is best understood by comparing it
to its opposite: monism. According to monists, there is a single ultimate value,
which apparently different values – such as beauty, friendship, courage, wisdom
and so on – are reducible to. For instance, the utilitarian Jeremy Bentham was
a monist who believed that valuable things (such as beauty, friendship etc.)

were valuable if and only if they contributed to the sensation of pleasure, which he regarded as the ultimate value (we examine contemporary versions of this theory in Chapter 9). In contrast, value pluralists believe there are many different valuable things *and* that these cannot be meaningfully compared or reduced to another. When values cannot be ranked or compared, value pluralists call them incommensurable. Moral philosophers continue to disagree with one another about whether or not value pluralism correctly describes the structure of morality. Meanwhile, the political theorists we discuss in this chapter all accept value pluralism, albeit to different degrees. However, they disagree about how we should respond to the fact that people actually do disagree about basic and fundamental matters of religion, morality and politics. Historically, such disagreements – and especially disagreements about religion – have been the source of political volatility and even violence.

One historically influential solution to the discord unleashed by the fact of religious diversity was to institutionalise the principle of toleration by separating church and state. Formulated as a doctrine, as in the First Amendment to the US Constitution or the 1905 Law on the Separation of the Churches and State in France, this strategy makes two demands. First, states should refrain from imposing any particular religious orthodoxy on their members and from interfering in their religious liberties. Thus it should take no views about theological controversies and should tolerate a variety of religious beliefs and practices. Second, religious influence over political decisions should be minimised and political power should not be exercised for religious purposes. Proponents of the first theory that we examine in this chapter – political liberalism – identify two shortcomings with this doctrine. First, because it focusses narrowly on the issue of establishing peace amongst different religious groups, it neglects other forms of disagreement. Second, because its goal is stability and not legitimacy, it does not supply moral reasons for citizens to endorse their common political arrangements. In response to these concerns, political liberals have sought to explain how citizens who otherwise disagree about morality, religion, politics and the good life can nevertheless reach a widely acceptable 'overlapping consensus' about shared political principles. For them, the challenge of pluralism is not simply to reduce the likelihood of conflict, but it is to justify fair terms of co-operation amongst free and equal people who hold very different views about the ultimate ends and purposes of human life.

Proponents of the second view we shall consider – *modus vivendi* – are sceptical about the possibility of reaching a meaningful consensus about the principles that should underlie an ideal political order. For these political theorists, pluralism runs deeper than political liberals acknowledge and it is naive to believe that we will find any genuinely shared political principles amongst our different worldviews. Instead, they argue that a stable peace may be the best we can aspire to, and that our best prospects for securing this are to find pragmatic compromises that the various groups in society might be willing to acquiesce to, even if they do so for reasons of self-interest.

Finally, proponents of the third view – agonism – agree that pluralism runs deeper than political liberals acknowledge and similarly reject the goal of reaching a consensus about shared political principles. However, they also reject the goal of stability and instead celebrate the dynamic and transformative potentials of disagreement and conflict. Agonists aspire to a political (dis)order in which all governing principles are always open to contestation and they are wary about the stifling effects of a political life that aspires to agreement and consensus. For these political theorists, the key challenge presented by pluralism is neither legitimacy nor stability, but is rather to convert potentially hostile forms of antagonism into 'agonistic' respect.

These three different views are set out briefly in Table 3.1, and will be explored in greater depth in the first half of this chapter. Some of the most difficult challenges posed by pluralism in contemporary societies are related to cultural

Table 3.1 Summary of rival perspectives on pluralism

	Political liberalism	Modus vivendi	*Agonism*
Goals	Political legitimacy and stability 'for the right reasons'	Social peace and stability	Vibrant confrontation amongst respectful adversaries, leading to the emergence of new possibilities/identities
Understanding of pluralism	A diversity of incompat-ible yet mostly reasonable 'comprehensive doctrines'; consensus about political principles is possible	Incommensurable value systems that cannot be rationally ranked or compared; sceptical about the possibility of consensus about political principles	Pluralism is an 'axiologic-al principle'; political language and concepts are unstable, ambiguous and contested; consensus about political principles is illusory and potentially oppressive
Criteria for political justification	Constitutional essen-tials to be based on a free-standing political conception of justice supported by an overlap-ping consensus; political consent should be moral and rational	Shared willingness to accept common political arrangements, which are usually a product of strategic negotiation, bargaining and compromise	Denies the possibility of fixed criteria of political justification; all principles of political order should be open to contestation
Favoured mode of political discourse	'Idealised' conception in which citizens accept the standards of 'public reason' and regard one another as free and equal.	'Realist' conception in which individuals and groups promote their own interests; the interests of the powerful are likely to prevail	Opposes the goal of consensus on philosophic-al and political grounds; celebrates adversarial and subversive contestation; acknowledges that politics is a space of power and conflict

diversity, and in the second half of the chapter we will examine how proponents of the three rival perspectives have sought to address them. We will begin by exploring how political communities might respond to cultural differences and to controversial cultural practices. After this, we will focus more narrowly on the question of whether or not political liberalism responds fairly to the needs, perspectives and interests of deeply religious citizens. Then, we will examine the relationship between pluralism and equality, focussing especially on the tensions between multiculturalism and feminism. Finally, to conclude the chapter, we will examine some of the ways in which our three rival perspectives have responded to the challenge of pluralism on the global stage.

Rival perspectives

Political liberalism

> How is it possible that there may exist over time a stable and just society of free and equal citizens profoundly divided by reasonable religious, philosophical, and moral doctrines? (Rawls, 1996, p. xxv)

This is the problem that political liberalism addresses. To find out what is distinctive about it, we should begin by looking at how its proponents – such as John Rawls, Charles Larmore, Gerald Gaus and Stephen Macedo – understand the phenomenon of pluralism. According to Rawls:

> A modern democratic society is characterized not simply by a pluralism of comprehensive religious, philosophical, and moral doctrines but by a pluralism of incompatible yet reasonable comprehensive doctrines. No one of these doctrines is affirmed by citizens generally. Nor should one expect that in the foreseeable future one of them, or some other reasonable doctrine, will ever be affirmed by all, or nearly all, citizens … Political liberalism assumes that, for political purposes, a plurality of reasonable but incompatible doctrines is the normal result of the exercise of human reason within the framework of the free institutions of a constitutional democratic regime. (Rawls, 1996, p. xviii)

Three features of this account are worth noting. First, pluralism includes philosophical and moral differences as well as religious ones. Second, under conditions of pluralism, citizens endorse rival comprehensive doctrines that are incompatible with one another. These doctrines cover 'the major religious, philosophical, and moral aspects of human life in a more or less coherent and consistent manner' (Rawls, 1996, p. 59) and give rise to contrasting visions about the good life and about the ultimate purposes of political association. Third, deep religious, moral and philosophical disagreements are to be expected in free societies – pluralism 'is not a mere historical condition that may soon pass away;

it is a permanent feature of the public culture of democracy' (Rawls, 1996, p. 36). One reason for this is that the freedoms of speech and conscience that liberalism insists upon make it almost inevitable that reasonable people will continue to disagree about ultimate questions.

Importantly, the fact that citizens disagree about the nature and significance of basic moral and political values is not the result of bad faith or ignorance on their part. Rather, it follows from what Rawls (1996, pp. 54–8) calls 'the burdens of judgement'. These burdens have to do with things such as the difficulties of assessing and interpreting evidence, the variances amongst people's experiences, the vagueness of concepts, and the complexity of moral, political and social issues. What Rawls's account suggests is that even if citizens had the opportunity and desire to thrash out their disagreements about truth, morality and religion, it is highly unlikely that they would come to any substantive agreements about them.

Why should pluralism of this kind pose a challenge for liberal political theory? Peter Lassman answers this by identifying a 'paradox' of liberal justification:

> Liberal theorists have generally insisted that justifications of the exercise of political power must be available and intelligible for all citizens. However, if pluralism, understood as the existence of conflicting but reasonable visions of the good, is itself a product of the liberal state, then this seems to limit the prospects of the emergence of a universally acceptable public philosophy ... Liberal political regimes seem to create a state of affairs that undermines their own requirements for legitimacy. (Lassman, 2011, p. 86)

A stable political system must be 'willingly and freely supported by at least a substantial majority of its politically active citizens' (Rawls, 1996, p. 38). Consequently, political communities require a shared conception of justice that can attract the support of most members. But at the same time, the possibility of agreement about values seems to be blocked by the inevitability of pluralism. Rawls's theory of political liberalism aims to overcome this paradox by making three important moves.

First, Rawls rejects the idea that a shared conception of justice needs to be wedded to a comprehensive theory about human nature, morality and truth. This possibility, of course, is what the fact of pluralism seems to rule out. Instead, he thinks that we can all agree to a more limited conception of justice provided that it satisfies two conditions: that it fall entirely 'under the category of the political' (Rawls, 1996, p. 133) and that it is free-standing. A political conception of justice has a limited scope. It applies solely to a society's major social, political and economic institutions and not to other controversial questions about human life (such as those concerning the proper conduct of personal relationships or which human excellences are the most valuable). Meanwhile, a free-standing conception of justice is 'presented independently of any wider comprehensive religious or philosophical doctrine' (Rawls, 1996, p. 223). Detaching the political conception from any particular comprehensive doctrine means that it will not compete with any of the moral and religious views already endorsed by citizens. Members should be able to endorse the free-standing political conception without abandoning their existing ideas about how they should lead their lives.

Second, the aim of a free-standing political conception of justice is to attract the support of an 'overlapping consensus' of reasonable comprehensive doctrines. The political conception represents a kind of common ground that can be endorsed by adherents of rival moral and religious traditions. Followers of these different traditions might endorse the shared conception for quite different reasons, including ones that are rooted in their own comprehensive doctrines and which are rejected by their fellow citizens. Importantly, citizens themselves will regard their shared political conception of justice as part of their own broader beliefs about morality, and not simply as something they 'go along' with for strategic purposes. As Rawls conceives of it, 'the political conception is a module, an essential constituent part, that fits into and can be supported by various reasonable comprehensive doctrines' (Rawls, 1996, p. 12).

Third, citizens will be able to agree on a political conception of justice only if they 'put aside their comprehensive moral and religious conceptions' (Macedo, 1995, p. 474). Political liberalism asks that the members of a political community adopt a particular style of deliberation, which Rawls terms 'public reason', when they address fundamental political questions. According to this view, citizens must refrain from appealing to controversial doctrines when justifying their views about basic political matters and instead draw only from a limited pool of widely accepted reasons and arguments. Like the 'civic virtue' theorists we examined in Chapter 2, Rawls requires citizens to internalise some demanding attitudes and dispositions:

> The ideal of citizenship imposes a moral, not a legal duty – the duty of civility – to be able to explain to one another on those fundamental questions how the principles and policies they advocate and vote for can be supported by the political values of public reason … The union of the duty of civility with the great values of the political yields the ideal of citizens governing themselves in ways that each thinks the others might reasonably be able to accept. (Rawls, 1996, pp. 217–18)

There are two aspects of the case in favour of a duty of civility. First, and pragmatically, public debate will quickly reach a stalemate if partisans of rival comprehensive doctrines insist on making assertions and counter-assertions that can only be understood in terms of their incompatible understandings of the 'whole truth'. Consequently, in order to achieve consensus, they must restrict themselves to standards of reasoning that are shared by their fellow citizens and to values which are widely accepted. Second, and morally, it would be unreasonable for partisans of particular comprehensive doctrines to seek to impose their world-view on others who disagree, since political power is something in which each citizen has an equal share.

Modus vivendi

Political liberalism is a much more ambitious doctrine than the separation of church and state, because it combines liberalism's historical concern with social peace with a demanding theory of legitimacy. According to Rawls, the basic institutions of society are legitimate not simply if they deliver stability but only if the principles underlying them also solicit an overlapping consensus. This requires that citizens do more than merely acquiesce to the principles governing the design of society's major institutions, or accept those institutions for strategic purposes. Rather, they must recognise the underlying principles as being in some sense 'their own'. To illustrate what he means by this, Rawls contrasts his view with a *modus vivendi*, which he characterises as 'a consensus on accepting certain authorities, or on complying with certain institutional arrangements, founded on a convergence of self- or group interests' (Rawls, 1996, p. 147). As an example of such an arrangement, he discusses the uneasy toleration of Catholics and Protestants in sixteenth- and seventeenth-century Europe. On his reading, this pragmatic pact for civil peace, entered into for reasons of mutual self-preservation, lacked 'stability for the right reasons', because had either group been able to do so, they would have imposed their 'own religious doctrine as the sole admissible faith' (Rawls, 1996, p. 479). The lesson Rawls draws from this is that it is dangerous for citizens to affirm their arrangements as being only 'second best', since this will lead to a weak commitment to the political order. Larmore makes a similar point by arguing that *modus vivendi* settlements are 'hostage to the shifting distribution of power: Individuals will lose their reason to uphold the agreement if their relative power or bargaining strength increases significantly' (Larmore, 1990, p. 346).

Meanwhile, a number of contemporary liberals – such as John Gray, Bernard Williams and John Horton – have embraced a *modus vivendi* view, albeit one that differs from Rawls's own description of it. For these authors, the purpose of a *modus vivendi* is to secure social order, minimise violence, avoid disruption and protect society against great evils, such as civil war. Its proponents acknowledge that many citizens may regard it as a 'second best' outcome, but even a 'mere' *modus vivendi* will very often be preferable to the *status quo* (Williams, 2005, p. 2). A *modus vivendi* simply requires an agreement that delivers peace, for whatever reasons and however rough-and-ready, and it drops the requirement that members must affirm a shared political conception of justice. Like political liberalism, it requires that citizens accommodate one another and accept common institutions, but unlike political liberalism it does not require citizens to reach an overlapping consensus about principles of justice. As Horton puts it, a *modus vivendi* only requires 'a kind of shared willingness to acknowledge the legitimacy of some particular set of political arrangements' (Horton, 2010, pp. 438–9). For its supporters, this makes the *modus vivendi* approach a more realistic and workable proposition.

John Gray's defence of the *modus vivendi* approach emphasises its anti-utopian credentials:

> [A] theory of *modus vivendi* is not the search for an ideal regime, liberal or otherwise. It has no truck with the notion of an ideal regime. It aims to find terms on which different ways of life can live well together. (Gray, 2000, p. 6)

On Gray's account, the *modus vivendi* approach is the authentic heir to classical liberalism because it accepts the full force of value pluralism. Political liberals took liberalism down the wrong path by putting so much emphasis on consensus, and in doing so they neglected the deep truth that 'humans will always have reason to live differently' (Gray, 2000, p. 5). Whilst political liberals tend to view disagreement about values as a regrettable consequence of our human limitations that can be overcome through public reason, *modus vivendi* approaches instead view value conflicts as deep and irresolvable. For Gray, there are many different ways of life, which cannot be rationally ranked and amongst which no single vision expresses the best way to live. The conflicts amongst these different ways of life cannot be overcome by settling on common political values, since there is no guarantee that any such values exist.

In support of their view, contemporary advocates of a *modus vivendi* approach draw attention to three important aspects of pluralism that seem to be brushed over by political liberalism. First, they point out that pluralism is as much a political phenomenon as a philosophical one, as it is more often experienced in the form of conflicts amongst groups with competing interests than as philosophical disagreements amongst individuals with different ethical beliefs and ideals. Proponents of a *modus vivendi* are sceptical about solving the problem of pluralism through the seminar-room exercise of finding common ground amongst rival ethical systems, because the tough cases that must be settled are rooted in 'the rival claims of ways of life' (Gray, 2000, p. 12). These rival claims might issue from groups that share similar moral values but disagree deeply about their political allegiances, as in Northern Ireland. Or they might come from groups that not only have different ethical beliefs and ideals but also refuse to associate with one another. In these cases (and others) finding common philosophical ground seems to be much less urgent than settling on a workable *modus vivendi*.

Second, advocates of a *modus vivendi* argue that political liberals do not pay enough attention to political power and how it is distributed. Political liberals operate within a stylised and highly abstract model of politics, in which free and equal individuals with different comprehensive moral doctrines attempt to reach an overlapping consensus through public reason. But real political bargains are not at all like this: they are made amongst political unequals and are often the product of negotiation, compromise, persuasion and even threats. Because the theoretical construct that sustains political liberalism is unrealistic, it cannot help to guide our practical reasoning about what we should actually do in the here and now.

Third, proponents of *modus vivendi* also think that political liberals overestimate the extent to which liberal values are widely endorsed. Although quintessentially liberal concepts – such as rights and freedom – are frequently invoked in political discourse, there is little real agreement about their meaning (think, for example, about the disagreements amongst those who favour a 'right to life' and those who favour a 'right to choose' with respect to abortion). Similarly, any shared commitment to liberal principles often seems to be, at best, very thin:

> In reality, though there is unprecedented lip-service to them, most late modern societies contain little consensus on liberal values. Many people belong at once in a liberal form of life and in communities which do not honour liberal values. At the same time, many who stand chiefly in liberal ethical life do not subscribe to some of its traditional values. The liberal ideal of personal autonomy is the idea of being part-author of one's life. For some, the pursuit of autonomy comes into conflict with allegiance to an established community. For others, it is in tension with the freedom to respond to the needs of the present. (Gray, 2000, p. 13)

The worry that Gray expresses here is that the prospects for reaching an overlapping consensus that is recognisably liberal are bleak. If this is true, then committed liberals might be better off settling for a 'mere' *modus vivendi*.

A *modus vivendi* is reached when members of a society accept some set of political arrangements, even if they do so reluctantly and even if they regard those arrangements as second-best. As Horton points out, there is no guarantee that a *modus vivendi* 'will always issue in an outcome that would generally be regarded as liberal' and one 'could be struck on terms that might not conform to (any plausible version of) liberal principles' (Horton, 2010, p. 438). This has led some political theorists to conclude that regardless of the attractions of a *modus vivendi*, it is not a *liberal* theory. However, liberal defenders of the approach have sought to placate this worry, as we explore in Box 3.1.

Agonism

Both *modus vivendi* and political liberal approaches offer different solutions to the problem of pluralism. Whilst political liberals want to resolve deep

---

BOX 3.1 LIBERALISM AND *MODUS VIVENDI*

Many proponents of a *modus vivendi* approach also claim to be liberals. According to them, a *modus vivendi* will qualify as liberal if it satisfies two conditions: it ought to be widely accepted and it should uphold minimal moral standards. Requiring a *modus vivendi* to be widely accepted disqualifies arrangements that maintain peace through fear and suppression or which do not satisfy people's basic interests. Meanwhile, requiring a *modus vivendi* to satisfy minimal moral standards rules out agreements that would permit people to be tortured, humiliated, persecuted or separated from their friends and family, since these are 'generically human evils' that make 'a worthwhile life unattainable' (Gray, 2000, p. 66). Both criteria face difficulties. Widespread acceptance of a *modus vivendi* might not be adequate, because people 'can be drilled by coercive power into accepting its exercise' (Williams, 2005, p. 6). In response, some *modus vivendi* liberals insist that agreements should not be 'the product of clear, wilful, systematic and comprehensive deception by those with political power' (Horton, 2010, p. 439). Meanwhile, ruling out agreements that permit 'generically human evils' would seemingly require consensus about values, which proponents of a *modus vivendi* are usually sceptical about. In response, John Gray maintains that our knowledge of these evils derives from a degree of 'constancy in human nature' rather than 'an agreement in opinions' (Gray, 2000, p. 66). As such, people who agree about little else might nevertheless acknowledge them.

Can liberals endorse the modus vivendi *approach? Would it ever be rational to accept a* modus vivendi *that secured stability but did not honour minimal moral standards?*

---

disagreements by locating common political principles that everyone can endorse, proponents of a *modus vivendi* believe that our best hopes for civil peace rest with forging practical accommodations that appeal to the self-interests of followers of different ways of life. Meanwhile, advocates of an agonistic politics – such as Chantal Mouffe, William Connolly and Bonnie Honig – have advanced a radical critique of the rationalistic pretensions of both approaches. Agonists are not just sceptical about the possibility of rational consensus but are hostile to the idea. For them, a politics of 'agonistic confrontation' is preferable to the search for an inaccessible agreement.

Recent formulations of the case for agonism have issued mainly from philosophers sympathetic to poststructuralism. Poststructuralism describes an intellectual movement that emerged during the second half of the twentieth century and was strongly influenced by the writings of French philosophers such as Jacques Derrida and Michel Foucault, whose work we will consider in greater detail in Chapter 6. Its followers reject appeals to objectivity and truth, instead arguing that meaning is dynamic and fluid, constituted through complex operations of power. A characteristic poststructuralist move is to 'destabilise' the 'foundations' upon which our knowledge claims are based, in order to reveal the precarious contingency of our settled beliefs. The influence of poststructuralist thinking is especially reflected in three features of the agonist project: its questioning of supposedly stable categories and concepts; its scepticism about overly rational approaches to political problems; and its attentiveness to the pervasiveness of power in social relations. Each of these can be seen in the radical rethinking of pluralism that agonists propose.

First, on the agonistic view, the pluralism of contemporary societies is not just amongst different people endorsing different comprehensive moral doctrines or following different ways of life. Rather, pluralism is an 'axiological principle' (Mouffe, 2000, p. 19) that reaches much further than liberals acknowledge, and includes the categories and ideas we use to make sense of political life. For instance, agonists stress that political concepts (such as equality, respect, democracy and freedom) as well as philosophical ones (such as reason, human nature and truth) are not fixed or stable entities, but are rather produced by distinctive histories of political contestation. This kind of 'deep pluralism' is reflected, for example, in Connolly's depiction of politics as an 'ambiguous and relatively open-ended interaction of persons and groups who share a range of concepts but share them imperfectly and incompletely' (Connolly, 1993, p. 6). The implication of this is that because the concepts which are used in political discourse are radically plural and unstable, any agreements or consensus that we believe ourselves to have reached are likely to be 'fictitious' (Mouffe, 2000, p. 19).

Second, agonists criticise rational approaches to politics, including *modus vivendi* and political liberalisms. Not only do these approaches fail to recognise the importance of political passions, but they are also exclusionary, because they involve removing from public contestation those things which mark us out as different. For example, Rawls's notion of 'public reason' excludes controversial religious doctrines if they do not contain reasons that would be acceptable to non-believers. Although this strategy offers a way to settle the problem of pluralism, it does so by relegating religious difference to the non-political sphere. On an agonistic interpretation, this purported solution is really nothing more than an evasion of the oppositional dimension of politics. As Mouffe sarcastically remarks, 'for Rawls, a well-ordered society is a society from which politics has been eliminated' (Mouffe, 2000, p. 29).

Third, on an agonistic reading, the liberal approach to pluralism is hypocritical, because it serves to disguise the role of power in shaping actual political agreements. Political liberals aim to treat people as equals by favouring political principles that are acceptable to all. But at the same time they exclude controversial views from politics on the basis that they are not widely shared. Although political liberals themselves present this exclusion in terms of a universal morality, agonists stress that it is actually deeply partisan and political (Mouffe, 2000, pp. 24–6). This is because, on their account, what is perceived as reasonable and what is perceived as unreasonable will always depend on the traditions, discourses and power relations that are currently in circulation. Thus, excluding purportedly unreasonable views from political discourse serves to reinforce the prevailing hegemony of the dominant tradition.

Agonists adopt a hard-headed attitude towards politics, regarding it as 'a space of power, conflict and antagonism' (Mouffe, 2005, p. 9). Passionate disagreement is built into the nature of modern democracy, and the liberal project of smoothing over pluralism by removing it from public contestation is fatally undermined once we recognise 'the ineradicable character of antagonism' (Mouffe, 2000, p. 20). Nevertheless, agonists do not think that pluralism should be left to run riot, and they acknowledge that 'some limits need to be put to the kind of confrontation which is going to be seen as legitimate in the public sphere' (Mouffe, 2000, p. 93). The aim of limiting political confrontation in this way 'is to transform *antagonism* into *agonism*' (Mouffe, 2000, p. 103), and this is achieved by altering the terms upon which people regard their political opponents, so that they are 'no longer perceived as an enemy to be destroyed, but as an "adversary"; that is, somebody whose ideas we combat but whose right to defend those ideas we do not put into question' (Mouffe, 2000, pp. 101–2). Connolly makes a similar point, referring to the possibility of moving from 'an antagonism in which each aims initially at conquest or conversion of the other' towards 'an agonism in which each treats the other as crucial to itself' (Connolly, 2002, p. 178). This is achieved by cultivating agonistic respect, which is 'a civic virtue that allows people to honor different final sources, to cultivate reciprocal respect across difference, and to negotiate larger assemblages to set general politics' (Connolly, 2002, p. xxvi). Cultivating this virtue will make citizens both friends and enemies of one another. They 'are friends because they share a common symbolic space but also enemies because they want to organise this common symbolic space in a different way' (Mouffe, 2000, p. 13). Mouffe concludes that converting antagonistic opponents into respectful agonistic adversaries 'is the real meaning of liberal-democratic tolerance, which does not entail condoning ideas that we oppose or being indifferent to standpoints that we disagree with, but treating those who defend them as legitimate opponents' (Mouffe, 2000, p. 102).

Agonists cite two main advantages of their approach. First, an agonistic politics is well placed to ward off the twin threats of citizen passivity and enmity. On their account, both the theory and practice of liberalism have negative effects because they tend to discourage citizen engagement. For instance, Bonnie Honig worries that the 'displacement of politics by law and administration engenders remainders that can disempower and perhaps even undermine democratic institutions and citizens' (Honig, 1993, p. 14). Similarly, Mouffe thinks that a consensus-orientated politics, directed towards minimising confrontation, will 'lead to apathy and disaffection with political participation' (Mouffe, 2000, p. 104). This is because politics is an inherently partisan activity, and 'for people to be interested in politics they need to have the possibility of choosing between parties offering real alternatives' (Mouffe, 2005, p. 29). What agonists recommend is a richer, more partisan and more dynamic politics that will comprehensively engage the passions of its citizens. At the same time, however, respectful agonistic contestation offers a pressure valve for political passions, thereby reducing the risk of an 'explosion of antagonisms that can tear up the very basis of civility' (Mouffe, 2000, p. 104).

The second advantage claimed by proponents of agonism is that their approach opens up political space for the creative reconfiguration of social and cultural identities. Because social and cultural identities are contested within public life, and not hidden away in the private sphere and immunised from criticism, citizens will be exposed to new and different ideas and their identities will be put under pressure. According to proponents, agonistic contestation will help to prevent people's identities from becoming settled, fixed and entrenched, and will instead encourage the emergence of more flexible, contingent and overlapping identities. As Connolly puts it:

> When democratic politics is robust, when it operates to disturb the naturalization of settled conventions, when it exposes settled identities to some of the contestable contingencies that constitute them, then one is in a more favourable position to reconsider some of the demands built into those conventions and identities. (Connolly, 2002, p. 192)

Agonistic confrontation might mean, for example, that new reconfigurations of gender will become possible, or that new religious identities emerge when the old ones are put under public scrutiny.

The dynamic subversion of social and cultural identities that agonists anticipate will no doubt be a disturbing experience for many people. But because the experience of having one's own identity put in question will be shared by all, this may discourage antagonistic hostility. For instance, in reference to religious differences, Connolly describes an ideal in which people respectfully contest their religious beliefs, and then suggests that this will be 'agonistic in two senses': 'you *absorb the agony* of having elements of your own faith called into question by others, and *you fold agonistic contestation* of others into the respect that you convey to them' (Connolly, 2005, p. 124). Because the possibility of having one's identity challenged is shared by everyone, this may discourage the kinds of passive hostility that minorities are currently exposed to in contemporary societies.

Key debates

How should society respond to cultural diversity?

Some of the most pressing cases of pluralism in contemporary politics are so because they involve the intersection of value pluralism and cultural pluralism.

Consider, for example, the fierce controversies surrounding the publication, initially in the Danish newspaper *Jyllands-Posten*, of cartoons depicting the Islamic prophet Muhammad, which are discussed in Box 3.2. Or alternatively, think about the opposition of many Jehovah's Witnesses to blood transfusions. In cases such as these, different cultural groups seem to be divided because of their opposing value systems and worldviews. Indeed, it is sometimes suggested that multiculturalism raises the stakes of pluralism, because of the special significances that people invest in their cultures and identities. For instance, whilst people are sometimes willing to back down in ordinary political debates, they may be less inclined to do so when their identity is at issue, and this may make the achievement of rational consensus, stable agreement or agonistic respect more difficult.

BOX 3.2 CARTOONS CONTROVERSY

The 'cartoons controversy' was triggered by the publication of 12 cartoons in the Danish newspaper *Jyllands-Posten* in September 2005, many of which depicted the Prophet Muhammad. After some peaceful demonstrations in Denmark, there were a number of international protests, some of which became violent and according to estimates resulted in over 200 deaths (Klausen, 2009). The ensuing controversy provoked discussion about the legitimate extent of free speech, about religious intolerance and the incitement of religious hatred, and about the place of Islam and Muslims in Europe. For proponents of a *modus vivendi*, the reaction to the publication of the cartoons revealed the precarious fragility of social peace and the volatility of political passions. Underlying the controversy were incompatible understandings of what kind of respect is owed to religious sensibilities, which perhaps indicated a deeper 'clash of civilisations'. Since advocates of a *modus vivendi* are sceptical about finding common ground or shared principles, they instead favour adopting political rules and institutions that are likely to secure political stability, even if these are restrictive. Meanwhile, political liberals are more optimistic about the prospects of securing principled agreement about how to balance the right to free speech against other concerns. Even when people hold different views about religious truth, they nevertheless share similar values, such as civility, respect and tolerance, and these might form the basis for a common agreement about whether or not the publication of offensive material should be prohibited. Finally, for agonists the controversy reflected a failure to convert antagonistic confrontation into respectful agonistic engagement. Whilst the editors defended their decision to commission the cartoons as an attempt to provoke debate about self-censorship and free speech, the subsequent and heated discussion was not genuinely dialogical, since neither side exhibited a willingness to listen to and learn from the other. In particular, each side sought to place their own cherished principles beyond discussion and refused to acknowledge their essentially fluid and contestable character.

Which approach to the cartoons controversy is preferable?

One proponent of a *modus vivendi* approach, John Gray, has drawn an explicit link between value pluralism and cultural pluralism, defining cultural pluralism as a condition 'in which society intimates a diversity of possibly incommensurable values and worldviews' (Gray, 1993, p. 253). Since Gray believes that a *modus vivendi* approach follows from an acceptance of value pluralism, he also thinks that a *modus vivendi* approach is the best response to multiculturalism. Whether or not one is convinced by this will depend on three things: whether one believes that value pluralism is true; whether one believes that value pluralism entails a *modus vivendi* approach; and whether one believes that cultural pluralism is a form of value pluralism. All three of these claims are contentious.

Other defenders of a multicultural *modus vivendi*, such as John Horton (2011) and Jacob Levy (2007), have developed theories that do not depend upon controversial views about value pluralism and its relationship with cultural pluralism. For these thinkers, a major attraction of a *modus vivendi* approach is that it seems to offer a realistic prospect for securing peace and stability amongst rival ethnic, cultural and religious groups. For example, Horton cites the case of the 1998 Good Friday Agreement, which he thinks succeeded largely as a consequence of its *modus vivendi* credentials. This agreement established a system of power-sharing amongst the two main communities in Northern Ireland and consequently was able to 'detoxify a deep-rooted and persistent religiously-defined conflict' (Horton, 2011, p. 134). Horton emphasises that this 'messy, ragbag of a document' was the result of back room bargaining and compromises amongst groups looking out for their own interests. The preceding political negotiations 'followed no established procedure, theory or principle' and were 'pretty much made up as the process developed' (Horton, 2011, pp. 132–3). The implication that Horton draws is that had participants in the peace process been limited to the kind of rarefied approach advocated by political liberals, they would have been unable to make the necessary compromises.

A more general defence of *modus vivendi* multiculturalism has been suggested by Chandran Kukathas (2003). Kukathas compares a multicultural society to an archipelago, suggesting an ideal in which different cultural groups achieve peace and stability by agreeing to leave one another alone. This is a radical version of the 'mosaic multiculturalism' discussed in Chapter 2, and each group in society is, in effect, left to govern itself. Kukathas characterises this as a liberal vision, since it realises a particularly demanding version of the principle of toleration. Of course, some groups in society, such as religious fundamentalists, might reject both liberalism and the principle of toleration. Nevertheless, they might be convinced to go along with archipelago-type arrangements on *modus vivendi* grounds, because they too have an interest in peaceful co-existence. One consequence of this view, as Kukathas acknowledges, is that it 'gives considerable power to the group, denying others the right to intervene in its practices – whether in the name of liberalism or any other moral ideal' (Kukathas, 1995,

p. 239). Critics have been especially worried about this, because it potentially leaves weaker group members vulnerable to oppression or exploitation (we return to this issue at the end of this chapter).

Whilst *modus vivendi* approaches to cultural differences tend to lean towards a mosaic form of multiculturalism, agonistic approaches lean closer to the hodgepodge ideal. For them, multiculturalism offers the exciting prospect of multiple and complex agonistic engagements across differences. For its proponents, respectful agonistic encounters are to be celebrated because they will disturb settled cultural identities and disrupt hegemonic political ideas. For example, according to Connolly:

> A *democracy* infused with a spirit of agonism is one in which divergent orientations to the mysteries of existence find overt expression in public life. Spaces for difference to be are established through the play of political contestation … The terms of contestation enlarge opportunities for participants to engage the relational and contingent character of the identities that constitute them, and this effect in turn establishes one of the preconditions for respectful strife between parties who reciprocally acknowledge the contestable character of the faiths that orient them and give them definition in relation to one another. (Connolly, 2002, p. 211)

Connolly acknowledges that in order for the 'politics of democratic agonism to flourish … the politics of generalized resentment must be subdued' (Connolly, 2002, p. 211). However, he does not supply much concrete guidance about how this might be achieved.

Critics of agonism, such as Monique Deveaux, have expressed scepticism about agonism's potential to subdue resentment in culturally diverse societies. For instance, Deveaux writes that the 'claim that an agonistic model of democracy could foster greater inclusion of diverse citizens as well as mutual respect between communities will remain an ineffectual bit of rhetoric in the absence of clearer ideas about how (or indeed whether) we can formalize such inclusion and recognition' (Deveaux, 1999, p. 14). Moreover, she speculates that agonistic engagement, with its emphasis on conflict and disagreement, could turn out to be counterproductive, leading 'to the entrenchment of social and cultural identities' and making 'it more difficult for diverse cultural communities to see that they do share at least some social and moral views, norms and interests' (Deveaux, 1999, p. 15). What Deveaux and the agonists disagree about is not the value of expressing and engaging cultural difference, but rather the form that such engagement is likely to take within a society that adopts a positive attitude toward conflict and disagreement.

Meanwhile, some multiculturalists have begun to develop more nuanced explanations of how society might encourage respectful engagement across cultural differences. One example of this is Bhikhu Parekh's model of 'intercultural dialogue', which shares some features in common with both political liberalism and agonism. Parekh is concerned to find out how culturally diverse societies might deal fairly with 'disputed practices', such as female genital mutilation, polygamy, animal slaughter methods, arranged marriages and ritual scarring. As he observes:

> A multicultural society is likely to include communities some of whose practices offend against the values of the majority. It cannot tolerate them indiscriminately because it has a duty both to raise its voice against morally outrageous practices and to safeguard the integrity of its own moral culture. However, if it disallowed all it disapproved of, it would be guilty of moral dogmatism and extreme intolerance and would miss the opportunity to take a critical look at its own values and practices. This raises the question as to how a multicultural society should decide which minority values and practices to tolerate within what limits. (Parekh, 2000, p. 264)

In common with the political liberals, Parekh thinks that these kinds of controversies should be settled through a dialogue that aims towards consensus. However, like the agonists, he acknowledges that real political dialogue does not come out of nowhere but instead always occurs within a particular social, cultural and political context. Thus, for him, intercultural dialogue cannot be free-standing and neutral, but must always begin from the prevailing values of a society. But unlike the agonists, he does not regard this as a form of hegemonic dominance. Rather, prevailing values are a helpful starting point for discussing disputed practices, because they can make the unfamiliar seem familiar.

Intercultural dialogue, on Parekh's model, should be orientated around society's 'operative public values'. He thinks that most societies already contain a set of dominant values and practices that are part of its 'moral structure and are embodied in its major social, economic, political and other institutions' (Parekh, 2000, p. 268). These operative public values 'form a complex and loosely-knit whole and provide a structured but malleable vocabulary of public discourse' (Parekh, 2000, p. 269). They are *values* in the sense that adherents cherish them, endeavour to live in accordance with them, and refer to them when evaluating the behaviour of others. Meanwhile, they are *public* in the sense that they are embodied in laws, institutions and practices, and because they regulate the public conduct of citizens. Finally, they are *operative* in the sense that they are not merely abstract ideals but are generally observed and constitute a lived social and moral reality. Importantly, these values are not fixed but instead are malleable and may change as circumstances alter. Similarly, they are not neatly structured, and will often overlap messily with one another and be subject to varying degrees of public contestation. Whilst some citizens may reject these values, they are nevertheless a generally reliable guide to 'how we do things here'. These values do not pretend to be neutral amongst different cultural traditions: they embody a distinctive way of life, reflecting a shared history and a partial perspective about what it is to be a human being. As a consequence, they will often be experienced as burdensome by cultural minorities who endorse very different value commitments (such as migrants and historically marginalised groups).

How can operative public values be used to arbitrate about disputed practices? Parekh rejects the idea of using them as a 'crude and non-negotiable standard' (Parekh, 2000, p. 270). Instead, he favours an open-minded dialogue about the relationship between the disputed practice and the operative public values. Importantly, and in contrast to political liberalism, Parekh places no limits on the kinds of reasons and arguments that participants in the dialogue might invoke (in other words, there is no equivalent to the idea of 'public reason'). Moreover, he emphasises that this kind of dialogue has no fixed destination and could have the kind of transformative potential that agonists celebrate. For instance, intercultural dialogue might lead to a minority group deciding to abandon a controversial practice by fostering a debate within that community about its legitimacy. But alternatively, it might also encourage majority society to reconsider its own values and their scepticism about the practice. The effects of dialogue will be difficult to predict, and will depend upon the practices and values that are under contestation, as well as the dispositions of the dialogical partners. The important thing is that dialogue gives both sides the opportunity to learn about one another, and to reconsider their views in light of the arguments, stories and perspectives to which they are exposed. As a consequence, intercultural dialogue may make for more informed and considered public policy, as each group is allowed to present its case. Furthermore, dialogue may help to embed a democratic culture, assisting in the cultivation of the virtues of tolerance, reciprocity and open-mindedness.

An interesting, perhaps surprising and certainly un-agonistic aspect of Parekh's approach is his reluctance about demanding rapid transitions in a society's operative public values. For instance, after a dialogue about a disputed practice, Parekh thinks that if the majority remain unconvinced about it then their values should prevail. He gives three reasons in support of this. First, operative public values are 'woven' into a society's institutions and practices which 'cannot be radically revised without causing considerable moral and social disorientation' (Parekh, 2000, p. 273). Second, majorities do not have a duty to accommodate minorities if doing so threatens their own way of life. Third, minorities – and especially immigrants – should 'defer' to majorities in contentious matters in order to 'counter the resentment their presence generally provokes among some sections of society' (Parekh, 2000, p. 273).

A further controversial point about Parekh's approach is that the terms of intercultural dialogue are established by the different views present within society, and do not make reference to universal moral values (in this respect, intercultural dialogue is closer to agonistic and *modus vivendi* approaches than to political liberalism). Some liberal critics, such as Brian Barry (2001b) worry about this. For instance, suppose that a society contains a large number of racists, and that the operative public values of this society reflect this. Parekh's approach seems to require that if an ethnic minority cannot convince the majority to alter its values, then it should defer to majority preferences.

Is political liberalism fair to religious believers?

Political liberals are committed to the ideal of justificatory neutrality. This means that any justifications we give – especially when discussing constitutional essentials but perhaps also when considering a law or a policy – should not depend upon controversial ideas about which other citizens reasonably disagree, such as religious doctrines. Within this view, public reason operates as a kind of constraint on the ideas that are allowed to enter into political reasoning (thus, Joseph Raz (1986) characterises it as the 'exclusion of ideals'). This aspect of political liberalism has inspired a substantial critical literature and in this section we will look at two serious objections to it: that political liberalism's claim to neutrality is unfounded, and that political liberalism unfairly discriminates against some religious believers.

The first objection has been advanced by both multiculturalists and communitarians. The basic claim is that political liberalism – like most other forms of liberalism – does not actually supply an impartial framework within which different moral and political views can resolve their differences. Rather, political liberalism is itself a contested doctrine that stands amongst (and not above) the different views within society. Parekh, for example, thinks that all forms of liberalism advocate 'a specific view of man, society, and the world' based on 'a particular cultural perspective' and as such 'cannot provide a broad and impartial enough framework to conceptualise other cultural perspectives and their relations with it' (Parekh, 2000, p. 14). For sceptics like Parekh, Rawls's theory 'presupposes a conception of man and society' that is not found 'in other traditions of thought' (Parekh, 2000, p. 87).

In addition to smuggling a set of controversial cultural assumptions through the back door, political liberalism has also been accused of promoting a distinctively liberal way of life. On the face of things, this accusation seems perplexing, since the aim of political liberalism is to find a mutually acceptable political conception of justice that leaves intact whatever comprehensive moral doctrines are currently in circulation. The problem, according to its critics, has to do with the conception of citizenship that political liberalism depends upon. As we have seen, Rawls thinks that citizens must 'have a sufficient degree of the "political virtues" ... and be willing to take part in public life' (Rawls, 1996, p. 205). The political virtues that citizens must exhibit include such things as 'toleration and mutual respect ... a sense of fairness and civility ... a spirit of compromise and a readiness to meet others halfway' (Rawls, 1996, pp. 122, 163).

The importance of these virtues is clear: if citizens lacked them, then it would be difficult for society to sustain democratic political institutions. If these virtues are necessary then society seems to have a duty to promote them, for instance through its school system. But promoting particular and controversial values seems to contradict the ideal of leaving the various comprehensive doctrines intact. Some of the difficult issues this tension gives rise to are discussed in greater detail in Box 3.3.

BOX 3.3 PROMOTING CIVIC VIRTUES IN SCHOOLS

The case in favour of promoting civic virtues is that inculcating certain dispositions and attitudes may be necessary if children are to become good citizens. For example, it is difficult to see how citizens could sustain a democratic community if they are intolerant of people who lead different ways of life, if they refuse to engage respectfully with different opinions, or if they are unwilling to compromise on political matters. Meanwhile, the case against promoting civic virtues is that doing so amounts to a form of indoctrination. This objection often seems particularly pressing when some individuals or groups in society reject the values or virtues that the state wishes to promote. A famous legal case in which these issues were contested was *Mozert v Hawkins County Board of Education* (1987). This case arose in Tennessee in the United States, after a group of parents objected to a decision that required public schools to use a particular 'reader', which was designed to help children develop positive values. Some parents objected to its content, which they believed conflicted with the literal truth of the Bible and compromised their ability to pass on their religious beliefs to their children. As one commentator describes it:

> The parents objected to teaching children to make critical judgments, to use their imaginations, and to exercise choice 'in areas where the Bible provides the answer.' They objected to assigning, among other things: (1) a short story describing a Catholic Indian settlement in New Mexico on grounds that it teaches Catholicism; (2) a reading exercise picturing a boy making toast while a girl reads to him ('Pat reads to Jim. Jim cooks. The big book helps Jim. Jim has fun.') on grounds that 'it denigrates the differences between the sexes' that the Bible endorses; (3) an excerpt from Anne Frank's *Diary of a Young Girl* because Anne Frank writes in a letter to a friend that nonorthodox belief in God may be better than no belief at all; and (4) a text that describes a central idea of the Renaissance as being 'a belief in the dignity and worth of human beings' because that belief is incompatible with their faith. (Gutmann, 1995, p. 571)

Ultimately, the Court of Appeals refused the claim made by the parents, holding that the reader did not impose an undue burden on their religious freedom.

Should the state attempt to promote civic virtues through the school system? To what extent should the wishes of parents be accommodated?

Suppose, for the sake of argument, that children could be socialised into accepting the political virtues of tolerance and civility without jeopardising their comprehensive moral doctrines (perhaps, for example, they could be taught how to be tolerant and civil in their political conduct, without requiring them to apply these virtues across all aspects of their lives). The problems do not end here for political liberalism, since the doctrine also seems to be committed to promoting the value of critical reasoning. This is more controversial because, as political liberal Stephen Macedo notes:

> [P]romoting core liberal political virtues – such as the importance of a critical attitude toward contending political claims – seems certain to have the effect of promoting critical thinking in general ... Even a suitably circumscribed political liberalism is not really all that circumscribed: it will in various ways promote a way of life as a whole. (Macedo, 1995, p. 477)

The value of critical reasoning is rejected by a number of comprehensive moral doctrines. For example, religious believers who accept scriptural authority as the whole truth may regard adopting a critical attitude towards religious texts as dangerous and heretical. Indeed, Rawls himself acknowledges that people 'may have, and often do have at any given time, affections, devotions, and loyalties that they believe they would not, indeed could not and should not, stand apart from and evaluate objectively' (Rawls, 1996, p. 31). What his position seems to require is that all citizens accept the value of critical reasoning within their political lives and in their public capacities as citizens, but that no member of society be required to accept the value of critical reasoning in their non-political lives. But as Macedo points out, this might be impossible to realise in practice.

The second objection to political liberalism is that the ideal of public reason unfairly restricts the democratic freedoms of religious believers. Recall, political liberals say that we should avoid making 'sectarian' appeals to controversial doctrines that our fellow citizens might reasonably reject when we are discussing constitutional essentials or basic matters of political justice. Instead, they think that we have a duty of civility to uphold the ideal of public reason, which means accepting the reasonableness of pluralism and adopting a restricted mode of political discourse, namely one in which we respect the freedom and equality of our fellow citizens by confining ourselves to commonly accepted truths of science and history as well as 'shared fundamental ideas implicit in the public political culture' (Rawls, 1996, p. 100).

One objection to the ideal of public reason is that society itself could lose out if religion were excluded from political debate, since this would disallow many praiseworthy forms of political activity. For instance, consider the abolitionist movement, which sought to outlaw slavery in antebellum America, or the civil rights movement led by Martin Luther King. In both of these cases, political activists used deeply religious speeches to support their causes and did not always back up their arguments in terms that would satisfy the stringent demands of public reason.

Another objection to the ideal of public reason is that not everyone can accept it, which is a possibility that Rawls himself acknowledged:

> [T]hose who believe that fundamental political questions should be decided by what they regard as the best reasons according to their own whole idea of truth – including their religious or secular comprehensive doctrine – and not by reasons that might be shared by all citizens as free and equal, will of course reject the idea of public reason. Political liberalism views this insistence on the whole truth in politics as incompatible with democratic citizenship and the idea of legitimate law. (Rawls, 1996, p. 447)

For example, some religious fundamentalists reject the idea of reasonable pluralism and as a consequence are unwilling to uphold the duty of civility. For them, a single religious *truth* really does exist, the rejection of which is always an error, and this truth should inform the use of political power. Furthermore, and perhaps more troublingly, Rawls's appeal to public reason could even treat non-fundamentalist religious believers unfairly, preventing them from invoking religious reasons during political discourse. This could lead to a kind of 'split identity' problem, in which religious believers end up hiding some of their values when deliberating about important political matters. Some critics worry that this will diminish religion, turning it into 'a kind of hobby' (Carter, 1987, p. 978). Worse still, others think that 'bracketing-off' religious beliefs is in effect to ask people to 'annihilate … essential aspects of one's very self' (Perry, 1988, p. 182). This could be because, for instance, religious beliefs are 'core beliefs that give meaning and purpose to many lives' (Galston, 2002, p. 116). Two of the different strategies that political liberals have deployed in response to this line of objection are explored in Box 3.4.

Can pluralism and equality be reconciled?

The relationship between pluralism and equality is fraught because some individuals and groups reject the value of equality, such as orthodox or fundamentalist religious groups. As a result, respect for pluralism may be incompatible with the principle of equal treatment. In this final section we will examine how the three rival approaches have balanced the competing demands of pluralism and equality, focussing especially on the case of sexual equality.

Proponents of a *modus vivendi* have said the least about equality, which they tend to regard as one of those ideals with which they have 'no truck'. Nevertheless, three distinctive features of a *modus vivendi* theory of equality can be identified. First, strong value pluralism of the kind that some *modus vivendi*

BOX 3.4   PUBLIC REASON AND RELIGIOUS DOCTRINES

According to its critics, Rawls's duty of civility treats religious believers unfairly. One response to this objection, suggested by Kwame Anthony Appiah, is to reconfigure public reason as an erudite and intricate set of 'debating tips'. According to this view, the duty of civility should be regarded:

> as rhetorical advice about how best, within a plural polity, to win adherents and influence policies. There's nothing coercive about such counsel. Sectarians may speak however they prefer, but if they seek to win over those who do not already share their sectarian convictions, they will be well advised to appeal, as much as possible, to those norms and premises that are most generally accepted. (Appiah, 2005, p. 81)

However, this seems unsatisfactory, because it deprives political liberalism of an explanation about why the use of sectarian reasons is objectionable. Moreover, turning the duty of civility into a purely pragmatic strategy means that it might be replaced, for instance if it turns out to be the case that zealous religious rhetoric were to do a better job of mobilising political support. Another response, favoured by Rawls, is to 'widen' the conception of public reason. For instance, in the introduction to a later edition of his *Political Liberalism* Rawls explicitly allows for the inclusion of non-public reasons (such as those of King and the abolitionists) provided that their arguments are also supported by public reasons 'in due course' (1996, p. xlix). That King and the abolitionists may not have done this does not trouble Rawls, since 'they could have' and 'had they known the idea of public reason and shared its ideal, they would have' (1996, p. l, footnote).

Is either of these strategies satisfactory? Does political liberalism treat religious believers fairly?

---

theorists endorse seems to rule out definitive statements about what the principle of equal treatment requires. This is because different worldviews embody rival accounts of human interests, and these generate different understandings of equal treatment. Thus John Gray concludes that 'there is no best interpretation of what equality means or requires' (Gray, 2000, p. 90). In this strong form, Gray's view casts doubt on any principled attempt to pursue a strongly egalitarian programme of government.

Second, equality could nevertheless perform an important instrumental function in a *modus vivendi*, if a *perception* of equal treatment could help to secure whatever compromises are necessary for political stability. Something like this idea can be found in John Horton's interpretation of the Good Friday Agreement. This agreement was recognisably egalitarian, in that it affirmed a principle of 'parity of esteem' amongst the Catholic and Protestant communities. Moreover, this positive instrumental valuation of equality is consistent with Gray's scepticism, since what mattered for Horton was that the agreement achieved its purpose of securing peace. From a *modus vivendi* point of view, nothing significant would have been lost had the agreement been reached without the egalitarian principle of 'parity of esteem'.

Third, where there is a conflict between respect for pluralism and the principle of equal treatment, advocates of a *modus vivendi* will tend to say that the former takes priority over the latter. Chandran Kukathas outlines a strong version of this view, arguing that 'attempts to promote one can only be made at the expense of the other' (Kukathas, 2003, pp. 214–15). For instance, consider the example of groups that are internally unequal because their cultural traditions are hierarchical. According to Kukathas (2003, p. 223), equality can only be upheld across society if we forcibly override the cultural practices of these groups. But this would be unacceptable, on his view, since there are strong reasons to refrain from intervening within the affairs of cultural minorities.

Controversially, Kukathas applies the same logic to the case of sex equality, arguing that the aims of feminism and multiculturalism will often clash with one another, because some cultural groups do not grant female members equal dignity or equality of opportunity. In such cases, his view is that toleration should prevail, even for groups that deny women the right to hold property, limit their access to education and practise forced marriage and female genital mutilation (Kukathas, 1997, p. 70). Meanwhile, as Box 3.5 indicates, liberal feminist authors have criticised Kukathas for not taking liberalism's commitments to freedom and equality seriously enough. They agree that feminism and multiculturalism are in tension, but say that securing women's equality is more important than tolerating cultural differences. Liberal feminism therefore demands much more than a *modus vivendi* can be guaranteed to deliver. Perhaps the parties to a *modus vivendi* will accept gender equality, in which case there need be no trade-off between equality and pluralism. However, if the different groups are not willing to endorse women's equality, then feminist and *modus vivendi* variants of liberalism must part company.

Although the tensions between feminism and political liberalism are less stark, feminists have raised two objections to this theory. First, political liberalism, because of its emphasis on consensus, is said to concede too much ground to comprehensive moral doctrines that do not take women's equality seriously enough. Consequently, the principles of justice delivered by political liberalism may be inadequately egalitarian. Second, political liberalism, because of its restricted 'political' scope, is too reluctant to intervene within associations such as the family, which are often important locations for the reproduction of gendered forms of inequality.

Can political liberals promote equality amongst the sexes, at least to a more demanding extent than a *modus vivendi*? On the one hand, political liberals are strongly committed to tolerating a wide diversity of moral doctrines. If political principles must be justified to all members of society, then it may turn out to be the case that any principles which are capable of soliciting an overlapping consensus

BOX 3.5   MULTICULTURALISM AND FEMINISM

According to Okin, multiculturalism and feminism are in tension since 'most cultures have as one of their principal aims the control of women by men' (Okin, 1998, p. 667). Both majority and minority cultural groups are typically strongly concerned with personal, familial, domestic and sexual morality, as well as with preserving and passing on cultural traditions for future generations. Because women are frequently associated with the reproduction of culture – for instance, through child rearing practices – the accommodation of minority cultural practices may reinforce gendered hierarchies and impose disproportionate burdens on them. There are at least three different ways in which the tension between respecting cultural identities and upholding women's rights could be settled. First, like Kukathas, we might say that if the two come into conflict, then the cultural traditions should have priority. Second, we might instead favour sex equality even if it comes at the expense of cultural pluralism. For example, in a famous passage Okin argues that women within patriarchal cultures:

> may be much better off, from a liberal point of view, if the culture into which they were born were either gradually to become extinct (as its members became integrated into the surrounding culture) or, preferably, to be encouraged and supported to substantially alter itself so as to reinforce the equality, rather than the inequality, of women – at least to the degree to which this is upheld in the majority culture. (Okin, 1998, p. 680)

A third alternative is to attempt to combat both sex and cultural inequality by strengthening the political voice of female group members 'through the expansion of sites of democratic contestation and the inclusion of women in formal decision making procedures' (Deveaux, 2005, p. 341). A central challenge for this more democratic approach is to find ways to contest and revise the various barriers to democratic participation that are often faced by women in traditional cultural groups.

Which of these alternatives is preferable?

will be weakly egalitarian at best, and therefore inadequate from a feminist point of view. On the other hand, Rawls himself is clearly concerned about sex inequality. For instance, in the preface to *Political Liberalism* he writes that '[t]he same equality of the Declaration of Independence, which Lincoln invoked to condemn slavery, can be invoked to condemn the inequality and oppression of women' (1996, p. xxix). Similarly, in a later essay he describes the equal rights of women as 'inalienable' and argues against the application of gender distinctions in the distribution of rights and liberties (Rawls, 1999c, p. 599).

An important issue here concerns the extent to which political liberalism must accommodate comprehensive moral doctrines that do not respect equality between the sexes. Clearly, since political liberalism grants free speech rights, it must favour a wide degree of liberty even for groups and individuals who wish to proselytise on behalf of sexist ideals. But at the same time, political liberalism rules out such groups and individuals imposing their ideals on others, if those ideals do not respect the freedom and equality of women as citizens. This means that groups are entitled to encourage their members to follow traditional gender roles, including deeply unequal ones, provided that society itself upholds a substantive ideal of equal citizenship (for example, granting men and women the same rights and opportunities).

For many feminists, the bargain that political liberalism strikes with patriarchal groups does not go far enough, since it conceivably permits sexist groups considerable discretion within the domestic sphere. Martha Nussbaum expresses the quandary in which political liberalism finds itself as follows:

> On the one hand, the family is among the most significant arenas in which people pursue their own conceptions of the good and transmit them to the next generation. This fact suggests that a liberal society should give people considerable latitude to form families as they choose. On the other hand, the family is one of the most nonvoluntary and pervasively influential of social institutions and one of the most notorious homes of sex hierarchy, denial of equal opportunity, and also sex-based violence and humiliation. These facts suggest that a society committed to equal justice for all citizens, and to securing for all citizens the social bases of liberty, opportunity and self-respect must constrain the family in the name of justice. (Nussbaum, 2003, pp. 499–500)

Rawls himself was notoriously ambiguous on the question of whether or not his theory sanctions intervention within the family, and we will return to this issue again in Chapter 9. Meanwhile, sympathetic critics, such as Okin (1989, 1994), have argued that if political liberalism is really committed to equal respect for persons, then it must also be committed to a critique of the traditional patriarchal family. One reason why intervening within families might be important has to do with the formative role they play in the creation of future citizens. If, for example, children are reared so that they internalise inegalitarian ideas about the proper gender roles of men and women, they may become citizens who are incapable of respecting the equal status of women.

Finally, the egalitarian potential of agonism rests primarily in the emancipatory possibilities that could follow in the wake of transformations in the symbolic order. Recall, one aim of agonism is to allow for the deconstruction of the apparent naturalness of settled identities, and instead to make it possible for new identities to emerge. If it is the case that dominant norms and identities reinforce inequality, then agonistic confrontation – with its potential for challenging and transforming these norms and identities – may conceivably have a radical and egalitarian impact. Consider, for example, the case of inequalities within the family, such as the unequal division of domestic labour. One possible explanation for such inequalities remaining widespread, despite the participation of both men and women in the workplace, has to do with the 'essentialising' tendencies of prevailing ideas about gender. For instance, dominant binary constructions of gender identities allocate distinctive roles to men and women, and associate each with a discrete bundle of tasks and responsibilities (for instance, child rearing and domestic labour in the case of women, home maintenance and breadwinning in the case of men). These prevailing ideas may have the effect of 'trapping' people into settled identities, stereotyping men and women, and preventing them from configuring new ways of relating to themselves and to one another. Meanwhile, agonistic confrontation may reveal and nourish new possibilities, allowing people to create new identities and to blur traditional divisions between the genders.

However, critics of agonism cast doubt upon the egalitarian potential of poststructural forms of political theory. In particular, they emphasise that poststructuralist scepticism about universal reason and foundational moral values, such as justice and equality, leave it unable to fully address substantive issues of inequality. For instance, in an earlier work written with Ernesto Laclau, Mouffe characterises the term 'equality' as a 'floating signifier', the meaning of which depends on the context and the discourse in which it is 'articulated' (Laclau and Mouffe, 2001). For them, equality has an essentially ambiguous meaning, which can be temporarily 'fixed' as a result of discursive political struggle. The appropriate aim for a feminist politics, on this view, is to work towards establishing a particular understanding of equality as the dominant (or hegemonic) one. Pragmatically, such a strategy might have profoundly equalising effects, if it were to succeed. However, given the poststructuralist reluctance to accept foundational political claims, it is difficult to see what theoretical resources would be available to us to condemn the persistence of gender inequality, if the discursive project were to fail.

Future challenges

Pluralism raises challenges not only within political communities but also between them. Consider, for example, the difficulty of reaching global consensus about complex issues such as the regulation of the global economic order, the practices and institutions of international relations, and how to respond to the environmental crisis. Not only is there disagreement about which solutions to favour, but there are also disagreements about how to understand these problems and about what values are at stake. By way of a conclusion, I will briefly sketch how our three rival perspectives might respond to the challenges presented by pluralism on the global stage.

The *modus vivendi* approach has been applied to international politics by 'realist' scholars of international relations, such as E. H. Carr, Hans Morgenthau and Reinhold Niebuhr. Realists believe that conflict and struggles over power are the basic components of international life and they criticise utopians and 'idealists' for failing to appreciate that relationships between states are inevitably governed by self-interest rather than morality. Realists make two important points about the role that self-interest plays in international politics. First, they argue that a world of self-interested actors can be a stable one, but only in a very limited sense. Realists accept that powerful states will always dominate weaker states, if they are given the opportunity, but since each state has an interest in its own survival, alliances will form to bring about a 'balance of power'. Such a system will be 'stable' in the sense that it will enable the general structures of state sovereignty to persist, but it will not be peaceful and war will remain an inevitable feature of international life. Second, realists also argue that attempts to reach consensus about political values – such as human rights or democracy – are unfeasible if they conflict with the interests of powerful actors. Indeed, on a realist worldview, 'value-talk' in international politics is more likely to be a rhetorical disguise used by dominant states to further their own self-interested goals and projects.

Meanwhile, some political liberals suggest that a deeper form of international stability might be possible and are more optimistic about the prospects of consensus about human rights and other basic political values. For example, in a work written towards the end of his life, called *The Law of Peoples* and discussed in Chapter 9, Rawls outlined his vision for a 'realistic utopia' in which different political communities formed an international 'Society of Peoples' by agreeing to shared principles for regulating global society. Rawls argued that different states could agree to respect the freedom and independence of one another, to uphold treaties and agreements, to honour a limited set of human rights and to observe restrictions in the conduct of war (Rawls, 1999b, p. 37). Although he acknowledged that there are constraints on the kind of consensus that might be possible at the global level – since disagreement about fundamental moral, religious and political values will be deeper at this level than within a single political community – he also suggested that co-operation amongst different political communities would increase as societies developed affinities for one another, such that they would 'no longer [be] moved simply by self-interest but by mutual concern for each other's way of life and culture' (Rawls, 1999b, p. 113). By rejecting the realist assumption that self-interest is always the dominant motive in international affairs, Rawls suggests the possibility of a deeper kind of international stability based on a widely shared 'allegiance to the Law of Peoples' (Rawls, 1999b, p. 18).

Two points are especially worth noting about Rawls's approach. First, it is a 'minimalist' view and he does not anticipate different political communities agreeing to the kind of substantive principles that he thinks the members of a single political community could agree to, such as principles of distributive justice or even rights to freedom of expression and association. Second, the agreement he envisages about the 'Law of Peoples' obtains only amongst liberal democracies and what he calls 'decent consultation hierarchies' (political communities that lack liberal or democratic institutions but nevertheless respect the basic rights of members and take their interests into account when making decisions). He accepts that some 'outlaw states' might refuse to comply with the generally recognised principles of international cooperation and instead 'think that a sufficient reason to engage in war is that war advances, or might advance, the regime's rational ... interests' (Rawls, 1999b, p. 90).

Finally, agonists have at least three reasons to be sceptical about Rawls's project of establishing a 'realistic utopia'. First, like realists, they are doubtful about the prospects of reaching a meaningful and sincere consensus about shared principles at the global level. Although different political communities might pay lip-service to the idea of sharing common values, for instance by signing up to human rights agreements, agonists emphasise that these agreements are likely to be superficial and unstable. Second, they also object to Rawls's exclusion of societies that do not qualify as liberal or decent. For them, this unfairly privileges the kind of views that are commonplace in wealthy societies, such as Rawls's own. Third, they also worry about the consequences of a global politics orientated around consensus. For example, Mouffe characterises Rawls's approach to international politics as 'profoundly alarming' and 'likely to lead to war' (Mouffe, 2005, p. 230). For her, the very project of attempting to reach a consensus about global principles risks stifling legitimate expressions of dissent and instead encouraging more militant forms of antagonistic politics.

4

Representation

Introduction

Representation is about making present what is absent, such as by standing, acting or speaking for another person or a group. In politics, representation can take many different forms. For instance, presidents and prime ministers can be said to represent their countries, politicians can be described as representing their constituents, and trade unions can be characterised as representing their members. Not all forms of political representation involve an electoral relationship. For instance, a scientist appearing on a television show might be said to represent the perspective or interests of the scientific community, or a member of a religious minority speaking at a council meeting might be said to represent the opinions or values of their co-religionists. In this chapter, we will examine some of the complexities of these different forms of representation, as well as exploring how they connect up to the idea of democracy.

Contemporary writing about representation has been strongly influenced by Hanna Pitkin's landmark *The Concept of Representation*, published in 1956. One aim of this book was to sort through the different ways in which we speak about representation and the different roles we attribute to representatives. In particular, Pitkin introduced two distinctions that will be helpful to us. First, she distinguished between 'formal' and 'substantive' conceptions of representation. Formal conceptions focus on the relationship between the representative and the represented, asking whether a representative has been properly 'authorised by' or is appropriately 'accountable to' those being represented. For example, we might describe a government as a representative because it was elected by its people and has thereby been authorised to negotiate international treaties on their behalf. Or, we might describe a politician as a representative because they can be held accountable at the ballot box. We look at some of the difficult issues that authorisation and accountability give rise to, focussing especially on their relationship to democracy, in the first two key debates.

Meanwhile, substantive conceptions of representation have to do with whether or not a representative acts in the interests of another. Distinguishing between formal and substantive representation is helpful because it allows us to make sense of cases in which a representative has been formally authorised to act on behalf of others and yet does not substantively represent them, as when an elected government negotiates a treaty that jeopardises the interests of its people, or when a politician favours a policy that is opposed by their constituents. In these cases, arguably, the government and the politician are both representatives (in the formal sense) and yet act unrepresentatively (in the substantive sense). We look at some particularly thorny issues associated with substantive representation, particularly as they apply to representatives of disadvantaged or oppressed groups, in the third key debate.

Pitkin's second distinction contrasts representatives who 'act for' others with those who 'stand for' others. A representative can 'act for' a person or a group either by following their instructions or by exercising independent judgement. These two basic models of 'acting for' make up the first pair of rival perspectives that we will discuss in the first half of the chapter. The first of these is *mandate representation*, which says that representatives are delegates who should not deviate from the instructions supplied by those whom they represent. On this view, representatives are like mouthpieces and do not need to consult their expertise or make judgements. The second is *trustee representation*, which says that representatives 'act for' others by using their own discretion, intellect and judgement rather than following directives. Whilst mandate representatives are instructed, trustee representatives are independent. As we shall see, many of the historical disputes about representative democracy concern the extent to which elected representatives should model themselves on one or the other of these ideals. This disagreement was eloquently captured by John Stuart Mill in the nineteenth century:

> Should a member of the Legislature be bound by the instructions of their constituents? Should he be the organ of their sentiment, or of his own? their ambassador to a congress, or their professional agent, empowered not only to act for them but to judge for them what ought to be done. (Mill, 1993, p. 341)

Although these controversies have not abated, few contemporary political theorists exclusively endorse one of the rival positions. Indeed, if there is a consensus, it is that political representatives should be 'a bit of both'. Nevertheless, the distinction between the two alternatives continues to shape much writing on representation.

Let us now turn to representation as 'standing for'. As in the case of 'acting for' representation, a representative might 'stand for' others in one of two ways. Either symbolically – as when a monarch stands for their people – or descriptively – as when a polling company populates a representative sample. Descriptive forms of 'standing for' representation have become increasingly important in contemporary politics, especially in debates about the under-representation of women, ethnic minorities and other disadvantaged groups. Consequently, the third rival perspective we shall consider is *descriptive representation*, according to which representatives 'stand for' others when they share some significant characteristic, such as gender, race or sexuality.

The fourth rival perspective we shall consider is *constitutive representation*, which has been especially associated with feminist and poststructuralist political theory. This view emphasises the dynamic and creative aspects of political representation, suggesting that representatives do not simply reflect the preferences, interests or identities of their constituents, but that they play an important role in constituting those preferences, interests and identities. Importantly, its proponents emphasise the provisional nature of representative claims and the importance of ongoing political contestation, arguing that effective political representation should aim to 'foster and institutionalize popular impatience with our rulers' and 'to both fuel and channel popular grievances against those in power' (Garsten, 2009, p. 91). Furthermore, this view characterises traditional forms of electoral representation as only one example of representation amongst others, and it draws attention to a wider economy of provisional and contestable 'representative claims' (Saward, 2010). This includes claims made by unelected representatives, such as celebrity advocates. In a sense, this perspective is of a different order to the other ones we consider, since mandate, trustee and descriptive representatives can all be understood as advancing 'representative claims'. However, it is also worth noting that because constitutive theories of representation share much in common with the agonistic theories of pluralism we discussed in Chapter 3, they are also committed to some controversial assumptions (Table 4.1).

After exploring mandate, trustee, descriptive and constitutive theories of representation, summarised in Table 4.1, we will examine three key debates, each of which connects these different modes of representation to the ideal of democracy. First, we will take up a difficult puzzle about why representatives are entitled to act or stand on behalf of their constituents. To address this, we will compare three different mechanisms that potentially explain how representatives are authorised, exploring the relationships between these different models and our four rival perspectives. Second, we will turn to the issue of accountability, comparing some different ways in which representatives might be held to account. A key issue here concerns identifying if electoral accountability – which consists in rewarding and

Table 4.1 Summary of rival perspectives on political representation

	Mandate	Trustee	Descriptive	Constitutive
Primary relation between representative and constituents	Representatives 'act for' constituents by following their instructions	Representatives 'act for' constituents by exercising their judgement	Representatives 'stand for' their constituents by virtue of resembling them	Representatives 'create' constituencies
Object of representation	Preferences of constituents	National or common interests	Identities of constituents	A (contestable) interpretation of the preferences, interests or identities of constituents
Subject of representation	Independently defined constituency, for instance by electoral rules or membership of a voluntary association	Independently defined constituency, for instance by electoral rules or membership of a voluntary association	Independently defined constituency, possibly with fluid boundaries (e.g. surrogate representation)	Constituency has fluid and contested boundaries, defined by both the representative and their audience
Role of representatives	Bargaining amongst other representatives, on behalf of constituents	Deliberating amongst other representatives, about the common good	Making identities 'present' and making shared interests or perspectives visible	'Constituting' political identities and discourse, by creatively interpreting the interests of constituents
Criteria for evaluation	'Congruence' of preferences	Exercising good judgement	Descriptive 'fit' amongst representatives and constituents; legislatures should be a 'mirror' to wider society	A 'reflexive' system that incentivises genuine dialogue between representatives and constituents
Primary mode(s) of authorisation	Instruction	Competitive election	Resemblance (and possibly election via a quota system)	Formal and informal audience 'acceptance'; representatives can be 'self-appointed' as well as elected
Primary mechanism(s) of accountability	Representatives are highly responsive to formal electoral sanctions (which ideally take the form of permanent revocability)	Representatives are subject to formal electoral sanctions (at periodic elections) but ideally are unresponsive to these	'Responsiveness' achieved mainly through informal deliberative accountability; limited role for (often ineffective) electoral sanctions	Emphasises informal and discursive modes of accountability, including public shaming and peer monitoring for 'self-appointed' representatives

punishing representatives at the ballot box – is adequate, or if it might need to be complemented by less formal modes of accountability. Third, we will concentrate on two objections that have been levelled against descriptive representation: that descriptive representatives might be less accountable to their constituents than other kinds of representatives, and that descriptive representation itself might not be feasible, given the complexity of social identities. Finally, to conclude the chapter, we will explore some of the challenges of global political representation, focussing especially on proposals to democratise the United Nations.

Rival perspectives

Mandate representation

Politicians often claim to be acting on a mandate. Consider, for example, a government enacting a legislative programme based on its election manifesto, or a troublesome politician tenaciously clinging to a point of principle because their constituents demand it, or a spokesperson articulating the demands of a pressure group. In cases such as these, and in many others, political representatives can credibly claim to be acting on the instructions of those whom they represent.

This view of political representation is described as the 'mandate' or 'delegate' view. For its proponents, a political representative is 'a "mere" agent, a servant, a delegate, a subordinate substitute for those who sent him' (Pitkin, 1967, p. 146). As one political theorist expresses it, mandate representatives 'serve as voiceboxes for the represented' (Pettit, 2009, p. 72). Thus, according to mandate theory, politicians are representatives of their constituents in much the same way as lawyers are representatives of their clients, since in both cases the representative is an 'agent' who defends and advances the interests of their 'principal'. For instance, one contemporary political scientist suggests that, according to this view, 'we can conceive of the citizens as principals represented by agents to whom the citizens temporarily delegate the power to make public policies' (Bingham Powell, 2004, p. 274). The role of a political representative is therefore strictly curtailed by mandate theorists, and it is 'to reflect purposively the preferences of [their] constituents' (McCrone and Kuklinski, 1979, p. 278) and 'to secure their constituents' interests as their constituents so define them' (Rehfeld, 2009, p. 218).

As a normative ideal, the significance of the theory of mandate representation lies mainly in its position as one of the defining alternatives in the mandate-trustee controversy, to which we will return later. Indeed, at least in its purest form, the theory is not widely endorsed by contemporary political theorists. Nevertheless, mandate representation resonates with an intuitively appealing conception of democracy, since it says that legitimate political representatives are 'agents' who have been 'authorised' by their 'principals' to act, speak and vote in particular ways. Consider, for example, how some trade unions work, whereby delegates follow the instructions of their branch members. If we think about a political community in similar terms, then political power would ultimately rest with the people and not with politicians, *if* those politicians acted as the theory of mandate representation prescribes. However, if interpreted strictly, the mandate view would be incredibly inefficient for governing the affairs of a large and complex society, since politicians would be required to continually seek instructions from their constituents. Consequently, some political theorists have explored some ways in which a looser form of mandate representation could be achieved.

One possibility is suggested by the following – highly stylised – characterisation of the underlying mechanisms of representative democracy:

> Parties or candidates make policy proposals during campaigns and explain how these policies would affect citizens' welfare; citizens decide which of these policies they want implemented and which politicians to charge with their implementation, and governments do implement them. (Manin et al., 1999, p. 29)

Jane Mansbridge associates this account with a 'promissory' model of political representation, according to which 'the representative promises to follow the constituents' instructions or expressed desires' (2003, p. 516). One difficulty it raises is discussed in Box 4.1. A further challenge it encounters is to ensure that politicians actually do honour their campaign promises. Interestingly, no current democratic regime legally requires this of political representatives (Manin, 1997). However, citizens themselves can informally sanction politicians and political parties who go back on their word, for instance by rejecting them at future elections. Consequently, in contemporary democracies, mandate representation of the kind described above will require politicians who are 'highly responsive to the threat of sanction' and who acknowledge their constituents to be the source of their judgements (Rehfeld, 2009, p. 218). We will look more closely at whether this is an attractive ideal in the second key debate below.

Another possibility for achieving a looser form of mandate representation was suggested by the Scottish historian and philosopher James Mill in the early nineteenth century. Mill believed that the great merit of representative government was that it allowed the interests of the many to be efficiently represented. This is because effective democratic institutions can be a microcosm of wider society, thus relieving ordinary citizens of the burden of articulating their own interests in legislative assemblies. For Mill's model to work, it is crucial to ensure that politicians themselves act on the interests of the people as a whole, rather than the 'sinister interests' of particular groups and established elites (Mill, 1992, p. 27). Mill himself thought that this would require there to be an 'identity of interests' between government and the population (Mill, 1992, p. 38) and

---

**BOX 4.1   MANDATE REPRESENTATION AND
KEEPING PROMISES**

There is an important tension within the ideal of mandate representation, since it seemingly requires politicians to both uphold their electoral promises *and* promote the interests of their constituents. In contemporary democracies these two requirements often run up against one another, especially when circumstances change or new information becomes available. For instance, a government might discover that implementing its promised tax cuts would impose greater burdens than it initially anticipated, perhaps as a consequence of changing economic circumstances. Under such conditions, it is not clear whether the theory of mandate representation would require the government to switch its policy and promote the interests of its constituents, or to stick to the original policy and honour its campaign promise.

Should representatives break promises?

---

he made two proposals to ensure that this happened. First, he emphasised the importance of voters choosing representatives who were likely to act according to the interests of the voters. He suggested that this would require free and open elections conducted by secret ballot, in order to protect poor and vulnerable voters from being unduly influenced by their employers. He also stressed the importance of voter education to render the electorate less susceptible to manipulation and capable of selecting policies and politicians to advance their own real interests. Second, he also suggested that representatives should hold their roles for relatively short periods, because term limits discourage elected representatives from forming separate interests of their own. Importantly, Mill did not argue that representatives themselves needed to be especially public spirited. Instead, he favoured careful institutional design to incentivise political representatives to advance the interests of everyone.

Trustee representation

The traditional rival to the mandate view is the trustee view, which was given its classic articulation by Irish political theorist Edmund Burke in the late eighteenth century. Having recently been elected as a Member of Parliament for Bristol, Burke argued against the idea that political representatives were duty bound to follow the instructions of their constituents. Burke's alternative position was nuanced. He agreed that a representative should 'live in the strictest union, the closest correspondence, and the most unreserved communication with his constituents' (1996, p. 68). Furthermore, he acknowledged that the wishes of constituents ought to 'have great weight' and 'in all cases' a representative should 'prefer their interest to his own' (1996, pp. 68–9). However, he also insisted that the first duty of political representatives was to their own 'unbiassed opinion ... mature judgment [and] enlightened conscience' (1996, p. 69). Burke's view was that good political representatives should not be beholden to the whims of their constituents but should rather be guided by their considered judgements and sympathetic understanding. As he told the voters of Bristol: 'Your representative owes you, not his industry only, but his judgment; and he betrays, instead of serving you, if he sacrifices it to your opinion' (1996, p. 69).

As was the case for James Mill, Burke's version of trustee representation also connects up with a distinctive and intuitively appealing theory of democracy. According to Burke:

> Parliament is not a *Congress* of Ambassadors from different and hostile interests; which interests each must maintain, as an Agent and Advocate, against other Agents and Advocates; but Parliament is a *deliberative* Assembly of *one* Nation, with *one* Interest, that of the whole; where, not local Purposes, not local Prejudices, ought to guide, but the general Good, resulting from the general Reason of the whole. (1996, p. 69)

Four features of Burke's view are especially worth noting. First, he emphasises the significance of judgement, intelligence and sympathetic imagination for good representation, and rejects the mandate theorist's view of representatives as 'agents and advocates'. Second, he opposes the factionalism that mandate theory potentially gives rise to, whereby politicians battle it out against one another, advocating for rival 'local prejudices'. Instead, he thinks that democratic institutions are venues in which the national or common interest is discussed and defined, and good representatives will advocate on behalf of what they believe to be the common good rather than for their constituents' local and narrow preferences. Third, Burke views democratic politics as something that happens between elections, in debating chambers and amongst enlightened representatives themselves. This contrasts with the mandate view, in which the real substance of democracy occurs before and during elections, amongst representatives and their constituents. Fourth and controversially, because trustee representatives seek to advance policies that will further the national interest, subjects and citizens can be 'virtually' represented even if they do not vote or are not permitted to vote.

The independence of trustee representatives brings at least four potential advantages by comparison with the mandate view. First, by weakening the connection between principal and agent, it removes some of the ambiguities that haunt the mandate model. For instance, as we saw in Box 4.1, mandate representatives face difficulties when the instructions of their constituents are unclear or when circumstances change. Trustee representatives, by contrast, are not bound by manifesto commitments or the instructions of their constituents, and are free to consult their own judgement and the expert opinions of others. Second, trustee representation acknowledges the complexity of political questions, which often require nuanced debate of a kind that is impossible in mass electoral politics. Third, trustee representation makes compromise more likely, since politicians are able to respond freely to the views and suggestions of their colleagues. Fourth, trustee representation allows for the possibility of 'virtual' political representation for people and things that are unable to give instructions to political representatives, such as children, future generations and even the environment.

Critics worry that because trustee representatives are not beholden to the wishes of those whom they claim to represent, they are neither representative nor democratic. For instance, at the beginning of the twentieth century, Hilaire Belloc and G. K. Chesterton characterised trustee representatives as 'oligarchs', noting that 'it is surely ridiculous to say that a man represents Bethnal Green [in London] if he is in the habit of saying "Aye" when the people of Bethnal Green would say "No"' (quoted in Pitkin, 1967, p. 150). In response to worries such as these, recent versions of trustee representation have sought to restore its democratic credentials by finding ways to close the gap between voter and representative, as discussed in Box 4.2.

Descriptive representation

The mandate-delegate controversy was the central preoccupation for political theorists writing about representation for much of the twentieth century.

BOX 4.2 GYROSCOPIC REPRESENTATION AND DEMOCRACY

Jane Mansbridge says that some representatives are 'like gyroscopes, rotating on their own axes, maintaining a certain direction, pursuing certain built-in (although not fully immutable) goals' (2003, p. 520). Like Burke's trustees, gyroscopic representatives make their own judgements and do not rely on instructions from constituents. Moreover, they act for 'internal' reasons and are not responsive to sanctions. Arguably, gyroscopic representatives are good for democracy, since voters often select representatives who share their views and whom they perceive as trustworthy and principled, because representatives like these 'can be expected to act in ways the voter approves without external incentives' (Mansbridge, 2003, p. 520). However, some gyroscopic representatives might be bad for democracy. For example, Suzanne Dovi notes that that they might cut themselves off from dissent, or refuse to read newspapers or to gauge public opinion (Dovi, 2012, p. 188).

Is gyroscopic representation democratic?

Meanwhile, since the 1990s political theorists and activists have become increasingly concerned about the under-representation of particular social groups in supposedly representative bodies, such as women, ethnic minorities, LGBT persons and the disabled. For example, Anne Phillips has noted that:

> Many of the current arguments over democracy revolve around what we might call demands for political presence: demands for the equal representation of women with men; demands for a more even-handed balance between the different ethnic groups that make up each society; demands for the political inclusion of groups that have come to see themselves as marginalized or silenced or excluded. (Phillips, 1995, p. 5)

Advocates of descriptive representation – such as Robert Goodin, Will Kymlicka, Jane Mansbridge, Anne Phillips, Melissa Williams and Iris Marion Young – worry about demographically unrepresentative legislatures not only because they signal the persistence of discrimination in wider society, but also because they indicate a failure of political representation itself. A characteristic example of this view can be found in Iris Marion Young's insistence that a democratic regime 'should provide mechanisms for the effective recognition and representation of the distinct voices and perspectives of those of its constituent groups that are oppressed and disadvantaged' (Young, 1990, p. 184).

Although demands for political presence are mostly advanced by or on behalf of historically disadvantaged groups, underlying them is a general theory of 'mirror representation', which says that a representative body or institution should be a statistically accurate sample of the wider society it represents, reflecting back to society a broadly accurate image of itself. This means that political representatives – taken as a whole – 'should faithfully reproduce significant differences among the population, and reproduce them in proportion to their realization within the community' (Pettit, 2009, p. 66). Thus, a representative body is truly representative if it is a 'microcosm of the larger society' (Birch, 2001, p. 96), or if it 'constitutes a recognisable image or likeness of the populace as a whole' (Skinner, 2005, p. 163). Proposals along these lines have a long history, and were canvassed amongst the American and French revolutionaries of the eighteenth century. For example, in America John Adams suggested that a legislature 'should be an exact portrait, in miniature, of the people at large' (quoted in Pitkin, 1967, p. 60). Similarly, in France Honoré Mirabeau claimed that a representative body 'is for the nation what a map drawn to scale is for the physical configuration of land; in part or in whole the copy must always have the same proportions as the original' (quoted in Pitkin, 1967, p. 62).

As these examples indicate, characterisations of descriptive representation often make use of figurative or pictorial metaphors, such as the mirror, the portrait or the map. These metaphors suggest that politicians are representative to the extent that they *resemble* those whom they represent. Thus, political representatives should exhibit or exemplify certain significant characteristics which they share in common with those whom they represent. As Mansbridge puts it:

> In 'descriptive representation', representatives are in their own persons and lives in some sense typical of the larger class of persons whom they represent. Black legislators represent Black constituents, women legislators represent women constituents, and so on. (Mansbridge, 1999, p. 629)

This aspect of descriptive representation points to distinctive accounts of both the role of representatives and the phenomenon of representation. First, whilst mandate and trustee representatives are said to 'act for' their constituents, for instance by following their instructions or advancing their interests, descriptive representatives are instead said to 'stand for' their constituents, 'by virtue of a correspondence or connection between them, a resemblance or reflection' (Pitkin, 1967, p. 61). Second, and relatedly, whilst someone is represented by a mandate or trustee representative by virtue of what that person does, someone is represented by a descriptive representative by virtue of who that person is.

Goodin identifies two logically distinct reasons for favouring descriptive representation. First is the idea that 'demographically unrepresentative assemblies cannot (or anyway usually do not, in practice) represent well the ideas and interests of excluded groups' (Goodin, 2004, p. 455). As discussed in Box 4.3, proponents of descriptive representation often argue that representatives need to share the same kinds of experiences and interests as the people they represent. Second is the idea that 'demographically unrepresentative assemblies cannot represent the identities and images of the excluded' (Goodin, 2004, p. 455). The symbolic exclusion of particular identities matters because, as we saw in Chapter 2, the 'nonrecognition' of particular identities can harm individual group members, by stigmatising them or reinforcing negative self-esteem. For instance, Mansbridge suggests that '[l]ow percentages of Black and women representatives … create the [social] meaning that Blacks and women cannot rule, or are not suitable for rule' (Mansbridge, 1999, p. 649). By contrast, incorporating descriptive representatives may have the positive effect of symbolically affirming the value of minority groups and the political equality of their members, reminding them and the rest of society that they are capable of participating in collective self-rule (Guinier, 1994).

As we shall see later, proposals for descriptive representation are controversial. On the one hand, some critics worry that it requires 'tokenistic' forms of political inclusion, and that these could exacerbate the stigmatisation of particular groups or identities as inferior. For example, quotas for minorities may convey the impression that these groups require special help to do something that others manage to do on their own. On the other hand, others worry that descriptive representation could undermine democracy, since if representatives can only speak on behalf of 'their own', and are not expected to understand the lives and

> ## BOX 4.3   SHARED EXPERIENCES AND
> ## COMMON INTERESTS
>
> Prior to the revolution of 1789, and whilst petitioning for a place at the general assembly (*Les États-Généraux*), a group of French women made the following observation:
>
> > Just as a nobleman cannot represent a plebeian and the latter cannot represent a nobleman, so a man, no matter how honest he may be, cannot represent a woman. Between the representatives and the represented there must be an absolute identity of interests. (quoted in Phillips, 1995, p. 52)
>
> On one reading, the petitioners believed that 'shared experience took precedence over shared ideas: no amount of thought or sympathy, no matter how careful or honest, could jump the barriers of experience' (Phillips, 1995, p. 52). Thus, female representatives were required because men were incapable of fully grasping the predicament of women, or would inevitably overlook issues and concerns that were important to women. On another reading, although men might be capable of understanding the needs and interests of women, they could not be trusted to effectively represent women, since they had rival and competing needs and interests of their own which they would favour whenever conflicts of interest arose (Mansbridge, 1999).
>
> *Must good representatives share the interests and experiences of those they represent?*

experiences of others, then the possibility of a democratic conversation about the common good is undercut and representatives may be discouraged from trying to understand other perspectives. For instance, Kymlicka believes that non-Maori representatives in New Zealand ceased taking responsibility for Maori affairs after the Maori obtained guaranteed seats in Parliament. This leads him to observe that 'the claim that whites cannot understand the needs of blacks, or that men cannot understand the needs of women, can become an excuse for white men not to try to understand the needs of others' (Kymlicka, 1995, p. 139).

Constitutive representation

According to the theory of descriptive representation, representatives should resemble those whom they represent, and the role of a representative is to 'stand for' their constituents, by articulating a common perspective. Likewise, for mandate and trustee representation, representatives 'act for' their constituents by following their instructions or advancing their interests. In all of these theories, the relationship between representative and represented is, in principle at least, transparent. Similarly, the interests and identities of constituents are treated as relatively fixed and given. Meanwhile, some political theorists have questioned the assumption that representatives are as passive or neutral as these views seemingly suggest. In particular, they have drawn attention to the active and creative ways in which representatives 'construct' or 'constitute' the political identities of their constituents. Thus, unlike the other theories of representation that we have considered, whereby the representative aims to make the preferences, interests or identities of their constituents visible, political theorists such as Linda Alcoff, Frank Ankersmit, Lisa Disch, David Plotke, Michael Saward, Judith Squires and Nadia Urbinati argue that representatives play a more creative, active and constitutive role.

An assumption underlying these theories of 'constitutive representation' is that representation itself is an interpretive activity. For example, according to Linda Alcoff:

In both the practice of speaking for as well as the practice of speaking about others, I am engaging in the act of representing the other's needs, goals, situation, and in fact, *who they are.* I am representing them *as* such and such, or in post-structuralist terms, I am participating in the construction of their subject-positions. This act of representation cannot be understood as founded on an act of discovery wherein I discover their true selves and then simply relate my discovery. (Alcoff, 1991, p. 9)

According to this view, when we represent something – including ourselves – we present a particular image to an audience. Such images cannot be comprehensive, fully depicting a constituency or an individual in all of its complexity. Rather, representations must be selective, emphasising some characteristics and playing down others. Moreover, in making selections, a particular representative act or 'claim' will define how something is seen and understood (or, in poststructuralist language, it will define the 'subject-position' of the represented). Thus, for example, Judith Squires points out that political representatives who claim to represent women are inevitably and 'actively engaged in making claims about women, participating in the construction of feminine subject-positions' (Squires, 2008, p. 192).

Political representation is not only interpretive but it is also productive, 'constituting rather than simply depicting what is seen' (Squires, 2008, p. 191). As such, it is a dynamic and creative activity that 'facilitates the formation of political groups and activities' (Urbinati, 2006, p. 37). For instance, Suzanne Dovi gives the example of James Curley, who was a four-time Mayor of Boston during the first half of the twentieth century (Dovi, 2012, pp. 155–6). Curley famously attributed Boston's progress to the hard work of the Irish, thereby helping to constitute both how other citizens understood Irish Americans and how they understood themselves. Michael Saward suggests that we can best make sense of phenomena like this through his 'claims-making' theory of representation, which says that 'at the heart of the act of representing is the depicting of a constituency *as* this or that, as requiring this or that, as having this or that set of interests' (Saward, 2010, p. 71). On his account, 'representatives "choose" their constituents in the sense of portraying them or framing them in particular, contestable ways' (Saward, 2006a, pp. 301–2). Similarly, according to Lisa Disch's 'mobilization' conception of representation, political representatives aim 'to call forth a constituency by depicting it as a collective with a shared aim' (Disch, 2011, p. 107).

According to Saward, political representatives are required to create constituencies and political identities because people's preferences and interests are never entirely 'transparent, patently evident, singular and obvious' (Saward, 2006a, p. 310). As he puts it: 'political representatives construct portrayals or depictions of the represented, in order to be able to represent them' (Saward, 2006b, p. 414). Frank Ankersmit makes a similar point, arguing that without representation 'we are without a conception of what political reality – the represented – is like' (Ankersmit, 2002, p. 115). For both theorists as well as for other proponents of constitutive representation, representation itself has an aesthetic dimension, since representatives have no choice but 'to mould, shape, and in one sense create that which is to be represented' (Saward, 2006a, p. 310).

Saward situates constitutive representation within a more general 'claims-making' theory of political representation (2006a, 2010). This theory starts from the assumption that representation is ubiquitous and comes in many different forms. Therefore, an adequate theoretical account of representation needs to explain representative claims that are both formal and informal, both electoral and non-electoral, and both national and global. On Saward's account, representation is neither a fact nor a thing but is rather an action, an event or a process 'that involves offering constructions or images of constituents *to* constituents and audiences' (2010, p. 14). Consequently, representation has to do with 'the practice of making *claims to be* representative, and varied efforts to substantiate or contest those claims' (Saward, 2006c, p. 185). More formally, he argues that all instances of political representation take the same basic form:

A maker of representations (M) puts forward a subject (S) which stands for an object (O) which is related to a referent (R) and is offered to an audience (A). (Saward, 2006a, p. 302)

This technical definition is best understood by working through examples. For instance, take the case of an elected representative who claims to be working on behalf of their decent and hard-working constituents (adapted from Saward, 2009, pp. 3–4). Here, the elected representative is both (M) and (S), since they are making a representative claim on their own behalf. Meanwhile, the thing being represented is not the flesh-and-blood constituents (which Saward labels (R) for referent), but is rather an idea of the constituency as decent and hard-working (which Saward labels (O) for object). Although the object (O) is related to the referent (R), it is a selective portrayal, and it is up to the audience (A) to accept, reject or ignore the representative claim. Alternatively, consider the example of anti-globalisation protestors who offer themselves to Western governments as speaking on behalf of marginalised and oppressed peoples (adapted from Saward, 2010, p. 37). Here, the protestors are (M), and they present their movements (S) as standing for interests of marginalised and oppressed peoples (O). Again, the object is related to a referent (R) (the real, flesh and blood people living in developing countries). However, in this case, the audience are Western governments (A), who are free to accept, reject or ignore the representative claim made by the protestors.

Two features of constitutive theories of representation are particularly worth noting. First, because it is not limited to cases of electoral representation, it can encompass claims made by self-appointed representatives. Saward, for instance, discusses the singer and political activist Bono, who was reported to have said: 'I represent a lot of people [in Africa] who have no voice at all … They haven't asked me to represent them. It's cheeky but I hope they're glad I do' (quoted in Saward, 2009, p. 1). Likewise, Dovi discusses the actress and United Nations 'goodwill ambassador' Angelina Jolie, who sought to encourage the US to fund peacekeeping initiatives in Darfur (2012, p. 62). Some non-governmental organisations might also qualify as representatives in this expanded sense, including Oxfam or Amnesty International, who portray themselves as representing the world's poor and the oppressed (Montanaro, 2012). These forms of representation are often politically very effective. For instance, Bono met with the leaders of the G8 countries, who subsequently made promises about debt relief programmes. Moreover, self-appointed representatives can also play an important role as representatives, making otherwise neglected constituencies visible in decision making procedures.

Second, constitutive representation also draws attention to the contestability of representation, since audiences may dispute or contest a representative claim. For instance, Saward argues that 'representative claims only work, or even exist, if "audiences" acknowledge them in some way, and are able to absorb or reject or accept them or otherwise engage with them' (Saward, 2006a, p. 303). This means, for example, that some constituents might reject a politician's interpretation of their needs, or they might deny that a particular politician is capable of acting in their interests. If this happens, and even if the politician has been elected, there is a sense in which the politician's claim to be a representative has failed. Thus, according to the constitutive view, and in contrast to the other three views we have considered, representative claims are fluid and not fixed, often unstable and subject to ongoing contestation.

Key debates

How are representatives authorised?

The idea that political representatives have been authorised is central to how we think about representative democracy. To say that a representative has been authorised typically means two things: that the representative has a right to perform certain actions on behalf of the represented, and that the represented bear at least some responsibility for those actions (Pitkin, 1967, pp. 38–9). These two dimensions of representative authorisation are brought out most clearly in thinking about representation as a principal–agent relationship. For example, consider a representative 'agent' who has been authorised to enter into a contract on behalf of their 'principal'. Provided that the agent really has been authorised by their principal, then that agent is entitled to enter into a contract that will have the effect of binding the principal to uphold whatever terms were agreed to. These two dimensions can also be observed in the more complex examples that we tend to associate with political representation. For example, representative governments are typically thought to be entitled to exercise political rule on behalf of their citizens, and at the same time 'the governed can be said to be responsible for their governors' actions' (Plamenatz, 1938, pp. 16–17).

However, beneath this apparent simplicity are a number of ambiguities and difficulties that we shall now explore by comparing three different ways in which political representatives might be said to have been authorised. First, according to the 'authorisation-by-instruction' model, associated with mandate representation, constituents authorise their representatives by issuing them with instructions. As will become clear, the idea that constituents can directly 'instruct' their political representatives is more problematic than it might first appear. Second, according to the 'authorisation-by-election' model, the people authorise their representatives by voting for them. This view is widely endorsed, and is compatible with descriptive, trustee and constitutive theories of representation, but it may struggle to explain both why some representatives are entitled to act on behalf of others and why the represented are responsible for the actions of their representatives. Third, according to the 'authorisation-by-an-audience' model, associated with constitutive theories of representation, political representatives are authorised if an audience accepts their representative claim as legitimate. This may happen through informal mechanisms, such as public recognition, as well as formal ones, such as instruction and election. This approach has the merit of capturing both traditional forms of political representation and less traditional ones, such as 'self-appointed' representatives, but it also potentially has some worryingly undemocratic implications.

Let us begin with the authorisation-by-instruction model. This view is suggested by the theory of mandate representation, which says that political representatives are instructed by their constituents in much the same way as lawyers are instructed by their clients. In both cases, if a principal is entitled to 'instruct' an agent, then it seems clear that the agent correspondingly acquires a right to perform certain actions on behalf of the principal, who in turn will bear responsibility for those actions. For instance, if the members of a political community 'instruct' their government to sign a peace treaty with a neighbouring state, and if the government actually does so, then we can describe the government as a representative of the people that has been authorised to act in a particular way. Moreover, because we can describe the government so, we can also say that the people themselves bear at least some responsibility for the government's actions.

Despite its theoretical clarity, the authorisation-by-instruction model is vulnerable to at least two objections. The first is that in the democracies we are familiar with today, there are few opportunities for constituents to meaningfully instruct their representatives. For example, Anthony Birch notes that there is typically 'no machinery whereby constituents may formulate instructions and communicate them to [representatives]' (Birch, 2001, p. 98). Although politicians frequently consult polling data and other information about the beliefs and preferences of the electorate, it would be an exaggeration to describe these as forms of instruction. Second, because constituents have competing interests, endorse rival values and make different judgements about matters of public policy, they may be incapable of providing their representatives with coherent and rational instructions (Brito Viera and Runciman, 2008, pp. 84–96; Pettit, 2009). This difficulty arises as a consequence of the so-called 'discursive dilemma' (Brennan, 2001; Pettit, 2001; List and Pettit, 2002, 2004), which suggests that groups of people may be prone to making collectively irrational judgements.

This dilemma can be illustrated by considering the predicament of a trade union delegate, who is representing a group of three employees (this example is adapted from Pettit, 2001, p. 272). Suppose that the employees (who we will label A, B and C) are trying to decide how to instruct their representative in a forthcoming round of pay negotiations with their employer. The issue under consideration is whether or not the employees should willingly forego a pay-rise so that the money saved can be directed towards a workplace safety measure. Importantly, all three agree about the correct way to settle this issue. Specifically, they each believe that they should accept a pay sacrifice if there is a serious enough danger *and* if the proposed safety measure would be effective. However, because they disagree about these two things, they cannot reach an agreement about whether or not a pay sacrifice would be acceptable.

This might seem bad enough, but matters are actually worse than they first appear, once we come to understand the different judgements that the employees have made, which are illustrated in Table 4.2. First, A opposes a pay sacrifice because although she accepts that there is a serious danger, she does not think that the proposed safety measure will be effective. Second, B disagrees with A about the effectiveness of the proposed safety measure, but also opposes a pay sacrifice because he is not convinced that the danger is serious enough. Third, C is the only employee to favour a pay sacrifice, because she is convinced about both the seriousness of the danger and the effectiveness of the proposed safety measure. Table 4.2 makes it clear that although a majority

Table 4.2 Employee judgments

	Serious danger?	Effective measure?	Pay sacrifice?
A	Yes	No	No
B	No	Yes	No
C	Yes	Yes	Yes
Majority	Yes	Yes	No

(adapted from Pettit, 2001)

of the employees oppose a pay sacrifice, a majority also think that there is a serious danger and another majority thinks that the proposed safety measure would be effective. But we also know that A, B and C agree that if there is a serious danger and if the safety measure would be effective, then a pay sacrifice would be justified. Thus, it is plausible to infer that as a group, they collectively favour a pay sacrifice, but as a set of individuals they collectively oppose a pay sacrifice! In this situation, it seems difficult to see how the employees could 'instruct' their representative about how to act. Furthermore, notice that each employee is individually rational, because their conclusions (about the pay sacrifice) follow from their premises (about the seriousness of the danger and the effectiveness of the proposed remedy). However, as a group they are irrational, since their (majority-endorsed) conclusion does not follow from their (majority-endorsed) premises.

Box 4.4 discusses the difficult predicament facing A, B and C's trade union delegate. If it is the case that many representatives will encounter similar 'discursive dilemmas', then this should prompt us to question the plausibility of the instruction model of authorisation. In its place, we might instead favour the 'authorisation-by-election' model. This way of thinking about authorisation is compatible with descriptive and constitutive theories of representation, but is perhaps most closely associated with trustee representation. According to this model, representatives are authorised to act within certain constraints, and their constituents are responsible for at least some of their actions, because of the status that is conferred on representatives through the process of election. Characterising political authorisation as a product of electoral success is widespread amongst political scientists, political theorists and ordinary citizens. Elections matter because they give the people an opportunity to choose their representatives, whom they are consequently likely to identify with.

If electoral success authorises a representative then it must be able to explain why the represented should be held responsible for the actions of their representatives. It is not clear that a 'one-off' act like voting really does this, since although constituents are present when representatives are selected they subsequently become a 'silent partner' in the relationship. This worry prompts

BOX 4.4   INSTRUCTING REPRESENTATIVES

Recall the workplace example discussed in the main body of the text. For the purposes of negotiating with their employer, the employees (A, B and C) have commissioned R to act on their behalf, and R wishes to act as a good mandate representative. Because the employees cannot issue unambiguous instructions, R is faced with two similarly unattractive options. On the one hand, they could follow the majority-endorsed conclusion and tell the employers that the workers will not accept a pay sacrifice. However, this would ignore the fact that majorities of the employees accept both that the danger is serious enough and that the measure is likely to be effective enough to justify a pay sacrifice. On the other hand, R could follow the collective logic of the employees and say that the workers will accept a pay sacrifice, provided that the safety measures are implemented. However, this would ignore the fact that a majority of the employees do not actually endorse this. Now suppose that during the pay negotiations R is presented with overwhelming evidence about effectiveness of the proposed safety measure, which R believes would be sufficiently weighty to change A's mind. Or imagine that during the negotiations R becomes personally convinced of the case in favour of a pay sacrifice.

Should either of these things affect how R should act? And if so, what does this imply about the theory of representation?

Pitkin to note that the authorisation-by-election is 'strongly skewed in favour of the representative':

> Representation is a kind of 'black box' shaped by the initial giving of authority, within which the representative can do whatever he pleases. If he leaves the box, if he exceeds the limits, he no longer represents. There can be no such thing as representing well or badly; either he represents or he does not. There is no such thing as the activity of representing or the duties of a representative; anything done after the right kind of authorization and within its limits is by definition representing. (Pitkin, 1967, p. 39)

Importantly, the authorisation-by-election model does not specify how much (if any) control a principal should have over its agent. Thus, it is neutral with respect to whether politicians should honour their promises or whether constituents should be encouraged to sanction unpopular representatives. We will look at these normative questions more closely in the next key debate. For the moment, however, it is worth noting a tension between the ideas of electoral authorisation and representation. For example, suppose that a democratically elected government adopts a policy that is opposed overwhelmingly by its citizens. On the one hand, we might say that the government has been formally authorised by the people to adopt *a* policy, as a consequence of the fact it was elected. On the other hand, we might also say that in adopting *this* policy, the government is no longer substantively representative of the people. Thus, at least in some cases, it seems doubtful that the simple fact of electoral success is sufficient to explain why a principal should be responsible for all of the actions of its agent.

The other dimension of authorisation has to do with how representatives come to have a right to act on behalf of others. The authorisation-by-election model seems to be under-inclusive here, since some representatives might conceivably be entitled to act on behalf of people who did not have the opportunity to vote for them. For example, Mansbridge has coined the term 'surrogate representation' to describe 'representation by a representative with whom one has no electoral relationship – that is, a representative in another district' (Mansbridge, 2003, p. 522). Surrogate representatives are elected, but they represent a different, usually wider, constituency than the one that voted for them. To illustrate this, Mansbridge proposes the (hypothetical) example of a member of Congress from Minnesota who leads the Congressional opposition to a war. Such a politician would be a 'surrogate representative' for 'voters in Missouri and Ohio whose own representatives support the war' (Mansbridge, 2003, p. 522).

In contemporary politics, surrogate representation 'plays the normatively critical role of providing representation to voters who lose in their own district' (Mansbridge, 2003, p. 523). It is often particularly important for minority groups, as surrogate representatives may also be descriptive representatives. For instance, Mansbridge discusses the case of Barney Franks, who was an electoral representative for Massachusetts but also saw himself as 'a surrogate representative for gay and lesbian citizens throughout the nation' (Mansbridge, 2003, p. 523). The problem that surrogate representation poses for the authorisation-by-election model is not that surrogate representatives lack authorisation, since they have in fact been elected. Rather, it is that they have not been elected by all of the people they represent. Consequently, if Barney Franks is entitled to act on behalf of gay and lesbian citizens from outside Massachusetts, it must be that he has been authorised to do so through some additional – unspecified – mechanism.

The final 'authorisation-by-an-audience' model potentially explains why Barney Franks was authorised to represent gay and lesbian citizens from outside his district. According to this view a representative is authorised as such if an audience recognises or accepts their claim to be a representative. For instance, in the case of elected representatives, authorisation might take the form of recognising or accepting the outcome of an election as legitimate. Meanwhile, in the case of non-elected and surrogate representatives, like Barney Franks and Bono, authorisation happens through non-electoral channels. It is worth noting that self-appointed representatives are not always high-profile figures, and might include, for instance, an immigrant who appears on a television programme claiming to represent other immigrants, or a working class single mother who claims to represent other working class single mothers when meeting with a politician. In cases like these, the authorisation of a representative often derives from their social identity or experiences. For example, Dovi notes that 'having certain experiences – such as having lost a son in a war – can lend authority to one's questioning and advocating for certain policies' (Dovi, 2012, p. 64). Similarly, a representative might derive their authority from their long-standing commitment to a political cause, especially if they are known to have made significant sacrifices for it.

Four points are worth noting about non-electoral audience authorisation. First, the audience that authorises a representative claim might be the represented themselves, but it could also be another group or individual. For instance, when Bono claimed to represent some Africans, this claim was accepted by the leaders of the G8 countries, rather than by the people of Africa (Rehfeld, 2006). Second, audience authorisation may be formal or informal. For example, the leaders of the G8 countries issued an official invitation to Bono, whilst an audience might informally authorise a representative claim made by a scientist to represent the interests of the scientific community by issuing regular invitations to publish newspaper articles, by taking their public pronouncements seriously, or by otherwise honouring that scientist with a particular public standing. Third, particularly when authorisation is informal, the membership of the audience may be quite fluid and could itself be a matter of contention (for instance, *who* is entitled to authorise the claim of a scientist to represent the scientific community?). Fourth, audience authorisation is always contestable. In particular, self-appointed representatives may face ongoing attempts to contest, challenge or 'de-authorise' their representative claims, as when the ostensibly 'represented' signal their dissent or disapproval (Montanaro, 2012, p. 1101).

How satisfactory is this model of authorisation? Some critics worry that audience authorisation could be elitist, as it leaves open the possibility that self-appointed representatives can be authorised – formally or informally – without seeking the approval of those whom they claim to represent. This may be the case for global public figures who self-appoint as representatives of the poor and disadvantaged, as discussed in Box 4.5. Meanwhile, audience authorisation might be more democratic when representatives themselves are held to account by those who they claim to represent. For instance, Laura Montanaro discusses the case of the Pro-Femmes/Twese Hamwe organisation, which represents Rwandan women to their government (Montanaro, 2012, p. 1104). The audience that authorises Pro-Femmes/Twese Hamwe includes both the government of Rwanda and Rwandan women themselves, who participate in its member organisations. Importantly, Rwandan women are able to express criticisms or dissatisfaction with Pro-Femmes/Twese Hamwe by refusing to participate in its programmes or by exiting its organisations. Thus, in this case, the represented have the opportunity to contest claims made on their behalf and even to de-authorise their self-appointed representatives.

BOX 4.5 CELEBRITY REPRESENTATIVES

Some global celebrities have engaged in political advocacy on behalf of the most seriously disadvantaged people in the world. Celebrity activists are often extremely effective mobilisers and spokespeople. Moreover, because of their visibility, they may be the only credible advocates for some people, such as those living under despotic regimes or in failed states and lacking a government that is willing or able to speak for them. However, disadvantaged groups are often unable to contest the representative claims made on their behalf, since they do not have access to global public forums, and this could have seriously undemocratic implications, as Monica Brito Viera and David Runciman point out:

> [T]he globally disempowered have no real opportunity to express their view of how they are being represented. They are more like spectators who have no choice but to support whichever team happens to be playing and claiming their support. International representation by self-appointed elites, however well directed and however well intentioned, lacks the 'expressive' element that makes electoral politics so dynamic. The audience have no means of contributing to the success or failure of the performance itself. (Brito Viera and Runciman, 2008, p. 167)

Is celebrity representation desirable? Can it be democratic?

How should representatives be held accountable?

Accountability is an important aspect of democratic representation. Indeed, one scholar – Carl Friedrich – takes accountability to be a necessary condition for representation in general, stipulating that 'if A represents B, he is presumed to be responsible *to* B, that is to say, he is answerable to B for what he says and does' (Friedrich, quoted in Pitkin, 1967, p. 55; see also Elster, 1999, p. 255). However, incorporating accountability alongside authorisation into our theoretical account of representation complicates matters considerably. This is because whilst authorisation has the effect of freeing representatives from particular responsibilities, accountability imposes new and special responsibilities upon them (Pitkin, 1967, p. 55). Recall, if a representative has been authorised, then they are entitled to perform actions that other people are at least partially responsible for. Meanwhile, if a representative is accountable, then they are responsible to those they represent.

There are two main ways in which representatives can be held accountable (Rehfeld, 2005, p. 189; Urbinati and Warren, 2008; Mansbridge, 2009). First, constituents can hold their representatives accountable by applying positive and negative *sanctions*, for example by rewarding or punishing their representatives at the ballot box. Second, representatives can also be held accountable in the more *deliberative* sense of giving an account of themselves or their actions. For example, a politician may be asked to explain why they voted for a particular piece of legislation, or a self-appointed representative may be asked to explain why they supported one initiative and not another. Of course, purely deliberative accountability – without *any* recourse to sanctioning – may turn out to be toothless (Rehfeld, 2005, p. 189). However, as we shall see, the practice of sanctioning political representatives may introduce some unexpected costs, whilst more deliberative forms of accountability may play an important role in supporting democratic reflexivity or responsiveness.

Let us begin by discussing sanctions. The strictest sanction potentially available to constituents is to recall their representatives on a discretionary basis. Although no current representative democracy allocates this right to its citizens, it would likely be required if the theory of mandate representation were to be fully implemented. A striking historical example of this sanction was the system of 'permanent revocability' established by the Paris Commune of 1871 (Manin, 1997, p. 165). Here, members of the ruling council were elected by universal suffrage and could be recalled by the voters at any time. As Manin points out, this institution resolves the problem of representatives being tempted to act without regard for the preferences of their constituents. Instead, it forces representatives to be accountable in the strictest sense, and 'guarantees congruence between the preferences of the electorate and the decisions of those in power, since voters can immediately punish and dismiss a representative whose decisions they disagree with' (Manin, 1997, p. 166).

A similar but weaker sanction is provided by the institution of periodic elections, which makes politicians accountable by requiring them to regularly seek the approval of voters. Indeed, political scientist James Fearon has noted the existence of 'an important tradition in democratic theory' that understands elections 'as a sanctioning device that induces elected officials to do whatever the voters want' (Fearon, 1999, p. 55). The idea here is that the threat of electoral defeat will incentivise political representatives to either follow the instructions or promote the interests of their constituents. However, it is worth noting that empirical social scientists have increasingly come to question the assumption that voters themselves conceive of elections as opportunities to reward or punish the past behaviour of their political representatives. Instead, at least in some cases, voters seem to understand their role in terms of 'selecting' good or trustworthy representatives (Mansbridge, 2009). But if voters are not – as a matter of fact – sanctioning politicians at elections, then elections cannot serve as mechanisms for holding elected representatives accountable for their past actions.

Self-appointed representatives can also be sanctioned, even when they are ostensibly 'independent'. For example, NGOs – such as Oxfam and Amnesty – can be held accountable through network monitoring by their peers and reputational sanctioning (Goodin, 2008, pp. 168–74). Additionally, such groups can be held accountable by the media, who are often able to 'produce the sanction of embarrassment and damage to reputation' (Keohane and Nye, 2003, p. 390).

Furthermore, volunteers, employees, funders and supporters can also sanction organisations, for instance by publicly criticising policies, contesting decisions or even by renouncing their association with the group. These forms of sanctioning are facilitated by a variety of formal and informal devices that have become commonplace, such as audits, inter-agency rivalries, a culture of professionalism and the publication of budgets and accounts (Majone, 1994, p. 118).

Regardless of whether sanctions are an *effective* mechanism for holding representatives accountable, it is worth noting that there may be some *normative* costs associated with the practices of monitoring and sanctioning. Mansbridge, for example, worries that electoral sanctions could turn out to be counterproductive if they have the effect of eroding the public-spiritedness of political representatives. To make this point, she quotes Onora O'Neill, who argues both that 'institutionalised suspicion undermines trust' and that '[p]lants don't flourish when we pull them up too often to check how their roots are growing' (O'Neill, quoted in Mansbridge, 2009, p. 379). The problem that Mansbridge and O'Neill identify is that if we conceive of accountability in narrow terms, as something that is realised primarily by rewarding or punishing politicians at the ballot box, then we may discourage virtuous politicians from using their judgement, and even from seeking political office in the first place. This objection might also be extended to apply to the monitoring of independent bodies such as NGOs, who might likewise experience perverse incentives if they are subjected to excessively close public scrutiny (for instance, by refraining from campaigning on potentially unpopular issues or by avoiding risks).

Let us now turn to deliberative accountability, which one scholar defines as follows: 'A is accountable with respect to M when some individual, body or institution, Y, can require A to inform and explain/justify his or her conduct with respect to M' (Philp, 2009, p. 32). Within democracies, deliberative accountability may take place in both official and unofficial venues, such as legislatures, review boards, public committees, official hearings, public meetings, newspaper columns, online forums, and the informal life of civil society. Young notes that accountability of this kind is especially important when representatives are required to make judgements under new or changing circumstances, since in these cases the 'responsibility of the representative is not simply to tell citizens how she has enacted a mandate they authorized or served their interests, but [is] as much to persuade them of the rightness of her judgement' (2000, p. 131). If deliberative accountability goes well, then it can help to nurture closer relationships between citizens and their representatives, preventing political representatives from becoming detached or estranged. Consequently, Young argues that the process of representation should be evaluated according to the extent it 'avoids separation' and 'renews connection' (Young, 2000, pp. 128–30).

Amongst contemporary political theorists, two rival accounts about how to prevent separation and ensure connection have emerged. First, a prominent view, which originated in Pitkin's work, emphasises the idea of 'responsiveness'. For example, Pitkin claims that a 'representative government must ... be responsive to the people' (Pitkin, 1967, p. 232) and that 'there must be a constant condition of responsiveness, of potential readiness to respond' (Pitkin, 1967, p. 233). Responsiveness can be understood as a virtuous disposition of both governments and individual political representatives, which requires them to engage with those whom they represent but does not require accountability in the strictest sense. This is because, as Albert Weale points out, 'political representatives can be responsive to their constituents without necessarily rendering them an account or giving an explanation of their actions' (Weale, 2007, p. 133). For example, a politician who adjusts their policy position in light of polling data is responding to their constituents without being held to account by them.

One attraction of the ideal of responsiveness is that it establishes a connection between public opinion and the decisions of political representatives. Interestingly, however, it sits uneasily alongside both the trustee and mandate theories of representation. On the one hand, mandate representatives need to do more than merely respond to their constituents, but must bind themselves to their instructions. On the other hand, trustees owe their constituents their good judgement and should not 'sacrifice' that judgement to popular opinion. Meanwhile, as we shall see in the next section, something like the virtue of responsiveness may be necessary if descriptive representatives are also to be substantive representatives.

The second view is associated with the constitutive theory of representation and appeals to the idea of reflexivity. Proponents of this theory question the assumption – widespread in political science – that the quality of political representation is primarily a function of 'congruence' between citizen preferences and the voting behaviour of elected representatives. Instead, as we have seen, they argue that political representation is a dynamic and creative activity. These theoretical assumptions imply that both the sanctions model of accountability and appeals to virtue of responsiveness are muddled, because they both aim to ensure that representatives articulate or respond to the views and interests of those they represent, as if those views and interests exist independently of the practice of representation. But according to proponents of the constitutive theory of representation, this neglects the fact that representatives themselves play a crucial role in shaping and forming the views, identities and interests of citizens.

Consequently, advocates of constitutive representation argue that when evaluating political representation we should not focus on how accountable or responsive individual politicians are to their constituents. Rather, we should focus on how 'reflexive' the system as a whole is. A reflexive system encourages contestation, ensures that the represented can communicate with and contest the actions of their representatives, and requires that representatives respond

BOX 4.6 REPRESENTATION AND DEMOCRACY

Representative democracy, in which citizens elect politicians to govern on their behalf, is sometimes said to be a poor substitute for direct democracy, in which citizens govern themselves. During this 'key debate' we have examined four potential responses to this objection. First, political representatives could be put under popular control by establishing the institution of permanent revocability. Second, political representatives could be held accountable by requiring them to stand for periodic election. Third, political representatives could maintain close relationships with citizens by being more responsive to their needs, opinions and interests. Fourth, a reflexive political system could encourage citizens to contest the provisional representative claims made on their behalf.

Do any of these approaches satisfactorily address the direct democrat's challenge?

to challenges from those whom they represent (Disch, 2011, p. 111). Such a system would incentivise representatives to engage in genuine dialogues with their constituents, who in turn would have multiple opportunities to register their objections about how they were being represented. For its proponents, a reflexive system of representation would be democratic if, as they believe is likely, it succeeds in 'expanding participation in representative forms; enhancing communication between representatives and constituents; increasing effective participation by previously excluded or underrepresented groups; and increasing sites and modes of representation' (Plotke, 1997, p. 33). Nevertheless, as Box 4.6 indicates, proponents of direct democracy believe that this would still fall short of the democratic ideal.

Can descriptive representatives represent minorities?

Proponents of descriptive representation favour greater representation for disadvantaged or marginalised social groups. However, some political theorists are sceptical about the capacity of descriptive representatives to substantively represent the voices and perspectives of oppressed groups. Whilst some critics worry that descriptive representatives are not sufficiently responsive or accountable to those whom they represent, others worry that groups are not sufficiently cohesive to allow for meaningful descriptive representation. In this final section, we will examine both of these objections. An additional concern, discussed in Box 4.7, is that even if the oppressed and disadvantaged are empowered to represent themselves politically, they may struggle to meaningfully convey their distinctive interests, perspectives and concerns.

BOX 4.7 SELF-REPRESENTATION AND THE SUBALTERN

The term 'subaltern' was introduced by Marxist intellectual Antonio Gramsci, who used it to denote subordinate or non-hegemonic groups, such as those living at the margins of society. In a rich and provocative essay entitled 'Can the Subaltern Speak?' (1988), postcolonial theorist Gayatri Chakravorty Spivak makes the arresting claim that they cannot. By this, she does not mean that the subaltern cannot talk, but rather that their utterances will often be unintelligible against the backdrop of dominant narratives and understandings, and therefore will not be meaningfully 'heard'. One implication of her argument is that oppressed and marginalised groups may find it difficult to represent themselves politically. This is a special problem for the 'politics of presence', since one argument in favour of descriptive representation is that it allows historically excluded groups to get 'their' issues, perspectives and interests onto the political agenda. Spivak's essay is complex, but her main claim can be illustrated with an example she discusses in the closing passages. Bhuvaneswari Bhaduri was a young woman who hanged herself in Calcutta in 1926. Nearly a decade later it was discovered that she had been a member of a group involved in the struggle for Indian independence. According to Spivak, Bhaduri had killed herself because she felt unable to carry out a political assassination with which she had been entrusted. Spivak interprets her suicide as a form of political speech – as an attempt to rewrite 'the social text of sati-suicide' (1988, p. 307). The evidence in support of this is that Bhaduri waited until the onset of menstruation before killing herself, in order to discourage others from misinterpreting her suicide as the result of an illegitimate pregnancy. Nevertheless, the 'illicit love' narrative took hold. Hence, Spivak concludes that '[t]he subaltern cannot speak' (1988, p. 308).

Is Spivak right? What does this imply about the theory and practice of political representation?

Let us begin with the objection that descriptive representatives cannot substantively represent their constituents because they are not responsive or accountable enough to them. This was initially suggested by Pitkin, who argued that because descriptive representation is essentially about 'standing for' other people with whom one shares a resemblance, it cannot make room for the ideas of accountability or responsiveness (1967, p. 89). As she puts it, 'a man can only be held accountable for what he has done, not for what he is' (1967, p. 90). Pitkin's objection, however, concerns the concept of representation itself rather than political practice. Her claim is that thinking about representation in terms of standing-for-those-whom-one-resembles is fundamentally different to thinking about representation in terms of responsiveness-to-those-one-speaks-for. On her account, if we endorse the descriptive conception of what representation really is, then we can no longer evaluate representatives in terms of their accountability or responsiveness, since unresponsive and unaccountable representatives could nevertheless resemble those whom they represent in the relevant ways.

Although Pitkin's conceptual point may be true, the descriptive representatives sitting in contemporary legislatures are typically elected, a fact that makes them vulnerable to the same electoral sanctions as other elected representatives. These representatives, then, can be held accountable, provided that there is meaningful competition for political office. However, some political scientists are sceptical about the effectiveness of electoral sanctions in holding descriptive representatives accountable. For example, Mansbridge suggests that the constituents of descriptive representatives can be lulled 'into thinking their substantive interests are being represented even when this is not the case' (1999, p. 640). In support of this, she quotes an African American member of Congress, who referred to the 'shameless loyalty' of his constituents and suggested that descriptive representatives often do not need to have '*any* vigilance about [their] performance' (Mansbridge, 1999, p. 640; quoting Swain, 1993, p. 73). The worry here is that even if descriptive representatives are held accountable at the ballot box, they might – in practice – be held to lower standards than their non-descriptive colleagues. Furthermore, some groups may also find it difficult to hold their descriptive representatives deliberatively accountable, since this would require some degree of self-organisation on the part of the relevant group (Phillips, 1995, p. 188), and this may be something that disadvantaged groups find difficult.

Even if descriptive representatives turn out to be less accountable than at least some of their non-descriptive counterparts, they might be more responsive. This is because responsiveness is facilitated by the presence of shared understandings, reciprocal trust, and mutual engagement. Representatives who share the 'view from the inside' may be able to better grasp the distinctive challenges faced by those they represent, and voters may be more willing to trust and engage with representatives with whom they share significant experiences and characteristics. For example, Mansbridge suggests that 'representatives and voters who share membership in a subordinate group can ... forge bonds of trust based specifically on the shared experience of subordination' (Mansbridge, 1999, p. 641). Similarly, minority voters may be more likely to contact representatives who descriptively resemble them, as Claudine Gay has demonstrated in the case of African Americans (Gay, 2002). Moreover, even if descriptive representatives are only weakly responsive, disadvantaged groups who lack them could experience an even more severe responsiveness deficit. For example, the historical experience of women in what are now liberal democracies suggests that non-descriptive representatives are often unaware of the interests, concerns or perspectives of disadvantaged groups (see, e.g., Sapiro, 1981). Similarly, Barbara Arneil has described how the repeated experiences of 'betrayal or broken promises' have left African Americans distrustful of whites (Arneil, 2006, p. 145), whilst Melissa Williams similarly argues that 'the repeated betrayals of marginalized group interests through history produces a profound – and often quite reasonable and understandable – distrust of privileged groups' (Williams, 1998, p. 149).

The second objection that we will consider is that descriptive representatives cannot substantively represent their constituents because their constituents do not share a single 'essential' identity. As Williams puts it, 'it would be absurd to claim that a representative, simply because she is a woman, therefore represents the interests or perspectives of women generally, or that an African American representative is automatically representative of all African Americans' (Williams, 1998, p. 6). To be fair, contemporary proponents of descriptive representation are particularly sensitive to the fact that social groups are typically neither 'monolithic' nor 'cohesive' (Guinier, 1994, p. 142). For example, Phillips observes that 'interests can be gendered without any implication that all women share the same set of interests; racial and ethnic minorities may have a strong sense of themselves as a distinct social group, but this can coincide with an equally strong sense of division over policy goals' (Phillips, 1995, p. 145). However, the fact that social groups tend to be internally diverse – both because members do not resemble one another in important ways and because they disagree over substantive political issues – suggests that a small number of descriptive representatives cannot adequately represent all of the members of the group.

These problems are exacerbated when one takes into account the fact that people may be members of more than one disadvantaged group. Phillips captures this predicament by observing that 'once men were dislodged from their role of speaking for women, it seemed obvious enough that white women must also be dislodged from their role of speaking for black women, heterosexual women for lesbians, and middle-class women for those in the working class' (Phillips, 1995, p. 9). Not only might people belong to two or three disadvantaged groups, but the conjunction of these identities might itself be another identity that deserves representation. For instance, Young points out that if the descriptive representatives of Latinos include only heterosexuals, then this may inadvertently silence or suppress the perspectives and experiences of homosexual Latinos (Young, 1997, p. 351). Likewise, Mansbridge argues that descriptive representation risks 'assimilating minority or subordinate interests in those of the dominant group without even recognizing their existence' (Mansbridge, 1999, p. 637). Consequently, she argues that attempts to institutionalise descriptive representation should aim to reflect 'the inner diversity of any descriptively denominated group' (1999, p. 638). In a similar fashion, Goodin suggests that if a lesbian Latina is discriminated against as a lesbian, as a Latina *and* as a lesbian Latina, then proponents of the politics of presence 'should require physical presence in the assembly not only of lesbians and Latinas but also of lesbians who are Latinas' (Goodin, 2008, p. 245). However, as he notes, achieving this for all relevant identities will likely require an assembly that contains an implausibly large number of representatives.

One solution to these problems is to relax the requirement that every single identity should be represented, and instead to design political institutions that represent 'the sheer fact of diversity' (Goodin, 2008, pp. 247–52). To achieve this 'some substantial diversity has to be made manifest in the assembly', but 'a fully representative sample is not necessary' (Goodin, 2008, p. 248). The aim is to remind legislators that society is diverse, so as to encourage them to account for this in their deliberations and decisions. Thus, when voting and speaking, legislators will hopefully be cognisant of the fact that not everyone thinks as they do or experiences the world in the same way. Goodin acknowledges that this solution is not optimal, since in many cases legislators will have to rely on their imaginations – projecting themselves into the shoes of others of whom they may have little knowledge. Indeed, if it were feasible, it would be better for legislators to be confronted with flesh-and-blood representatives of minority groups, with whom they could talk, listen and argue. Nevertheless, Goodin concludes that 'simply reflecting upon the fact and extent of differences across the community might make legislators more cautious and circumspect in their policy ... [encouraging them to] avoid imposing "one-size-fits-all" policies' (Goodin, 2008, p. 251).

Future challenges

In this chapter we have largely focussed on the challenges that existing practices of political representation pose for political theory. Unsurprisingly, most of these have to do with representation inside the state, and especially with the democratic credentials of elected politicians and representative systems. Of course, as the activities of celebrity representatives and international advocacy groups indicate, international forms of political representation are becoming increasingly important, and are likely to demand greater critical scrutiny from political theorists in the future. Another challenge that has recently arisen concerns the representative qualities of international organisations, and we will conclude this chapter by examining some possibilities that have been suggested for democratising these bodies.

Critics of globalisation often protest that international institutions and organisations are too distant from ordinary people. They argue that institutions like the World Bank, the International Monetary Fund or the United Nations lack clear mechanisms of democratic authorisation, or are inadequately accountable or responsive, or privilege wealthy groups and individuals in their composition. As we have seen, shortcomings like these can plausibly be described as a failure of political representation, and the rival perspectives we have surveyed suggest various possibilities for improving the quality of representation in these bodies. One proposal, which we shall focus on here, is that the United Nations should be more deeply democratised by establishing a World Parliament that would sit alongside, or in place of, its General Assembly (Held, 1995; Falk and Strauss, 2001; Archibugi, 2008; Goodin, 2010).

In order to evaluate this proposal, we need first to examine the existing mechanisms of representation in the United Nations, since at least two of its principal organs have putative claims to being both representative and democratic. The first of these – the General Assembly – contains representatives from each member state, each of which is equipped with a single vote. In turn, these representatives are responsible for electing the non-permanent members of the second major body – the Security Council – who sit alongside the five permanent members (China, France, Russia, the UK and the US). The case in favour of saying that the United Nations represents the global population is that each country has its own representative, and these represent the peoples of their respective countries. Thus, ordinary people are represented in the General Assembly via their states. On comparable grounds, the Security Council could also be described as representative, because it contains members who were selected by the General Assembly. Meanwhile, the case against saying that the United Nations represents the global population is that membership of the General Assembly is made available to non-democratic countries. As such, in many cases it is implausible to say that representatives in the General Assembly represent the citizens of their countries, since they have not been authorised by them and are not accountable to them, and citizens in non-democratic states have few opportunities to contest the representative claims made on their behalf. Thus, even if it is true that the members of the General Assembly represent their respective member states, it is a stretch to say that they all represent their peoples. Consequently, it seems difficult to resist the conclusion that the United Nations, in its current formation, is inadequately representative.

Establishing a World Parliament, to sit alongside or in place of the General Assembly, might correct this deficiency. This is not a new idea, and before the United Nations was established the British Foreign Secretary Ernest Bevin advocated a 'study of a house directly elected by the people of the world' (quoted in Goodin, 2010, p. 177). More recently, cosmopolitan democrat David Held has argued for a global assembly composed of directly elected members, representing territorially defined constituencies, and accountable to their electorates (Held, 1995). In a similar proposal, Richard Falk and Andrew Strauss (2001) have argued for a single system of global electoral districts, combined with election rules to prevent manipulation or elite domination. Finally, John Galtung (2000) recommends a multi-tiered scheme, containing different assemblies for peoples, governments, corporations, local authorities and non-governmental organisations. Within this framework, the final three assemblies are allocated a 'consultative' role, and something like the existing General Assembly would act as a kind of executive. Meanwhile, a (global) 'People's Assembly' would 'function as any other parliament, making laws, budgets and appointments' (Galtung, 2000, p. 156).

Is a World Parliament the most effective means to ensure adequate global representation? A positive answer can be given to this question if one thinks that democratic representation must feature authorisation-by-election. If this is the case, then establishing a World Parliament is likely to be the most feasible means to ensure that each global citizen is represented. Something similar can also be said by those who believe that representatives should be held accountable through electoral sanctions. Meanwhile, if one believes that non-electoral modes of descriptive or constitutive representation can also be legitimate, then it might be possible to have adequate global representation without instituting a World Parliament. Indeed, there are plausible reasons to think that some individuals and groups might be more effectively represented on the global stage through existing informal mechanisms. For instance, geographically dispersed groups, whose representatives are unlikely to be elected under the proposed schemes, might fare better by being represented by celebrities or grassroots campaigns, especially if those campaigns are well funded. Finally, if one thinks that a representative system should be evaluated according to how responsive or reflexive it is, then alternative institutional solutions may be preferable to a World Parliament. For example, Kuper proposes a 'responsive' system of global governance in which unelected representatives of non-governmental organisations, local authorities, regional organisations, trade unions and professions are incorporated into a Global Assembly alongside states (2004, pp. 165–70). Although this scheme is clearly unrepresentative by the standards of the theories we have examined, overall it might be more responsive to the changing needs and interests of the global population.

5
Democracy

Introduction

Democracy is one of those things that everyone seems to be in favour of. Unfortunately, the glow of approval that surrounds the term can be misleading. This is because, as Bernard Crick once suggested, '[d]emocracy is perhaps the most promiscuous word in the world of public affairs' (1962, p. 56). For example, a person who says that they want more democracy might mean that governments should be more responsive to citizens, that politicians should be more socially representative, that people should have more control over political decisions, or that more institutions should be subject to popular control. Confusingly, however, someone could also oppose any of these things on democratic grounds. For instance, being responsive to popular opinion might neglect the interests of minorities, and a socially representative legislature might need to implement a quota scheme in place of free and open elections. Similarly, empowering people to directly control political decisions might impoverish democratic deliberation by focussing attention on blunt and simplistic referenda questions, and democratising institutions like the workplace might undermine the freedom of employers to run their own businesses. Democracy, then, might be something that nearly everyone favours, but not everyone favours the same kind of democracy.

One way in which scholars have responded to these ambiguities is to distinguish amongst different 'models' of democracy (Held, 2006), such as by identifying 'direct' and 'indirect' forms of democracy. Direct democracy refers to popular self-government, whereby citizens rule themselves directly without transferring that responsibility to elected officials. This requires particular

107

kinds of institutions, such as assemblies where citizens can gather together or technologies that allow them to express their political preferences. A strong (but highly exclusive) form of direct democracy was practised by the ancient Athenians, and something similar continues today in 'town-hall' democracies, such as those found in parts of New England and Switzerland. Occasional manifestations of direct democracy also occur when governments solicit the views of citizens in popular referenda. Meanwhile, 'indirect' democracy refers to government by elected officials, and is sometimes called 'representative democracy'. As we saw in Chapter 4, the democratic credentials of this model are often thought to rest on whether politicians have been authorised or are accountable to those whom they represent.

Although the distinction between direct and indirect democracy can help to explain some of the disagreements that we began with, it obscures as much as it illuminates. We can see this by asking if the two models are different versions of the same ideal, or if they are different ideals. If we say they are manifestations of the same ideal, then it may appear as if indirect democracy is a less complete but more feasible version of direct democracy. This might be true, but as we shall see later, many political theorists think that representative democracy has some distinctive virtues that cannot be realised in a direct democracy. Meanwhile, if we say that they are different ideals, then it becomes difficult to say whether there is a single underlying ideal of democracy. This has important practical consequences, because many political systems combine features of both models, for instance by allocating some decision making competences to elected representatives and reserving others for the people themselves. If we want to know how to make these systems more democratic, then we need an account of democracy that can stand apart from these two models.

One way to do this is to map out the various values and principles that we associate with democracy. For example, all theories of democracy connect it to the idea of political equality, albeit in different ways. Some political theorists also associate democracy with freedom, since they believe that only in a democracy can people be truly free. Although this claim is controversial, it has a strong intuitive appeal, as we often describe people living under non-democratic rulers as being unfree. Others connect democracy to political legitimacy, arguing that only democratic procedures can yield outcomes that are authoritatively binding. Again, although this is controversial, it is implicit in many everyday sentiments about the authority of democracy. Furthermore, some political theorists think that democracy is valuable because it leads to better quality decision making, or because it enables citizens to cultivate virtuous dispositions.

As will become clear, different theories of democracy configure this cluster of values and principles in different ways, giving priority to some and excluding others. Although it is possible to discriminate amongst different approaches to democracy by mapping out the various ways to arrange these values, this would not illuminate the full scope of disagreements among contemporary political theorists. This is because they disagree not only about the value of democracy, but also about what kind of an activity democratic politics is. Consequently, the three rival perspectives we shall explore in this chapter, and which are summarised in Table 5.1, have been selected because they each capture a different sense of what it means for citizens to 'do' democratic politics.

According to the first view, competitive elections are the key democratic institution and voting is the fundamental democratic activity. Competitive democrats believe that democracy is simply a method for selecting political leaders and that it has nothing to do with identifying policies or institutions to serve the common good or the public interest. Contemporary advocates tend to present this theory as a realistic alternative to the other theories we shall consider, not least because it closely resembles actually existing democracies. Nevertheless, competitive democracy does have a prescriptive component, since advocates are concerned about establishing institutional and social conditions that allow for meaningful political competition amongst parties, candidates and policies.

Meanwhile, participatory democrats associate the democratic ideal with living in a participatory society. This is a social form in which citizens collectively control the institutions that shape their lives, including not only laws and government, but also the component parts of civil society, such as the workplace, schools and universities, and even the family. Thus, unlike competitive democrats, participatory democrats believe that democratic activity is ongoing rather than sporadic, and involves thoroughgoing and active engagement rather than simply ticking boxes. The intellectual progenitors of this view include Jean-Jacques Rousseau in the eighteenth century and Hannah Arendt in the mid-twentieth century. During its heyday – which spanned the 1960s, 1970s and early 1980s – it was the leading radical alternative to both the theory of competitive democracy and to the actual practices of Western capitalist democracies. Although participatory democracy became 'unfashionable' during the 1980s and 1990s (Pateman, 2012, p. 7), it has resurfaced in recent years.

Finally, the theory of deliberative democracy identifies public argument and reasoning as the key democratic acts. This view has risen to prominence in recent years, and is certainly the most widely discussed amongst contemporary political theorists. According to this view, what makes a society democratic is the quality of deliberation that precedes decision making, rather than the gathering of votes. A society upholds the ideal of deliberative democracy to the extent that its members deliberate on an equal basis about how to arrange their institutions. Deliberation does not simply mean expressing one's preferences, but rather involves a collective search for solutions to shared problems, in which participants aim to reach a rationally motivated consensus by suggesting and criticising arguments. Importantly, deliberation involves both speaking and listening, and citizens must be willing to recognise the force of the better argument, even when doing so goes against their own self-interest.

Table 5.1 Summary of rival perspectives on democracy

	Competitive	Participatory	Deliberative
Aim	To establish legitimate rule	Popular control by citizens of their own affairs	Rationally motivated consensus about basic political principles, and perhaps about specific laws and policies
Site	Democracy occurs during election campaigns, when politicians position themselves in order to capture the largest share of the vote	Ideally, all institutions or 'common activities' should be democratised, including universities and the workplace	Deliberation may be dispersed throughout civil society or it might occur in specially designed fora (legislatures, mini publics, deliberative polls)
Frequency	Periodic voting at elections	More participation is better than less, and ideally participation should be ongoing; otherwise, one-off 'participatory experiments' are to be favoured	More deliberation is better than less, and ideally all decisions should be reached through deliberation; otherwise, ongoing or one-off 'deliberative experiments' are to be favoured
Popular control	Political outcomes are not subject to popular control	Political and civil society institutions should be subject to popular control	Political principles, laws and policies should attract the consent of those who are subject to them
Citizen attributes	Voters are self-interested and may be poorly informed; voter preferences are assumed to be fixed	Participation has a 'developmental' aspect, transforming the *character* of citizens, ideally making them better informed and authentically orientated towards the common good	Deliberation forces citizens to adopt an orientation to the common good; good deliberators are responsive to reasons and the force of the better argument
Values	Respects equality (formal), promotes stability and efficiency; potentially responsive to the needs and interests of citizens; nourishes virtuous dispositions amongst citizens (e.g. individuality)	Respects equality (formal and substantive); honours (positive) freedom; nourishes virtuous dispositions (e.g. civility) and skills (e.g. critical reasoning) amongst citizens	Respects equality (formal and substantive); achieves legitimacy; encourages good government; nourishes virtuous dispositions (e.g. civility) and skills (e.g. critical reasoning) amongst citizens
Favourable conditions	Adequate political competition; political parties offering a range of alternatives	Approximate material equality; engaged citizens; opportunities for meaningful democratic participation that will determine outcomes	Citizens are informed and rational, and able to deliberate as equals; adequate opportunities for meaningful deliberation and to allow citizens to influence political outcomes

Each of these rival perspectives makes different assumptions about the nature and value of democracy, as well as delivering different recommendations about how to realise the democratic ideal. We will begin the second half of the chapter by comparing them across two dimensions. First, we will address the nature of democracy, focussing especially on whether democratic citizens and societies should aim to promote the common good. Whilst deliberative and participatory democrats think that they should, competitive democrats favour a model of democratic politics that puts the self-interests of voters and politicians at its centre. Second, we will turn to the value of democracy, and explore some different normative explanations that have been given in support of democratic institutions. Whilst some political theorists think that democracy is intrinsically valuable, others believe that it is valuable because it delivers good outcomes. Each of our rival perspectives associates democracy with different clusters of values, and comparing them in this way illustrates some of the fundamental divisions amongst them. Third, since it has captured the greatest amount of attention amongst contemporary political theorists, we will look more closely at deliberative democracy, exploring whether it is a feasible ideal for large and complex societies. Finally, we will conclude the chapter by addressing a future challenge for democratic theory, which has emerged from a radical critique of consensus-orientated forms of democratic politics.

Rival perspectives

Competitive democracy

The theory of competitive democracy, which is also sometimes described as the elitist theory of democracy, was given its classic formulation by Joseph Schumpeter in the middle of the twentieth century and has been defended more recently been by Samuel Huntingdon, Richard Posner and Ian Shapiro. Proponents say that democracy is fundamentally a method for establishing legitimate leadership. For example, Posner describes democratic politics as 'a competition among self-interested politicians, constituting a ruling class, for the support of the people, also assumed to be self-interested, and none too interested or well informed about politics' (Posner, 2003, p. 144). From the perspective of the majority of citizens, popular involvement in politics is limited to periodically voting at elections. Advocates identify three main attractions of this vision of democratic politics. First, by granting citizens the right to 'throw the rascals out', competitive democracy empowers people to protect themselves against bad rulers. Second, because elections tend to be a stable mechanism for transitioning between different rulers, competitive democracies are less likely than other political formations to experience instability and violence. Third, because it does not expect much in the way of citizen involvement in politics, competitive democracy is a feasible and realistic theory.

The classic articulation of the competitive theory of democracy can be found in Schumpeter's *Capitalism, Socialism and Democracy*, first published in 1942. At the centre of his vision of democratic life was an image of multiple political parties competing against one another in open and regular elections. Schumpeter, an economist, understood political competition for votes to operate in a similar fashion to competition in an economic market. Voters are like consumers, choosing amongst the different policy packages offered by political parties. However, just as consumers are often poorly informed and vulnerable to manipulation from advertisers, Schumpeter was also sceptical about the independence and rationality of voters, at one point concluding that the 'electoral mass' are 'incapable of action other than a stampede' (1956, p. 272). However, not all proponents of competitive democracy paint so bleak a picture of the electorate. Posner, for example, writes that '[t]he people are the repository of common sense, which, dull though it is, is a barrier to the mad schemes, whether of social engineering or foreign adventures, hatched by specialists and intellectuals' (2003, p. 168).

Schumpeter formally defined democracy as 'that institutional arrangement for arriving at political decisions in which individuals acquire the power to decide by means of a competitive struggle for the people's vote' (Schumpeter, 1956, p. 269). He presented this characterisation as a realistic alternative to what he termed the 'classical' theory of democracy, which took democracy to be 'that institutional arrangement for arriving at political decisions which realises the common good by making the people itself decide issues through the election of individuals who are to assemble in order to carry out its will' (1956, p. 250). Schumpeter did not specify which political theorists endorsed the classical view, and it is not clear that any particular thinker to be found in the history of ideas really did (Pateman, 1970, p. 17). Nevertheless, his juxtaposition between the two ideals helps to bring out four of the most distinctive features of his own view.

First, unlike the classical model, Schumpeter's definition of democracy does not include the idea that the people themselves should directly influence or control political outcomes. Instead, decision making responsibility is allocated to elected officials, who are entitled to this power because they have captured a sufficient share of the vote. Thus, Schumpeterian democracy is not a means to empower the people to 'control their political leaders' (Schumpeter, 1956, p. 272), and it is less rule-by-the-people than rule-of-the-elected-politician (Schumpeter, 1956, p. 285). Second, although elections are crucial to both theories, they perform different roles in each. In the classical theory, elections are an opportunity to define the popular will. For example, if voters prefer anti-war to pro-war candidates or parties, then this sends a signal to the government about which decisions have popular support. Meanwhile, Schumpeter denied that voters could convey meaningful information at elections, which for him were simply a vehicle for selecting political decision makers. Third, whilst the classical theory of democracy assumes that representatives will act more or less as delegates, advancing the common good as the people themselves perceive it, Schumpeter instead favours a trustee model, in which politicians act independently and according to their own judgements (see Chapter 4). Fourth, whilst the classical model connects democracy to the ideal of realising the common good, Schumpeter's model explicitly disavows moralistic or utopian rhetoric. His was a defiantly 'realist' theory, which characterised democracy simply as 'a political method, that is to say, a certain type of institutional arrangement for arriving at political – legal and administrative – decisions' (1956, p. 242).

Schumpeter supported his controversial theory of democracy by casting doubt on the rationality of voters, which led him to conclude that the popular will (or the will of the people) could not serve as a legitimate basis for law, administration and government. Schumpeter's scepticism about individual rationality stemmed from his observation that people tend to respond emotionally rather than rationally in the political domain. For instance, in a famous passage he claims that when talking about politics, most citizens exhibit little more than 'an indeterminate bundle of vague impulses loosely playing about given slogans and mistaken impressions' (1956, pp. 253–4). This was because, on his account, people only fully grasp things that are fully 'real' to them, and this usually does not include political affairs:

[T]he typical citizen drops down to a lower level of mental performance as soon as he enters the political field. He argues and analyses in a way that he would readily recognise as infantile within the sphere of his real interests. (Schumpeter, 1956, p. 262)

Because people tend to reason poorly about politics, Schumpeter infers that they are vulnerable to manipulation and are easily swayed by outside forces. Consequently, he concludes that what the people believe themselves to want – what they perceive to be the popular will – is often the product of interest group and elite manipulation, and lacks an independent rational foundation (1956, pp. 256–68). Even if the people think they have come to an agreement about what is in their shared interests, this agreement is likely to have been 'manufactured'. As Schumpeter puts it:

If all the people can in the short run be 'fooled' step by step into something they do not really want, and if this is not an exceptional case which we could afford to neglect, then no amount of retrospective common sense will alter the fact that in reality they neither raise nor decide issues but that the issues that shape their fate are normally raised and decided for them. (1956, p. 264)

As a consequence, if we are to have democracy then Schumpeter thinks that we need to give up on the idea that the people themselves should choose what they want, since they are not capable of making such decisions.

**BOX 5.1   VOTER RATIONALITY,
INFORMATION AND INCENTIVES**

As we have seen, Schumpeter's case against 'classical democracy' rested partly on what he perceived to be the intellectual shortcomings of citizens in existing democracies. One response to Schumpeter's pessimism – suggested by deliberative democrat James Fishkin (1991, 1995) and drawing on Anthony Downs (1957) – is to accept that voters in actually existing democracies are often poorly informed about politics, but to attribute this to a rational calculation on their part. The logic of this calculation is that since becoming informed about politics is costly (in terms of the time and effort that must be invested), and since individuals have only a limited influence on political outcomes, then it is rational for voters in a competitive democracy to delegate the responsibility of learning and thinking about politics to their representatives. If this logic is convincing, then it is unwarranted for Schumpeter to infer that ordinary people are always poor political thinkers, because increasing voter influence over political outcomes could have the effect of encouraging voters to become more informed.

Are voters more likely to become informed about politics if they believe that their voice counts? What does this imply about the theory and practice of democracy?

Schumpeter's critics have suggested that his view is unduly pessimistic and contains unjustified inferences. One objection, discussed in Box 5.1, is that Schumpeter's depiction of voters as irrational confuses something produced by a competitive democratic system with an enduring quality of voters themselves. According to critics who press this objection, it is unwarranted for Schumpeter to infer that voters could never be capable of making informed and rational decisions (Parry, 1969). Meanwhile, supposing that Schumpeter's scepticism about voter rationality is correct raises another problem, because it would imply that we should give up on the democratic project entirely. As Held rhetorically asks: 'If the electorate is regarded as unable to form reasonable judgements about pressing political questions, why should it be regarded as capable of discriminating between alternative sets of leaders?' (Held, 2006, p. 154).

A final objection is that Schumpeterian democracy is not competitive enough. For instance, participatory democrat C. B. Macpherson has suggested that Schumpeter's view is more 'oligopolistic' than democratic, since it allows political parties a lot of discretion in selecting the range of political alternatives presented to voters (Macpherson, 1977, p. 89). Similarly, contemporary competitive democrat Ian Shapiro suggests that 'Schumpeterian democracy leads to less than fully adequate political competition' (Shapiro, 2003a, p. 203). One basis for these worries is that politicians, at least in many capitalist societies, need to campaign for financial contributions as well as for votes. As a consequence, the agendas of wealthy elites will often influence and constrain the proposals that politicians are able to offer to the people. In response to this, contemporary proponents of competitive democracy have suggested that adequate political competition will require things such as the tighter regulation of political financing and the dismantling of large political parties (Posner, 2003). Furthermore, according to one commentator, 'if competitive democracy is to survive, voters must be provided with a space in which they can voice their political opinions' (Kelly, 2012, p. 51). Shapiro makes a similar point, suggesting that 'meaningful political competition requires that there be opposition parties waiting in the wings, criticising the government and offering voters potential alternatives' (Shapiro, 2003a, p. 59). At the very least, this implies that competitive democracies must secure rights to free speech and political participation. More demandingly, it may also require citizenship education to ensure that voters can think critically and evaluate the options that are put before them.

Participatory democracy

Participatory democrats – such as Carole Pateman, Archon Fung, Benjamin Barber and C. B. Macpherson – regard competitive theories of democracy as unduly minimalist. Whilst Schumpeter argued that the public should be discouraged from participating in politics between elections – even suggesting that citizens should refrain from 'back-seat driving' (1956, p. 295) – participatory democrats favour greater public involvement in decision making. For them, public participation is at the heart of democratic politics, since 'democracy is control by citizens of their own affairs' (Cunningham, 2002, p. 126). Participatory democrats understand this to mean that citizens must be willing and able to participate in decision making at a variety of different levels, not only in the formal political system but also in everyday institutions such as universities, the workplace and the family. Ultimately, the aim of participatory democrats is to create a 'participatory society' (Pateman, 1970), and this will require radically transforming citizens themselves as well as the social and political structures they inhabit.

  Participatory democrats believe that people need to be afforded meaningful opportunities to participate in collective self-government. However, in many societies the opportunity to participate often does not seem to translate into actual participation. In response, participatory democrats argue that contemporary political disenchantment is the product of existing (competitive) democratic institutions, which fail to empower citizens (Pateman, 1970, p. 104). For example, Benjamin Barber suggests that people are 'apathetic because they are powerless' (Barber, 1984, p. 272). Thus, instead of seeing democratic disenchantment as an obstacle to the participatory project, participatory democrats see their own proposals as solutions to it.

Notwithstanding this, many participatory democrats accept the Schumpeterian premise that people will be less interested in 'high politics' than in local matters that impact directly upon them. For instance, Pateman concedes 'that it is doubtful if the average citizen will ever be as interested in all the decisions made at national level as [they] would in those made nearer home' (1970, p. 110). Consequently, she argues that we first need to encourage greater participation in 'local' forms of politics, such as in the workplace, and that this could have the effect of enabling people to 'better appreciate the connection between the public and the private spheres' (1970, p. 110). Ultimately, Pateman accepts that the institutions of 'high politics', even in a participatory society, are likely to resemble those in a competitive democracy, and she acknowledges the need for parties, political representation and competitive elections in a mass society. However, and importantly, she argues that a more participatory society would alter the 'context within which all political activity was carried out' (1970, p. 110). In particular, she thinks that participation has an educative or developmental aspect. As a consequence, citizens who participate locally, and who live in a participatory society, will be 'better able to assess the performance of representatives at the national level, better equipped to take decisions of national scope when the opportunity arose to do so, and better able to weigh up the impact of decisions taken by national representatives on his own life and immediate surroundings' (1970, p. 110).

Participatory democrats want citizens to participate in decision making in a range of institutions, and one of their most significant theoretical contributions has been to expand the range of sites that might be imagined to fall under democratic or popular control. For example, participatory democrats supported the student movements in the 1960s, which sought greater democratic involvement in matters such as curriculum design and university administration. Similarly, they have argued for democratising the workplace, claiming that we need to modify 'the orthodox authority structure' and to move away from the model whereby 'decision making is the "prerogative" of management, in which workers play no part' (Pateman, 1970, p. 68). There are at least two participatory rationales for democratising the university and workplace. First, as we have seen, participatory democrats believe that 'local' participation trains people to become more effective citizens, thus improving the quality of 'national' politics. Second, these institutions have a profound impact upon people's lives, are 'political systems in their own right' (Pateman, 1970, p. 83), and should therefore be subject to democratic control. Pateman puts special emphasis in this regard on workplace democracy, arguing that 'industry, with its relationships of superiority and subordination, is the most "political" of all areas in which ordinary individuals interact and decisions taken there have a great effect on the rest of their lives' (1970, pp. 83–4).

Participatory democrats are sensitive to the fact that managers and administrators can manipulate the language of participation. For instance,

Pateman points to the phenomenon of 'pseudo participation', giving the example of a 'supervisor [who] instead of merely telling the employees of a decision, allows them to question him about it and to discuss it' (Pateman, 1970, p. 69). Although cases such as these may create a 'feeling' of participation, they are not genuinely participatory, if employees have little influence over the decision itself. In other cases, students and employees may be given some say about how their organisations are run, but they may not have an equal influence if the final decision is made by administrators and managers, and Pateman labels this 'partial participation' (Pateman, 1970, p. 70). Although partial and even pseudo participation may have beneficial educative effects, they are inadequate when considered as forms of democratic control. What democracy really requires, on Pateman's account, is 'full participation', in which everyone has 'equal power to determine the outcome of decisions' (Pateman, 1970, p. 71). Moreover, full participation must apply both at the lower level (such as to decisions about the shop floor and everyday work process) and at the higher level (such as to decisions about investment strategies and marketing) (Pateman, 1970, pp. 70–3). Achieving this in the workplace will require a radical overhaul of the structure of industrial authority, for instance along the lines of workers' self-government. Consequently, Pateman dedicates a substantial portion of her book to examining the feasibility of such a model (Pateman, 1970, ch. 5).

Critics of participatory democracy have drawn attention to its seemingly 'utopian cast' (Bohman, 1996, p. 9), in one case suggesting that it is 'beset by a fuzzy utopianism that fails to confront limitations of complexity, size and scale of advanced industrial societies' (Warren, 1996, p. 242). For example, many citizens lack both the time and the disposition to learn about and participate in political life. Conceivably, this problem could be solved by legally requiring people to participate in politics, but as Habermas notes, this solution 'has something totalitarian about it' (Habermas, 1996, p. 120). Furthermore, mandatory participation would not guarantee that citizens would participate responsibly, for instance by researching political issues and seriously exploring the alternatives. Thus, if the project of creating a participatory society is to be realised, it will require a substantial transformation in citizens themselves. Although participatory democrats have suggested that the radical alterations in authority structures they favour will bring about such a change (Macpherson, 1977, pp. 108–14; Barber, 1984, p. 307), it is difficult to see what evidence could be appealed to in support of this.

Although few contemporary scholars embrace the call for a participatory society, many of the central themes elaborated by the participatory democrats continue to inspire political theorists, scientists and activists today, albeit in a piecemeal fashion. For example, building on the work of participatory democrats, political scientists have appealed to the idea of 'social capital' to explain why democracies are more likely to flourish when citizens are

BOX 5.2   PARTICIPATORY BUDGETING IN PORTO ALEGRE

Since 1989, an influential experiment in public participation has been attempted in the Brazilian town of Porto Alegre. There, all citizens are able to contribute to open meetings, where they can raise local concerns, and which inform decisions about municipal budget priorities and about the distribution of investments. Studies of this process suggest that it has brought about some of the transformative effects that political theorists attribute to participation. First, it seems to have enhanced participants' awareness of political procedures and issues. For instance, one participant – reflecting on their experience – remarked: 'I had to learn about the process as the meetings took place. The first time I participated, I was unsure, because there were people there with college degrees, and I don't [have one]. But in time I learned' (Baiocchi, 2005, p. 43). Second, it also seems to have empowered participants, who came to more vividly appreciate that administrators and politicians were accountable to them (Hilmer, 2010, p. 57). Third, it also seems to have led to substantive changes in policy priorities. For example, one observer noted that the proportion of citizens with access to water and sewage in one district of Porto Alegre nearly doubled between 1989 and 1996 (Santos, 2006, p. 313).

Should participatory budgeting be attempted in other towns and cities?

actively involved in civic associations (Putnam, 2000). This work has inspired politicians in Western democracies to advocate a variety of measures intended to strengthen and encourage participation in civil society. For example, the World Bank has published a *Participation Sourcebook* (1996) and a report on *Participatory Budgeting* (2008). Likewise, development agencies and NGOs have become increasingly concerned to promote political participation, and have become especially interested in participatory budgeting schemes, such as the one discussed in Box 5.2.

Deliberative democracy

Whilst the profile of participatory theories of democracy has waned in recent decades, theories of deliberative democracy have flourished. Although the two approaches are recognisably distinct, important elements of the participatory project have filtered into deliberative accounts of democracy. For example, deliberative democrats agree that citizens should make a greater contribution to decision making than either contemporary democratic formations or the competitive theory of democracy allow. They also agree that political participation has a transformative effect, enabling citizens to better perceive their own interests and those of their fellow citizens. Furthermore, deliberative democrats agree that citizens will make more reasoned and intelligent contributions to political debate if they are convinced that their voice counts. However, although they are committed to improving the quality of democracy in the real world, deliberative democrats tend to have less radical ambitions than participatory democrats, and their theory can perhaps be realised without a thorough over-haul of existing social and political structures.

At its core, deliberative democracy describes a normative ideal in which free and equal citizens publicly exchange reasons with one another with a view to reaching a consensus about some issue or policy, or about the principles underlying the political system as a whole. The central claim endorsed by its proponents – such as Joshua Cohen, Seyla Benhabib, Jürgen Habermas, James Fishkin, John Dryzek, Amy Gutmann and Dennis Thompson – is that a political decision or system is legitimate if it can command 'free and reasoned agreement among equals' (Cohen, 1989, p. 22). Thus, a political decision or system is ideally or maximally legitimate if it attracts the reasoned support of citizens, each of whom had an equal opportunity to make their voice heard, to listen to their fellow citizens, and to exchange views and reasons amongst one another. Clearly, this is an idealised conception, of which contemporary political life – with its partisan rivalries and messy compromises – often falls short. Nevertheless, underlying the deliberative ideal is a powerful moral intuition about the nature of truly democratic association, according to which 'the justification of the terms and conditions of association proceeds through public argument and reasoning among equal citizens' (Cohen, 1989, p. 21).

Alongside their demanding theory of political legitimacy, deliberative democrats also have a demanding conception of deliberation. Deliberation is valuable as it offers citizens a way 'to live with moral disagreement' (Gutmann and Thompson, 1996, p. 361). Disagreement in politics applies both to public policy decisions and to the basic rules and procedures of democratic association (for instance, about who should participate in political life, or about what constitutionally guaranteed rights people should have). Political disagreement is often quite deep, involving not only practical disagreements about how to reach desirable goals but also moral disagreements about what those goals should be (Gutmann and Thompson, 1996, pp. 40–41). For instance, whilst we might disagree about what policies are likely to encourage economic growth, we might also disagree about how important economic growth is and about how it should be balanced against other political concerns, such as the welfare of the least advantaged or the protection of the environment. Deliberation, at least according to its proponents, offers us the best democratic means to negotiate these deep and complex disagreements.

Four important features of deliberation are especially worth picking out. First, deliberation is 'reasoned' and non-coercive. As Habermas puts it, when deliberation goes well, then 'no force except that of the better argument is exercised' (1976, p. 108). This means that deliberators must offer arguments in support of their positions and be open to persuasion. It also means that domination, manipulation, deception and threats should not influence political outcomes. Second, parties deliberate on equal terms, and this means both that the voice of each counts equally and that each participant has an equal opportunity to influence the outcome. As Cohen puts it:

In ideal deliberation parties are both formally and substantively equal. They are formally equal in that the rules regulating the procedure do not single out individuals. Everyone with the deliberative capacities has equal standing at each stage of the deliberative process. Each can put issues on the agenda, propose solutions, and offer reasons in support of or in criticism of proposals. And each has an equal voice in the decision. The participants are substantively equal in that the existing distribution of power and resources does not shape their chances to contribute to deliberation, nor does that distribution play an authoritative role in their deliberation. (Cohen, 1989, p. 23)

The requirement of 'substantive' equality might turn out to be quite demanding, since it requires ensuring that inequalities in power and/or resources do not influence political discourse. For some critics of deliberative democracy, such as competitive democrat Shapiro, this is hopelessly idealistic, and it ignores the reality that, fundamentally, 'politics is about interests and power' (Shapiro, 1999, p. 36).

Third, deliberative democrats emphasise that deliberation can be transformative, because it involves speaking *and* listening. Proponents often contrast this aspect of their theory with the notion of 'aggregation' underlying traditional conceptions of democracy. According to aggregative views, if we want to resolve political disagreements democratically, then we should tally up the preferences of citizens, for instance by convening a referendum or an election. By contrast, deliberative democrats emphasise that democracy is not just about preference aggregation, but is also about the processes of preference formation and transformation. Proper deliberation ought to induce citizens to reflect on their preferences (Dryzek, 2000, p. 68), and (non-deliberative) democratic procedures are unsatisfactory if they do not offer citizens a meaningful opportunity to listen and learn. For instance, suppose that a group of citizens are divided over a political issue, such as healthcare policy, and imagine that each citizen begins from a set of preferences about what services should be provided and how. The significance of deliberation is that in the course of arguing and giving reasons those citizens may acquire new information, learn about the different experiences of others, realise that they have neglected important possibilities, or discover that they have misunderstood how the healthcare system operates. The process of deliberation, then, should reduce prejudice and ignorance, resulting in a more informed citizenry who are better equipped to make informed and well-reasoned political judgements.

Fourth, deliberative democrats have traditionally required that participants aim at consensus, which means that they ought to seek to persuade all of their fellow citizens and not simply a majority of them. Not only does this reduce the likelihood of citizens invoking self-interested reasons during political debate, or adopting bargaining strategies to get their own way, but it also 'forces the individual to think of what would count as a good reason for all others involved' (Benhabib, 1996, pp. 71–2). Indeed, because citizens must try to communicate with (and convince) others who do not share their point of view, who have different interests and who are moved by different values, then a particular ideal of reciprocity is built into the idea of consensus-orientated deliberation (Gutmann and Thompson, 2004). In this context, reciprocity refers to citizens offering justifications in support of their views that are intelligible to people with different perspectives. Thus, the arguments that citizens propose to one another must be comprehensible, stated publicly, and draw upon evidence and beliefs that others can understand and assess. Some deliberative democrats go even further, and appeal to an ideal of public reason that is very similar to the one defended by political liberals, who we examined in Chapter 3. For these authors, deliberators should evaluate the different proposals by using evidence and reasons that are acceptable to all, and this means excluding 'sectarian' views, whose 'justification depends on a particular view of the human good' (Cohen, 1989, p. 27).

An important objection to deliberative democracy is that it is unfeasible, since it seemingly requires that all citizens deliberate in an informed and restrained way about every political decision, and that legitimate decisions attract the rational support of everyone. Competitive democrats such as Posner, for example, think that ordinary citizens are generally too muddled, confused and ignorant to act as deliberative democrats require them to (Posner, 2003, p. 163). Even if deliberative democrats can overcome this problem, they still face what Michael Walzer has called the 'central problem' of deliberative democracy, which is that deliberation is not meaningfully possible in large-scale nation-states (2004, p. 109). As we shall see in the final key debate, deliberative democrats have recently proposed a variety of solutions to this challenge.

Key debates

Should democracy promote the common good?

Should democratic citizens vote, act and speak on the basis of what they believe is good for society, or on the basis of what they believe is good for themselves? Whilst participatory and deliberative democrats argue that democracies should aim to promote the common good, competitive democrats argue that the idea of a common good is both conceptually confused and a normatively unattractive basis for democratic politics. Instead, they favour a democratic politics in which citizens aim only to promote their self-interest. In this key debate we will compare these alternatives.

The *locus classicus* for the view that democracy should promote the common good is Jean-Jacques Rousseau's *Social Contract*, written during the eighteenth century. Rousseau thought that democratic procedures should ensure that political rule is based on the 'general will', by which he meant principles that would advance the public interest. This is captured most clearly in the contrast he draws between the 'general will' and the 'will of all', which was his shorthand for the sum of private preferences. The 'will of all' can be discerned, for example, by convening a referendum in which each person votes for whatever outcome will best satisfy their own self-interest. Although a society governed on this basis might appear to be democratic, it would allow for the possibility of citizens voting for policies that they know to be bad for society but good for themselves. Consequently, a society governed by the 'will of all' is unlikely to be democratic by Rousseau's standards, because it does not guarantee that government will advance the public interest.

Rousseau's alternative to the 'will of all' was the 'general will'. Unfortunately, his account of this concept is notoriously ambiguous (Bertram, 2012). On the one hand, it might refer to principles that the people themselves have voted for, after being asked to reflect on the common good. On the other hand, it might refer to principles that actually are in the public interest, defined independently of what the people themselves say. Regardless of this interpretive issue, it is clear that Rousseau believed that if democratic procedures are to result in decisions that have the effect of promoting the common good, then citizens must be moved by a concern to put the public interest above their own narrow self-interest. This raises a motivational challenge, which on his account could only be solved in small city states, since only in such settings do citizens share enough in common to be willing to make sacrifices for one another. For many political theorists, including competitive democrats, this solution is sufficient to render Rousseau's project irrelevant to contemporary political life. Meanwhile, participatory and deliberative democrats have sought to rehabilitate the idea that democratic politics could advance the common good, and have explored different ways in which this could be achieved in large and complex societies.

Some participatory democrats are committed to a very strong interpretation of what a democratic politics of the common good requires. For example, Barber suggests that real (or 'strong') democracy will require citizens to set aside their self-interest and to express themselves only in terms of the common good. As he puts it, '[i]n place of "I want Y" the strong democrat must say "Y will be good for us"' (Barber, 1984, p. 200). Because many of us do not approach politics in this way, Barber's theory encounters a particularly stark motivational challenge. One solution might be found in the developmental or educative dimensions of political participation, since participatory democrats believe that experience of participation has the potential to yield an orientation toward the common good amongst citizens. According to them, political participation is not just about voting, making decisions and protecting one's interests. Rather, it is a rich, multifaceted and ongoing activity that requires us to speak and act amongst people from different backgrounds, with different perspectives, and with different interests. In the course of doing so, we learn that we need to take those perspectives and interests seriously if we are to gain the co-operation of others. Consequently, greater participation could discourage us from pursuing self-interest and instead induce us to adopt an orientation toward the common good.

This line of argument is endorsed by Pateman, who believes that the experience of participation 'attaches the individual to [their] society' and 'increases the feeling among individual citizens that they "belong" in their community' (Pateman, 1970, p. 27). Thus, for her, a willingness to look towards the common good (rather than self-interest) 'is provided by the transformation of consciousness that is gradually brought about through the participatory process' (Pateman, 1985, p. 156). Barber makes an even stronger claim, arguing that active participation in a common life, where people regularly and openly confront one another's different desires and interests, can help citizens to form a 'creative consensus' (Barber, 1984, p. 224). For him, widespread and ongoing participation can both stimulate citizens to search for the common good and help them to find out what it is. However, as discussed in Box 5.3, some political theorists think that this solution to the motivational challenge is paradoxical, since it implies that participatory democracy requires something that it is designed to give us.

BOX 5.3 THE PARADOX OF PARTICIPATORY DEMOCRACY

Participatory democrats argue that the experience of participation has a developmental or educative quality, since exercising power with others can increase people's capacities as citizens and empower them with a sense of their own political efficacy. For example, participating in a grassroots campaign might equip someone to become a more effective political activist or organiser, whilst the experience of talking and arguing amongst both their fellow campaigners and opponents might help someone to finesse their debating skills. Furthermore, democratic participation might also enhance someone's capacities for empathy and understanding, allowing them to gain a richer appreciation of how their fellow citizens think and feel. However, an early advocate of participatory democracy noted a 'paradox of democratic participation', which is that people who have not experienced participation may lack the capacities to be good democratic citizens (Kaufman, 1968). The paradox is that a participatory society seems to require something of its members which they currently lack, and which they can only gain by participating in a good participatory society.

How much of a problem is the paradox of participatory democracy? Can it be solved?

Meanwhile, deliberative democrats argue that deliberation, properly understood, already has an orientation toward the common good built into it. This follows from their conception of deliberation, in which participants are required to justify themselves to one another whilst aiming to reach a rational consensus. Thus, although citizens may begin from different standpoints, with competing interests and preferences, once they start trying to convince their fellow citizens they have no choice but to reason 'from the point of view of others' (Benhabib, 1992, pp. 9–10). Indeed, at least according to some deliberative democrats, appealing to self-interest will often be incompatible with a proper commitment to deliberation:

> There are certain arguments that simply cannot be stated publicly. In a political debate it is pragmatically impossible to argue that a given solution should be chosen just because it is good for oneself. By the very act of engaging in a public debate – by arguing rather than bargaining – one has ruled out the possibility of invoking such reasons. (Elster, 1986, pp. 112–13)

Consequently, deliberative democrats believe that 'through public deliberation, citizens transform their preferences according to public-minded ends, and reason together about the nature of those ends and the best means to realize them' (Young, 1996, pp. 120–1).

Like theorists of participatory democracy, then, deliberative democrats believe that properly constructed democratic procedures can help to 'transform' citizens, encouraging them to set aside considerations of self-interest and instead to focus on the interests we share in common. One possible advantage of the deliberative conception, at least as described so far, is that it supplies a clearer explanation as to why citizens should adopt an orientation toward the common good. This is because whilst self-interested participation is still participation – albeit possibly of a bad kind – self-interested deliberation would not count as real deliberation at all. However, as discussed in Box 5.4, some recent formulations of deliberative democracy have questioned the assumption that deliberation either can or should exclude appeals to self-interest, instead suggesting that at least some self-interested claims might have a legitimate role to play in political deliberation.

By contrast, proponents of competitive democracy think it is conceptually muddled to require voters to be guided by a concern to promote the common good. In Schumpeter's case, this was because – much like the *modus vivendi* and agonistic pluralists we discussed in Chapter 3 – he believed that people have radically different wants, interests, values and needs. On his account, these result in profound disagreements that cannot be overcome through rational argument and persuasion, since disagreements about values are 'beyond the range of mere logic' (Schumpeter, 1956, p. 251). The lesson that Schumpeter draws from this is that:

> [There is] no such thing as a uniquely determined common good that all people could agree on or be made to agree on by the force of rational

BOX 5.4 DELIBERATION AND SELF-INTEREST

In strict formulations of deliberative democracy, deliberators are not permitted to appeal to their own interests and must instead adopt an impersonal or dispassionate point of view. Some philosophers propose relaxing this requirement. For example, Simone Chambers allows for self-interested deliberators, provided they introduce such concerns with a 'public spirited attitude' (Chambers, 2003, p. 318). Similarly, Jane Mansbridge and her co-authors say that deliberative democracy should accommodate 'suitably constrained forms of self-interest' (Mansbridge et al., 2010, p. 66). Deliberative democrats have given two reasons for incorporating self-interest. First, 'statements of self-interest' should be permitted so that deliberators can 'present information' to one another (Cohen and Rogers, 2003, p. 247). For example, a deliberator might (self-interestedly) explain to their fellow citizens that some proposed policy will disproportionately burden the members of their group (Pettit, 2006, p. 100). Second, and more controversially, appeals to self-interest may serve to help justify some policy or principle. For instance, we might think that individual self-interest is 'worthy of being counted' on the grounds that satisfying an individual's interests will be good for them (Mansbridge et al., 2010, p. 76). To illustrate this, Mansbridge and her co-authors discuss the following example:

> One member of a married couple has a job offer in Chicago and the other an offer in Boston. It would distort their communication and decision-making to 'force' them to discuss the issues solely in terms of what is good for 'us', e.g., for the 'marriage' or for the children. Only by recognizing their self-interests and the conflict between them can the couple negotiate a fair ... agreement. In the good that they forge through their deliberative negotiation, their self-interested claims are intrinsically justifiable, that is, self-justifying in the absence of negating considerations. (Mansbridge et al., 2010, p. 76)

What role, if any, should self-interest play in deliberative democracy?

argument. This is due not primarily to the fact that some people may want things other than the common good but to the much more fundamental fact that to different individuals and groups the common good is bound to mean different things. (Schumpeter, 1956, p. 251)

He then goes on to suggest that even if citizens did unanimously agree to particular principles, we should not expect this agreement to yield further consensus about concrete policy proposals. For instance, each citizen might accept that the state should secure adequate health for its citizens, but they might continue to disagree about what treatment options should be available, or about whether medical insurance should be mandatory, and so forth.

How far reaching is Schumpeter's critique? At the very least, his position is that it is unfeasible to expect democratic procedures to yield an agreement about the common good, because there is no way to combine people's different preferences, opinions and desires to form something 'that could in any convincing sense be called the will of the people' (1956, p. 254). In addition to this, Schumpeter advances the more controversial claim that there is no such thing as a common good, as people have radically different wants, needs and desires. Moreover, at least according to some scholars, Schumpeter also endorses an even stronger claim, which is that a democratic politics orientated around the common good might be dangerous, as it could have the effect of marginalising minority perspectives that do not easily fall in step with majority conceptions of the common good (Held, 2006, p. 148). This final claim has been taken up by others and directed against participatory theories of democracy. For example, Frank Cunningham suggests that 'there would be enormous pressure to conform to majority sentiment in a participatory-democratic community' because '[m]inority dissent is easily taken to be evidence of a lack of will or ability to seek consensus and hence of being a bad citizen' (2002, p. 134).

Given this scepticism about the common good, it is unsurprising that the logic of competitive democracy points towards a vision of political life based on 'the will of all' rather than the 'general will'. For competitive democrats, democratic citizens should act on the basis of self-interest and behave like consumers, voting for whichever candidate or party promises to satisfy most of their (individual) preferences. One problem with this type of view, however, is that it fits uneasily alongside many of our considered views about what we are doing when we engage in democratic politics, which involves arguing with others about what it is that *we* should do. For instance, according to the democratic pragmatist Robert Talisse, competitive democrats misrepresent many of the ordinary and mundane features of democratic practice. To support this, he points out that 'citizens generally take their political beliefs to stand in need of arguments and evidence, they often believe their opponents *mistaken* rather than simply *craven*, and they think that political *argument* is possible as something distinct from political *bargaining*' (Talisse, 2007, p. 110). Thus, a conception of democracy in which politics is conducted purely on the basis of self-interest, without reference to the idea of the common good, is descriptively inadequate, since it does not capture what most of us think we are doing during political discussion and debate.

Why is democracy valuable?

Explaining why democracy is morally desirable is crucial for any theory of democracy, because such an account is needed to inform decisions about how democratic procedures and institutions should be designed or reformed. In this key debate we will begin by examining two different ways in which democracy might be valuable, before going on to explore some of the different explanations of democracy's value that have been given by proponents of our three rival perspectives.

One way in which democracy could be valuable is *instrumentally*. Something has instrumental value if it is 'valued for the sake of something else' (Korsgaard, 1996, p. 250). For example, money and cleaning are instrumentally valuable, since although they have no value in themselves, having or doing them allows you to bring about some desirable state of affairs. Thus, to describe democracy as instrumentally valuable is to imply that it is a means to achieve some good end or consequence, such as better quality government or political stability. If we discovered that democracy did not lead to these outcomes, or if we realised that these outcomes were not themselves valuable, then they would no longer count as instrumental reasons for valuing democracy. Another way in which democracy might be valuable is *intrinsically*. For example, suppose we find that democracy has destabilising effects, perhaps because the people keep electing incompetent governments. We might nevertheless say that it was good that the people had the opportunity to choose their government. This might be because democracy has 'goodness in itself' (Korsgaard, 1996, p. 250). If we say that democracy is intrinsically valuable, then we imply that it is valuable regardless of its consequences.

An important argument for the conclusion that democracy is intrinsically valuable, which can be endorsed by all three rival perspectives, is that it is the only system of political rule that treats people as equals (Waldron, 1999). Importantly, however, each of our rival perspectives interprets political equality differently. Whilst competitive democrats think that it is satisfied provided that votes are distributed equally, participatory democrats tend to argue that certain material preconditions must be satisfied if people are to participate on equal terms. For example, unless people are sufficiently educated and have enough leisure time, they are unlikely to be able to defend their interests against those who occupy more fortunate social positions. Similarly, as we have seen, deliberative democrats argue that proper deliberation presupposes formal and substantive kinds of equality, meaning that, for example, citizens should both be able to shape the political agenda and to exercise meaningful influence over the outcome of deliberations. One implication of these different interpretations, as we shall see below, is that proponents of one conception of democracy can use their understanding of political equality to criticise other conceptions as being not truly democratic.

Let us now turn to competitive theories of democracy. Schumpeter denied that democracy could possess any intrinsic value because he thought it was merely a political 'method' – 'like a steam engine or a disinfectant' (Schumpeter, 1956, p. 266) – and 'incapable of being an end in itself' (1956, p. 242). He was also unsympathetic to the claim that democracy is instrumentally valuable. Although he noted that democrats themselves are often 'convinced that democracy will guarantee … ideals and interests such as freedom of conscience and speech, justice, decent government and so on', he pointed out that the 'democratic method' could also be used to support various immoral practices, such as 'the persecution of Christians, the burning of witches, and the slaughtering of Jews'

(1956, p. 242). Thus, as one commentator summarises it, Schumpeter's own view was that '[d]emocracy is just a method, neither valuable in itself nor tending to right action or good ends' (Mackie, 2009, p. 129).

Many of Schumpeter's critics concur that *his* conception of democracy cannot be valuable. For example, Amy Gutmann and Robert Dahl have both pointed out that Schumpeter did not require a democracy to grant everyone the vote or to count each vote equally. Because he was not committed to political equality, then (incredibly) 'by Schumpeter's understanding, South Africa in 1992 (with an exclusively white electorate) [was] democratic and Stalinist Russia would [have been democratic] if only members of the Communist Party could vote' (Gutmann, 2007, p. 522; see also Dahl, 1989, pp. 121–2).

Notwithstanding this, recent defenders of competitive democracy, who generally are committed to political equality, have suggested that political competition is instrumentally valuable because it supports important goods. For instance, Shapiro describes it as 'truth's ally' (Shapiro, 2003b, p. 200) because political competition provides a mechanism to hold politicians to account, allowing opposition parties to publicly identify when governments 'fail to live up to their promises and misrepresent reality' (Shapiro, 2003b, p. 200). Similarly, Posner suggests that political competition encourages governments to be responsive to the interests of the electorate and to avoid unpopular policies, since they face the threat of electoral 'punishment' (Posner, 2003, p. 182). Additionally, political competition could also perform an important role in preserving stability, ensuring peaceful transitions from one government to the next, if citizens generally perceive the institutions of competitive democracy to be legitimate.

Another grounds for believing that competitive democracy is instrumentally valuable is that it fosters important moral or civic virtues (see Chapter 2), a possibility that has been suggested by George Kateb. His account begins from the observation that competitive electoral systems tend to have the effect of 'chastening', 'demystifying' and 'desacralizing' political authority by continuously reasserting its 'artificial' nature:

> When political authority is, at every moment, a temporary and conditional grant, regularly revocable ... a major moral distinctiveness enters the life of society. Society is taught – society teaches itself – a fundamental lesson about the nature of all authority ... The overall lesson can be expressed in a number of ways. Most commonly, we speak of a pervasive skepticism toward authority; a reluctance to defer; a conviction that those who wield authority must themselves be skeptical toward their roles and themselves and that necessary authority must be wielded in a way that inflicts minimum damage on the moral equality of all people. Furthermore, there is a tendency to try to do without authority wherever possible or to disperse or disguise it, and thus to soften it. (Kateb, 1981, p. 358)

According to Kateb, 'chastened' political authority, of the kind that one might expect to find in a competitive democracy, nourishes particular political dispositions, and these 'spill over' into our non-political (or everyday) lives. For example, he suggests that electoral democracy supports 'independence of spirit' by encouraging 'individuals to be less fearful of all authority' (1981, p. 360). Similarly, he thinks that political competition encourages tolerance or even affection for diversity, discouraging the belief that there is a single best way to lead one's life, or a single best answer to a difficult problem. Thus, if Kateb is right, then competitive democracy might be valuable because of the positive effects it has on the moral qualities of society and its members.

As we have seen, participatory and deliberative democrats have reached similar sounding conclusions, since they also believe that meaningful involvement in politics could have an educative or developmental aspect. For example, political participation might be intellectually edifying, because it requires us to solve collective problems by thinking through different issues, gathering and analysing information, listening and responding to arguments, presenting our views clearly, and so forth. Moreover, political participation or deliberation that is orientated around the search for a common good might improve our moral characters, since it requires us to address the needs of others, to treat them respectfully, to think about what is good for them, and to modify our own claims in light of their interests.

However, competitive, participatory and deliberative democracies might conceivably yield different kinds of moral virtues. For example, Kateb suggests that forms of political engagement which are orientated around a search for the common good could lead to 'modesty, denial of gratification, obedience to legally constituted authority..., self-control ... and a decent propriety' (Kateb, 1981, p. 387). These virtues, clearly, are different to the independence of spirit and tolerance that he thinks would be engendered by self-interested forms of engagement in a competitive democracy. Moreover, the virtues encouraged by one form of democratic practice might be 'gravely weakened' by another form of democracy (Kateb, 1981, p. 367). This suggests that one way to arbitrate between the rival perspectives is to reflect on which does the best job of stimulating genuine human excellences.

Some participatory democrats have also argued that participatory democracy is intrinsically valuable, suggesting at least three different arguments to this effect. First, as discussed in Box 5.5, participatory democracy could be intrinsically valuable because the *activity* of political participation is itself intrinsically valuable. Second, as discussed earlier, participatory democracy could be intrinsically valuable because it is the only form of decision making that treats people as equals. Third, as we shall discuss now, participatory democracy could be intrinsically valuable because it is the only form of political organisation that respects human freedom.

BOX 5.5 PARTICIPATION AND THE GOOD LIFE

Some civic republicans believe that political participation represents 'the highest form of human living-together that most individuals can aspire to' (Oldfield, 1990, p. 6). This view depends on a distinctive conception of the human excellences, in which political participation itself is understood to be part of each person's individual good. If political participation is something that everyone should find rewarding and valuable, then a life without it is stunted, inadequate or incomplete. However, Mark Warren characterises the idea that 'democratic participation is an attractive activity, one that people would naturally choose if only they had the opportunity' as a 'romantic dogma' (Warren, 1996, p. 243). Similarly, Philip Pettit, a contemporary republican, describes this demanding vision of citizenship as 'romantic' and 'other-worldly' (Pettit, 2012, p. 227). Certainly, in contemporary liberal democracies, many citizens seem to lack the disposition to learn about and participate in politics, in many cases because they find other things in life more rewarding (such as their families, careers and hobbies). Consequently, Will Kymlicka and Wayne Norman conclude that the participatory ideal is 'markedly at odds with the way most people in the modern world understand both citizenship and the good life' (1994, p. 362).

Must participatory democrats be committed to the idea that participation is part of the good life? How plausible is this idea?

The connections between political participation and freedom were first suggested by Rousseau, who argued that a people can only be truly free if they live together under laws they have given to themselves. The attraction of this view is that it brings out the difference between a people collectively participating in self-government and a people having their affairs arranged for them, for instance by an elite or by an occupying power. For many people, only the first kind of society respects freedom. However, Rousseau's own argument has attracted controversy, especially because it relies on his ambiguous notion of a 'general will'. One recent attempt to rehabilitate Rousseau's position has been suggested by Carol Gould (1988), who favours a rich form of participatory democracy on the grounds that it supports a conception of freedom as self-development. On her account, freedom refers to 'the freedom to develop oneself through one's actions' (Gould, 1988, p. 40). Because we each have an equal right to the 'conditions of self-development' (1988, p. 60), then 'every person who engages in a common activity with others has an equal right to participate in making decisions concerning such activity' (1988, p. 84). To put her point another way, unless people can shape the institutions that in turn shape their self-development, they cannot truly be free. The implication is that outside of a participatory society human beings are not (and cannot be) free to develop themselves. Like Rousseau, Gould endorses a controversial 'positive' conception of freedom, which we shall examine more fully in Chapter 7.

Finally, deliberative democrats have developed two distinctive arguments to explain why deliberation is morally desirable. According to the first of these, deliberation is instrumentally valuable as it results in better quality decisions. For example, according to Gutmann and Thompson:

> A well-constituted deliberative forum provides an opportunity for advancing both individual and collective understanding. Through the give-and-take of argument, participants can learn from each other, come to recognize their individual and collective misapprehensions, and develop new views and policies that can more successfully withstand critical scrutiny. When citizens ... deliberate, they can expand their knowledge, including both their self-understanding and their collective understanding of what will best serve their fellow citizens. (Gutmann and Thompson, 2004, p. 12)

According to this argument, deliberation – at least when conducted appropriately – transforms and enhances our understanding of political issues, resulting in better quality decisions. As discussed in Box 5.6, empirical evidence derived

BOX 5.6 THE BENEFITS OF DELIBERATION

Deliberative democrats believe that deliberation has transformative and beneficial effects. For example, John Dryzek suggests that studies of citizens' juries and assemblies reveal that 'given the opportunity, ordinary citizens can make good deliberators' and that 'in many cases individuals come in with little or no interest or capability in politics, yet leave as energized and competent actors' (Dryzek, 2010, p. 158). Moreover, he thinks that these benefits obtain even when citizens are asked to deliberate about difficult and contested political issues (Dryzek, 2010, p. 158). One source of evidence for this conclusion has been provided by James Fishkin, who has conducted a number of 'deliberative polls', which he describes as follows:

> Take a national random sample of the electorate and transport those people from all over the country to a single place. Immerse the sample in the issues, with carefully balanced briefing materials, with intensive discussions in small groups, and with the chance to question competing experts and politicians. At the end of several days of working through the issues face to face, poll the participants in detail. (Fishkin, 1995, p. 162)

By comparing polls from before and after deliberation, Fishkin has found that 'it is routine to find large and statistically significant changes of opinion' (2009, p. 26). In particular, he has found that after the process of deliberation, the judgements of citizens tend to be more informed and considered (Fishkin, 2009, p. 35).

Suppose that deliberators routinely alter their judgements after deliberation – should democrats accord their later judgements greater weight or credibility?

from small-scale deliberative experiments seems to support this conclusion. However, some political theorists believe that deliberation is likely to result in worse decisions. Rousseau, for example, thought that it would open the door to factionalism and manipulation, and instead proposed that citizens should reason about politics in isolation from one another. More recently, Cass Sunstein has suggested that the effects of deliberation are often negative, since rather than encouraging people towards consensus on the common good, deliberation tends to entrench and widen disagreements, because people are more likely to deliberate amongst those with whom they already agree (Sunstein, 2002).

The second distinctively deliberative argument in favour of democracy says that deliberative democracy is intrinsically valuable because it manifests a correct understanding of the ideal of political justification. Deliberative democrats hold that the 'justification of the exercise of collective political power is to proceed on the basis of a free public reasoning among equals' (Cohen, 1996, p. 99). This means that not all putatively democratic decisions are binding on those who are subject to them – just as laws enforced by dictators lack democratic legitimacy, so too do ostensibly democratic laws that have been arrived at by non-deliberative procedures. For deliberative democrats, only some kinds of (deliberative) democratic procedure are adequate to justify legitimate and binding decisions.

In summary, there are a number of different instrumental grounds to favour democracy. For instance, democracy might encourage transparency, responsiveness and stability, or it might nourish morally desirable character traits or improve the quality of decision making. If one (or more) of these grounds really is adequate to justify democracy, then proponents must demonstrate that democracies consistently and reliably promote these consequences. A different way to argue for the value of democracy is to say that it is intrinsically valuable, for instance by appealing to equality, freedom or political legitimacy. Although I have suggested that some of these instrumental and intrinsic reasons 'fit' more closely with one or another of the rival perspectives, in principle proponents of all three theories could lay claim to them. Crucially, whatever understanding of the value of democracy one settles on will have prescriptive implications, suggesting ways in which our democratic institutions need reform.

Is deliberative democracy possible?

This final key debate explores two serious challenges to the prospects of implementing deliberative democracy: that deliberation may be impossible in large and complex societies, and that the ideal of deliberation may be unrealistically narrow and restrictive. The first challenge has been described as the 'scale' problem (Dryzek, 2010, p. 24), which Michael Walzer captures by suggesting that 'deliberation is not an activity for the demos ... [since] 300 million of them, or even one million or a hundred thousand, can't plausibly reason together' (2004, p. 109). We will begin by exploring three different strategies for addressing this problem. The first strategy is to relax one or another of the conditions for political legitimacy. Recall, deliberative democrats have a demanding theory of political legitimacy, according to which only laws that meet with the reasoned assent of all citizens in a deliberative setting are legitimate (Habermas, 1996, p. 110). Since it would be difficult for a whole society to realise this demanding standard, some deliberative democrats propose lowering the bar. One possibility for doing so is to replace the requirement that laws command everyone's actual agreement with a test of hypothetical consent. This has been suggested by Cohen, who believes that 'outcomes are legitimate if and only if they *could* be the object of a free and reasoned agreement among equals' (1989, p. 22, *emphasis added*). Thus, a law that people could assent to, even if they in fact did not, might still be legitimate, provided that the deliberative procedures were appropriately designed and that participants proceeded by aiming 'to find reasons that are persuasive to all' (Cohen, 1989, p. 23). However, although this solution solves the feasibility problem, it struggles to explain why people who disagreed with a decision should regard it as binding upon them.

Another possibility is to relax the requirement that *all* political decisions be reached through a discursive process, and to retain the demanding standards of deliberative democracy only for matters of basic justice, such as when society is deciding on its constitutional essentials (Rawls, 1996). According to some scholars, society-wide deliberation can and does occur at critical historical moments. For example, writing about the US, Bruce Ackerman (1991) suggests that the debates surrounding the constitutional founding, the reconstruction amendments and the New Deal all qualify as deliberative. However, other scholars have also observed that 'high politics' is often anything but deliberative. For example, Dryzek argues that the Australian debates about whether to replace the British monarch with a republic were deliberative failures (Dryzek, 2010, p. 25). Moreover, even if 'high politics' can be adequately deliberative, restricting deliberation to these occasions would arguably empty deliberative democracy of much of its radical promise.

A further possibility is to relax the condition that all citizens must participate in deliberation, either by making participation voluntary or by establishing 'mini-publics'. The first of these alternatives has been suggested by Bernard Manin, who argues that deliberative outcomes are legitimate provided that 'the right of all to participate in deliberation' is satisfied (Manin, 1987, p. 352). On this view, the outcomes of a deliberative procedure can justifiably be imposed on those who did not participate, provided that they had the opportunity to do so. Although this conceivably addresses the scale problem, it comes at the cost of accepting (and even requiring!) a large dose of political apathy. The second alternative, discussed in Box 5.7, is to limit participation to a small representative sample of the population, for example one that has been selected by lot. In support of this, Fishkin has argued

BOX 5.7   MINI-PUBLICS AND THE SCALE PROBLEM

Suppose an advanced democratic country were to create a 'minipopulus' consisting of perhaps a thousand citizens randomly selected out of the entire demos. Its task would be to deliberate, for a year perhaps, on an issue and then to announce its choices. The members of the minipopulus could 'meet' by telecommunications. One minipopulus could decide on the agenda of issues, while another might concern itself with a major issue. Thus, one minipopulus could exist for each major issue on the agenda. A minipopulus could exist at any level of government national, state, or local. It could be attended – again by telecommunications – by an advisory committee of scholars and specialists and by an administrative staff. It could hold hearings, commission research, and engage in debate and discussion. (Dahl, 1989, p. 340)

Dahl envisaged the minipopulus serving as a complement to ordinary democratic procedures, providing an additional input. Now generally referred to as a mini-public, versions of this innovation have been attempted in various parts of the world (see Smith, 2009 for a survey). For example, the British Columbia Citizens Assembly met over the course of 2004. There, a random sample of voters discussed their electoral system and put forward their recommendations for reform to a popular (and binding) referendum. Similar experiments were attempted in Iceland (in 2009–10) and Ireland (in 2013–14), although both of these involved the participation of elected politicians.

Can 'mini-publics' solve deliberative democracy's scale problem?

that the results of properly designed 'deliberative polls' offer 'a representation of the considered judgements of the public – the views the entire public would come to if it had the same experience of behaving more like ideal citizens immersed in the issues for an extended period' (1995, p. 162). Thus, he suggests that deliberative polls have a 'recommending force'. However, as Fishkin notes, it is not clear whether such polls could (or should) be binding on the rest of society.

A different strategy for overcoming the 'scale' problem is to adopt a 'systemic' perspective, focussing on the outcomes of the system as a whole rather than the procedures adopted within particular deliberative institutions (Habermas, 1996; Parkinson, 2006; Goodin, 2008; Parkinson and Mansbridge, 2009). Proponents of this approach emphasise that deliberation can and does occur at multiple sites within the political system, such as, for example, legislatures, town halls, bureaucracies, political parties, trade unions, interest groups, new and traditional forms of media, universities, petitions, protests, elections, citizens' juries and public hearings. These different sites encourage different forms of deliberation, are accessible to different kinds of deliberators, and should be held to different standards of legitimacy. What matters is that they are interdependent, in the sense that what happens in one site influences what happens elsewhere.

The systemic approach seems promising, since it begins by identifying existing and potential deliberative sites and moves outwards to ask whether – as a whole – the political system encourages 'a talk-based approach to political conflict and problem-solving' (Mansbridge et al., 2010, pp. 4–5). Although many of the individual sites within a deliberative system are unlikely to satisfy the strict procedural requirements of deliberative democracy, taken as a whole they might nevertheless contribute to achieving deliberative outcomes. This would be the case if we were able to conclude that the decisions reached are the product of informed judgement and reflection, and that they are acceptable to citizens who each had an opportunity to make their voice heard by participating in one or another deliberative site. If we conclude that our current systems fail to meet this standard, for instance because some citizens had restricted access to deliberative fora, or because the decisions made are not the product of informed judgement, then this can be addressed by adjusting our institutional arrangements.

A final strategy for addressing the 'scale' problem has been suggested by Robert Goodin, who has proposed a theory of 'democratic deliberation from within' (Goodin, 2003, pp. 169–93). Goodin argues that instead of trying to facilitate society-wide democratic conversations, deliberative democrats should focus on the quality of the deliberation that occurs within individual minds. He points out that good deliberators internalise the perspective of others, empathising with them and engaging in an imaginary dialogue. The importance of empathy has also been stressed by other democratic theorists, since unless citizens actively listen to one another, and take into account their different interests, beliefs and feelings, then democracy will be unable to 'fulfil its promise to give equal consideration to all citizens' (Morrell, 2010, p. 12). Distinctively, Goodin thinks that some of the merits of deliberative democracy can be realised even when others are not 'conversationally present', provided that they are 'imaginatively present'. One potential implication of this is that actual deliberation could play a more modest role in political life, if it was complemented by 'deliberation from within'. If this strategy is to work, then it will be crucial that citizens are actually able to imaginatively construct the lives of others, free from prejudice and distortion. Interestingly, this means that deliberative democrats would need to pay greater attention to the production and distribution of things such as 'the literary, visual, and performing arts' (Goodin, 2003, p. 171).

The second serious challenge to the feasibility of deliberative democracy is that the ideal of deliberation itself might be too narrow and restrictive. As we have seen, in its earliest formulations, deliberative democracy was an idealistic and demanding theory, and deliberation itself was presented as a highly stylised form of communication, distinct from familiar forms of political speech. Good deliberators were required to satisfy a demanding list of conditions, such as speaking truthfully and sincerely, justifying their preferences with reasons and arguments, treating their fellow citizens respectfully, listening to one another's views in an open-minded way, and yielding to the force of the better argument. Proponents were aware that such manifestations 'have an improbable character and are like islands in the ocean of everyday praxis' (Habermas, 1996, p. 323). Nevertheless, their point was that a demanding ideal of deliberation was required for us to envisage the form a truly democratic politics might take.

Many political theorists who are otherwise sympathetic to the deliberative project believe that this idealistic conception of deliberation is excessively narrow. For example, it seems to neglect the healthy contribution to political discourse that non-deliberative forms of political communication often make, such as protests and demonstrations (Warren, 2007, p. 278). Similarly, it seems to ignore the role and significance of passions and emotions in democratic life (Walzer, 2004; Hall, 2007; Krause, 2008). Accounting for these would arguably require a much wider conception of what qualifies as deliberation. For example, if citizens are to empathetically engage with the lived experiences and political preferences of one another, then narratives and storytelling might sometimes be more important than reasons and arguments. To illustrate this, Michael Morrell has suggested that since 'white people tend to have few experiences analogous to living as a black person in a racist society', they are more likely to empathise with the experiences of black people if they listen to their stories than if they are exposed to abstract arguments (Morrell, 2010, p. 142).

Another objection to the ideal of deliberation has been suggested by difference theorists (see Chapter 2), who have criticised the 'identification of reasonable open public debate with polite, orderly, dispassionate, gentlemanly argument' (Young, 2000, p. 49). On their account, a restrictive model of deliberation could turn out to disadvantage socially marginalised groups. For instance, according to Lynn Sanders:

> [T]aking deliberation as a signal of democratic practice paradoxically works undemocratically, discrediting on seemingly democratic grounds the views of those who are less likely to present their arguments in ways that we recognize as characteristically deliberative. In our political culture, these citizens are likely to be those who are already underrepresented in formal political institutions and who are systematically materially disadvantaged, namely women; racial minorities, especially Blacks; and poorer people. (Sanders, 1999, p. 348)

Relatedly, others have worried that the requirement that deliberation be both public and reasonable might have the effect of stifling unpopular or radical views, the articulation of which might otherwise benefit political discourse (Kuran, 1998, p. 536).

In response to objections such as these, some deliberative democrats have begun to develop 'realistic' models of deliberation. Characteristically, these views entail relaxing one or more of the demanding criteria associated with proper deliberation and permitting forms of communication that would otherwise be forbidden. For instance, Dryzek suggests that deliberation should be broadened to allow not only rational argument, but also 'rhetoric, humour, emotion, testimony or storytelling, and gossip' (Dryzek, 2000, p. 48). Similarly, Bohman thinks that when other deliberators are 'deceived by their own ideologies and self-deceptions', it may be acceptable to use 'irony, jokes, metaphors and other jarring ways of expressing something' to 'achieve understanding' (Bohman, 1996, p. 205). Likewise, Young (2000) praises the use of narratives and testimony to enable disadvantaged individuals and groups to convey their distinctive experiences and perspectives, since as we saw in Box 4.7, marginalised groups often face special difficulties in conveying their perspectives.

Each of these proposals entails a departure from the original ideal of deliberation. Although the use of rhetoric, irony, jokes, narratives, testimony and even gossip might enhance our understanding of some situation, they might also jeopardise the requirements that deliberators yield to the force of the better argument, speak sincerely, and justify their preferences by appealing to reasons and arguments. Consequently, although these modifications may make deliberation more feasible, they might also have a 'diluting' effect, rendering deliberation indistinguishable from other forms of communication. Perhaps more importantly, they could also undermine one of the fundamental aims of deliberation, which is to reach a *rational* consensus.

Future challenges

Schumpeter's critique of 'classical' theories of democracy has recently been revived by a group of political theorists styling themselves as 'radical democrats'. These authors object to the connections that deliberative democrats have drawn between consensus, reason and the common good, and they claim that deliberative democracy both neglects the conflictual aspects of politics and underestimates the scope and depth of disagreement. We will conclude by examining this critique and exploring one response to it.

Radical democrats argue that deliberative democrats have an otherworldly tendency to 'spirit away the moment of antagonism as if it were marginal to the experience of the public sphere' (Martin, 2009, p. 97). This is mistaken, they argue, because conflict is a permanent and central feature of politics. According to them, deliberation orientated towards consensus is an evasion of the democratic ideal, since it marginalises oppositional and radical perspectives and reduces the scope for genuine political engagement (Rancière, 1999, 2009). This critique overlaps with the agonistic challenge to political liberalism, which we examined in Chapter 3, and in both cases the quest for a rational consensus is associated with a deadening conformity. The radical critique is not that deliberation in practice will most likely fail to yield a consensus. Rather, it is that consensus can only be reached at the cost of stifling genuine disagreements, which is too high a price to pay.

Some deliberative democrats have seemingly accepted the spirit of this critique, and have begun to explore the possibility of reconciling deliberative democracy with radical pluralism. One promising line of argument has been suggested by John Dryzek and Simon Niemeyer, who argue that 'the purpose of deliberation is *not* to secure consensus' but is rather 'to produce meta-consensus that structures continued dispute' (Dryzek, 2010, p. 15). Meta-consensus refers to an agreement about which values, judgements and discourses do (and do not) have a bearing on some problem or issue. We can therefore reach a meta-consensus without forming an actual consensus about what to do. Although meta-consensus is still a form of consensus, and may still be exclusionary in the sense that radical democrats oppose, it does not eliminate the possibility of continued disagreement.

We can get a sense of this proposal by looking at an example of what Dryzek and Niemeyer call 'normative meta-consensus' (adapted from Niemeyer, 2004). Imagine that a community is deciding whether or not to build a road, a proposal opposed by some citizens who believe it will be ugly and environmentally destructive, but supported by others who think it will bring economic benefits. Dryzek and Niemeyer accept that deliberation is unlikely to yield uniform agreement about what to do. However, they suggest that deliberation could have the more modest goal of reaching agreement about what values are relevant to settling the issue, and this is what they call normative meta-consensus. For example, after deliberation the participants might agree that economic and environmental values legitimately have a bearing on the issue, and that aesthetic ones do not. Thus, they would have reached a meta-consensus despite not agreeing about how economic and environmental values should be ranked – in other words, without agreeing about what they should actually do.

In addition to normative meta-consensus, Dryzek and Niemeyer also suggest that deliberation should aim towards epistemic and preference meta-consensus. Epistemic meta-consensus refers to an agreement about what kinds of knowledge claims should (and should not) inform some particular policy domain. So, for example, deliberation might yield an agreement that both epidemiological studies and personal testimony supply evidence that is relevant to deciding whether a nuclear power station should be built, but that evidence based on religious revelation does not. Meanwhile, preference meta-consensus refers to an agreement about what policy alternatives are acceptable and about how those alternatives are to be compared. Deliberators reach preference meta-consensus when they agree about how policy alternatives should be ordered (for example, on a left-to-right scale) even when they disagree about which alternatives are preferable.

As discussed in Box 5.8, one attraction of Dryzek and Niemeyer's approach is that it potentially reveals how people who disagree deeply can make progress by deliberating with one another, without requiring them to reach a substantive

BOX 5.8   META-CONSENSUS AND THE GOOD
         FRIDAY AGREEMENT

Dryzek and Niemeyer believe that theirs is an eminently realistic theory, and they cite the Good Friday Agreement of 1998 (discussed in Chapter 3) to illustrate how meta-consensus already happens in practice:

> In the wake of that agreement, Protestant Unionists and Catholic Republicans still find their own identities in the rejection of the other side, and still oppose the core project of the other side (be it a republic encompassing all thirty-two counties of Ireland, or continued union with Britain). But each side's leadership has come to recognize the legitimacy of the discourse underlying the aspirations of the other side, even as both leaderships remain strenuously opposed to those aspirations. (Dryzek, 2010, p. 110)

Of course, because meta-consensus is not substantive agreement, it leaves open the question of how outcomes are to be settled on. Consequently, even after reaching a meta-consensus some additional decision procedure may need to be employed, such as bargaining or a majority vote.

Are decisions that are 'structured' by free and reasoned meta-consensus legitimate? Does this approach adequately accommodate deep disagreement and value pluralism?

agreement about what course of action to take and without unfairly constraining the range of views expressed by deliberators. Meanwhile, what should radical democrats say about Dryzek and Niemeyer's proposal? On the one hand, they might be sceptical about it, since meta-consensus is still exclusionary, in the sense that deliberation may result in the exclusion of certain values, knowledge claims and policies. However, this kind of exclusion is of a different order to the one that radical democrats object to. Radical democrats believe that deliberation which aims at consensus will be stifling since citizens will have to communicate in a contrived and limited fashion. Meanwhile, Dryzek and Niemeyer favour 'open-ended' deliberation, in which exclusion is not constitutive to deliberation itself but occurs after deliberation. On the other hand, radical democrats might also have reasons to be sympathetically disposed towards Dryzek and Niemeyer's approach, because it might strengthen the disposition of citizens to treat one another with civility and respect. Recall, as we saw in Chapter 3, a key concern of agonistic pluralists is to find ways in which antagonism can be converted into agonistic respect. According to Dryzek and Niemeyer, deliberation orientated around the pursuit of normative meta-consensus might achieve this by making it more likely that citizens 'will engage in a creative search for outcomes that respect the basic values of all parties, however different these values remain' (Dryzek, 2010, p. 103).

6

Power

Introduction

According to Terence Ball, 'power is arguably the single most important organising concept in social and political theory' (Ball, 1992, p. 14). Like the other
concepts we have examined in this book, although we are often able to employ
the word in a serviceable enough fashion, things become more difficult when
we try to pin down exactly what 'power' is. Indeed, as one leading theorist of
power has observed, although scholars are able to discuss how 'to gain, resist,
seize, harness, secure, tame, share, spread, distribute, equalize or maximize'
power, they cannot agree 'about how to define it, how to conceive it, how to
study it, and if it can be measured, how to measure it' (Lukes, 2005, p. 61). In
this chapter we try to sort through some of these disagreements about power by
comparing four different views about what it is, and by exploring their complex
relationships with democracy and freedom. Before doing so, however, it will
be helpful to establish some general features of power and to explore a closely
related concept – domination.

According to Bertrand Russell, power is 'the production of intended effects'
(1938, p. 25). This captures perhaps the most basic sense in which we use the
term 'power'. For instance, a bully might have the power to insist that another
schoolchild hands over their lunch money, a committee chair might have the
power to decide when a vote should be taken in order to bring a discussion
to a close, or an army might have the power to overthrow a government. In
these cases, power is power-to, which Keith Dowding defines as 'the ability

of an actor to bring about or help bring about outcomes' (1991, p. 48). When power is understood in this way, it is an ability or a capacity, or what Peter Morriss calls a 'dispositional concept' (2002). Power is also sometimes used in what seems to be a different sense. For instance, suppose that the schoolchildren, the committee or the government are consistently terrorised by the bully, the chair or the army. If this were the case, then we might say that the latter has power-over the former. Power-over, in contrast to power-to, refers to an individual or group holding another individual or group in their power. Some political theorists, such as Morriss (2002), think that power-over is ultimately a form of power-to. For instance, instead of saying that the bully has power-over the others because they are terrified of him, we might say that the bully has the power-to terrify the others into submission. Meanwhile, other political theorists maintain that there is a genuine distinction and that power-over is the more interesting concept, because of its relationship with domination. For example, Steven Lukes thinks that if political theorists were to focus their attentions solely on power-to, this would remove 'the central interest of studying power relations in the first place' (Lukes, 2005, p. 34, although also see pp. 65–9; Morriss, 2006).

Like power, domination is an amorphous concept. One influential definition of it was introduced by the German sociologist Max Weber, who described it as 'the probability that a command with a specific content will be obeyed by a given group of persons' (1978, p. 53). To be sure, Weber's term for domination (*Herrschaft*) does not translate easily into English – it also has connotations of rule or leadership and is sometimes rendered as 'authority'. Nevertheless, his description helpfully captures two important ideas: that domination is a matter of degree, and that it is a property of particular social relationships in which one person or group has the ability to direct others. Another distinguishing feature of domination is that it persists over time. Thus, in contrast to power-to, which can be exercised on a one-off basis, domination is usually reserved for relationships in which one party has power over another for a protracted period. This is captured by sociologist Jonathan Hearn's definition:

> *Domination* refers to a situation where an agent exercises relatively stable, ongoing control over the actions of other agents ('agents' taken broadly to mean anything from individual persons, to social groups, to organisations and institutions). Domination is not episodic. Relations of domination are, by definition, firmly established, and often naturalised and taken for granted. (Hearn, 2011, p. 203)

As we shall see later, some political theorists think that enduring relations of domination can be secured both overtly, as when subordinates are terrified into submission, and covertly, as when subordination is achieved through apparently innocuous mechanisms.

So, then, power-to describes the ability to achieve outcomes, whilst power-over describes an enduring asymmetrical social relation, and domination is a particular kind of power-over. Recall, however, that domination might also be describable as a form of power-to, for instance if we say that an individual or group has the power-to dominate another individual or group. Whilst power-to is sometimes described in neutral or positive terms, domination is nearly always understood as unwelcome, repressive and objectionable ('nearly always' because, as we shall see later, authors like Michel Foucault are ambivalent about this). A common explanation of domination's harm is that it frustrates or inhibits the ability of subordinates to determine their own fate – to decide what to do and the terms on which to act. For example, according to Cécile Laborde:

> When we are dominated we are either deprived of the ability to form our own perspective (we are indoctrinated, manipulated, socialised into submissive roles) or, if we possess the capacity, we are prevented from using it (we are silenced, humiliated, threatened). (Laborde, 2008, pp. 153–4)

Exactly how domination undermines individual self-determination is a contested issue, to which we shall return during the key debates, and again in Chapter 7.

In this chapter, we will focus on four different perspectives, which are summarised in Table 6.1. Whilst the first two treat power primarily as power-to, the other pair treat it mainly as power-over. The first perspective – power as decision making – says that power is the ability to get others to do something that they would not otherwise do. For example, politicians exercise power in this sense when they overcome their opponents and get their own way over a contested issue. An attraction of this conception is the simplicity with which it can be deployed by political scientists. For instance, they can identify venues where decisions are made – such as town halls, legislatures and international organisations – and try to figure out which individuals or groups are powerful by asking whose policy was adopted or who succeeded in blocking the preferred policies of others. Meanwhile, critics of this view believe that focussing on official decision making fora is unduly limiting, since it leads us to neglect the ways in which power can be exercised in informal or unofficial venues. For example, imagine a society in which liberals and feminists want to alter abortion laws, and conservatives want to preserve the status quo. If the conservatives use backroom dealing to prevent the issue from being discussed in the national legislature, then it seems to make sense to say that they have exercised power, even though they did not get their own way in an actual decision. To explain this, proponents of the second rival perspective – power as agenda setting – say that power can also take the form of nondecision making. As we shall see, although power as nondecision making can be exercised in different ways, it always involves individuals and groups managing to suppress political issues that challenge their own interests or values.

Taken together, these perspectives suggest that power can be exercised at both the decision making and agenda setting stages, when the preferences of one individual or group are satisfied against the wishes of another individual or group. Proponents of the third perspective – power as preference manipulation – suggest that there is another and more insidious way in which power might be exercised, namely by influencing, shaping and determining people's beliefs and desires. For example, radical social critics often point out that subordinate individuals and groups seem to internalise norms about how they should behave, about what they can reasonably expect, about how society should be arranged, or about what their role or social status is. If those norms, expectations and beliefs are at odds with their 'real' interests, then we might conclude that power has been exercised by causing people to accept a false or distorted impression of who they are and how they should behave. As we shall see later, however, a difficulty with this view is that it assumes that people have real interests of which they have no knowledge, and which they do not endorse.

The final rival perspective is even more radical, since it says that people's interests – as well as their preferences – are a product of power. An important difference between the constitutive view of power and the preference manipulation view is that the constitutive view says that people do not have 'real' interests. Rather, it says that interests, preferences and identities are an effect of power. Interestingly, this view denies that power is necessarily repressive, and instead says that it produces meanings and social orders. Amongst other things, this means that our self-understandings are the product of distinctive formations of power/knowledge. Power, then, is not something that is exercised by getting others to do what you want them to do, or manipulating their preferences so that they voluntarily do what you want them to do. Instead, it is a ubiquitous feature of social life that operates by normalising or producing a complex set of dispositions, desires and behaviours.

In the second half of the chapter we will explore these perspectives in greater depth by analysing three key debates. The first compares the decision making and agenda setting approaches by contrasting their respective analyses of domination. Although both views treat domination as a failure of democracy, they offer competing solutions, in one case favouring a form of competitive democracy, in the other favouring a form of participatory democracy (see Chapter 5). Importantly, both of these perspectives agree that dominated people are generally aware of the fact of their domination, and they take it for granted that dominated people would prefer it if their grievances were addressed. Meanwhile, the other two perspectives both allow for the possibility that domination could be covert, in the sense that subordinate people could be unaware of their predicament. We will address these two theories directly during the second key debate, asking whether covert domination really is possible. As we have already seen, whilst the preference manipulation view treats covert domination as repressive,

Table 6.1 Summary of rival perspectives on power

	Decision making	Agenda setting	Preference manipulation	Constitutive
Type	Power-to	Power-to	Power-over	Power-over
Basic manifestation	Getting another to do something they would not otherwise do	Thwarting a challenge to one's values or interests	Influencing, shaping or determining the wants and desires of another	Producing meanings, social orders and subjectivities by moulding identities and regimes of truth
Primary site	Official decision making fora	Informal venues, such as the 'corridors of power'	Beliefs, norms, values, ideologies, social expectations	Power is dispersed and decentred – it 'comes from everywhere'
Visibility	Power can be observed by analysing formal decision making procedures	Power can be observed by analysing informal agenda setting mechanisms and by getting 'insider information'	Power is often insidious and difficult to observe; it can be interpreted by comparing people's 'preferences' with their 'real interests'	Since power is ubiquitous, it cannot be observed; its effects can be traced through 'archaeological' and 'genealogical' studies that seek to explain how particular practices became 'possible'
Conflict	Manifest conflict is a necessary condition for power	Conflict is a necessary condition for power, and can be manifest or 'latent' (e.g. if 'losers' acquiesce to defeat)	Conflict is a necessary condition for power, and is often 'latent' – apparently voluntary submission does not always indicate 'real consent'	Conflict is not a necessary condition for power; power is consensual, since it shapes our wants, desires and who we really are
Character	Power is sometimes repressive	Power is often repressive	Power is always repressive	Power is productive; it creates subjectivities and regimes of knowledge
Domination	Occurs when a ruling minority repeatedly gets its own way; subverts democracy; can be prevented by competitive democracy	Occurs as a result of the 'mobilisation of bias'; subverts democracy; can be prevented by institutional design	Covert and apparently consensual; dominated people have a false impression of their own interests; a pervasive feature of capitalist democracies; potentially escapable	Covert and consensual; constraining and constitutive; inevitable and inescapable

Table 6.1 (Continued)

	Decision making	Agenda setting	Preference manipulation	Constitutive
Awareness	Power is exercised intentionally; both dominator and dominated are aware of its effects	Power is exercised intentionally; both dominator and dominated are usually aware of its effects	Power may be exercised intentionally or unintentionally; both dominated and dominator may be unaware of its effects	Power is largely invisible and we are typically unaware of its effects
Distribution	Power can be concentrated in the hands of an elite or dispersed amongst different groups	Power tends to be concentrated amongst those who can mobilise bias and control agendas	Power may be disproportionately held by ideology dispensers and opinion formers, such as newspapers, educationalists, advertisers etc.	Power cannot be distributed since it cannot be held
Preferences and interests	Preferences and interests are identical and unaffected by power	Preferences and interests are identical and are largely unaffected by power	Preferences may be formed by power, if they are contrary to someone's 'real' interests	Preferences and interests are formed by power

the constitutive view treats it as productive. This generates a series of further disagreements about the relationships between power, freedom and resistance. Meanwhile, in the third key debate we will focus on the constitutive theory of power, asking whether it is compatible with a genuinely emancipatory politics. On the one hand, radical social critics – including both feminists and postcolonial theorists – have found resources within this view to support their own emancipatory projects. On the other hand, constitutive theories of power also seem to counsel a form of political quietism, since they imply that domination will always be with us – when one dominating structure is overturned another one will emerge in its place. Finally, we will conclude the chapter by exploring whether political theory itself might be implicated in a covert form of domination, and if it is, what might be done about it.

Rival perspectives

Power as decision making

The conception of power as decision making was given its classic formulation by political scientists Robert Dahl and Nelson Polsby during a series of academic debates that came to be known as the 'community power' debates. These were conducted during the 1950s, 1960s and 1970s, and concerned the nature and distribution of power in the US. On one side of the debate, 'elite theorists' such as the sociologists C. Wright Mills and Floyd Hunter argued that power was concentrated in the hands of a relatively small number of individuals. For example, Mills argued that influential figures drawn from the worlds of business, politics and the military collectively held a 'power unequalled in human history' (Mills, 1959, p. 361; see also Mills, 2000). Elite theorists were scathing about the democratic credentials of the US, criticising the detachment of the powerful from the experiences of ordinary men and women, to whom they were largely unresponsive. On the other side of the debate, 'pluralists' such as Dahl and Polsby argued that power was dispersed, albeit unequally, amongst different groups and individuals. As such, the pluralist view was more optimistic about the state of contemporary democracy in America, at least as a form of 'polyarchy' that resembled the competitive theory of democracy we discussed in Chapter 5. For our purposes, the most significant aspects of these debates concern how the various protagonists understood power itself, rather than how they thought it was distributed. Significantly, Dahl and Polsby's conception of power as decision making emerged from a methodological critique they levelled against Mills and Hunter. Consequently, to make sense of this understanding of power, we need to look briefly at some of the methodological concerns animating social scientists at this time.

The community power debates were triggered by Hunter's book *Community Power Structure: A Study of Decision Makers* (1953), which is discussed in Box 6.1. Hunter aspired to map the 'power structure' of Atlanta (disguised as 'Regional City') by using what came to be known as the 'reputational method'. He started from the assumption that having a reputation for being powerful was a reliable predictor of actually being powerful. He then asked people who were supposedly in the know to locate the identities of the 'power elite' and to map the relationships between them. Meanwhile, his pluralist critics condemned this approach for being unsatisfactorily circular and unscientific, since they believed that a reputational study could only reveal who was perceived to be powerful, rather than who actually was powerful (Wolfinger, 1960; Polsby, 1963, ch. 3). Their methodological critique was informed by the 'behaviouralist' revolution in political science, which according to one of its leading figures had attempted 'to improve our understanding of politics by seeking to explain the empirical aspects of political life by means of methods, theories, and criteria of proof that are acceptable according to the canons, conventions, and assumptions of modern empirical science' (Dahl, 1961b, p. 767). Thus, when it came to studying power, the pluralists aspired to adopt a more scientific approach, which they took to mean dispassionately observing relations of cause and effect. Consequently, they

BOX 6.1   POWER AND REPUTATION

Hunter sought to map the power structure of his 'Regional City' by presenting a list of 175 community leaders to a panel of 14 'insiders', drawn from religious, professional and business circles. He asked them to identify who the most important leaders were, which gave Hunter a list of 40 people, about whom there was considerable agreement. He then interviewed some of these individuals, along with an additional group comprising welfare workers and representatives of the African American community. They were all asked to identify the most powerful leaders, and to give their impressions about 'who knows who' and about how local issues were formulated and decided. The interviewees agreed that the 40 people initially specified included the most significant leaders in 'Regional City' and added another 5 names to the list. On the basis of the data he had collected, Hunter concluded that power in Atlanta had a 'pyramidal' structure, dominated by a small number of individuals, linked both socially and institutionally by their membership in overlapping 'cliques' or 'crowds'. Moreover, his interviews suggested that successful policy initiatives were typically nurtured within these cliques, and were often discussed informally and in private settings before being advanced publicly. Significantly, and in common with many other elite theorists, he argued that '[t]he test for admission to this circle of decision-makers is almost wholly a man's position in the business community' (Hunter, 1953, p. 79).

Is the 'reputational method' an adequate approach for studying the distribution of power?

proposed a 'decisional' method, which involved observing how actual decisions are made. This method was preferable to the reputational one, they believed, because it involved studying 'specific outcomes in order to determine who actually prevails in community decision making' (Polsby, 1963, p. 113).

On the pluralist account, the existence of a power elite could be confirmed only by identifying a significant range of occasions in which a defined group of people (the 'elite') managed to get their own way against the wishes of others (Dahl, 1958, p. 466). Dahl set out to test this hypothesis in his own landmark study of New Haven politics, *Who Governs: Democracy and Power in an American City* (1961a), discussed in Box 6.2. On the face of things, Dahl and Hunter endorsed similar conceptions of power. For instance, according to Hunter power was 'the ability of men to command the services of other men' (1953, p. 4) and 'the ability of personnel to move goods and services toward defined goals' (1953, p. 139). Similarly, Dahl depicted his 'intuitive idea of power' as 'something like this: *A* has power over *B* to the extent that he can get *B* to do something that *B* would not otherwise do' (Dahl, 1957, pp. 202–3). In both cases, power involves one party altering the behaviour of another. Although Dahl used the language of power-over rather than power-to, this is a red herring, and his basic understanding of power – like Hunter's – is the ability to achieve outcomes (see Morriss, 2002, pp. 12–13). However, in their studies of Atlanta and New Haven, the two authors operationalised their conceptions in very different ways, mainly as a consequence of their contrasting methodological stances. Whilst Hunter associated 'holding power' with having the reputation of being powerful, Dahl

BOX 6.2   POWER AND DECISIONS

In his study of politics in New Haven, Dahl tried to 'determine for each decision which participants had initiated alternatives that were finally adopted, had vetoed alternatives initiated by others, or had proposed alternatives that were turned down' (Dahl, 1961a, p. 336). If he could reliably conclude that an individual or group was more likely to have their preferred policies adopted, or were better able to veto the policies of others, then he would have grounds for declaring them to be powerful. He focussed his research on three 'key issues' (political nominations, urban redevelopment and public education), selected because in each case there was actual disagreement amongst different groups in society about what to do. Thus, they lent themselves to the observation of power, since for a group to 'win' it needed to prevail over its opponents. Significantly, his findings undermined the elitist view, because he found that different groups were able to get their own way in different domains, and that no single 'elite' dominated decision making. As he put it: 'a leader in one issue-area is not likely to be influential in another' and 'leaders in different issue-areas do not seem to be drawn from a single homogenous stratum' (1961a, p. 183).

Is a 'decisional method' an adequate approach for studying the distribution of power?

was committed to relying on observational rather than anecdotal or impressionistic evidence. Hence, for him, power could only be revealed by analysing 'who gets their way' in political decision making. Despite the clear advantages of this approach, Dahl's conception of power raises two difficulties that are worth noting.

First, Dahl's method makes conflict a necessary condition for the exercise of power. For him, identifying winners and losers under conditions of conflict and competition was 'the best way to determine which individuals and groups have "more" power in social life' (Polsby, 1963, p. 4). This was because we can only know that A exercised power over B if we (a) observe B doing x, (b) know that B would prefer not to do x, and (c) can attribute B's doing of x to A. One consequence of this is that, for Dahl, power is not simply about getting others to do things, but is about getting others to do things that they would not otherwise do. However, as we shall see later, this is arguably too restrictive, as it excludes from the definition of power the possibility that A could exercise power over B by shaping B's wants and desires.

Second, because Dahl thought that we can only know that power is present when it can be observed, he was suspicious of talk about 'potential power'. In his analysis, power is treated as something that is exercised rather than as something that individuals or groups can hold, or be able to exercise, should they so wish. However, this seems to be a mistake, as Peter Morriss illustrates in the following example:

> It is, of course, true that one cannot tell whether an actor is powerful unless *some* set of observations 'attests to' his power. But there is no reason whatsoever why these observations should be of the actualization of that power. When I go to a zoo, I can see that a lion is powerful enough to eat me up by observing its jaws, teeth and muscles, and combining these observations with my general knowledge of animals' masticatory performances. If I am still in doubt, I can observe what the lion does to a hunk of meat, and induce. Not even the most dogmatic positivist would declare that he couldn't know if the lion could eat him up until it had actually done so. (Morriss, 2002, p. 16)

Morriss concludes that views such as Dahl's risk committing the 'exercise fallacy', since they treat the 'power to do something' as 'nothing more than the doing of it' (2002, p. 15).

Power as agenda setting

The conception of power as agenda setting also emerged during the community power debates. It was formulated by political scientists Peter Bachrach and Morton Baratz, who published two critical articles (1962, 1963) in response to Dahl's study of power in New Haven (1961a). In these, as well as in a later book (1970), they argued that Dahl's conception of power as decision making only captured one of its 'faces' and, as such, needed to be supplemented. Key to Bachrach and Baratz's view is the idea that political issues, such as those studied by Dahl in New Haven, do not simply appear. Rather, issues are raised or made by groups and individuals, who can also suppress and marginalise them. Consequently, they suggested that there was a second 'face' of power, which took the form of excluding issues from the political agenda.

Let us begin by looking at Bachrach and Baratz's critique of Dahl. Recall, Dahl had selected three issues to study in New Haven, and found that different groups had 'won' in each of them, thereby falsifying the elitist hypothesis and supporting the pluralist one. These issues were selected on methodological grounds, since in each case there was disagreement over the outcome. Potentially, had Dahl studied three other issues then he might not have been able to falsify the elitist hypothesis (perhaps, for instance, a single group would have got its own way in each decision). However, according to Bachrach and Baratz, even if Dahl had been able to study every political issue that was contested in New Haven that year, the resulting picture would still have been incomplete in two important ways:

> One is that the model takes no account of the fact that power may be, and often is, exercised by confining the scope of decision making to relatively 'safe' issues. The other is that the model provides no *objective* criteria for distinguishing between 'important' and 'unimportant' issues arising in the political arena. (Bachrach and Baratz, 1962, p. 948)

Their conception of power as agenda setting was intended to correct these deficiencies. Incorporating agenda setting into the definition of power allowed Bachrach and Baratz to argue that power could be exercised surreptitiously, when groups ensured that issues which threatened their interests never reach the decision making stage.

Bachrach and Baratz drew special attention to ways in which the powerful suppress challenges to the existing order, ensuring that 'demands for change in the existing allocation of benefits and privileges in the community can be suffocated before they are even voiced; or kept covert; or killed before they gain access to the relevant decision making arena' (Bachrach and Baratz, 1970, p. 44). For instance, in their own study *Power and Poverty* (1970), they sought to demonstrate that issues of particular significance for poor African Americans were persistently excluded from the political agenda. Similarly, in a study of the politics of air pollution, Matthew Crenson (1971) found that corporations often succeeded in keeping pollution off the political agenda. Bachrach and Baratz referred to this kind of activity as 'nondecision making', which they defined as 'a decision that results in suppression or thwarting of a latent or manifest challenge to the values or interests of the decision-maker' (1970, pp. 43–4). As discussed in Box 6.3, nondecision making often takes place outside the formal political arena (for instance, in the

BOX 6.3 OBSERVING NONDECISION MAKING

Agenda setting is less visible than decision making, because it often happens outside formal political institutions and takes the form of creating or reinforcing 'barriers to the public airing of policy conflicts' (Bachrach and Baratz, 1970, p. 8). For instance, an oppositional movement might be effectively silenced because it is unable to access the media, lacks the resources required to form a cohesive organisation, because it is tied up in red tape, because its leading members are bribed, or because they are subjected to threats or intimidation. Similarly, powerful groups might ensure that a decision is indefinitely postponed by commissioning endless committees and reports, by misplacing important files, or by declaring an issue to be private and off limits. In some cases, the powerful do not need to deliberately erect barriers, since 'the common knowledge that certain decisions would be unacceptable to the local "godfather" is sufficient to remove whole ranges of potential options from the agenda of the town meeting entirely' (Hyland, 1995, p. 194). In each of these cases, because power has the effect of preventing an issue from reaching the point where a decision is required, then it will not even appear 'on the radar' of approaches such as Dahl's.

How can we know when power as agenda setting has been exercised?

'corridors of power', in newspaper offices, and in social clubs). It is exercised when 'A devotes his energies to creating or reinforcing social and political values and institutional practices that limit the scope of the political process to public consideration of only those issues which are comparatively innocuous to A' (1970, p. 7).

An unambiguous implication of Bachrach and Baratz's view is that a group exercises power if it intentionally and successfully keeps an issue off the political agenda. More problematic are those cases in which the political agenda is shaped unintentionally, for instance by 'dominant values ... political myths, rituals, and institutional practices' (Bachrach and Baratz, 1970, p. 11). The difficulty is that dominant values (etc.) often both favour the interests of privileged groups and contribute to the exclusion of issues that would challenge the interests of those groups. Thus, they can serve to ensure that certain issues are kept off the political agenda, even where no individual or group has consciously decided that this should be the case. For instance, Stephen Holmes has pointed out that:

> In the United States, unlike European nations with Communist parties, the legitimacy of private property is never debated in formal legislative settings. But the issue was never deliberately suppressed because, for a variety of reasons, it was never raised. (Holmes, 1988, p. 26)

In this case, an issue has been (consistently) excluded from the political agenda, and this exclusion clearly benefits some members of society (e.g. those who hold private property). However, it is not clear that anyone has actually suppressed the issue – in other words, no one has consciously and intentionally acted to bring about a non-decision. Consequently, although we might want to characterise the exclusion of this issue as a manifestation of power, it is difficult to do so in Bachrach and Baratz's language of agenda setting, since on their account, a nondecision is still a decision.

Power as preference manipulation

If we combine the two 'faces' of power discussed so far, then A can exercise power over B either by getting its own way in a political decision or by limiting the scope of decision making to 'safe' issues. In a book originally published in 1974, Stephen Lukes (2005) characterised this as a 'two dimensional' view of power and argued that although it was an improvement on Dahl's original conception, it was still too narrow. Lukes argued that the two dimensional view neglected the conditions under which individuals and groups form their preferences and beliefs. This is because it locates the operation of power in the satisfaction or frustration of people's wants and desires, which are treated as 'givens'. But as Lukes (rhetorically) asks: 'is it not the supreme exercise of power to get another or others to have the desires you want them to have – that is, to secure their compliance by controlling their thoughts and desires?' (Lukes, 2005, p. 27). This leads him to favour a wider conception of power, according to which 'A may exercise power over B by getting him to do what he does not want to do, but he also exercises power over him by influencing, shaping or determining his very wants' (Lukes, 2005, p. 27).

Lukes's broader conception of power aims to account for the possibility that power can be exercised by causing subordinate groups to accept their position, by shaping how they perceive of themselves and their interests. One implication of this wider view is that it facilitates a number of radical political claims that would otherwise remain obscure (hence, Lukes labels it a 'radical' view of power). For example, Marxists have argued that capitalism works by imposing a 'false consciousness' on workers, so that they fail to recognise their true (revolutionary) interests. Similarly, many feminists believe that patriarchal societies preserve themselves by ensuring that women internalise gendered norms and understandings, and thus fail to recognise their own true interests in female emancipation. Whilst examples such as these cannot be classified as power if power is conceived of in terms of decision making and agenda setting, they can be if power is understood in terms of preference manipulation. Thus, Lukes's account of power as preference manipulation potentially makes visible a form of domination that would otherwise be obscure, namely one in which the dominated acquiesce to the values and ideologies implicated in their domination, either by resigning themselves to them or by willingly embracing them (Scott, 1992). This radical conception of power was operationalised in a striking manner by John Gaventa, in his *Power and Powerlessness: Quiescence and Rebellion in an Appalachian Valley* (1980), discussed in Box 6.4.

BOX 6.4 POWER AND QUIESCENCE

Like Hunter and Dahl, Gaventa studied power in a local, community setting. He sought to explain why oppressed mineworkers in Clear Fork Valley did not challenge their domination. Key to his explanation was the idea that quiescence was produced and maintained by power relations, and especially by the recurring experience of political defeat on the part of the powerless. In the course of making this argument, Gaventa developed an illuminating analysis of the ways in which power as decision making and agenda setting can help to sustain power as preference manipulation. On his account, if a group repeatedly loses out in political decisions, then it might rationally withdraw from political competition, thus lessening its capacity to shape the political agenda. Over time, calculated withdrawal from politics may turn into 'an unconscious pattern of withdrawal', which might bring about 'extensive fatalism, self-deprecation, or undue apathy about one's situation' (Gaventa, 1980, pp. 16–17). Furthermore, the 'sense of powerlessness may also lead to a greater susceptibility to the internalisation of the values, beliefs, or rules of the game of the powerful as a further adaptive response – i.e. as a means of escaping the subjective sense of powerlessness, if not its objective condition' (Gaventa, 1980, p. 17). Thus, for Gaventa, the powerful need not intentionally manipulate the beliefs and preferences of the powerless. Rather, the 'internalisation' of dominant values and beliefs may occur in a seemingly 'natural' way, as a result of the situation in which subordinate people find themselves.

Can subordination produce political quiescence?

An important feature of the conception of power as preference manipulation is that it relaxes the requirement that power be accompanied by open and explicit disagreement over political outcomes. Recall that, according to the first two faces of power, conflict is a necessary condition for power, since if *A* is to exercise power over *B*, then *A* must get *B* to do something that *B* would not otherwise do, which means that *A* must meet with (and overcome) some kind of opposition, either in the decision making process itself, or during the earlier agenda setting phase. Thus, on these views, if there is no opposition, for example because *A* and *B* are known to favour the same outcome, then it does not make sense to say that power was exercised over *B* when *A* gets their way, since *B* shared *A*'s preference. Indeed, according to Dahl:

> [I]f everyone were perfectly agreed on ends and means, no one would ever need to change the way of another. Hence no relations of influence or power would arise. (Dahl, 1970, p. 59)

However, as Lukes and Gaventa point out, treating conflict as a necessary condition for power can cause us to misinterpret political submission, for example by taking the quiescence of the mineworkers in Clear Fork Valley as evidence that power had not been exercised. As Lukes asks, again rhetorically:

> [I]s it not the supreme and most insidious exercise of power to prevent people, to whatever degree, from having grievances by shaping their perceptions, cognitions and preferences in such a way that they accept their role in the existing order of things, either because they can see or imagine no alternative to it, or because they see it as natural and unchangeable, or because they value it as divinely ordained and beneficial? To assume that the absence of grievance equals genuine consensus is simply to rule out the possibility of false or manipulated consensus by definitional fiat. (Lukes, 2005, p. 28)

To solve this problem, Lukes argues that power can be exercised in the absence of explicit conflict, provided that there is what he calls 'latent conflict'. He defines this as 'a contradiction between the interests of those exercising power and the *real interests* of those they exclude' (Lukes, 2005, p. 28). Thus, instead of saying that A exercises power over B by getting B to do something that B would not otherwise do, Lukes says that 'A exercises power over B when A affects B in a manner contrary to B's interests' (Lukes, 2005, p. 37). Consequently, A can exercise power over B without B being aware of it, and when A and B appear to share the same preferences, provided that A affects B in such a way as to subvert B's own 'real' interests.

Lukes's definition of power thus rests upon a distinction between perceived and real interests, and it associates the exercise of power with the subversion of the latter. A person's real interests – on Lukes's account – are objective, and may be different to the interests that people believe themselves to have, or the interests they reveal through their actions. This puts his position at odds with the other views we have considered so far:

> Extremely crudely, one might say that the liberal [e.g. Dahl] takes people as they are and applies want-regarding principles to them, relating their interests to what they actually want or prefer, to their policy preferences as manifested by their political participation. The reformist [e.g. Bachrach and Baratz], seeing and deploring that not everyone's wants are given equal weight by the political system, also relates their interests to what they want or prefer, but allows that this may be revealed in more indirect and sub-political ways – in the form of deflected, submerged or concealed wants and preferences. The radical [e.g. Lukes], however, maintains that people's wants may themselves be a product of a system which works against their interests, and, in such cases, relates the latter to what they would want and prefer, were they able to make the choice. (Lukes, 2005, pp. 37–8)

For many of Lukes's critics, the distinction between real and perceived interests is problematic. He insists that people have real interests which – unlike perceived interests – are not 'a product of a system' but are what people 'would want and prefer' if they were able to reflect on their own interests, unimpaired by ideological manipulation. However, although dominated people themselves are unable to perceive their own real interests, Lukes does imply that they are, in principle, discoverable by others, a view that Colin Hay describes as 'both logically unsustainable and politically offensive':

> The problem with [Lukes's] formulation is the deeply condescending conception of the social subject as an ideological dupe that it conjures. Not only is this wretched individual incapable of perceiving his/her true interests, pacified as s/he is by the hallucinogenic effects of bourgeois (or other) indoctrination. But, to confound matters, rising above the ideological mists which tame the masses is the enlightened academic who from a high perch in the ivory tower may look down to discern the genuine interests of those not similarly privileged. (Hay, 2002, p. 179)

However, despite Hay's objection, it is worth noting that Lukes's claim is a relatively modest one: he says that people are *not always* the best judges of their own interests, not that they are *never* the best judges of their own interests. Indeed, on Lukes's account, people can ascertain their own 'real' interests, if they exercise 'choice under conditions of relative autonomy ... independently of A's power (e.g. through democratic participation)' (Lukes, 2005, p. 37).

Power as constitutive

As Lukes construes it, power is repressive, because preference manipulation has the effect of leaving dominated individuals with a false or distorted impression of their real interests. An even more radical view of power, suggested by Michel Foucault, is that power is constitutive rather than repressive, since human subjects are produced by its 'disciplining' effects. Foucault denies that people have real interests in the way Lukes implies. Instead, his view proceeds from the assumption that the human subject lacks a fixed or permanent essence, and as such is malleable. To make this argument, he proposed a radical rethinking of the concept of power, which drew attention to its relationships with knowledge and subjectivity. Although Foucault's account of power is complex, it has three main components that we shall examine in turn.

The first of these is that power is ubiquitous. As Foucault put it, 'power is everywhere, not because it embraces everything, but because it comes from everywhere' (1998, p. 93). By this, he did not mean that power indiscriminately saturates all aspects of our social lives. Rather, Foucault's intention was to displace three commonplace beliefs. First, that power is exercised only at particular moments or in particular settings (as when, for example, we conceive of power as decision making or agenda setting). Second, that power is a commodity, which can be exchanged amongst individuals and institutions (as when, for example, we say that power is transferred from the people to their government, or from a government to a supranational body). Third, that relations of power are 'bad in themselves' and are something 'from which one must free one's self' (1987, p. 129). Foucault's insistence on the ubiquity of power led him to criticise the 'sovereignty model' of power, in which power is associated with the making and enforcing of laws. Such views are too narrow, since they focus only on power that is held or exercised by specific individuals and institutions, such as monarchs, parliaments, police officers, parents and teachers. Instead, Foucault preferred a 'capillary model' of power, in which power is dispersed and decentred, circulating through the social body. In order to study power of this kind we need to resist the temptation to see it as a 'top-down' phenomenon, and Foucault instead advocated a 'bottom-up' approach, or what he termed a 'microphysics of power' (1991, p. 26).

The second component of Foucault's conception of power is that it is productive, since it moulds our identities and how we understand ourselves. Thus, he argues that:

> [R]ather than asking ourselves what the sovereign looks like from on high, we should be trying to discover how multiple bodies, forces, energies, matters, desires, thoughts and so on are gradually, progressively, actually and materially constituted as subjects. (Foucault, 2004, p. 28)

Foucault developed the idea that power is productive in his historical studies of madness, punishment and sexuality. For example, in his work *Discipline and Punish* (1991) he criticised those who believe that power always works to frustrate human freedom, arguing that:

> We must cease once and for all to describe the effects of power in negative terms: it 'excludes', it 'represses', it 'censors', it 'abstracts', it 'masks', it 'conceals'. In fact power produces; it produces reality; it produces domains of objects and rituals of truth. The individual and the knowledge that may be gained of him belong to this production. (1991, p. 194)

Similarly, in *The History of Sexuality* (Foucault, 1998), he identified and criticised the 'repressive hypothesis', which associated power with prohibition. He challenged this view both by pointing out that repression often turns out to be paradoxical, encouraging rather than constraining desire, and by arguing that properly understood, power produces meanings, social orders and – most importantly – subjects.

Finally, the third component of Foucault's account consists in the connection he drew between power and knowledge, which he fused together into the term 'power/knowledge' (1980). He captured the basic relationship between power and knowledge as follows:

> No body of knowledge can be formed without a system of communications, records, accumulation and displacement which is in itself a form of power and which is linked, in its existence and functioning, to the other forms of power. Conversely, no power can be exercised without the extraction, appropriation, distribution or retention of knowledge. On this level, there is not knowledge on one side and society on the other, or science and the state, but only the fundamental forms of knowledge/power. (Foucault, quoted in Sheridan, 1997, p. 131)

Foucault did not claim that power is knowledge, or that knowledge is power. Rather, his more nuanced claim was that particular formations of knowledge (or 'discourses') serve as regimes of truth, and that these simultaneously govern and constitute us as subjects. Thus, on his account, knowledge and truth are inherently political concepts:

> Truth is a thing of this world: it is produced only by virtue of multiple forms of constraint. And it induces regular effects of power. (Foucault, 1980, p. 131)

The connection that Foucault draws between power and knowledge is mediated by a distinctive view about how we should understand human history and society. He was sceptical about putting human beings and their ideas centre stage, and thought it was naive to exaggerate the capacity of individuals to shape their lives. Instead, he emphasised the significance of discourses, which refer to the kinds of thoughts and utterances that are possible in a given setting (such as, for example, the discourses of health and illness, of madness, or of politics). Discourses shape how we understand ourselves and how we arrange our affairs, and they do so by naturalising a particular and bounded range of terms, categories, values and beliefs. In this sense, they are constitutive, since they express a particular kind of truth about subjects, and because they contribute to the formation of particular kinds of subjects.

Foucault's conception of power as ubiquitous, productive and constitutive can be illustrated by examining some of his own research, such as *Discipline and Punish*, discussed in Box 6.5. Another important and uncompleted work was his *The History of Sexuality*, where Foucault argued that the new sciences of sexuality (including psychoanalysis) had led to the emergence of a variety of discourses about sexuality and its control, introducing new categorisations of the normal and abnormal. One consequence of these was that individuals began to monitor both their actions and their desires, measuring themselves against the ideals established by the new sciences. Thus, he thought that power/knowledge could be observed in the attempts made by individuals to conform to what the sciences expected of them, which in turn had the effect of producing them as

BOX 6.5   POWER AND DISCIPLINE

In his *Discipline and Punish*, Foucault identified the emergence of a 'disciplinary society', modelled on transformations in the penal system during the eighteenth and nineteenth centuries, in which incarceration, surveillance and reform had gradually replaced more primitive and brutal forms of punishment. These reforms were the product of both legal and scientific developments, and served as a model to be expanded into schools, hospitals, factories and elsewhere. The 'disciplinary society' represented a new formation of power/knowledge and played an important role in creating new kinds of human identity (or, in Foucault's terms, new 'subjectivities'). Foucault's primary example of pervasive discipline and surveillance was Jeremy Bentham's 'Panopticon', which was a blueprint for a new kind of prison, designed so that inmates would be isolated from one another and under continual observation from guards. Since inmates would never know whether they were actually being watched, they would have no choice but to always act as if they were under observation. On Foucault's reading, the 'major effect of the Panopticon' was 'to induce in the inmate a state of conscious and permanent visibility that assures the automatic functioning of power' (Foucault, 1991, p. 201). This 'perfection of power' resulted in a more thoroughgoing disciplining of inmates than would previously have been possible. Importantly, the aim of disciplinary surveillance was not to enact revenge on inmates, but was rather to encourage reform and to correct deviant behaviour. Foucault suggests that these new techniques of disciplinary control became possible only because new forms of knowledge had emerged, introducing the ideas that human beings are equipped with interior lives, were capable of guilt and remorse, and could therefore be reformed (or normalised). Moreover, these new forms of knowledge, reinforced by disciplinary techniques, were productive, in the sense that they worked to constitute and reinforce a distinctive understanding of what it is to be a good citizen.

Can power both discipline and produce?

particular kinds of (self-forming) subjects. Foucault put special emphasis on the double-sidedness of apparently 'progressive' developments: in emancipating ourselves from (old) sexual inhibitions we imposed a (new) domination, based on a demanding form of 'knowledge' about how healthy and fulfilled human beings should live.

Key debates

Can democratic institutions prevent domination?

Different theories of power yield different explanations about the relationship between democracy and domination. For radical theories, like the final two, domination is a pervasive feature of Western liberal democracies and many of our social practices have covert forms of domination built into them. Meanwhile, the first pair of rival perspectives both conceive of domination as a transparent phenomenon, in which the dominated are aware of their subordination. Furthermore, as we shall now see, advocates of these perspectives agree that domination subverts democracy and should be addressed by careful institutional design. For Dahl, the solution to domination is political competition, whilst for Bachrach and Baratz it is a matter of ensuring that institutions cannot be used to 'mobilise bias' against the interests of weaker social groups. In this key debate we will compare these two perspectives and their different solutions to the problem of domination.

As we saw in the introduction, to be dominated is to be part of an ongoing social relationship that undermines one's self-determination, to a greater or lesser extent. According to the conception of power as decision making, an individual or group dominates another individual or group, or society as a whole, if it repeatedly gets its own way on issues that are put forward for decision. This captures the sense in which a minority can be said to dominate society if it monopolises the major political offices, such that it can be confident of consistently getting its own way. Thus, in *Who Governs*, Dahl was able to argue that no single group dominated New Haven politics, as the elite theorists had alleged, since there were multiple centres of power, as evidenced by the observation that different groups got their own way in different decisions. During this debate, both Dahl and the elitists agreed that it would have been detrimental to democracy had New Haven politics been dominated by an identifiable elite.

Nearly 30 years after this study, Dahl returned to the topic of domination in his *Democracy and its Critics* (1989). Again, he took the elite theorists – including Mills and Hunter as well as their predecessors such as Gaetano Mosca, Robert Michels and Vilfredo Pareto – to be his primary opponents. Here, he identified two criteria for domination: the presence of a ruling minority and the absence of competitive democracy. This led him to argue that a society in which the ruling minority 'controls all matters on the agenda of government decision' and 'encounters only negligible opposition' is dominated (Dahl, 1989, p. 278). Meanwhile, if there was some degree of meaningful political competition, or what Dahl called 'polyarchy', then he took that to be evidence against the presence of domination:

If oppositions are granted the right to form political parties, if the parties are entitled to participate in elections, if the elections are fair and free, and if the highest offices in the government of the state are held by those who win elections, then competition among political elites makes it likely that the policies of the government will respond in time to the preferences of a majority of voters. (Dahl, 1989, p. 276)

Thus, in this text, Dahl's view is that domination is the subversion of democracy for which robust and free political competition is the solution. Moreover, he claimed that the elite theorists had been too eager to diagnose the presence of domination, because they had underestimated the capacity of political competition to serve as a bulwark against it.

Is Dahl's view of domination convincing? Like other theories of domination, he identifies an ongoing social relationship (in his case, between the dominant minority and everyone else), in which the self-determination of the subordinate partner is frustrated (in his case, as a result of the absence of democracy). Because Dahl defines democracy in competitive terms, the implication of his view is that domination is impossible under conditions of adequate political competition. However, this potentially leaves his account vulnerable to some of the objections that have been levelled at competitive theories of democracy, such as those discussed in Chapter 5. For instance, recall participatory democrat Carol Gould's claim that freedom requires individuals to participate in the governing of those institutions which shape their self-development. On her account, the institutions of competitive democracy are too weak to secure the self-determination of each individual, since they leave many citizens unable to effectively influence the institutions that govern their lives. Thus, she would argue that individuals could remain dominated even if they had access to the political rights and liberties associated with competitive democracy. Moreover, even if one rejects this demanding conception of individual self-determination, Dahl's view might still be objectionably narrow, since assuming that domination is impossible in a minimally functioning competitive democracy seems to rule out drawing intuitively plausible distinctions amongst stronger and weaker forms of domination. Some of the implications of this are explored in Box 6.6.

Dahl's conception of domination seems best suited to identifying its most extreme manifestations, such as those which are found in authoritarian political societies. Meanwhile, the conception of power as agenda setting suggests a more nuanced view, in which domination is compatible with free and robust political competition. On this account, an individual or group dominates another individual or group, or society as a whole, either when it repeatedly gets its own way on issues that require a decision, or when it consistently succeeds in stifling issues that would potentially threaten its interests. This understanding allows for the possibility that domination occurs when democratic institutions 'operate systematically and consistently to the benefit of certain persons and groups at the expense of others' (Bachrach and Baratz, 1970, p. 43). Importantly, domination of this kind might not be produced by direct discrimination, but could be the result of the 'mobilisation of bias' – an idea Bachrach and Baratz borrowed from E. E. Schattschneider:

> All forms of political organisation have a bias in favour of the exploitation of some kinds of conflict and the suppression of others because *organisation is the mobilisation of bias*. Some issues are organised into politics while others are organised out. (Schattschneider, 1960, p. 71)

BOX 6.6 POLITICAL COMPETITION AND DOMINATION

Consider the following (hypothetical) society, discussed by Robert Dahl:

> A minority generally succeeds in securing policies it considers favourable to its most essential interests. It does so both by directly influencing governmental decisions and by indirectly influencing beliefs. However, it does encounter significant opposition and it rarely is able to succeed except in coalition with other groups. Moreover, on matters that do not deeply affect its most essential interests its influence is much weaker, its allies fewer, its opponents much stronger, and its failure to control outcomes more common. On many matters, in fact, the minority makes little or no effort, directly or indirectly, to influence policies. What is more, elected officials compete vigorously for office. As a result other minorities are also 'dominant' (in the same sense) on matters they regard as most important: farmers, say, on farm subsidies, older persons on old-age pensions and medical care, environmentalists on air and water pollution, military heads on defence expenditure... (Dahl, 1989, p. 278)

Dahl describes this society as a 'system of minorities rule' and suggests that it is not a case of elite domination (Dahl, 1989, pp. 278–9). This is because, on his account, elite domination obtains only when society lacks meaningful political competition. Meanwhile, for Bachrach and Baratz, political competition is compatible with domination, if dominant groups are consistently able to stifle issues that would potentially threaten their interests.

Which conception of domination, if any, is preferable?

Thus, according to this second conception, domination may be the result of institutional arrangements that have the effect of ensuring that the interests of weaker or marginal social groups remain peripheral.

Again, this conception of domination identifies an ongoing social relationship that has the effect of frustrating the self-determination of subordinates, in this case because they are unable to influence political decisions or the political agenda. Unlike Dahl's conception, this account allows for the possibility that individuals and groups might be dominated even if the governing elite does not get its own way in every political decision, and even if there is meaningful political competition, provided that those (dominated) individuals or groups are consistently prevented from effectively raising issues and concerns that directly affect their interests. Thus, for example, if the political agenda simply does not address the concerns of women, workers or ethnic minorities, and especially if representatives of those groups are unable to alter the political agenda, then according to this conception we have grounds to characterise those groups as being dominated.

A noteworthy implication of this view is that it identifies democratic institutions as both the vehicle through with domination is facilitated and the vehicle through which it can be corrected. On the one hand, domination is facilitated by the 'mobilisation of bias', in which institutions (as well as values, beliefs and rituals) operate to the benefit of some and the expense of others, ensuring that some issues never reach the political agenda. On the other hand, removing the conditions for domination means adjusting those institutions (and values, beliefs and rituals) so that previously marginalised groups are able to participate as full equals in the democratic arena. In turn, reducing the scope for democratic domination may require turning away from a minimalist conception of competitive democracy and instead embracing a more 'demanding' theory of participatory or deliberative democracy.

Even though this understanding of domination is more subtle than Dahl's, and allows for the possibility that groups and individuals might be dominated within functioning competitive democracies, it is still a very restrictive view. This is because Bachrach and Baratz make it a condition of domination that the dominated themselves are aware of being dominated. That is to say, they take it for granted that dominated individuals and groups will know that 'their' interests are not reflected in the political agenda, and that they are capable of registering this as a grievance during political participation (in order to demand change). To be sure, Bachrach and Baratz do not assume that dominated individuals and groups will always resist their condition, since it might be rational to acquiesce to one's fate, for instance as a result of anticipating that an attempt to influence the political agenda is unlikely to bear fruit. Nevertheless, they do not consider the possibility that individuals and groups might be dominated without being aware of it. This shortcoming can be illustrated by recalling Laborde's definition of domination noted earlier. Whilst Bachrach and Baratz successfully account for at least some of those experiences of domination that take the form of being 'silenced, humiliated, [and] threatened', they do not account for those which are the result of being 'deprived of the ability to form our own perspective' by being 'indoctrinated, manipulated, [or] socialised into submissive roles' (Laborde, 2008, pp. 153–4). Thus, a possible shortcoming of their view is that it neglects the possibility that individuals and groups might be dominated when they are prevented not only from realising but also from recognising their own real interests. It is to these 'hidden' dimensions of domination that we shall now turn.

Is covert domination repressive?

Both Lukes and Foucault are concerned to unmask 'hidden' or 'covert' forms of domination by identifying structures and relations of social control that are not apparent to the dominated themselves. In many respects, these rival perspectives share similarities with the agonistic theories of pluralism we examined in Chapter 3 and the theories of radical democracy we touched upon in Chapter 5. On the face of things, this way of thinking about domination is puzzling, since ordinarily it is associated with the experience of being harmed or repressed in a transparently objectionable fashion. If the dominated themselves are unaware of their domination, then this raises a difficult question about why their predicament is objectionable. One way to address this question is to explore the relationship between domination and freedom, since we have already seen that domination might be objectionable because it frustrates individual self-determination. Moreover, this is something that Lukes and Foucault take different views about. On the one hand, Lukes argues that even when the dominated are unaware of being dominated, they are nevertheless made less free by virtue of it. Thus, he tends to present domination as a repressive form of 'power-over' that renders those subject to it 'less free ... to live as their nature and judgment dictate' (Lukes, 2005, p. 114). On the other hand, Foucault emphasises the productive rather than the repressive dimensions of domination, arguing that it is both constraining and constitutive, and that it has a more complex relationship with freedom than Lukes suggests.

Before comparing Lukes and Foucault's accounts, we should begin by discussing some of the general ways in which domination conceivably represses the dominated, with or without their knowledge. The repressive dimension of domination has both relational and structural aspects. In relational terms, domination is repressive because it is an asymmetrical relationship of social control, in which A exercises power-over B on an ongoing basis. Meanwhile, in structural terms, domination is repressive because it constrains and conditions what B is able to do and say, leaving B unable to fully develop and exercise their capacities. For example, Iris Marion Young associates domination with:

> institutional conditions which inhibit or prevent people from participating in determining their actions or the conditions of their actions. Persons live within structures of domination if other persons or groups can determine without reciprocation the conditions of their actions. (Young, 1990, p. 38)

Often, both of these aspects reinforce one another. For example, as we shall see in Chapter 7, contemporary republicans equate domination with being vulnerable to arbitrary interference. On this account, domination is a relationship in which A is at liberty to interfere in B's affairs on an arbitrary basis, rather than according to norms and rules that are the subject of collective agreement. In turn, B might be vulnerable to A's interference as a result of inhabiting 'structures of domination' (for instance, by virtue of B's social class or gender). If this is the case, then the very fact of occupying a structural position that leaves B vulnerable to arbitrary interference may have the effect of constraining and conditioning B's attitudes and behaviour. One example of this can be found in the writings of eighteenth-century feminist philosopher Mary Wollstonecraft, who argued that women, as a result of their subordinate position within gendered social hierarchies, and their resulting dependency on men, were more likely to cultivate subservient or pleasing dispositions.

Let us now turn to Lukes's account of domination, which says that domination frustrates freedom not only through threats of physical violence, but also by ensuring that the subordinate internalise dominant values. According to Lukes, to 'speak of power as domination is to suggest the imposition of some significant constraint upon an agent or agents' desires, purposes or interests, which it frustrates, prevents from fulfilment or even from being formulated' (Lukes, 2005, p. 113). On this account, domination is a form of 'power-over' that can be manifested in two different ways. First, A can impose some constraint that prevents B from fulfilling their desires, purposes or interests. Thus, as we have seen, a dominant ethnic group could prevent another from influencing political decisions or the political agenda, dominating them by leaving them unable to realise their purposes. Clearly, domination of this kind can be repressive, since not being so dominated would increase a group's freedom. Second, and alternatively, A can prevent B from formulating or recognising their real desires, purposes or interests. Thus, for example, the preferences of women might be manipulated, ensuring that they internalise prevailing patriarchal values. Or, capitalist societies might perpetuate themselves by securing widespread acceptance of their institutions and values. Although this second kind of domination is distinctive to Lukes's view, explaining why it undermines freedom is not so straightforward, as we shall now see.

Typically, we believe that a person's freedom is undermined when they are coerced to do or be something, but not when they consent to do or be something (see Chapter 7). The possibility of preference manipulation complicates matters, since it suggests that people might be coerced into consenting to something. For example, suppose that A has manipulated B's preferences such that B is made to agree with A about some policy P. If P is subsequently adopted, then it will appear as if both A and B got their own way. The point of Lukes's theory is to get us to be careful about taking such appearances at face value, since apparent consensus is not the same as genuine consensus. Thus, if we follow Lukes, the appearance of agreement (between A and B about P) is not enough to know with certainty that B has consented to P, since B may have been manipulated. If B has been manipulated, then we will have grounds for believing that B's freedom has been undermined.

However, how are we to know whether or not B really has been manipulated? In answer to this Lukes identifies three conditions that must be satisfied: A and B should be divided by a latent and unarticulated conflict of interests; B should act against their own 'real' interests; and in so acting, B should benefit A. This answer is controversial in two respects. First, Lukes assumes that if there is a latent conflict of interests between A and B, such that it would be in B's (real) interests to prefer something other than P, then we should infer that B's apparent consent to P is actually a reflection of the fact that they have been dominated by A. But there is a difference between saying that A and B are divided by a latent conflict of interests and saying that A has manipulated B's preferences. For example, suppose that voters from a particular social class or ethnic group consistently vote against their 'real' interests. Lukes's position seems to be that knowing this is evidence enough to support the conclusion that those voters have been manipulated (and thereby dominated).

Second, Lukes complicates his account of preference manipulation by arguing that 'the notion of "interests" is an irreducibly evaluative notion' (Lukes, 2005, p. 37). This means that because different political theories will supply rival accounts of A and B's interests, there are different – and equally valid – standards that could be used to identify when there is a latent conflict of interests between A and B, or when B acts against their own interests, or when B benefits A. Consequently, as Lukes acknowledges, it is impossible to formulate an overarching and general theory of preference manipulation, since different political theorists will have different views about what B's 'real' interests are (2005, pp. 110–24). For example, suppose that a woman willingly sacrifices food and her health for the good of her husband or children (Sen, 1987). On one reading, this is a clear example of patriarchal domination, in which there is a latent conflict over scarce domestic resources that is resolved by a vulnerable partner acting against her own interests for the benefit of others. Meanwhile, on another reading, the sacrifices made by the mother and wife are a praiseworthy manifestation of her free and voluntary choice. Noticeably, both readings preserve Lukes's claim that domination undermines freedom, since in the first case the dominated women is unfree, and in the second her freedom is taken as evidence that she is not dominated. Lukes's theory is controversial not because he refrains from specifying which, if either, of these readings is correct, but because he insists that there is no rational means to arbitrate between the pair. This follows from his claim that power is an 'essentially contested' concept (Gallie, 1956), which we explore in greater detail in Box 6.7.

Lukes's analysis of power as preference manipulation is driven by the challenge of explaining why dominated people acquiesce to their subjection. Charles Tilly captures this puzzle as follows:

[I]f ordinary domination so consistently hurts the well-defined interests of subordinate groups, why do the subordinate comply? Why don't they rebel continuously, or at least resist along the way? (Tilly, 1991, p. 594)

One answer to this, implicit in the theories of Dahl, Bachrach and Baratz, is that the dominated acquiesce as a result of their powerlessness. By implication, if the weakest members of society had the means or the capacity to rebel effectively, then they would do so. Meanwhile, as we have seen, Lukes's theory suggests that domination can be consensual, albeit imperfectly so, as when the subordinate are hoodwinked into accepting those dominant values and institutions that sustain their oppression. The implication of his view is that subordinated peoples will

BOX 6.7 ESSENTIALLY CONTESTED CONCEPTS

As we saw in Chapter 1, some philosophers believe that some evaluative concepts – like democracy, art, fairness and justice – are 'essentially contested'. This means that disputes about their proper use cannot be settled rationally, for instance by appealing to facts, language or logic. According to Lukes, power is another such concept, because different views about power are grounded in non-comparable moral and political perspectives. Thus, he argues that all definitions of power are 'inextricably tied to a given set of (probably unacknowledged) value-assumptions' (2005, p. 30) and that different views about power are 'ineradicably value-dependent' (2005, p. 30). As we have seen, Lukes proposes one conception of power, according to which it is exercised by frustrating interests. If power really is essentially contested, then this must be one conception amongst others (and tied to a given set of value assumptions). Furthermore, he also argues that 'the notion of "interests" is an irreducibly evaluative notion' (2005, p. 37). Thus, even within his essentially contested conception of power he leaves ample space for further disagreement about when power has been exercised, as we observed in the case of the woman who willingly sacrificed her food and health for the sake of her family. However, Lukes's insistence that power is essentially contested has puzzled many of his readers (Barry, 1975; Gray, 1977), because he also argues that his 'three dimensional' view of power is rationally preferable to its rivals (Lukes, 2005, pp. 16, 25, 34).

Can power be an essentially contested concept?

only be able to formulate and register grievances once they perceive their situation with greater clarity. Meanwhile, as we shall now see, Foucault offers an even more radical take on this issue. On his account, subjects do not resist, comply with or unintentionally consent to their own domination. Instead, they are constituted and formed by it.

According to Foucault, modern power is 'disciplinary power'. This form of power does not simply render subjects 'docile', for instance by directing, corralling or repressing them. Rather, it operates more intimately, helping to bring about new rationalities and subjectivities:

What is to be understood by the disciplining of societies in Europe since the eighteenth century is not, of course, that the individuals who are part of them become more and more obedient, nor that they set about assembling in barracks, schools or prisons; rather that an increasingly better invigilated process of adjustment has been sought after – more and more rational and economic – between productive activities, resources of communication, and the play of power relations. (Foucault, 1982, p. 788)

Disciplinary power works to construct particular kinds of people (or 'subjectivities') that are compatible with particular regimes of 'power/knowledge'. Thus, within this framework, domination does not take the form of punishing, threatening, prohibiting or manipulating, but rather works by inculcating, normalising, forming, producing and making possible certain kinds of dispositions, desires and behaviours, such as those exhibited by the 'good' or productive or sane or healthy citizen. Thus, disciplinary power makes subjects of us in two ways: we are both subjected to it and created as particular kinds of subjects by it:

> This form of power applies itself to immediate everyday life which categorises the individual, marks him by his own individuality, attaches him to his own identity, imposes a law of truth on him which he must recognise and by which others have to recognise him. It is a form of power which makes individuals subjects. There are two meanings of the word 'subject': subject to someone else by control and dependence, and tied to his own identity by a conscience or self-knowledge. Both meanings suggest a form of power which subjugates and makes subject to. (Foucault, 1982, p. 781)

In his later work, Foucault extended his analysis of disciplinary power and domination by introducing the concept of 'governmentality', which refers to an encompassing and subtle form of domination particular to the modern era. On Foucault's reading, the challenge of political organisation, in an era of mass societies, was to create 'a system of regulation of the general conduct of individuals whereby everything would be controlled to the point of self-sustenance, without the need for intervention' (1984, p. 241). Unlike earlier modes of domination, which took commands and rules as their paradigm, modern governmentality operates through the conduct of conduct. Thus, modern domination takes the form of shaping how individuals regulate themselves, which prompts Wendy Brown to compare the effects of governmentality to 'regularised orchestration' (Brown, 2006, p. 73).

What kind of freedom is compatible with disciplinary power and governmentality? Foucault's disconcerting answer is to say that contemporary democracies offer only the illusion of freedom. On his account, because the human subject is the product of power, and because power is ubiquitous, then there is no way to escape it and no sphere in which a person might stand apart from it. Indeed, perhaps there is not even a subject capable of standing apart from it. Thus, although liberal regimes of governmentality purport to grant extensive freedoms to their citizens – for example by invoking the values of limited government, freedom of speech or individual autonomy – these freedoms are the product of a particular regime of power/knowledge, and do not reflect an independent reality. Thus, at least on a radical reading of Foucault's writings, the very ideal of a 'rational, autonomous moral agent' that lies at the heart of liberal governmentality is nothing more than the 'effect' of a particular form of domination (Hindess, 1996, p. 149). If this is true, then although we might experience a sensation of freedom within liberal societies, these experiences are really a manifestation of our own domination, since we ourselves are the product of a particular regime of power/knowledge.

Is constitutive power compatible with an emancipatory politics?

As we have seen, Foucault's general theses about power are that it is pervasive, that it operates by disciplining subjects, and that it does so in ways that are productive rather than simply repressive. As one commentator summarises his view, 'power operates "through" individuals rather than "against" them and helps constitute the individual who is at the same time its vehicle' (Garland, 1990, p. 138). One implication of Foucault's conception is that individual people are merely an effect of power, and are therefore neither free nor responsible in the senses that we usually ascribe to them. Foucault's critics have suggested that two unattractive conclusions seem to follow from this: that individuals are entirely imprisoned within all-embracing structures of power, and that emancipatory political movements are paradoxically doomed to confine individuals in new but similarly insidious ways. In this final key debate we will evaluate whether these objections are fair by exploring Foucault's mixed reception amongst feminist scholars. Additionally, Box 6.9 will consider an influential 'postcolonial' application of Foucault's ideas.

Although Foucault had much to say about sexuality and sexual identities, he did not engage with the concept of gender, which refers to the socially constructed meanings attached to biological sex differences. Nevertheless, some feminist scholars have found in Foucault's writings an illuminating framework from which to understand the complex operations of patriarchy (the rule, or domination, of men). Meanwhile, as we shall see, not all feminists have embraced Foucault's conception of power, and some have rejected it.

Some of Foucault's supporters have noted that his conception of power might play an important role in an emancipatory feminist politics. For example, as explored in Box 6.8, it can be used to reveal the ways in which certain 'self-imposed' disciplinary practices, which burden women more than men, can be the product of domination. Furthermore, according to Judith Butler, Foucault's idea of power/knowledge can also be used to radically destabilise the basic categories associated with both gender and biological sex. She thinks that this is an essential task, since 'feminist critique ought ... to understand how the category of "women," the subject of feminism, is produced and restrained by the very structures of power through which emancipation is sought' (Butler, 1990, p. 2). One of Butler's most influential arguments is that because the categories of 'woman' and 'women' are problematic, it is a mistake for feminists to insist that 'women' are a definable group with shared interests, because in doing so they perform 'an unwitting regulation and reification of gender relations' (1990, p. 7).

> ## BOX 6.8 FEMINISM AND
> ## SELF-SURVEILLANCE
>
> According to Foucault, surveillance is a form of disciplinary power that can be 'exercised continuously and for what turns out to be minimal cost':
>
> > There is no need for arms, physical violence, material constraints. Just a gaze. An inspecting gaze, a gaze which each individual under its weight will end by interiorisation to the point that he is his own overseer, each individual thus exercising this surveillance over, and against, himself. (Foucault, 1980, p. 155)
>
> As a number of feminist scholars have observed, self-surveillance might be a gendered practice, as it is manifested in ways that apply to women but not to men. For example, according to Sandra Bartky:
>
> > The woman who checks her make-up half a dozen times a day to see if her foundation has caked or her mascara run, who worries that the wind or rain may spoil her hairdo, who looks frequently to see if her stockings have bagged at the ankle, or who, feeling fat, monitors everything she eats, has become, just as surely as the inmate in the Panopticon, a self-policing subject, a self committed to relentless self-surveillance. (1990, p. 80)
>
> Thus, although surveillance has the effect of policing all subjects – men and women – it might play a special role in sustaining inequalities of gender, since 'it is women who practice this discipline on and against their own bodies [whilst] men get off scot-free' (Bartky, 1990, p. 80).
>
> *Is self-surveillance a gendered form of domination?*

To make this case, Butler proceeds from the assumption, endorsed widely by feminists and others, that gender is a product of society. At its most basic, this implies that our ideas about women and men derive from customs and power relations, and not from anything that is rooted in nature. Butler's initial twist on this argument is to argue that since gender is artificial, then there is no necessary reason for there to be two (rather than three, or more) gender identities. She then makes an additional – and more radical – move, which is to argue that differences of biological sex, just as much as differences of gender, are the product of power and society. To support this view, she refers to Foucault's own work on hermaphrodites, which reveals how expert categorisation of people into distinctive biological sexes can act as a form of disciplinary power, ushering each individual into a box. On the basis of this, Butler argues that the body itself is constituted by power, which means both that bodies are shaped by social norms, and that the division between the sexes is a product of human artifice. As such, Butler appeals to Foucault to extend the traditional feminist argument that gender is a social construct to incorporate the more radical claim that biological sex is also a social construct. On this view, biological differences between 'men' and 'women' are no less the product of power than gender differences.

However, not all feminists have embraced Foucault's conception of power. Often, the origins of feminist criticisms of Foucault are to be found in a wider antipathy about poststructuralism. Stated in very general terms, the crux of this objection is that whilst feminism entails a clear and unequivocal moral condemnation of patriarchy, poststructuralism intentionally disrupts and undermines the standards according to which such a condemnation might proceed. Here we will focus on two variants of this objection. Whilst the first suggests that Foucault's approach cannot distinguish between better and worse forms of domination, the second suggests that Foucault's theoretical commitments imply an antifeminist form of political quietism.

The first version of the objection is that because Foucault assumes that the constraining and constitutive effects of power are ubiquitous, his approach is incapable of discriminating amongst innocent, praiseworthy and objectionable usages of power. Central to this line of argument is Foucault's ambivalence about normative arguments, reflected in his reluctance to specify what alterations should be made to society in order to make it more just, or equal, or free. According to Nancy Fraser, this reluctance means that Foucault is unable to explain why domination ought to be resisted, since '[o]nly with the introduction of normative notions could he begin to tell us what is wrong with the modern power/knowledge regime' (Fraser, 1989, p. 29). Some feminist scholars go further than Fraser, arguing that Foucault's approach actually reinforces inequalities of gender. For example, Nancy Hartstock argues that 'poststructuralist theories such as those put forward by Michel Foucault fail to provide a theory of power for women' (1990, p. 158). Hartstock's worry is that Foucault's emphasis on discourses and disciplinary techniques leads him to adopt the perspective of the dominator rather than the dominated. But this is problematic, since 'domination, viewed from above, is more likely to look like equality' (Hartstock, 1990, p. 168).

The second version of the objection is that Foucault's vision of politics undermines emancipatory forms of political action by encouraging passivity and an acceptance of existing affairs. For example, both Linda Alcoff (1990) and Seyla Benhabib (1992) have suggested that Foucault's theory of power delivers an impoverished account of agency and resistance, since it suggests that subjects are the product of a particular regime of power/knowledge from which they are incapable of standing apart. As Benhabib puts it, for Foucault 'there is no history of the victims but only a history of the construction of victimisation ... for Foucault every act of resistance is but another manifestation of an omnipresent discourse-power complex' (Benhabib, 1995, pp. 113–14).

Martha Nussbaum has registered a similar criticism of Butler's extension of Foucault's ideas, arguing that they offer only a 'narrow vision of the possibilities for change' (2012, p. 207). On Nussbaum's reading, the message of Butler's writings is to warn her readers 'that the dream of escaping altogether from the oppressive structures is just a dream: it is within the oppressive structures that we must find little spaces for resistance, and this resistance cannot hope to change the overall situation' (Nussbaum, 2012, p. 210). Even to the extent that Butler believes that resistance to inequality and oppression is possible, it is of a decidedly minimalist form. For example, her preferred form of resistance to socially imposed gender and sexual identities is to disrupt dominant identities through subversive and parodic performances of sex and gender (for instance, through drag), but she accepts that these can 'never destabilise the larger system' (Nussbaum, 2012, p. 206). Nussbaum identifies at least two further difficulties with Butler's conception of political resistance as parodic performance. First, it offers little to women whose lives are marked by severe oppression and disadvantage. This is because for 'women who are hungry, illiterate, disenfranchised, beaten, raped, it is not sexy or liberating to reenact, however parodically, the conditions of hunger, illiteracy, disenfranchisement, beating, and rape' (Nussbaum, 2012, pp. 211–12). Second, Butler's poststructuralist reluctance to invoke normative standards potentially leaves her unable to criticise parodic performances that are motivated by antifeminist goals, such as students engaging in 'subversive performances of making fun of feminist remarks in class, or ripping down the posters of the lesbian and gay law students' association' (Nussbaum, 2012, p. 209). If Nussbaum is right, then embracing Foucault's conception of power to its fullest extent, as Butler purports to be doing, seems to leave feminists with at best a passive model of political change, and at worst with an amoral quietism.

Future challenges

An important insight yielded by Foucault's theory of power is that intellectual and scientific concepts and categories are productive because they constitute and shape our identities and lived experiences. As can be seen in Box 6.9, some scholars have employed this theory to argue that some academic discourses and ways of knowing might be implicated in subtle forms of domination. Interestingly, some postcolonial scholars have recently suggested that the practices and concepts of political theory might themselves be implicated in this kind of domination. This poses an important challenge for political theorists, and by way of a conclusion we will explore some of its different dimensions and compare two responses that have been given to it.

One way in which political theory might be implicated in domination is because ideas and authors from Europe and North America are more likely to acquire canonical status, thereby marginalising non-Western discourses and traditions. For example, ideas associated with the 'West' often appear 'natural' and 'commonsensical', even for scholars from other countries, and local discourses and traditions risk becoming relegated to a subaltern status. Dipesh Chakrabarty gives the following example to illustrate this phenomenon:

BOX 6.9   POWER/KNOWLEDGE AND ORIENTALISM

In his path-breaking book *Orientalism*, Edward Said applied ideas derived from Foucault to argue that 'Orientalism', as a body of knowledge, reproduces the subordination of formerly colonial peoples. On Said's account, Orientalism is not only a collection of academic studies, but is also a 'style of thought' based on a binary distinction between the 'Orient' and the 'Occident'. One effect of this discourse is that it enables Europe to define itself in relation to its 'other': '[t]he Oriental is irrational, depraved (fallen), childlike, "different"; thus the European is rational, virtuous, mature, "normal"' (Said, 1979, p. 40). Following Foucault, Said drew attention to the relationship between power and knowledge, arguing that Western 'knowledge' of the Orient was implicated in the project of dominating it, and that the effects of power/knowledge persisted long after former colonial powers withdrew. Thus, he describes Orientalism as a persistent manifestation of domineering authority, arguing that it is 'formed, irradiated, disseminated; it is instrumental, it is persuasive; it has status, it establishes canons of taste and value; it is virtually indistinguishable from certain ideas it dignifies as true, and from traditions, perceptions, and judgments it forms, transmits, reproduces' (1979, p. 20). Overall, Said depicts Orientalism as a way of 'dealing with the Orient – dealing with it by making statements about it, authorising views of it, describing it, by teaching it, settling it, ruling over it: in short, Orientalism [is] a Western style for dominating, restructuring, and having authority over the Orient' (Said, 1979, pp. 2–3).

What does it mean to describe Orientalism as a form of power that is both constraining and constitutive? Is this claim convincing?

Faced with the task of analyzing developments or social practices in modern India, few if any Indian social scientists or social scientists of India would argue seriously with, say, the thirteenth-century logician Gangesa or with the grammarian and linguistic philosopher Bartrihari (fifth to sixth centuries), or with the tenth- or eleventh-century aesthetician Abhinavagupta. Sad though it is, one result of European colonial rule in South Asia is that the intellectual traditions once unbroken and alive in Sanskrit or Persian or Arabic are now only matters of historical research for most – perhaps all – modern social scientists in the region. They treat these traditions as truly dead, as history … And yet past European thinkers and their categories are never quite dead for us in the same way. South Asian(ist) social scientists would argue passionately with a Marx or a Weber without feeling any need to historicize them or to place them in their European intellectual contexts. (2007, pp. 6–7)

Moreover, even when they are not neglected, non-Western traditions are often treated in a glib or superficial way that reinforces prevailing ideological assumptions about the 'clash of civilisations'. For example, Islamic and Confucian ideas are often branded as illiberal, anti-democratic and irrational, using terms of reference that derive from self-ascribed ideals of the 'West'. Not only do crude caricatures like these essentialise cultures, treating complex traditions as mono-lithic entities, but they arguably sustain colonial assumptions about the cultural, political and intellectual superiority of the 'West'. Furthermore, non-Western contributions to ostensibly 'Western' political traditions are often constitutively excluded from narratives about their origins and development. An example of this tendency has been identified by Michel-Rolph Trouillot, who notes that the ideals of freedom and universal citizenship are typically associated with the French and American revolutions, but not with the Haitian Revolution (Trouillot, 1995).

Another way in which political theory might be implicated in domination is if hegemonic ideals and standards confine political possibilities, thereby frustrating the self-determination of people to whom they are inappropriately applied. Historically, many European political theorists were acutely aware of the difficulties of applying their ideals to non-Western political societies. For example, and with no small dose of hypocrisy, British liberals in the nineteenth century argued that colonial subjects should be ruled from above, and that their own values of freedom and democracy should be reserved for societies in a full state of maturity (Mehta, 1999). Meanwhile, postcolonial theorists emphasise that decolonisation did not displace the hegemonic status of Western political ideas, which were inherited by the constitutional orders of the newly independent states seeking to realise the values and principles that they had been denied. According to Partha Chatterjee, the hegemonic status of Western ideals creates anomalies in postcolonial societies, which experience distinctive circumstances and challenges of their own (Chatterjee, 2013, p. 84). For example, the Indian constitution formally guarantees equal citizenship for all, and in that respect it simply applies the 'Western' norm. However, the practice of citizenship devi-ates from this, since scheduled castes and tribes are guaranteed various special educational and political rights. As we saw in Chapter 2, this is a form of 'differ-entiated citizenship', and we are inclined to characterise it as an exception to the norm of unitary citizenship (whether or not we think it is justified). However, we might just as conceivably regard the unitary citizenship norm as flawed, or standing in need of redefinition, or inappropriate for the case at hand. The fact that this thought does not come naturally, both within India and outside, reflects both the hegemonic status of one ideal of citizenship and the way in which this norm potentially serves to constrain political possibilities.

The gist of one response to these challenges, favoured by some anticolonial nationalists as well as some religious fundamentalists, is that subaltern peoples need to liberate themselves from the domineering influence of Western political ideals. This typically involves doing two things: reaching back into indigenous traditions to rediscover local principles and ideals, and purifying indigenous intellectual culture by ridding it of foreign elements. In effect, this is a 'protective' strategy that extends the border-guarding model of multiculturalism we discussed in Chapter 2. However, critics point out that a 'pure' culture, uncontaminated by colonial influences, is an elusive fiction, since colonial identities are 'hybrid' identities, situated ambivalently between the identities of both the coloniser and the colonised (Bhabha, 1994). If this is right, then 'Western' ideals are not foreign to postcolonial societies, but are already part of their complex and multifaceted intellectual traditions.

A different solution is to reconsider the practice of political theory itself. According to proponents of 'comparative political theory' – such as Fred Dallmayr, Roxanne Euben, Brooke Ackerly and Andrew March – political theorists should self-consciously engage with a wider diversity of intellectual traditions. Minimally, this would involve expanding the range of thinkers and texts taught in political theory courses and studied by professional political theorists. More strongly, it might also involve 'crosscultural encounters, mutual learning, and (what has been called) "dialogue among civilizations"' (Dallmayr, quoted in March, 2009, p. 542). A more widespread adoption of a comparative approach to political theory might bring at least three different kinds of benefits.

First, it might be philosophically enriching, since comparing the different approaches that have been taken to the 'universal' challenges of living together could reveal new and important insights and possibilities. For example, Brooke Ackerly (2005) argues that Confucian thought contains distinctive formulations of the principles of democracy and political equality. This suggests that the connection between liberalism and democracy may not be as close as many Western political theorists believe. Thus, by demonstrating that a non-liberal form of democracy is intellectually coherent, a comparative form of political theory can help us to more fully grasp the idea of democracy.

Second, a comparative approach could unsettle the assumed intellectual hierarchies that implicitly divide 'the West' from 'the rest', and which constitute an important part of political theory's postcolonial legacy. For instance, if political theorists engaged in a genuine dialogue with other traditions, in which they sought to grasp the ideas of non-Western thinkers on their own terms, then this would displace the Eurocentric focus of political theory by introducing new substantive concerns and methods. As Fred Dallmayr observes, this might be challenging for many political theorists, since 'the Western practitioner of political theory/philosophy must relinquish the role of universal teacher (buttressed by Western hegemony) and be content with that of fellow student in a crosscultural learning experience' (Dallmayr, 1999, p. 422). Nevertheless, a reorientation along these lines might be necessary, given the emergence of globalisation, because 'one segment of the world's population cannot monopolize the language or idiom of the emerging "village," or global civil society' (Dallmayr, 2004, p. 249).

Third, a comparative approach to political theory could also 'demystify the divide between contemporary Western standards and the views or practices of a non-Western tradition' (March, 2009, p. 542). For example, a comparative political theory could undermine the assumption that rigorous and careful thinking about politics is an exclusive privilege of the 'West'. Similarly, it might reveal the ways in which non-Western ideas are less alien than they might initially appear. For example, closer inspection often reveals that there are important similarities underlying apparently different intellectual traditions (Parel and Ketih, 1992). In addition to revealing that non-Western traditions contain points of familiarity as well as unfamiliarity, locating points of overlap might also play an important role in justifying support for some basic political values, such as human rights, and this is a possibility to which we will return in Chapter 10.

7

Freedom

Introduction

In 1958, the political theorist and historian of ideas Isaiah Berlin gave an Inaugural Lecture at the University of Oxford, which was subsequently published as an essay entitled 'Two Concepts of Liberty'. Almost certainly the most influential English-language essay in twentieth-century political thought, it continues to be included in nearly every philosophical anthology that touches on the topics of freedom or liberty (in this chapter we will use these two terms interchangeably). Berlin was addressing a difficult and persistent puzzle about the multiple and often contradictory purposes to which these terms can be put, which will also serve as our starting point here. For example, sometimes we speak of people being unfree to dine at a fine restaurant because they cannot afford to do so, or being free to publish a novel or to give up smoking because no one is stopping them from doing so. In different contexts, we might say that democratic citizens are free in a way that subjects of dictators cannot be, or that a people can become free by throwing off their colonial masters. Furthermore, some social and political theorists associate structural inequalities, such as patriarchy or racism, with unfreedom, arguing that oppressed people can only become free if those structures are reformed or abolished. In all of these cases, and in the many others that we use on a regular basis, it seems unlikely that the word 'freedom' signifies the same thing. This raises an obvious question: what is it that we mean when we invoke the concept of freedom?

For Berlin's audience during the Cold War, the most timely example of this puzzle was found in the competing claims then being made by radically different societies to be the true defenders of liberty. Such claims were advanced not only by liberal and democratic states in North America and Western Europe, but also by authoritarian and totalitarian ones, such as Stalin's Soviet Union. One way to explain this puzzle is to say that one side or the other was mistaken about the nature of liberty, or to say that their claim to uphold liberty was deceptive or manipulative. However, even if these solutions might have satisfied some of the Cold War ideologues, they would still leave us with a number of unresolved cases in which the term liberty is used in conflicting and contradictory ways. Berlin's contribution was to identify two different interpretations of liberty, which he labelled 'positive' and 'negative' conceptions (these terms were taken from an earlier liberal philosopher called T. H. Green). Berlin's positive conception of freedom is positive not in the sense of being praiseworthy, but rather in the sense of involving the presence of self-control or self-mastery. As he put it, '[t]he "positive" sense of the word "liberty" derives from the wish on the part of the individual to be his own master' (Berlin, 2002, p. 178). Meanwhile, the negative conception of freedom is negative in the sense of it involving the absence of impediments. Although Berlin did not explicitly argue that these two conceptions of liberty mapped directly onto the Cold War divisions, the thrust of his essay, combined with his other writings, suggests that he intended to motivate scepticism about the positive conception of liberty and to reveal the various ways in which it might lend itself to an authoritarian and perhaps totalitarian political morality.

The most straightforward way to grasp Berlin's distinction is to think of the two conceptions as ways of responding to different kinds of questions about freedom. On the one hand, negative liberty is involved in the answer to the question 'What is the area within which the subject – a person or group of persons – is or should be left to do or be what he is able to do or be, without interference by other persons?' (Berlin, 2002, p. 169). Thus, a person or a group is negatively free to the extent that they have opportunities which are not impeded by another person or group. On the other hand, positive liberty is involved in the answer to the question 'What, or who, is the source of control or interference that can determine someone to do, or be, this rather than that?' (Berlin, 2002, p. 169). Thus, a person or a group is positively free to the extent that they are self-governing, or to the extent that they can achieve things that amount to their self-determination. A key difference between the two views is that the theorist of positive liberty connects freedom to something like self-mastery or the realisation of one's potential or the expression of one's nature, whilst the theorist of negative liberty connects it to the absence of external obstacles and impediments. One simple illustration of this distinction is that I might simultaneously be negatively free to smoke if I may do so unimpeded *and* positively unfree if I am a slave to my addiction to nicotine.

One reason why Berlin's essay has attracted controversy is that it can be read in at least two different ways, and can therefore be evaluated according to different, and similarly demanding, sets of standards. For instance, the essay might be read as a contribution to the history of ideas, which was Berlin's own stated profession. Indeed, in the course of the essay, and often without much in the way of supporting evidence, Berlin attributes a negative view of freedom to thinkers as various as Occam, Erasmus, Hobbes, Locke, Bentham, Constant, Tocqueville, Jefferson, Burke and Paine, and a positive view to Plato, Epictetus, Montesquieu, Spinoza, Kant, Herder, Rousseau, Hegel, Fichte, Marx, Bukharin, Comte and Green. If we were to evaluate Berlin's essay from the perspective of an intellectual historian, then we would need to ask detailed and careful questions about how each of these thinkers conceived of freedom, what they share in common, and what distinguishes them. Much subsequent scholarship has addressed the question of whether Berlin's interpretations of various historical political thinkers are fair and accurate. Importantly, as we shall see below, a number of historians have taken Berlin to task for failing to appreciate a 'third' conception of liberty, developed most thoroughly in the writings of republican political theorists (Skinner, 1998, 2002). This understanding does not associate freedom with the absence of obstacles, or with the attainment of self-mastery, but rather with absence of domination. On this account, a person is unfree if they are subject to the arbitrary power of another, in the way that a slave is to the will of their master, or a subject is to the will of an absolute monarch.

A different way to read Berlin's essay is as an exercise in conceptual analysis, and this is how we shall approach it. On this approach, what really matters is whether Berlin's distinction enhances our philosophical understanding of freedom itself. Frustratingly, Berlin's initial formulation of the two conceptions was not as clear as it might have been. Indeed, according to one influential account, the distinction does not even hold up as a distinction, and the two different views ultimately collapse into a single 'triadic' concept of liberty (MacCallum, 1967). Nevertheless, in this chapter we shall treat the different views of freedom as genuine rivals, focussing on how subsequent political theorists have developed them and paying special attention to some of the difficulties they encounter. Thus, in the 'rival perspectives' part of the chapter we will explore the negative, positive and republican conceptions of liberty, which are summarised in Table 7.1. Then, in the 'key debates' section we will address three questions about the value of freedom, exploring some of the ways in which different conceptions of freedom generate contrasting answers to important political questions. First, we will examine the relationship between freedom and poverty, asking whether poverty relief programmes can be justified in the name of freedom. Second, we will explore the relationship between freedom and democracy, looking at some of the different ways in which proponents of the rival perspectives have connected the two values. Third, we will turn to a question that has been prominent in many of the debates surrounding multiculturalism (see Chapter 2), which concerns whether promoting the freedom

Table 7.1 Summary of rival perspectives on freedom

	Negative	Positive	Republican
Basic manifestations	Absence of obstacles imposed by others	Self-mastery; personal or political autonomy	Absence of domination
Type	Opportunity concept – freedom is being 'unprevented' from being and doing things	Exercise concept – freedom is doing and being things	Status concept – freedom is not being subject to the arbitrary will of another
Freedom constraints	Actual external interferences, sometimes understood narrowly to include physical obstacles only; 'impure' versions also include threats and laws	Can be both internal and external; internal constraints may be the result of external circumstances	Potential external interferences, understood broadly
Conditions for freedom	Absence of coercion	Appropriate social, political, economic, cultural and psychological circumstances	Independence, and being empowered to 'check' domination
Democracy	Democracy is not necessary for freedom, and may threaten it	Democracy is necessary for 'political autonomy', which may be 'co-original' with 'private autonomy'	Democracy protects freedom, and may be necessary for it

of members of cultural minorities requires subsidising, protecting or promoting their cultural identities. Finally, we will close the chapter by considering some different implications of our three rival perspectives for the ethics of international society.

Rival perspectives

Negative freedom

Accounts of negative freedom have mostly been propounded by liberals, such as David Miller and Ronald Dworkin, and by libertarians, such as Robert Nozick and Hillel Steiner. As we shall see, the disagreements amongst these theorists are just as significant as those which divide the negative, positive and republican camps. In particular, proponents of this view disagree about the concept and value of liberty, and about how it relates to other political concepts, such as justice and equality. In this section we will begin by discussing negative freedom in very general terms, before examining its complex relationship with coercion. During the key debates, we will explore its relationship with economic inequality and democracy.

Let us begin with the idea that freedom has to do with the absence of external impediments, which is endorsed in some form or another by all proponents of negative liberty. Berlin captures this as follows:

> I am normally said to be free to the degree to which no man or body of men interferes with my activity. Political liberty in this sense is simply the area within which a man can act unobstructed by others. (2002, p. 169)

As such, the extent of a person's negative liberty can be revealed by asking how far others interfere with them, and the less someone is interfered with the greater their freedom. One implication of this view is that being unable to do something does not imply that one is unfree to do that thing, as there is a difference between possessing an ability and having a freedom. Thus, although I might be unable to understand string theory or play the accordion, I am not unfree to do so. A further – and more controversial – implication is that being unable to afford to do something, such as attend university or eat in a fine restaurant, does not imply that a person is unfree to do that thing. However, as we shall see during the first key debate, some left-wing political theorists have questioned this, arguing that a lack of money can make a person negatively unfree.

As Berlin initially formulated the idea, negative liberty is frustrated only when people are prevented from doing what they *desire* to do. Thus, a law that prohibits dancing does not intrude on the negative liberty of people who do not like to dance. However, this way of defining negative liberty seems to invite two unwelcome implications. First, it counterintuitively suggests that contented slaves – who desire to do whatever their master asks of them – are free, since they are not prevented from doing what they desire. Second, it implies that a person could be made less unfree by suppressing their desires, since people whose desires are frustrated could liberate themselves by adapting their preferences or lowering their horizons. But as Berlin later pointed out, 'to teach a man that, if he cannot get what he wants, he must learn to want only what he can get may contribute to his happiness or his security; but it will not increase his civil or political freedom' (2002, p. 32). In response to these difficulties, Berlin reformulated his conception of negative liberty, and in a subsequent introduction to his essay he summarised his mature view as follows:

> The sense of freedom in which I use this term entails not simply the absence of frustration (which may be obtained by killing desires), but the absence of obstacles to possible choices and activities – the absence of obstructions on roads which a man can decide to walk. Such freedom ultimately depends not on whether I wish to walk at all, but on how many doors are open, how open they are, and upon their relative importance in my life, even though it may be impossible, literally to measure this is any quantitative fashion. (Berlin, 2002, p. 32)

As a result of modifying his original view, Berlin's mature position is that negative freedom is about having unimpeded options, and not about being able to do what one wants to do.

According to Charles Taylor, negative liberty is an 'opportunity concept' of freedom, since it suggests that 'being free is a matter of what we can do, of what it is open to us to do, whether or not we do anything to exercise these options' (1985, p. 213). A difficulty with treating liberty as an 'opportunity concept', according to Taylor, is that it leaves us unable to discriminate amongst greater and lesser invasions of freedom. As discussed in Box 7.1, Taylor compared the installation of a new traffic light system with a law that prohibits religious freedom. On his analysis, the proponent of negative liberty should regard both as infringements of freedom, since they both close doors that were previously open. Furthermore, if the traffic light system closes more doors than the law that prohibits religious freedom, then it looks as though the proponent of negative liberty ought to conclude that it is a greater affront to liberty. The problem here, according to Taylor, is that an opportunity concept of freedom cannot make sense of qualitative differences amongst constraints on freedom if it lacks 'a background understanding that certain goals and activities are more significant than others' (Taylor, 1985, p. 218). Perhaps this objection is overstated, since as we saw, Berlin explicitly says that negative liberty depends not only on 'how many doors are open [and] how open they are', but also on 'their relative importance in my life'. Nevertheless, Berlin does not supply explicit guidance about how we can distinguish relatively important and relatively trivial options, and – as we shall see – is sceptical about attempts to prescribe answers to such questions.

BOX 7.1   NEGATIVE FREEDOM AND THE DIABOLICAL DEFENCE

In 1979, when Albania had banned the preaching of religion, Charles Taylor asked his readers to '[c]onsider the following diabolical defence of Albania as a free country':

> We recognize that religion has been abolished in Albania, whereas it hasn't been in Britain. But on the other hand there are probably far fewer traffic lights per head in Tirana than in London ... Suppose an apologist for Albanian socialism were nevertheless to claim that his country was freer than Britain, because the number of acts restricted was far smaller. After all, only a minority of Londoners practise some religion in public places, but all have to negotiate their way through traffic. Those who do practise a religion generally do so on one day of the week, while they are held up at traffic lights every day. In sheer quantitative terms, the number of acts restricted by traffic lights must be greater than that restricted by a ban on public religious practice. So if Britain is considered a free society, why not Albania? (Taylor, 1985, p. 219)

Must proponents of negative liberty accept that Albania was freer than Britain?

Another ambiguity in Berlin's initial formulation of negative liberty has to do with whether the absence of interference is a sufficient condition for freedom. In his original essay, Berlin summarised his view by saying that 'by being free I mean not being interfered with' (Berlin, 2002, p. 170). Read literally, this might mean that a person could be made unfree by a boulder that obstructed their intended path, or by a debilitating illness that left them unable to leave their house, since both are obstructions that block particular options. However, Berlin's view is that liberty is a *social* relation; that is to say, a relationship between persons (see also Nozick, 1974, p. 262; Steiner, 1994, p. 8). If liberty is a social relation, then a person can only be made negatively unfree by the interferences of other people and their freedom will be unaffected by boulders and illnesses. Meanwhile, the same person could be made negatively unfree by an angry neighbour who blocks their way or by a thief who steals their car. On the face of things, it might seem peculiar to discriminate between the boulder and the neighbour, or between the illness and the thief, since they could have the same overall result on the options that are available to someone. However, the crucial difference is that the neighbour and the thief – but not the boulder or the illness – act coercively, as they intentionally frustrate the activities of another person. Consequently, one way to characterise the idea of negative liberty is to say that people are made unfree when they are coercively interfered with by other people in ways that reduce the options available to them.

Although this formulation of negative liberty has greater precision than our starting point, it contains another ambiguity about what qualifies as coercive interference. Most proponents of negative liberty, including Berlin, believe that negative liberty can be undermined by threats as well as by physical force. However, some philosophers, such as Steiner, insist that threats are not – properly speaking – a form of freedom-undermining coercion, since people can resist them. For example, consider Janet, whose angry neighbour attempts to impede her journey into the local town by blackmailing her. If her neighbour succeeds, causing Janet to alter her plans, they must exercise power over her in Dahl's sense; that is to say, by getting Janet to do something that she would not otherwise do (see Chapter 6). In support of Berlin's view, it seems plausible to say that successful blackmail threats have freedom-undermining effects, as they apparently close doors that would otherwise be open. Meanwhile, in support of Steiner's view, it also seems plausible to say that Janet could have accepted that going to town carried the risk of her secrets being exposed, but did not undermine her freedom, because she nevertheless could have done so.

Let us look more closely at Steiner's view. On his account, 'a person is unfree to do an action if, and only if, his doing that action is rendered impossible by the action of another person' (Steiner, 1994, p. 8). The phrase 'rendered impossible' indicates that this is a strict view, according to which the freedom to do something is extinguished only if another person makes it physically impossible to do that thing. As we have seen, threats do not make actions physically impossible but rather aim to alter the intentions of an actor. Consequently, they do not make people unfree according to Steiner. One point worth noting about Steiner's view is that it seems to be consistent with Berlin's mature view that negative freedom is about having options rather than being able to do what one desires. By contrast, the opposite view – that threats can make people unfree by getting them to change their intentions – seems to presuppose that freedom has something to do with being able to do what one (really) desires, which is a thesis supposedly repudiated by the mature Berlin.

To further support his claim that threats do not make people unfree, Steiner draws attention to their similarity with offers, noting that both are 'interventions by others in persons' practical deliberations' that 'are intended by their authors to influence how their recipients act' (Steiner, 1994, p. 22). Threats and offers are similar to one another in the sense that acceding to them 'promises to make their recipients better off than not doing so' (1994, p. 23). Moreover, according to Steiner, 'it is not necessarily true that offers are more resistable or exert less influence than threats' (1975, p. 40). Suppose, for example, that instead of threatening Janet, her neighbour had offered her a large sum of money to stay at home. If the offer was generous enough, then a bribe might have as similarly powerful an effect on Janet's deliberations as a blackmail threat. In any case, Steiner's point is that threats (and offers) operate by altering the incentives faced by an actor, making some options more or less desirable than they might otherwise be. On his account, both might alter the opportunities available to someone, but they do not make that person unfree, since they do not make it physically impossible to carry out any particular course of action. In other words, threats and offers do not undermine freedom, as they are not coercive in the strict sense.

One surprising implication of Steiner's view is that draconian laws do not really make us unfree, but merely attach negative sanctions to possible courses of action. As Steiner puts it, '[t]he existence of an invariably enforced legal rule prohibiting the doing of B does not imply that persons subject to it are unfree to do B' (Steiner, 1994, p. 32). For instance, suppose that a law is enacted to the effect that people who wear red clothing are to be fined for doing so. On Steiner's account, such a law does not make subjects unfree to wear red clothes, but rather makes a preference for red clothing an expensive taste. Likewise, a law that prohibits murder does not make its subjects unfree to kill one another, even if it does make murder an option that is publicly known to carry punitive sanctions. The underlying intuition that drives Steiner's analysis here is that any descriptively accurate conception of liberty must account for the thought that 'persons are free to do what they actually do' (Steiner, 1994, p. 8). Consequently, Steiner's conception of negative liberty is 'pure' in the sense that it is 'purely descriptive' and lacks evaluative (or moral) content. As such, it is not an implication of his view that Janet being free to journey into town, people being free to wear red, or murderers being free to murder, are good or valuable or desirable states of affairs.

Steiner's view strikes many readers as peculiar. If a conception of negative freedom is to incorporate the intuition that draconian laws reduce liberty, then it will need to show that freedom can be compromised by interventions which alter the desirability of courses of action. However, it will not do for the theorist of negative liberty to argue that any action which renders an option less desirable reduces freedom, since that would capture too much. For example, suppose that my nemesis is dining in my favourite restaurant, thereby making it less desirable for me to dine there too. It would seem strange to say that in doing so they make me unfree. One solution to this problem, suggested by Nozick, is to argue that only some kinds of intervention are coercive, and that this cannot be said of choices of individuals who are acting 'within their rights' (1974, p. 262). Unlike Steiner, Nozick does think that at least some laws and threats can coerce people, thereby making them negatively unfree, and on his account a person is coerced when someone else restricts the options available to them in such a way that violates their rights. For example, if my nemesis knew that I could not stand to be in the same room as them and intended to prevent me from dining in my favourite restaurant by arriving there 30 minutes before I did, then Nozick should conclude that they did not coerce me, since they were acting within their rights. By contrast, if they were to threaten to kill me for eating in 'their' restaurant, then that would be coercive, because they do not have a right to do so.

Nozick and Steiner endorse rival conceptions of coercion, which in turn suggest different conceptions of negative liberty. For example, on Nozick's account, a thief is not free to enter my house if they lack a (moral) right to do so. Meanwhile, on Steiner's account, the same thief is free to enter my house if they are physically able to do so. Both views seem intuitively plausible and are consistent with ordinary language, even though they contradict one another. One feature of Nozick's view, which is not shared by Steiner's, is that negative freedom depends on an understanding of the proper content of (moral) rights, since liberty is restricted only when others stop you from doing things that you have a right to do. Hence, Nozick's account of negative liberty has been described as 'moralised' (Cohen, 1995, p. 66). A peculiarity of this is that it implies that it would be a mistake to describe a justly imprisoned prisoner as unfree, because their imprisonment does not violate their rights (Cohen, 1995, pp. 59–60). Moreover, as we shall see in Chapter 9, Nozick's own conception of rights has been criticised extensively, since he does not believe that extreme poverty necessarily violates rights. For example, one implication of Nozick's view, which we shall return to during the first key debate in this chapter, is that having an extremely restricted set of opportunities as a result of poverty does not itself restrict freedom, provided that one's poverty is not the result of a rights violation.

Positive freedom

The positive conception of liberty encompasses an even wider range of views than the negative conception. Amongst contemporary political theorists, it has been endorsed by liberals such as John Christman, Joseph Raz and Will Kymlicka, by socialists such as Carol Gould, by communitarians such as Charles Taylor and Michael Sandel, and by participatory democrats such as Benjamin Barber. Often, as we shall see, sympathy for the positive conception emerges from either conceptual or normative dissatisfaction with the negative conception. Here we will focus on two strands within this tradition, one that connects the idea of freedom to individual autonomy and another than connects it to political autonomy.

The individual autonomy strand of positive liberty has been defended by Taylor and Christman. On this view, free agents must exercise control over their lives. Thus, '[t]he free person must be guided by values that are [their] own' (Christman, 1991, p. 345) and 'one is free only to the extent that one has effectively determined oneself and the shape of one's life' (Taylor, 1985, p. 213). Importantly, proponents disagree with the assumption, made by advocates of negative liberty, that constraints on freedom must be 'external'. For example, even though Steiner, Nozick and Berlin disagree about what kinds of interferences frustrate negative freedom, they all agree that only the interferences of other people count. By contrast, both Taylor and Christman argue that people can also be made unfree by 'internal' constraints, such as fears, desires and addictions. These can undermine freedom because they can have the effect of preventing people from becoming effective masters of themselves, or living authentically, as when someone's fear of public speaking hampers their career, or when a smoker is a slave to their addiction.

Internal constraints are complicated and multifaceted. As illustrated in Box 7.2, sometimes they are the result of external factors, such as being socialised under oppressive conditions. In other cases, their origins may be obscure. Although sometimes we are not aware of internal constraints, sometimes we are, in which case we might experience them as unwelcome obstacles. For example, an alcoholic might believe their addiction to be a fetter, and an aspiring politician might welcome the opportunity to rid themselves of a fear of public speaking. But sometimes an internal constraint, whether or not it is known to us, can be an authentic aspect of our character. For example, someone with a powerful desire to become a successful entrepreneur might willingly accept that pursuing their ambitions could jeopardise their social life. Whilst the alcoholic and the aspiring politician understood their addictions and fears as unwelcome and regrettable, the entrepreneur might understand their career aspirations to be an acceptable obstacle to achieving other goals. For them, it would be wrong to say that overcoming this internal constraint would make them free. According to Taylor, one difference between the three scenarios is that an addiction to alcohol and a fear of public speaking are brute desires, whilst the entrepreneur's desires are 'import-attributing', since they are bound up with their identity (1985, p. 224). Often, 'import-attributing' desires are not experienced as constraints on freedom, since they are part of who we are. Sometimes, however, 'import-attributing'

BOX 7.2 POSITIVE FREEDOM AND INTERNAL CONSTRAINTS

Imagine ... a woman who is raised in a culture which fiercely inculcates in her the idea that women should never aspire to be anything but subservient and humble domestic companions to their husbands, no matter how unhappy this makes them or how abusive their husbands are. Imagine further that this person is suddenly placed in a new culture where opportunities abound for women to pursue independent activities. She nevertheless shuns these opportunities and remains married to an oppressive husband from the old culture. The only 'restraint' she faces (to pursuing the opportunities for an independent life-style) are her desires themselves (which remain the sort she was taught to have). She simply does not wish to act in any other way, turning a deaf ear to the reasons people give her to consider a less subservient posture. (Imagine that her husband abuses her but tells her she can leave him any time she wants, and she continues to want to stay.) (Christman, 1991, pp. 344–5)

The woman in this example has at least one negative freedom, since her oppressive and abusive husband does not block the option of exiting her marriage. Meanwhile, the positive conception concludes that she is unfree, as her character and values are not fully 'her own'. On Christman's reading, the negative conception is inadequate for explaining the nature of her unfreedom, since 'the presence of opportunities – the absence of restraints – is irrelevant' (1991, p. 345).

Which conception of freedom can better tell us whether the woman is free or unfree?

desires can be experienced as undermining freedom. For example, suppose that our entrepreneur later comes to believe that they had initially been mistaken about their priorities, and that their social life was more important than they had earlier believed. Now they think that pursuing their career at the expense of nurturing relationships with others was a mistake, leaving them less fulfilled than they would otherwise have been. Is there any way for us to tell whether the entrepreneur's later views are more accurate than their earlier ones?

One answer, suggested by Taylor, is that a desire is a fetter when it is experienced as alien, as not expressive of our personality (Taylor, 1985, p. 219). Another way to make this point, suggested by Gerald Dworkin, is to say that a person is autonomous if 'he identifies with his desires, goals, and values' (Dworkin, 1989, p. 61). However, initially at least, the entrepreneur did not experience their desires, goals and values as alien, but instead identified with them. Although Taylor argues that we 'must admit the possibility of error, or false appreciation' (Taylor, 1985, p. 226), this does not tell us whether the entrepreneur's earlier or later evaluation is the false one. A different approach to the same problem has been suggested by Christman. On his account, a person is positively free if their desires and goals have not been oppressively imposed upon them. On this view, what matters are the circumstances in which a character is formed:

> Self-mastery [positive freedom] means more than having a certain attitude toward one's desires at a time. It means in addition that one's values were formed in a manner or by a process that one had (or could have had) something to say about … whatever forces or factors explain the generation of changes in a person's preference set, these factors must be ones that the agent was in a position to reflect upon and resist. (Christman, 1991, p. 346)

Thus, if we know that the entrepreneur initially formed their beliefs under the influence of an overbearing father, and was not in a position to reflect upon those beliefs or resist that influence, then we should conclude that their earlier judgement was not fully autonomous. Similarly, if we know that their subsequent change of mind was clear-headed and carefully considered, then we should regard the regretful judgement as the accurate one.

A final point worth noting about the individual autonomy strand of positive liberty is its emphasis on the social, material and cultural preconditions for freedom. For example, Carol Gould (1981) argues that the freedom to realise oneself and to achieve one's purposes depends on having the right kinds of social and material circumstances. For her, being free presupposes that one inhabits social relations which are not contaminated by domination or exploitation, and that one has access to whatever resources are required to achieve your purposes. If Gould is right, then achieving positive freedom will have implications for the kinds of social or distributive justice that we should aim to realise (we shall return to this theme in Chapter 9). Another possible necessary condition for positive liberty, stressed by multiculturalist Will Kymlicka (1995), is that people have stable cultural memberships. According to this view, which we shall examine in the final key debate in this chapter, a person's ability to make meaningful choices depends on their having access to their culture, and individual freedom might be jeopardised if languages and cultures become vulnerable.

Let us now turn to the second conception of positive liberty, endorsed by political theorists such as Barber and Sandel, which stresses political, rather than personal, autonomy. The most distinctive feature of this conception is the link it draws with democracy, since it says that citizens are free if and only if they participate in the governing of their collective affairs, for instance by actively taking part in deliberations about law and public policy. For example, according to Sandel 'I am free insofar as I am a member of a political community that controls its own fate and am a participant in the decisions that govern its affairs' (Sandel, 1996, p. 25). Contrastingly, a person would be unfree according to this view if they lacked the effective ability to participate in democratic politics and to influence political decisions. There is a clear contrast with the negative conception here, since on that view freedom is typically located in the spaces between the laws, where options are permitted and not prohibited. Meanwhile, according to this conception of positive liberty, true freedom is possible only in a self-governing democratic community. As discussed in Box 7.3, this conception of positive freedom seems to support a participatory form of democracy. However, as we shall see during the second key debate, some proponents of negative liberty have suggested that the relationship between freedom and democracy is more awkward than these positive liberty theorists suggest.

Republican freedom

A group of contemporary political theorists and intellectual historians – including Philip Pettit, Quentin Skinner, Cécile Laborde and Frank Lovett – have suggested that there is a 'third' conception of liberty, generally referred to as the republican conception or as 'freedom as non-domination'. (Skinner originally suggested the label 'neo-Roman' (1998, 2002), but he now acknowledges (2008, p. 84) that his preferred term did not catch on.) As we saw in the introduction, this conception of liberty, like Berlin's distinction between positive and negative freedom, was initially formulated as an exercise in intellectual history. However, the republican conception of liberty is not a mere historical relic, and a growing number of political theorists are actively reviving this tradition by applying it to a range of challenges faced by contemporary political societies (Lovett and Pettit, 2009).

BOX 7.3 POSITIVE FREEDOM AND PARTICIPATORY DEMOCRACY

According to some positive liberty theorists, if citizens do not govern themselves, then they must be governed by someone else, and this would mean that they cannot truly be masters of themselves. Proponents of this view tend to favour participatory or deliberative models of democracy, and are sceptical about competitive democracy (see Chapter 5). For example, Barber argues that citizens can only be truly free in a participatory democracy:

> Men who are not directly responsible through common deliberation, common decision and common action for the policies that determine their common lives are not really free at all, however much they enjoy security, private rights and freedom from interference. (Barber, 1984, pp. 145–6)

Barber's claim is that non-participatory forms of democracy, such as competitive democracy, are capable of delivering only an impoverished – negative – form of liberty.

Does positive freedom require participatory democracy?

In order to grasp what is distinctive about this conception of freedom, we need first to look at republicanism as a tradition of political thought. Classical republicanism emerged as a distinctive theory of politics in medieval and Renaissance Italy, most especially in the writings of Machiavelli. It was later developed in seventeenth- and eighteenth-century Europe, by authors such as Milton, Harrington and Montesquieu, and again in revolutionary America, by Jefferson and Madison. One thing that unites these various political theorists, and which marks them out as republicans, is that they were animated by ideas which they traced back to the Roman republic. In different ways, these thinkers agreed that a good political community – or *res publica* – should be a community of equals, in which people are governed by laws and not men, and are citizens not subjects. This means that people should be empowered to face one another on equal terms, and should not be the playthings of their rulers.

In the course of defending their preferred ideal of political community, the classical republicans developed a distinctive understanding of what it is to be free. For them, the paradigm of unfreedom was slavery. Analogously, they thought that a person who lived under a tyrant was also unfree, since they too had a master whose arbitrary will they were subject to. Thus, within the republican tradition, being a free person became synonymous with living as an equal citizen, and not suffering vulnerability to arbitrary interference.

Amongst contemporary republicans someone is unfree if they are dominated, and a person can be said to be dominated if another agent has control over their choices, on an arbitrary or unchecked basis (Pettit, 1997; Lovett, 2001, 2010). This was the situation that the classical republicans believed the English people found themselves in during the seventeenth century, as discussed in Box 7.4, and it also describes the situation in which many people find themselves today. Thus, contemporary republicans argue that modern societies are rife with unfreedom, even if modern domination often takes a less explicit form. For example, Pettit offers the following list to illustrate the range of cases of domination in modern societies:

Think … of how you would feel as a student if you depended for not failing a course on the whim of an instructor. Or as a wife if you had to rely on the mood of your husband for whether you could enjoy an unmolested day. Or as a worker if you hung on the favour of a manager for whether you retained your job. Or as a debtor if you were dependent on the goodwill of a creditor for whether you had to face public ignominy. Or as someone destitute if you had to cast yourself on the mercy of others just to survive or maintain your family. Or think about how you would feel as a member of a cultural minority if you had to rely on the humour of majority groups for whether you escaped humiliation; or as an elderly person if you depended on escaping the notice of youth gangs for walking safely home; or as a citizen if you were dependent on winning the favour of some insider group for whether you or your kind ever caught the eye of government. (Pettit, 2012, pp. 1–2)

BOX 7.4   REPUBLICAN FREEDOM AND MONARCHY

In seventeenth-century England, during the disputes that preceded the outbreak of civil war, republican opponents of the Stuart monarchy argued that the King's ability to undermine the rights and liberties of his people with impunity was an affront to freedom (Skinner, 1998, 2008; Pettit, 2002). The republican view was not that the English people were made less free by the actual constraints imposed by the King, as proponents of the negative conception of freedom would argue. Rather, it was that the English people were unfree because they lived under a ruler who had the power to interfere with them on an arbitrary basis. For republicans, it was the presence of arbitrary power that makes a person unfree, and not any specific interference, impediment or obstacle that is imposed upon them. It was also in this vein that Locke was to later characterise unfreedom as being 'subject to the inconstant, uncertain, unknown, Arbitrary Will of another Man' (1988, p. 284).

In what sense were the English people subject to the arbitrary will of another? Did this make them unfree?

On the republican conception, each of these situations is not merely unpleasant or morally objectionable. Rather, because one agent holds sway over another – in other words, dominates them – they are all potential instances of unfreedom.

The understanding of domination deployed by republicans resonates with the one discussed in Chapter 6. According to Pettit, 'someone has dominating power over another, someone dominates or subjugates another, to the extent that (1) they have the capacity to interfere (2) on an arbitrary basis (3) in certain choices that the other is in a position to make' (1997, p. 52). To be dominated in this sense is to be vulnerable to the interferences of another, who has the capacity to arbitrarily worsen your situation, for instance through physical obstruction, coercive threats or manipulation. For Pettit, being able to worsen someone's situation means being able to reduce the range of options available to them, or being able to reduce the payoffs associated with those options. So, for example, a thug might be able to reduce the range of options available to a traveller by intimidating them so as to prevent them from using the bus service. Or, a bus company might increase their fares and thereby reduce the payoff associate with using public transport. However, having the ability to worsen the traveller's situation in either of these ways only counts as domination if the dominating agent has the capacity to interfere with impunity and at will. Thus, if the thug will suffer legal sanctions for attempting to intimidate bus passengers, or if the bus company knows that it will reduce its profits by increasing its fares, then they are not in a position to dominate the passenger. Republicans therefore argue that we can make people free by equipping them with 'anti-power', to guard them against the power of others (Pettit, 1996).

Because domination is a status, it does not entail that someone else actually does interfere with you, only that they could do so. Being vulnerable in this way is objectionable because dominated people have to live at the mercy of those who dominate them, and the resulting hierarchical relationship can have harmful psychological effects on both parties:

> Domination is generally going to involve the awareness of control on the part of the powerful, the awareness of vulnerability on the part of the powerless, and the mutual awareness – indeed the common awareness among all the parties to the relationship – of this consciousness on each side. The powerless are not going to be able to look the powerful in the eye, conscious as each will be – and conscious as each will be of the other's consciousness – of this asymmetry. Both will share an awareness that the powerless can do nothing except by the leave of the powerful: that the powerless are at the mercy of the powerful and not on equal terms. (Pettit, 1997, pp. 60–1)

Domination therefore potentially upsets equality as well as freedom. It does so because being aware of the fact of one's own domination – that is to say, being aware that one is subject to the arbitrary power of another – will frustrate the achievement of a community of equals. Thus, according to republicans, one of the evils of domination is that it is likely to nourish a destructive psychology of dependency, in which the subordinate defer to and fear their superiors.

Republicans argue that a person is dominated (that is to say, unfree) when someone else has the capacity to interfere in their choices. Two important points follow from this, each of which marks a distinction with the negative conception of freedom. First, a person may be dominated even if they are not interfered with. For example, suppose that a person lives under the arbitrary power of another who decides not to exercise their capacity to interfere. On the republican view, whether this person is free or unfree has nothing to do with the extent to which they are actually interfered with, as proponents of the negative conception believe. Rather, it has to do with whether the dominator may choose whether or not to interfere, and whether the dominated can resist or check this capacity. Thus, a slave whose master decides to permit them the widest sphere of negative liberty (that is to say, unimpeded options) is unfree on the republican view, since the master may later choose to reverse their decision. In situations such as these, the slave lives at the mercy of the master, and is dependent on them.

Second, someone might be interfered with without being dominated. To illustrate the possibility of non-dominating interference, Pettit suggests the following example:

> Suppose you wish to restrict your alcohol consumption and hand over the key of your alcohol cupboard to me, making me promise to return the key only at twenty-four hours' notice and not in response to a request for its immediate

return. When I refuse a request for the immediate return of the key, I interfere with your choice, removing the option of having a drink now. I deny you the possibility of choosing according to your current will. But do I subject you to my will? ... Surely not. (Pettit, 2012, p. 57)

In this case, since interference takes the form of acting under instructions, it does not involve the key holder imposing their will on the drinker (or the aspiring drinker). Rather the drinker imposes their will on themselves. Thus, the key holder does not dominate the drinker, even though they do impede them. Things would be different if the key holder was acting paternalistically rather than under instructions. For instance, suppose that a second key holder restricted the drinker's access to alcohol because they thought that doing so was in the drinker's best interests, regardless of the drinker's own preferences. The second key holder would then be dominating the drinker, since their interference would be at their own discretion.

Importantly, Pettit suggests that the public officials – such as police officers, judges and prison officers – could be like either of the key holders (Pettit, 1997, p. 65). If institutions are well designed, then officials will have little or no discretion over how they treat people and will be required to act under constitutionally determined rules. If they are designed badly, then they will permit office holders to dominate those who are subject to them, since they will have a greater scope to exercise their own discretion and the people themselves will have few or no opportunities to check or resist their power. Thus, according to the republican conception, a properly arranged and law governed democratic community could, in principle at least, respect the freedom of its members. We return to this possibility in the second key debate.

Key debates

Would relieving poverty promote freedom?

Money can't buy love, so they say, but can it buy freedom? Or to put the question another way, does having less money make a person less free? Most proponents of negative liberty answer these questions with a 'no'. This is because they draw a distinction between ability and freedom and argue that being unable to do something – for instance because one lacks the required strength, skills or resources – does not mean that one is unfree to do that thing. On this view, being poor might mean that a person lacks the conditions to exercise their freedom, but it does not mean that a person lacks freedom as such. If this is correct, then relieving poverty will not have the effect of promoting freedom. Indeed, poverty relief programmes could actually reduce freedom, if they are funded through taxes, which are a form of interference. Some right-wing political theorists have embraced these implications of the negative conception of liberty. For them, tackling inequality is not required for promoting freedom and a political community can honour the value of liberty despite being marked by serious inequalities of wealth. In this key debate, after first setting out the right-wing argument more carefully, we will examine three ways in which advocates of poverty relief, redistributive taxation and the welfare state have responded to it.

Cohen (2011, p. 168), a Marxist, summarises the right-wing argument as follows:

1. Freedom is compromised by (liability to) interference (by other people), but not by lack of means.
2. To lack money is to suffer not (liability to) interference, but lack of means.
3. [Therefore] Poverty (lack of money) does not carry with it a lack of freedom.
4. The primary task of government is to protect freedom.
5. [Therefore] Relief of poverty is not part of the primary task of government.

A preliminary point to note about this argument is that it contains two conclusions. The first – (3) – is a conceptual claim concerning the nature of (negative) freedom, and it follows from steps (1) and (2). Meanwhile, the second – (5) – is a normative claim concerning what governments should do, and it follows from steps (3) and (4). To resist the second conclusion – (5) – advocates of poverty relief must demonstrate that at least one of the earlier steps in the argument is faulty, and each of the three responses we shall examine does so in a different way. The first accepts steps (1), (2) and (3) but rejects (4) and consequently (5). Political theorists who take this view concede the right-wing conceptual claim (that poverty does not undermine negative freedom) but do not believe that it supports the normative conclusion (5). Meanwhile, the second response rejects (2) and therefore (3) and (5). Political theorists who take this view reject both the conceptual and normative conclusions of the right-wing argument. Instead, they argue that poverty does undermine negative freedom, properly understood, and that reducing poverty will increase freedom. Finally, the third response rejects (1) and the concept of negative liberty entirely. Political theorists who take this view instead endorse one of the other two conceptions of freedom. As we shall see, both positive and republican conceptions of freedom have been used to support the conclusion that poverty is a condition of unfreedom that governments should relieve.

Let us begin by examining the first response, which has been suggested by liberals such as Rawls and Berlin. These political theorists accept that poverty does not undermine freedom, but do not accept that the primary task of government is to protect freedom. Thus, for them, relieving poverty might be justified, even if doing so undermines freedom. For example, Berlin reaches this conclusion because he thinks that freedom is one value amongst many others (recall the idea of value pluralism we discussed in Chapter 3). His approach is neatly captured in the following passage, where he begins by endorsing (3) before rejecting (4) and (5) in the final, longer, sentence:

> It is important to discriminate between liberty and the conditions of its exercise. If a man is too poor or too ignorant or too feeble to make use of his legal rights, the liberty that the rights confer upon him is nothing to him, but it is not thereby annihilated. The obligation to promote education, health, justice, to raise standards of living, to provide opportunity for the growth of the arts and sciences, to prevent reactionary political or social or legal policies or arbitrary inequalities, is not made less stringent because it is not necessarily directed at the promotion of liberty itself, but to conditions in which alone its possession is of value, or values which may be independent of it. (Berlin, 2002, p. 45)

Berlin's commitment to value pluralism allows him to argue that even if poverty and inequality do not have anything to do with freedom, a government might still be justified in seeking to eliminate or reduce these things in order to secure other important values. One attraction of this strategy is that it maintains a descriptively clear concept of liberty, and thereby reduces the possibility of confusion or muddle. Berlin himself was adamant on this point, insisting that 'liberty is liberty, not equality, or fairness, or justice, or culture' (Berlin, 2002, p. 172). This commitment prompted him to argue that if political theorists wanted to defend redistributive taxation or the welfare state, they should appeal to values other than freedom, such as justice or equality.

The second response attacks the conceptual conclusion (3) by rejecting step (2), thereby also calling the normative conclusion (5) into question. Defenders of this view – who include liberals such as Jeremy Waldron and Marxists such as Cohen – argue that promoting negative liberty may require relieving poverty and reducing material inequalities. Waldron's views are discussed in Box 7.5, so we shall focus on Cohen's argument here. Cohen agrees with the general claim, endorsed by all negative liberty theorists, that people are made unfree by the interferences of others. However, he disagrees with the contention that when people lack money they lack the means to exercise their liberty but not liberty as such. Instead, Cohen claims that to lack money is to be prey to interference. If he is right, then poverty can be a form of negative unfreedom.

To make sense of Cohen's argument, it will be helpful to recall Berlin's view that liberty is not 'annihilated' when a person is 'too poor or too ignorant or too feeble' to exercise it. Cohen accepts that being unable to do something as a result of being 'too ignorant' or 'too feeble' does not make a person unfree. However, he thinks that being 'too poor' to do something is different, since 'poverty demonstrably implies liability to interference' (Cohen, 2011, p. 175). On his account, lack of money – at least in a capitalist society – can have the effect of leaving a person vulnerable to certain kinds of interferences. For example, a person who seeks a good or a service they cannot afford is liable to be subject to (freedom-undermining) interference. Indeed, as Cohen puts it, '[t]he only way you won't be prevented from getting and using things that cost money in our society – which is to say: most things – is by offering money for them' (Cohen, 2011, p. 177).

Cohen supports his view that to lack money is to lack freedom with the following two examples:

Suppose that an able-bodied woman is too poor to visit her sister in Glasgow. She cannot save enough, from week to week, to buy her way there. If she attempts to board the train, she is consequently without the means to overcome the conductor's prospective interference. Whether or not this woman should be said to have the *ability* to go to Glasgow, there is no deficiency in her ability to do so which restricts her *independently* of the interference that she faces. She is entirely capable of boarding the underground [the metro system in London] and traversing the space that she must cross to reach the train. But she will be physically prevented from crossing that space, or physically ejected from the train. Or consider a moneyless woman who wants to pick up, and take home, a sweater on the counter at Selfridge's [a department store]. If she contrives to do so, she will be physically stopped outside Selfridge's and the sweater will be removed. (Cohen, 2011, pp. 176-7)

In both of these cases, on Cohen's reading, 'money confers freedom, rather than merely the ability to use it' (Cohen, 2011, p. 176). As he sees it, a person who lacks money in a capitalist society will face obstacles and impediments in just the same way as with any other kind of freedom-undermining interference. He reinforces this point with a third example:

Suppose that two people are prevented from boarding a plane, one because she lacks a passport and the other because she lacks a ticket. Was only the first unfree to board it? What the airline does to the ticketless passenger is exactly what the state does to the passportless one: blocks her way. (Cohen, 2011, p. 179, fn. 29)

In this case, we can either say that a passport and a ticket are both means to exercising a freedom, or we can say that lacking a passport or a ticket both leave one liable to interference. Since there is no relevant difference between the two cases, at least from the point of view of negative freedom, then if you believe that the person without a passport is negatively unfree to board the plane, then you should also believe that the person without a ticket is negatively unfree to board the plane. Cohen favours the second reading, and if he is right, then to lack money in at least some circumstances is not merely to lack the means to do something, but is to lack the negative freedom to do that thing.

So far we have seen that proponents of negative liberty disagree about whether poverty is an obstacle to freedom. Those who believe that it is open the door to a normative argument in favour of redistributive taxation based on a negative conception of freedom. Meanwhile, those who believe that it is not draw contrasting normative conclusions, in some cases opposing redistributive taxation and in other cases supporting it. A third and final response to the right-wing argument is to reject step (1) and instead endorse an alternative conception of freedom. For example, as we saw earlier, proponents of the positive conception of liberty do not draw a strict distinction between freedom and ability. Instead, political theorists such as Gould argue that a lack of money does frustrate liberty, properly understood. One very general way to argue for this conclusion is to say that poverty can prevent a person from living autonomously, in the sense of having control over their own fate. On this view, if freedom is about exercising control over one's own life, then a free person must have the effective – and not merely the formal – ability to achieve the things they value. Consequently, promoting positive liberty will go hand in hand with alleviating poverty.

An influential argument for the view that freedom has to do with the ability to do things has been suggested by Amartya Sen (1992). Sen claims that some 'capabilities' are substantive freedoms, if they provide us with a real opportunity to achieve well-being. For him, well-being is constituted by various 'functionings', such as being in good health, being happy and having self-respect. In turn, a person has the 'capability' to achieve a functioning if they are effectively able to do so. Thus, on his view, if a person lacks the capability to achieve the functioning of being in good health, for example because they lack access to adequate medical care, then they lack a substantive freedom. Conversely, if social arrangements are adapted, giving that person a real opportunity to access medical care, then on Sen's view they would now have the capability to achieve the relevant functioning, and would thereby possess a substantive freedom they previously lacked. Thus, to be deprived of certain 'capabilities' is to be less free than one would otherwise be. Sen's account allows us to say that if a person is unable to achieve a functioning then they are unfree. However, it does not imply that to be unable to achieve *any* particular thing is an unfreedom, since he discriminates between certain beings and doings, suggesting that a person's freedom is deprived only when they lack the capability to achieve particular functionings.

Finally, the republican conception of freedom can be used to support two objections to the right-wing argument against poverty relief programmes. First, it does not support the conclusion that taxing the rich undermines their freedom. Recall, taxation is said to reduce freedom because it is a form of interference. By contrast, republicans believe that freedom is a status, and that a person is unfree only if they are vulnerable to arbitrary interference, which is to say, if they are dominated. Not all forms of interference involve domination, and a government that 'taxes people under a well-ordered system of law ... need not dominate them, since the interference involved should not be arbitrary' (Pettit, 1997, pp. 148–9). This means that a poverty relief programme which is enacted by a legitimate democratic government, who themselves form policies on the basis of procedures that track the interests of their citizens, will not undermine the republican freedom of its taxpayers.

The second republican objection to the right-wing argument is that poverty itself will often leave people vulnerable to domination. For example, Pettit argues that promoting freedom as non-domination will require promoting the socio-economic independence of citizens. Independence in this context means that people should 'have the wherewithal to operate normally and properly in your society without having to beg or borrow from others, and without having to depend on their beneficence' (1997, p. 158). Unless people are independent, they will have the status of being unfree, since they will be vulnerable to exploitation, perhaps living at the mercy of others or by their grace and favour, or otherwise exposed to forms of arbitrary treatment that they are unable to check or resist. For example, suppose that a person is unable to afford medical care in the event of them or their child falling sick. A medical emergency would leave that person vulnerable to domination, since unscrupulous doctors or benefactors could take advantage of their situation. Even if the person or their child did not become ill, they might still be disposed to tolerate arbitrary treatment from those on whom they are likely to depend in the future (Pettit, 1997, p. 160). Alternatively, consider the plight of the homeless, discussed in Box 7.5. Many homeless people have no option but to depend on the kindness of friends, family or strangers for food and shelter. As such, they are likely to expose themselves to a risk of arbitrary treatment, making them vulnerable to domination. What this suggests, then, is that republican freedom will require ensuring both that the least advantaged members of society have access to whatever resources are required for socio-economic independence, and that their access to such resources should not take the form of a gift but of a right or entitlement.

Does freedom require democracy?

The values of freedom and democracy are often connected in ordinary speech. For example, we might say that only a democratic people can be free, or we might associate the absence of democracy with unfreedom, or we might connect the promotion of democracy to the promotion of freedom. Whilst some political theorists believe that the link between the two is empirical, others say that it is conceptual. We shall explore these two possibilities in this key debate.

According to the first view, democracy tends to protect freedom, either because liberties are most effectively or reliably secured by the vigilance of democratic citizens, or because democratic institutions are the best means to ensure that governments respect the freedom of their citizens. Importantly, this view does not say that democracy is necessary for freedom, only that democracy is an effective means for realising or promoting freedom. It has been endorsed by proponents of both the negative and republican views, each of which have argued that democracy is instrumentally valuable, either because democratic societies tend to reduce freedom-undermining interferences, or because democratic societies offer the best guarantee against being dominated (Patten, 1996).

As illustrated in Box 7.6, some proponents of negative liberty, such as Berlin, are wary about this line of argument. Furthermore, as we saw in Chapter 5, competitive democrats like Schumpeter emphasise the potential for majorities to trample on the liberties of vulnerable minorities in democratic societies. Against this, recent work by comparative political scientists suggests that societies which have democratised are more likely to respect the liberties and rights of their members (Landman, 2005, pp. 557-8). The disagreement here is one that should be settled empirically, since it concerns the causal relationship between democratic decision making procedures and political outcomes. Nevertheless, it is worth noting an additional point on the side of democracy, and this is that democratic societies must be committed to protecting some fundamental or basic liberties. For instance, if democratic citizens are to be able to debate issues

BOX 7.6 DEMOCRACY AND NEGATIVE FREEDOM

According to the negative conception, freedom has to do with the extent to which one is interfered with, or the range of unimpeded options that a person has available to them. Berlin thought that it was a logical implication of this view that a person's freedom was unaffected by whether or not they live under a democratic system of government. This is because a person living under a benevolent dictator, who governed them sparingly, might have more negative liberty than a citizen in a heavily regulated democracy. Thus, Berlin noted that negative liberty 'is not incompatible with some kinds of autocracy, or at any rate with the absence of self-government' (Berlin, 2002, p. 176). Moreover, he also suggested that democratic institutions could turn out to have destructive effects on negative liberty, as they might 'deprive the individual citizen of a great many liberties which he might have in some other form of society' (Berlin, 2002, p. 176). For example, suppose that your fellow citizens vote to prohibit a practice that is permitted by the dictator of a neighbouring state. This might leave you with less negative freedom than the people of that state. Consequently, although Berlin was a supporter of liberal democratic institutions, he was adamant that freedom and democracy were independent of one another. However, his critics have argued that there is something peculiar, shallow, and perhaps absurd about a political conception of freedom that sees freedom and democracy as unconnected (Taylor, 1985, pp. 211–29; Skinner, 1998).

How are freedom and democracy related? Is it possible to have one without the other?

of public concern and to influence public policy, then they must have the freedoms to associate and to speak freely. Thus, in a non-trivial sense, democracies must have a beneficial effect on at least some negative and republican freedoms.

The other view about the connection between freedom and democracy suggests that the two have a more intimate connection, and it has been endorsed by proponents of both positive and republican conceptions of freedom. According to this view, freedom and democracy are conceptually connected. If this is true, then real freedom can be achieved only in a properly constituted democratic community, because democracy is a necessary condition for freedom.

One way to capture the conceptual link between democracy and freedom is suggested by the 'political autonomy' strand of positive liberty, which we discussed in the first part of this chapter. Recall that, according to this view, citizens are free if and only if they are active participants in an independent democratic community. This requires both that the participation of each member is meaningful, and that the community itself is not dependent on foreign or external powers. As such, this version of the positive conception equates political freedom with the status of being a 'free people', suggesting that a people is free if it governs itself and if its members are citizens not subjects. As stated, however, there might be something unsatisfactory about this way of capturing the link between positive freedom and democracy, since it ties the concept of freedom exclusively to our lives as citizens. In other words, it does not explain why democracy is a necessary condition for positive freedom in our personal lives, in the sense of a person either being a master of themselves or living a self-directed life. A more subtle view that perhaps does capture this has been suggested by Jürgen Habermas (1996), whose theory of deliberative democracy we examined in Chapter 5. On his account, explored in Box 7.7, personal freedom and political freedom each presuppose one another since they have an 'internal' and 'conceptually necessary' connection (1998, p. 208). Because they can only be realised jointly, then a democratic order that is to secure the political freedom of its citizens must also secure the personal liberties of its members (and vice versa).

Another way to capture the idea that freedom and democracy are conceptually linked has been suggested by contemporary republican political theorists. For example, Philip Pettit argues that a properly constructed democratic order 'holds out the prospect of our being able to enjoy an important benefit that would otherwise escape us', which he calls 'status freedom' (Pettit, 2012, p. 181). This freedom 'consists in the objective and subjective status of enjoying your freedom as non-domination, equally with fellow citizens' (2012, p. 181). Status freedom connects up to the idea of democracy in two ways. First, having the

BOX 7.7 HABERMAS AND FREEDOM

Habermas believes that personal freedom (or what he calls 'private autonomy') is 'co-original' or 'equiprimordial' with political freedom (or what he calls 'public autonomy'). This thesis can be illustrated from both directions. On the one hand, we can start from the rights that are standardly invoked as guarantors of personal freedom or private autonomy, such as the rights of free association or the right to be free from unwarranted interferences. Clearly, a modern legal order that failed to uphold these rights would not adequately protect our private autonomy. However, these rights are expressive of our freedom only if we recognise ourselves as their authors – that is to say, if we can think of ourselves as co-legislators who imposed them upon ourselves. Thus, private autonomy assumes public autonomy. On the other hand, we can also start from the exercise of public autonomy, in which citizens deliberate amongst one another about how to regulate their common affairs. This activity assumes that democratic participants are privately autonomous, in the sense of being able to freely articulate their own views and beliefs. We can see this by imagining a democratic order in which citizens faced sanctions for holding unpopular opinions, or in which they were required to support the positions favoured by their superiors. In such a society public autonomy would be jeopardised by the failure to adequately secure private autonomy. Thus, public autonomy assumes private autonomy.

Are personal and political freedoms 'co-original'?

status of being a free person requires being able to form relationships with one's fellow citizens that rule out the possibility of domination (2012, p. 91). This not only means that people must have sufficient resources and protections to ensure that others cannot interfere in their affairs with impunity, but also that each of us can 'walk tall' and 'look others in the eye' without fear or deference (2012, p. 84). Unless political influence is distributed equally, then it seems difficult to see how citizens will be able to achieve this. Second, status freedom also involves a person having the right kind of relationship with their state. In particular, it means that they must be able to exercise control over their government, since otherwise they will be subject to the arbitrary rule of another. Thus, if someone is to enjoy the status of being a free person, and if freedom is understood as non-domination, then political power must be subject to popular democratic control.

Does freedom require us to protect and promote vulnerable cultures?

The cultures, traditions and languages of many indigenous peoples and national minorities are currently under threat. For example, Ethnologue reports that 373 languages have become extinct since 1950, and that of the 7,106 languages which are currently spoken in the world, 915 are 'dying' and 1,519 are 'in trouble' (Lewis et al., 2014). Even where cultures do not face the immediate prospect of extinction, minorities are often concerned about the long-term prospects of their ways of life and traditions. The causes of cultural vulnerability are complex and contested, and might include things such as globalisation, migration and the pressures exerted by dominant cultural identities. As we saw in Chapter 2, many multiculturalists take it for granted that the loss of different ways of life, different practices and traditions, as well as different ways of understanding the world, is a matter of urgent moral concern. However, others think that these transformations are not self-evidently objectionable. In this final key debate we will examine an influential argument, suggested by Will Kymlicka (1989a, 1995), which appeals to the value of freedom to explain why cultural vulnerability harms the members of cultural minorities. If this argument is convincing, then protecting and promoting vulnerable cultures might be required in the name of freedom.

Kymlicka's basic claim is that 'freedom is intimately linked with and dependent on culture' (1995, p. 75). To understand what he means by this we first need to get a handle on how he understands the concept of freedom. Kymlicka endorses a positive conception of freedom, which has to do with a person's capacity 'to choose their own plan of life' (1995, p. 80). A person lives freely on this view if they are autonomous, in the sense of living their life 'from the inside' (1995, p. 81). At the very least, this means that people should be able to direct themselves and be moved by their own purposes, not by those of another. It also means that they should not be hindered in their projects by fear of discrimination or undeserved sanctions. More strongly, people must be capable of reflecting critically on their goals and decisions, and be equipped to rationally revise them if they so choose.

Like other proponents of positive liberty, Kymlicka emphasises that the enjoyment of individual freedom depends on the satisfaction of particular political, social and cultural conditions. For instance, protecting individual freedom of choice will require a variety of civil and political liberties, such as the rights of conscience and association. Similarly, enabling people to design their own lives and to reflect critically on their chosen plans will require making them aware of different views about what it is to lead a good life. In turn, this will require educating and empowering people so that they can examine, compare, adopt and adapt those views. Most importantly for our current purposes, Kymlicka also thinks that the enjoyment of freedom will require ensuring that a person's culture remains viable, for two reasons. First, he thinks that cultures supply us with options about how to lead our lives. Second, he also thinks that cultures provide us with the concepts and narratives that we need in order to make sense of those different options. As he puts it, '[o]ur language and history are the media through which we come to an awareness of the options available to us, and their significance; and this is a precondition of making intelligent judgments about how to lead our lives' (Kymlicka, 1989a, p. 165). Thus, '[f]or meaningful individual choice to be possible, individuals need not only access to information, the capacity to reflectively evaluate it, and freedom of association and expression. They also need access to a societal culture' (1995, p. 84).

Before analysing the link that Kymlicka draws between cultural membership and freedom, it is worth pausing to look more closely at how he uses the term 'culture'. Kymlicka focuses on what he calls 'societal cultures', which he says 'tend to be territorially concentrated and based on a shared language' (1995, p. 75). The key function they perform is to provide members 'with meaningful ways of life across the range of human activities, including social, educational, religious, recreational, and economic life, encompassing both public and private spheres' (1995, p. 75). Groups like teenage gangs, religious congregations or associations of sports fans are not societal cultures in Kymlicka's sense, since they are not rich and varied enough. Rather, societal cultures tend to correspond to the cultures of national groups or indigenous peoples, and are accompanied by institutional frameworks. Often, political communities contain more than one of these. For instance, according to Kymlicka: 'American Indian tribes and Puerto Ricans, like the Aboriginal peoples and Quebecois in Canada, are not just subgroups within a common culture, but genuinely distinct societal cultures' (1995, pp. 78–9). When this is the case, minority societal cultures may require special supports and assistance, if they are to continue to offer their members a meaningful range of options.

Kymlicka's view, then, is that 'freedom involves making choices amongst various options, and our societal culture not only provides these options, but also makes them meaningful to us' (1995, p. 83). For him, a cultural structure provides its members with a 'context of choice'. If political theorists are interested in promoting freedom, then they should be especially 'concerned with the fate of cultural structures, not because they have some moral status of their own, but because it's only through having a rich and secure cultural structure that people can become aware, in a vivid way, of the options available to them, and intelligently examine their value' (1989a, p. 165). Consequently, Kymlicka concludes that cultural membership is a 'primary good'. As we shall see in Chapter 9, 'primary good' is a term of art used to describe things that are good for anyone, irrespective of their particular life plan. In describing culture in this way, Kymlicka means to convey that it is something to which everyone is entitled, as a matter of justice, because he thinks that without it we would lose our capacity for autonomy.

Kymlicka's argument has been challenged in a number of different ways. Perhaps most importantly, as we saw in Chapter 3, feminists such as Susan Okin have raised the concern that protecting sexist or patriarchal cultures might turn out to undermine the freedom of women and girls. A different objection, which we shall examine in Box 7.8, is that Kymlicka is mistaken to say that autonomous people need access to a stable cultural context. Here we will consider another objection, which says that even if people do need access to culture to exercise their autonomy, Kymlicka's argument can only justify a right to a culture, and not a right to their own culture. Avishai Margalit and Moshe Halbertal offer the following example to illustrate this point:

> If the native Canadians' culture were destroyed by the presence of a white majority in their territory, but the individual members of the minority were able to assimilate, albeit against their will, into the white culture, then Kymlicka would not see any reason to grant this minority privileges. This is because their assimilation into the majority culture guarantees them what is important in a culture from Kymlicka's point of view – the ability to evaluate and choose among various life options. (Margalit and Halbertal, 1994, pp. 504–5)

A similar version of this objection has also been suggested by John Tomasi, who points out that Kymlicka's 'context of choice' view of culture cannot generate any special rights, since a 'context of choice' remains even if the character of a culture is radically changed. Consequently, Tomasi concludes that 'cultural membership is only a primary good only in the same uninteresting sense as is, say, oxygen: since (practically) no one is differentially advantaged with respect to that good, it generates no special rights' (Tomasi, 1995, p. 589).

In response to this, Kymlicka emphasises the powerful bonds that people often have with their own ancestral cultures, arguing that 'we should treat access to one's culture as something that people can be expected to want' (1995, p. 86). This is a claim about what people usually want, which Kymlicka uses as the basis for

BOX 7.8 MULTICULTURALISM AND COSMOPOLITANISM

Jeremy Waldron proposed a cosmopolitan objection to Kymlicka's view about the relationship between freedom and culture. Waldron begins from the observation that some people manage to flourish by constructing their identity from a wide variety of cultural sources. From this, he concludes that immersion in a single, pristine culture cannot be a *necessary* precondition for having available the kinds of choices that make a good life possible:

> [Because a] freewheeling cosmopolitan life, lived in a kaleidoscope of cultures, is both possible and fulfilling ... rich and creative, and with no more unhappiness than one expects to find anywhere in human existence ... [then]... one argument for the protection of minority cultures is undercut. It can no longer be said that people need their rootedness in the particular culture in which they and their ancestors were reared in the way that they need food, clothing and shelter. (Waldron, 1995, pp. 99–100)

Kymlicka has responded to Waldron's cosmopolitan critique by arguing that he overestimates the extent to which people move between different cultures. On Kymlicka's reading, the examples that Waldron gives – such as Irish-Americans eating Chinese food and reading German fairy tales to their children – do not describe genuine movement *between* cultures, but rather movement *within* a single diverse societal culture. Thus, according to Kymlicka, Waldron has not shown that people really can move between different societal cultures with ease.

What do Waldron and Kymlicka disagree about? What are the implications of their disagreement for how we think about freedom?

a stronger claim about what people are entitled to, as a matter of justice. According to this stronger claim: '[l]eaving one's culture, while possible, is best seen as renouncing something to which one is reasonably entitled' (Kymlicka, 1995, p. 86). To support this move, Kymlicka argues that stable cultural communities contribute to human well-being by providing members with an unconditional sense of identification and belonging. Moreover, he argues that they support other important values, such as social solidarity, mutual trust and intergenerational bonds. However, although these things may be true, it is worth noting that these additional functions often depend upon the character of a culture remaining stable over time. Thus, they suggest that if Kymlicka's argument is to support a right to *your* culture, it is a right to a cultural character, and not merely a right to a cultural structure, or a 'context of choice'. But this perhaps goes too far, since preserving the character of a particular cultural group may have the effect of undermining the freedom of its members to alter and adapt that culture to new circumstances.

Future challenges

The three conceptions of liberty that we have examined in this chapter capture different senses in which a person or a group might be described as free or unfree and they each suggest different ways to address substantive political questions. For example, advocates of negative liberty generally believe that people who lack resources do not lack freedom as such. This does not mean that they believe that tackling social or economic inequality are inappropriate goals for a political community, only that doing so will not promote freedom. The same theorists also tend to deny that democracy is necessary for freedom, arguing that although democracy might help to protect some negative liberties, it could also threaten them. Again, this does not mean that negative liberty theorists must oppose democracy, only that they should reject arguments that justify it by appealing to freedom. Meanwhile, advocates of positive and republican liberty are much more likely to associate poverty and inequality with unfreedom, and democracy with freedom. In the case of the positive conception, this is because exercising positive freedom assumes the presence of appropriate material, social and political circumstances. In the case of republican freedom, this is because political and social equality are necessary conditions for people to have the status of free persons. Moreover, in addition to informing normative disagreements about democracy and social justice, each of our rival perspectives also has implications for how we think about some contemporary puzzles of international society. By way of a conclusion I will briefly sketch out three interesting proposals, taking one from each conception of freedom. These all concern some of the different ways in which existing global practices and institutions potentially subvert freedom.

On nearly any formulation of the negative conception of freedom, immigration restrictions are a significant obstacle to individual liberty. As the libertarian Chandran Kukathas notes:

[C]losed borders restrict freedom of movement. Borders prevent people from moving into territories whose governments forbid them to enter; and to the extent that they cannot enter any other territory, borders confine them within their designated boundaries. (Kukathas, 2005, p. 210)

Border controls are coercive, since they are enforced by states (Abizadeh, 2008; for a rival view, see Miller, 2010). Amongst other things, they prevent people from seeking employment outside their country of citizenship, or to associate with friends and family living in other countries. Dismantling them – as has partly been achieved within the European Union – would therefore have the effect of increasing negative freedom. However, although most negative liberty theorists accept that borders restrict freedom, relatively few of them are committed to removing them. One explanation for this is that negative liberty theorists are often pluralists, who believe that freedom might justifiably be sacrificed for the sake of other values. For example, as we saw in Chapter 2, one communitarian has argued that a global regime of open borders would jeopardise democracy and sovereignty, since it would fail to respect the right of a political community to determine its own terms of association (Walzer, 1983). A related reason for rejecting open borders, suggested by liberal nationalist David Miller, is that the *value* of free movement could be more effectively realised within closed political communities, rather than in a global regime of open borders (Miller, 2005, pp. 195–6; also see Miller, 2008). According to this view, provided that each society offers its members an adequate range of options, dismantling borders would add very little, and might even compromise some things that we should cherish, such as national cultures.

The positive conception of freedom, or at least one version of it, has had a significant influence on development ethics, especially through the United Nations Development Programme and the Millennium Development Goals. As we saw earlier, the capability approach, which is also sometimes called the human development approach, associates unfreedom with capability deprivation (Sen, 1992; Nussbaum, 2011). According to this view, a person is unfree if they are unable to achieve particular functionings, such as being healthy, having bodily integrity, living imaginatively or being able to critically reflect on their beliefs and plans. Proponents of this view argue that people who lack these capabilities are unable to lead truly human lives, or to flourish, or to live with dignity. One practical implication of this view is that international development programmes ought to focus on equipping people in developing societies with the effective ability to achieve particular functionings. This might mean introducing comprehensive literacy and healthcare programmes, or advocating for institutional change when oppressive social, political or economic structures prevent people from functioning adequately. The capability approach also says that we can measure how successful development efforts have been by looking at what kinds of lives people are able to lead, and what they are able to do and be (in other words, by looking at whether their positive freedom has increased). This is more radical than it sounds, since it suggest that international organisations and aid agencies should be less concerned than they currently are with increasing the rate of economic growth, or with transferring resources to poorer societies. Although these things might be desirable, proponents of the capability approach emphasise that they are only instrumentally valuable, insofar as they increase the positive liberty of individuals themselves.

Finally, proponents of the republican conception of freedom have recently used their theory to argue that since the international order is rife with domination, many political communities are substantively unfree. For example, Pettit has identified three kinds of international domination (2010, pp. 77–8). First, powerful states dominate weaker states, for instance by using threats of military force, economic sanctions, bribery or espionage. Second, powerful corporations dominate states, for instance by threatening to move their activities overseas, or by lobbying politicians, or by manipulating democratic procedures. Third, inter-national bodies dominate states, for instance by threatening to impose sanctions. Unlike the previous two examples we have explored, the international unfreedom that republican theorists identify is experienced by states themselves, and not by their members. Moreover, republicans emphasise that because international domination does not require active interference, many political communities may be unfree even when they are not coerced by outsiders. For these authors, it is the structure of international society, and especially the massive inequali-ties of wealth and power, that are the source of international unfreedom. Thus, Laborde points out that powerful global actors are often able to take advantage of the vulnerability of poor and weak states. For instance, 'offers are made to them on terms they cannot refuse, and threats do not need to be carried out or even issued to be successful' (Laborde, 2010, p. 59). According to republicans, even where there is no active interference, there is a sense in which weaker states are unfree, since they are subject to 'alien control' over their affairs.

8

Equality

- INTRODUCTION
- RIVAL PERSPECTIVES
    Distributive equality • Social equality
- KEY DEBATES
    Is distributive equality an ideal that should be promoted? • Should equality be
    sensitive to responsibility? • Should equality be sensitive to difference?
- FUTURE CHALLENGES

Introduction

Political theorists refer to the concept of equality in a number of different contexts. For instance, sometimes equality is understood to mean the principle of formal or legal equality, which refers to the idea that each of us should have the same status before the law, and prohibits applying different legal rules to people because of things like their race, religion, gender or social class. Additionally, equality is also sometimes understood to mean political equality, and as we saw in Chapter 5, political theorists defend different views about what kinds of democracy and citizenship are required to uphold this ideal. Despite disagreements about how to formulate them, both of these ideals are now widely supported amongst political theorists and in wider society. In this chapter, we will address a more controversial and demanding kind of equality, concerned with social and economic inequalities, called equality of condition. This principle is defended by egalitarians, who believe that inequality itself is bad or unjust (Parfit, 1998). However, as we shall see, egalitarians take different views about which inequalities matter, which prompts Richard Arneson to describe egalitarianism as a 'protean doctrine' (2013).

Very roughly, contemporary egalitarians fall into two camps, and these form our rival perspectives, summarised in Table 8.1. On one side are distributive egalitarians, who believe that equality means equal shares of something, such as money, welfare, or the ability to do valuable things. On the other side are social egalitarians, who believe that equality means that people enjoy an equal status,

Table 8.1 Summary of rival perspectives on equality

	Distributive	Social
Distinctive feature of an equal society	Equal shares of something (opportunity for resources, welfare, opportunity for welfare, access to advantage, capabilities)	A 'society of equals', defined by equal status, egalitarian relationships or an egalitarian ethos
Distinctive feature of an unequal society	An unequal distribution of something (opportunity for resources, welfare, opportunity for welfare, access to advantage, capabilities)	The presence of unequal status or social relations, such as hierarchies, oppression, subordination, domination, misrecognition, etc.
Permissible inequalities	Inequalities that arise from responsible choices are permissible; inequalities that are the result of circumstances or bad luck are impermissible	Limited material inequalities are permissible provided they do not compromise unequal status or social relations
Likely indicators of gender inequality	Unequal opportunities for men and women	Patriarchal social relationships
Likely indicators of cultural inequality	Unequal distribution of 'recognition space'	Misrecognition

or relate to one another as equals. Both of these perspectives support broadly similar outlooks – for instance they both condemn the inequalities of wealth and opportunities currently found in most liberal democracies. However, the disagreements between and amongst them are both philosophically and politically significant, since they paint different pictures of what an egalitarian society would look and feel like, and offer competing justifications of why we should favour such a society. Of course, plenty of political theorists object to the ideal of equality of condition, and we will examine some of these different objections in both this chapter and the next.

Distributive egalitarianism refers to a family of related views, whose members disagree about two important and overlapping issues: about which inequalities matter and about whether holding people responsible for their actions licenses an unequal distribution of shares. We shall explore the first of these during the 'rival perspectives' part of the chapter and the other during the second key debate. Meanwhile, in the first key debate we will explore a challenge to distributive egalitarianism, which says that equality itself is not a distributive ideal and that instead we should ensure that everyone has enough or prioritise the needs of the least advantaged. Social egalitarianism describes a looser bundle of ideas, concerned with the quality of the relationships that obtain within society. Advocates of this view believe that egalitarianism should aim at the eradication of hierarchy, subordination, oppression and domination, so that people form a society of equals in which members are able to face one another as equals.

Although they acknowledge that distribution may be morally significant, they think that it is so because of the ways in which it shapes the character of social relationships (Scheffler, 2003, p. 23). In the third key debate we will compare this ideal to the distributive one by examining how each of them responds to the particular challenges raised by sexual and cultural inequality. These cases are interesting because, amongst other things, feminists and multiculturalists have been divided amongst themselves about whether equal treatment requires special rights and policies for women and cultural minorities. Finally, we will conclude by exploring some of the challenges of realising equality as a global ideal, focussing especially on a proposal for global equality of opportunity.

Rival perspectives

Distributive equality

Is inequality objectionable because some people have more money than others, because some people are happier than others, because some have a better quality of life than others, because of all of these things, or because of something else entirely? Distributive egalitarians – such as Richard Arneson, G. A. Cohen, Ronald Dworkin, John Roemer and Amartya Sen – agree that these are the kinds of questions which egalitarians should ask, because they each think that a society is unequal when people have greater or lesser shares of something. However, they take different views about what it is that should be distributed equally (the 'equalisandum', to use the technical term). Whilst Amartya Sen (1992) describes this as the 'Equality of What?' problem, G. A. Cohen (2011) calls it the currency question, and formulates it as follows: '[w]hat aspect(s) of a person's condition should count in a *fundamental* way for egalitarians, and not merely as a cause of or evidence of or proxy for what they regard as fundamental?' (Cohen, 2011, p. 3). For example, imagine a society in which there are many different inequalities – some have more money, friends, power or leisure time, and others are happier, funnier, better looking or more confident. Some of these inequalities might be significant without themselves being fundamental in Cohen's sense, and some distributive egalitarians believe that inequalities of wealth are like this. On the one hand, they say that what matters most fundamentally is that some people are less happy or satisfied than others, or that they are less able to do or be the things that they value. On the other hand, they nevertheless believe that inequalities of wealth are significant, since in a market society one's wealth may influence how satisfied one is, or what one is able to be or do.

Here we will explore some of the different views that contemporary distributive egalitarians have defended about which inequalities fundamentally matter. According to the first of these, it is the distribution of *resources* that egalitarians should be fundamentally concerned about. Resources are crucial to living well, since we need them to achieve various ends, such as satisfying our needs, fulfilling our desires, or completing our projects. Although advocates of this view acknowledge that it is these ends that are really essential to living well, they believe that distributive equality is satisfied by equalising the means to them, and not the ends themselves. In capitalist societies, one of the most important means to the satisfaction of ends is money. However, political theorists interpret resources much more broadly than this, and include various things that people might want in order to lead happier or more fulfilling lives. The most influential proponent of this approach is Ronald Dworkin, who calls his theory 'equality of resources' (Dworkin, 2000).

Dworkin distinguished between two different kinds of resource. First are impersonal resources, including things like wealth, property, goods, opportunities and services. These are transferable and can be reassigned by social institutions. For instance, the distribution of opportunities can be altered by outlawing (or initiating) discriminatory employment practices, and the distribution of wealth can be altered by implementing a new taxation scheme. Second are personal resources, which cannot be transferred amongst people, as they include things like 'physical and mental health and ability ... general fitness and capacities ... [and] wealth-talent, that is, [the] innate capacity to produce goods or services that others will pay to have' (Dworkin, 2000, pp. 322–3). On Dworkin's account, an equal distribution obtains when each person has an equally satisfactory overall share of resources, counting their personal resources in combination with their impersonal resources. Dworkin has a complex account of the properties that such a distribution should exhibit, which we shall examine in the second key debate. For the moment, we need only note one vital implication of his scheme, which is that because personal resources are not transferable, inequalities in their distribution should be compensated by allocating people greater or lesser shares of impersonal resources.

Dworkin summarises this aspect of his theory by saying that an egalitarian political community 'should aim to erase or mitigate differences between people in their personal resources' (Dworkin, 2000, p. 286). This might mean, for instance, that people with disabilities, or with fewer marketable talents, are entitled to financial subsidies or to additional opportunities, so as to preserve equality in the overall distribution. This kind of compensation scheme has a strong intuitive appeal. For example, consider a society in which impersonal resources, such as wealth and property, are distributed equally, and suppose that one of its members has a physical disability that requires them to expend some of their impersonal resources meeting their medical needs. Another member, meanwhile, does not have a physical disability, and is therefore able to devote more of their impersonal resources to fulfilling their aims. Unless the first person is allocated a greater share of impersonal resources than the second, it would seem 'forced' to describe the distribution that obtains amongst the pair as equal, at least in any sense that we should care about (Arneson, 1989). Consequently, equality seems to require something like a Dworkinian redistribution of impersonal resources, to mitigate against the effects of a prior inequality in the distribution of personal resources.

Dworkin outlined his theory as an alternative to a rival view, which he termed *equality of welfare*. Modified versions of this theory have subsequently been defended by Richard Arneson, G. A. Cohen and John Roemer. Welfare, in this context, refers either to preference-satisfaction or to happiness (we return to the question of defining welfare in Chapter 9). Thus, one person has more welfare than another if more of their preferences are satisfied, or if they subjectively experience their life as being more enjoyable. In turn, we can evaluate whether a society succeeds or fails to uphold the ideal of equality not by considering how wealthy people are, or how many resources they have, but by looking at whether they enjoy similar levels of welfare. Something like this view about the currency of equality is often implicitly assumed by condemnations of gross material inequality. For example, critics of the current global distribution of wealth often point out that it leaves large numbers of people unable to live fulfilling lives, and critics of capitalist societies often complain that they immiserate the poor. The common denominator in criticisms like these is that material inequality matters because of its effect on welfare. Consequently, there is a strong intuitive appeal to thinking about equality in these terms, which even Dworkin acknowledges, since 'welfare is what really matters to people, as distinct from money and goods, which matter to them only instrumentally, so far as these are useful in producing welfare' (Dworkin, 2000, p. 31).

Despite its appeal, adopting welfare as the currency of equality has two counter-intuitive implications. The first of these was noted by Amartya Sen, and it follows from the observation that people often alter their desires and ambitions in light of their circumstances (this phenomenon is called 'adaptive preferences'). As a result, '[a] thoroughly deprived person, leading a very reduced life, might not appear to be badly off in terms of the mental metric of desire and its fulfilment, if the hardship is accepted with non-grumbling resignation' (Sen, 1992, p. 55). If egalitarians adopt welfare as the currency of distributive equality, the danger is that they may fail to recognise that some people have been short changed, if those people have already lowered their horizons in light of their oppressive circumstances. A second counter-intuitive implication of the welfare view, noted by Dworkin and discussed in Box 8.1, is that equalising welfare would seemingly recommend giving more resources to people with 'champagne tastes, who need more income simply to achieve the same level of welfare as those with less expensive tastes' (Dworkin, 2000, pp. 48–90). Whilst the resourcist view recommends mitigating the effects of disablement by allocating supplementary resources to people with disabilities, the welfarist view recommends the same scheme on the subtly different grounds that people with disabilities cannot

BOX 8.1   EQUALITY AND EXPENSIVE TASTES

Consider the following example, suggested by Cohen:

Paul loves photography, while Fred loves fishing. Prices are such that Fred pursues his pastime with ease while Paul cannot afford to. Paul's life is a lot less pleasant as a result: it might even be true that it has less meaning than Fred's does. I think the egalitarian thing to do is to subsidize Paul's photography ... Paul's problem is that he hates fishing and, so I am permissibly assuming, could not have helped hating it – it does not suit his natural inclinations. He has a genuinely involuntary expensive taste, and I think that a commitment to equality implies that he should be helped in the way that people like Paul are indeed helped by subsidized community leisure facilities. (Cohen, 2011, p. 20)

Should Paul's photography be subsidised? Would things be different if his was not 'a genuinely involuntary expensive taste'?

convert their initial share of resources into an equal amount of welfare. But this rationale also applies to people like Louis, who does not have a disability, but who has cultivated 'expensive tastes', such as a preference for fine wine or opera (Dworkin, 2000, p. 49). Equalising Louis' welfare will require allocating him a greater share of impersonal resources than people with comparatively 'cheaper tastes' (for beer and television, for instance). Moreover, it would require this even if Louis had intentionally cultivated his preferences for wine or opera.

According to Dworkin, it is counter-intuitive to allocate additional resources to Louis because he identifies with and endorses his preferences, and should therefore be held responsible for them. Although Dworkin thinks that things would be different if Louis regretted his preferences (Dworkin, 2000, p. 291), his general position is that inequalities which are the result of a person's character, convictions, preferences, motives, tastes and ambitions do not demand correction or compensation, since an egalitarian political community should not 'aim to mitigate or compensate for differences in personality' (Dworkin, 2000, p. 286). As we shall see in the second key debate, some of Dworkin's critics worry that his refusal to compensate people for their ambitions, tastes and preferences is too hasty, since at least some aspects of someone's personality might be the unchosen product of their circumstances, such as their childhood socialisation (Arneson, 1989; Roemer, 1996; Cohen, 2011). Notwithstanding this, proponents of equality of welfare have largely accepted the underlying point that Dworkin was registering. For instance, Cohen agrees that egalitarians should not 'finance expensive tastes which people choose to develop' and that 'a person with *wantonly* expensive tastes has no claim on us' (Cohen, 2011, p. 20). In a similar fashion, Arneson claims that '[i]ndividuals can arrive at different welfare levels due to choices they make for which they alone should be held responsible' and that it would be 'inappropriate to insist upon equality of welfare when welfare inequality arises through the voluntary choice of the person who gets lesser welfare' (Arneson, 1989, pp. 83–4).

Defenders of welfare have consequently proposed reformulating their view so as to permit welfare inequalities that are 'due to factors which lie within each individual's control' (Arneson, 1989, p. 86). One way to do this, suggested by Arneson, is to say that egalitarians should aim to equalise people's *opportunity for welfare*, and not welfare itself. On this view, Louis' welfare shortfall is permissible, provided that he initially had an equal opportunity for welfare and chose to cultivate his expensive tastes. Arneson explains his view as follows:

> [W]hen an age cohort reaches the onset of responsible adulthood, they enjoy equal opportunity for welfare when, for each of them, the best sequence of choices that it would be reasonable to expect the person to follow would yield the same expected welfare for all, the second-best sequence of choices would also yield the same expected welfare for all, and so on through the array of lifetime choice sequences each faces. (Arneson, 1999, p. 488)

Arneson's view is complex because the choices a person makes at one time, such as their dietary or exercise choices, may influence the opportunities available to them later. Thus, holding people responsible for some of their choices cannot mean equalising their opportunities for welfare at each particular moment, since people could have greater or lesser opportunities at one time as a result of their prior choices.

A difficulty with Arneson's view has been suggested by Cohen (2011, p. 23), drawing on an example initially suggested by Dworkin (2000, p. 58). Suppose that Jude begins with fewer resources than everyone else, but has equal welfare, since his wants and desires are easily satisfied. Now imagine that Jude decides to cultivate some more expensive tastes (Dworkin suggests that he takes up bullfighting, requiring regular trips to Spain). Since Jude has so few resources, he now finds himself with less welfare than everyone else, and thus requests additional resources to equalise the distribution. Cohen thinks that Arneson must refuse Jude's request, because Jude chose to cultivate his subsequent preferences, and could have avoided doing so at no great cost to himself. In other words, Jude already had an equal opportunity for welfare, and chose to squander that opportunity by cultivating expensive tastes. But Cohen thinks that Arneson's solution is unfair, since Jude started out with fewer resources than everyone else. At the same time, Cohen also argues against Dworkin's resourcist alternative, on the grounds that it would be a mistake to neglect inequalities of welfare entirely. To make this point, he asks us to consider an 'unfortunate person' who is able to move his arms effectively, but only at the cost of experiencing serious pain (Cohen, 2011, p. 16). This pain can be relieved by expensive medicine, and Cohen thinks it is obvious that egalitarians should favour providing it for him. This is a compensation scheme, but it seems impossible to justify it without appealing to the idea of welfare, since it is pain and not resource-deficiency that is being corrected. The lesson that Cohen draws from these examples, and others like them, is that we need a hybrid currency of equality (which he calls *access to advantage*), incorporating both a person's resources and their welfare.

A final answer to the currency question has been suggested by Amartya Sen (1980, 1992, 2009), and developed by Martha Nussbaum (1990, 1992, 1999, 2011). According to this view, we should compare how well people are faring by looking at their *capabilities* to function in particular ways. As we saw in Chapter 7, a 'functioning' is what a person can do or be. These might be simple (such as being nourished, literate or healthy) or more complex (such as being happy, having self-respect or participating in social life). In turn, a capability is the effective ability to achieve a functioning, or a combination of functionings. Not all functionings are equally valuable, and capability theorists emphasise the importance of particular functionings which they believe to be essential for living a truly human life (Sen, 1992, pp. 44–6). For them, if we want to find out whether a society is unequal in ways that we should care about, we should begin by comparing the extent to which people can achieve valuable functionings.

The difference between the capability approach and the theories already discussed is that it requires egalitarians to compare people's effective abilities (or real freedoms), rather than what they have or how satisfied they are. As Nussbaum puts it:

> We ask not only about the person's satisfaction with what she does, but about what she does, and what she is in a position to do (what her opportunities and liberties are). And we ask not just about the resources that are sitting around, but about how those do or do not go to work, enabling [the person] to function in a fully human way. (Nussbaum, 2000, p. 71)

One advantage of using capabilities as the currency of equality is that it directly draws our attention to morally significant phenomena. For example, a person with limited vision might lack the capability to secure meaningful employment, if society is arranged so that there are inadequate supports for employers who hire people with disabilities. This strikes many people as an important inequality, quite independently of whether or not people who lack this capability have an equal share of resources, or have an equal opportunity for welfare. Moreover, focussing on capabilities reveals why it would be inadequate to compensate people by allocating them additional resources or welfare, if doing so did not address the capability deprivation at hand.

Considered as an answer to the currency question, the capability approach runs into two related difficulties. First, applying it will require a definitive list of human functionings, if we are to compare different people's respective levels of advantage and disadvantage. Perhaps unsurprisingly, attempts to come up with a list of basic functionings (such as Nussbaum's, discussed in Box 8.2) have

BOX 8.2 TEN CENTRAL CAPABILITIES

Nussbaum (2011, pp. 33–4) has proposed the following list of ten central capabilities, which she thinks are essential ingredients of a dignified human life:

1. *Life.* Being able to live to the end of a human life of normal length
2. *Bodily Health.* Being able to have good health, including reproductive health
3. *Bodily Integrity.* Being able to move freely from place to place; to be secure against violent assault, including sexual assault and domestic violence; having opportunities for sexual satisfaction and for choice in matters of reproduction
4. *Senses, Imagination, and Thought.* Being able to use the senses, to imagine, think, and reason – and to do these things in a 'truly human' way, a way informed and cultivated by an adequate education
5. *Emotions.* Being able to have attachments to things and people outside ourselves; to love those who love and care for us, to grieve at their absence
6. *Practical Reason.* Being able to form a conception of the good and to engage in critical reflection about the planning of one's life
7. *Affiliation.* (A) Being able to live with and towards others, to recognise and show concern for other human beings, to engage in various forms of social interaction; to be able to imagine the situation of another and have compassion for that situation; to have the capability for both justice and friendship. (B). Having the social bases of self-respect and non-humiliation; being able to be treated as a dignified being whose worth is equal to that of others
8. *Other species.* Being able to live with concern for and in relation to animals, plants, and the world of nature
9. *Play.* Being able to laugh, to play, to enjoy recreational activities
10. *Control over one's Environment.* (A) Political. Being able to participate effectively in political choices that govern one's life. (B) Material. Being able to hold property (both land and movable goods); having the right to seek employment on an equal basis with others; having the freedom from unwarranted search and seizure

Nussbaum thinks that each of these is essential to human flourishing, and her list has attracted controversy because it is presented in universal terms, as something that applies to all countries and should be guaranteed by all constitutions.

Is the capabilities approach compatible with respect for pluralism?

attracted controversy, as they are likely to include things that others regard as inessential to a truly human life. An example of this that is often cited is Nussbaum's insistence that '[b]eing able to live with concern for and in relation to animals, plants, and the world of nature' is a basic human functioning (Nussbaum, 2000, p. 79). Second, even if it was possible to get people to agree to a list of basic functionings, ensuring that each person had the capability to achieve them might still fall short of equality, comprehensively understood. For instance, everyone might have the full complement of capabilities and yet some people could be richer or happier than others, or equipped with the capabilities to achieve additional functionings not specified on the list. In response to this, some advocates of the capability view prefer to describe their goal as bringing everyone to a 'minimum threshold' of capability (Nussbaum, 2011, p. 76). On this account, the capability approach aims to an ideal of 'sufficiency' rather than 'equality' (we return to this issue in the first key debate below, and again in Chapter 10).

Social equality

Not all egalitarians believe that distributive equality is the best way to capture egalitarianism as a moral or political ideal. A rival theory of social equality has recently been sketched out by authors such as Elizabeth Anderson, Nancy Fraser, Axel Honneth, David Miller, T.M. Scanlon, Samuel Scheffler, Charles Taylor, Michael Walzer, Jonathan Wolff and Iris Marion Young, albeit under a variety of names, including 'democratic equality' (Anderson, 1999, 2010), 'structural equality' (Young, 1990, 2000, 2010), 'relational equality' (Scheffler, 2010), 'complex equality' (Walzer, 1983) and 'equality of status' (Miller, 1999). Because this view has not been as thoroughly worked out as its rival, there is less agreement about what it is that social egalitarians believe, and about what divides them. Here, we will consider three different characterisations that have been given of the ideal of social equality. However, it is important to note that these overlap in important ways, and that many theorists incorporate elements from each of them.

The first characterisation contrasts social equality with status hierarchy. For example, David Miller describes social equality as an 'ideal of a society in which people regard and treat one another as equals – in other words, a society that does not place people in hierarchically ranked categories such as classes' (Miller, 1999, p. 232). To support this kind of view, discussed in Box 8.3, Samuel Scheffler argues that 'there is something valuable about human relationships that are, in certain crucial respects at least, unstructured by differences of rank, power, or status' (Scheffler, 2010, p. 225). Stark examples of status hierarchy include aristocratic and caste societies, where nobility and honour are associated with a person's title or ancestry. Contemporary liberal democracies tend to have more subtle hierarchies, marked by the influence of social categories such as class, gender and race.

Some social egalitarians object to hierarchies because they associate them with domination. For instance, as we saw in Chapter 7, Philip Pettit argues that the test for whether people are free from domination is to see whether they are able to 'walk tall, live without shame or indignity, and look one another in the eye without any reason for fear or deference' (Pettit, 2012, p. 3). The more hierarchical a society is, the more likely it will fail the 'eyeball test'. In some circumstances, hierarchy might also open the door to a particular form of tyranny, if high-status groups are able to exercise leverage, using their control or superiority in one

BOX 8.3   EQUALITY AND HIERARCHY

Social hierarchies often shape how people act towards one another. For instance, in a hierarchical society people might greet one another by bowing rather than by shaking hands, they might communicate in a reticent or deferential or arrogant manner, members of different groups might use terms like 'boy' or 'boss' or 'your honour' to address one another, and they might socialise exclusively amongst members of the same 'set' or caste or clan. Where social practices like these are ubiquitous, then status inequalities are likely to have had a pervasive influence on how people make sense of their social world. Meanwhile, some social egalitarians aspire to a society in which there will be 'no more bowing and scraping, fawning and toadying; no more fearful trembling; no more high-and-mightiness' (Walzer, 1983, p. xiii). This means that each member of the community must enjoy an 'equal standing' with everyone else (Miller, 1999, p. 239). Walzer illustrates this by invoking the idea of a 'society of misters' (Walzer, 1983, p. 252). On his reading, the gradual decision to adopt a uniform mode of address marked an erosion of the aristocratic dynamics of superiority, snobbery and deference. Once people began to address one another on equal terms, Walzer argues, it was clear that status inequality had loosened its grip on their imaginations.

Is the abolition of social hierarchy a fundamental goal of egalitarianism?

domain to extend control elsewhere. For example, Michael Walzer (1983) points out that elites in hierarchical societies may be able to convert their success in one sphere into advantages in another, such as when the wealthy exercise disproportionate influence over political decisions, or when political representatives have preferential access to medical care, or when bureaucrats allocate themselves superior living quarters. To correct this, he proposes a form of 'complex equality', the aim of which is to ensure that inequalities in the distribution of one good do not influence or distort the distribution of other goods.

The second characterisation contrasts social equality with oppression. If social equality is understood in this way, then egalitarians should prioritise rectifying oppression, for instance by favouring mechanisms to empower or protect its victims. A formative influence on this type of view is feminist philosopher Iris Marion Young's theory of oppression, aspects of which were later developed by other multiculturalist and feminist political theorists. Young developed a rich and nuanced account of the multifaceted character of oppression in the modern world, which she thinks has two distinctive features. First, oppression is experienced by groups, such as women, ethnic minorities, immigrants, homosexuals, the elderly, the poor and the disabled. Second, oppression is a structural injustice, which is woven into the institutions that govern our collective lives.

According to Young, groups can be oppressed in at least five different ways (1990, pp. 48–63). First, groups may be exposed to violence, which includes 'harassment, intimidation, or ridicule simply for the purpose of degrading, humiliating, or stigmatizing group members' (1990, p. 62). For example, sexist, racist and homophobic societies oppress women, ethnic minorities and homosexuals if they leave them vulnerable to assaults of this type. Second, groups may be marginalised, such as when people with disabilities, indigenous peoples, asylum-seekers and undocumented migrants have little or no opportunity to participate meaningfully in major social activities, especially the workplace. Third, groups may be oppressed by virtue of being powerless, such as when people are unable to meaningfully influence the decisions that shape their lives. For example, workers may lack the opportunity to influence decisions made by their employers, immigrants may lack the right to vote or to run for election, and indigenous peoples may lack the appropriate social standing for their demands to be listened to by others. Fourth, oppression might take the form of cultural imperialism, when the worldview of a dominant social group is imposed on subordinates. As a result, groups that do not 'fit' the norm may be stereotyped as deviant, or written off as inferior, or rendered invisible, as discussed in Box 8.4. Finally, oppression may also take the form of exploitation, 'when the energies of the have-nots are continuously expended to maintain and augment the power, status, and wealth of the haves' (Young, 1990, p. 50). Although the term 'exploitation' is typically used to describe the benefits that employers extract from their workers, Young extends it to cover other social relations, including those between men and women (1990, p. 51). For example, female spouses often perform unpaid domestic labour that advantages their male partners, since it frees them up to pursue other – often higher-status – activities. Similarly, in the workplace, female employees are often expected to perform traditionally feminine tasks, such as nurturing or smoothing over workplace tensions. In both settings, Young thinks that women are exploited, and therefore oppressed, since their 'energies are expended in jobs that enhance the status of, please, or comfort others, usually men' (Young, 1990, p. 51).

Other social egalitarians have added additional forms of oppression to Young's list. For example, Anderson (2010, p. 15) suggests 'stigmatization', pointing out that subordinate groups are often represented in ways that associate them with negative traits, such as being stupid, criminal, incompetent, irrational or weak. Anderson thinks that stigmatisation is oppressive, since it can be demeaning and because it can justify excluding groups from positions of authority. In addition, stigmatisation might also lead to groups suffering what Miranda Fricker has labelled 'testimonial injustice' (2007), which occurs when a listener gives the assertions of a speaker lesser weight because of their prejudices. This is facilitated by the dispersal of assumptions and biases about the competences and credibility of different social groups. For example, if a police officer does not believe you because you are black, or if your work colleagues talk over you because you are a woman, or if your views are not taken seriously because you are a member of an indigenous people, then you have been a victim of testimonial injustice in

BOX 8.4   MISRECOGNITION AND OPPRESSION

Proponents of the politics of recognition, such as Charles Taylor and Axel Honneth, associate misrecognition with oppression. These political theorists start from the idea that people have unique identities, by which they mean distinctive ways of living in and understanding the world. Because identities are formed and negotiated 'dialogically', through interactions with others, they believe that it is important for people to be recognised and esteemed for who they really are, and not to be misrecognised or ignored by their fellow citizens or by social institutions. For example, according to Taylor:

> [O]ur identity is partly shaped by recognition or its absence, often by the misrecognition of others, and so a person or group of people can suffer real damage, real distortion, if the people or the society around them mirror back to them a confining or demeaning or contemptible picture of themselves. Non recognition can inflict harm, can be a form of oppression, imprisoning someone in a false, distorted or reduced mode of being. (Taylor, 1994, p. 25)

One example of the harm of misrecognition is the experience of being a member of a racially stigmatised group in a racist society. People who find themselves in this situation can be oppressed not only by physical insecurity and material deprivation, but also by the way in which they are represented within the public space, for instance as lazy or violent or dangerous. As Honneth points out, 'the experience of this kind of social devaluation typically brings with it a loss of personal self-esteem, of the opportunity to regard themselves as beings whose traits and abilities are recognised' (1995, p. 134). Misrecognition may also take more subtle forms. For instance, linguistic and national minorities may experience recognition deprivation if their culture or language is not supported or valued by their political community. Or, homosexuals might experience a failure of recognition if educational and social practices persistently represent heterosexuality as the norm.

Is misrecognition a form of oppression?

Fricker's sense. No doubt other forms of oppression could also be added to this list. However, one shortcoming with this approach, discussed in Box 8.5, is that some objectionable forms of social inequality are not oppressive, but might still qualify for egalitarian concern.

The final characterisation of social equality equates an egalitarian society with an egalitarian social ethos. A version of this view has been defended by Jonathan Wolff, and similar ideas also animate the later work of distributive egalitarian G. A. Cohen. Motivating this approach is a belief that distributive equality, at least as it is ordinarily formulated, can seem 'rather soulless' (Wolff, 2010, p. 337). As Wolff puts it 'there is more to a society of equals than a just scheme of distribution of material goods' (1998, p. 104). In particular, distributive egalitarians seem to fail to appreciate the existence of 'goods that depend on the attitude

BOX 8.5 SOCIAL INEQUALITY AND OPPRESSION

Although social egalitarians should be committed to eradicating oppression, there are other forms of disadvantage and inequality which are not oppressive, and these should perhaps concern social egalitarians too. For example, in a fashion-conscious social context, such as a school in a capitalist society, being unable to afford high-status brands might mark a pupil out as inferior. Students who find themselves in this position might be ridiculed, but in a sense that falls short of what Young means by violence. Likewise, they might be left off invitation lists and be excluded from some social activities, but in a sense that falls short of what Young refers to as marginalisation. Although social egalitarians might want to refrain from describing those students as oppressed, they might nevertheless want to insist that the culture or the ethos of the school is inegalitarian.

Should social egalitarians be troubled by inequalities that are not oppressive?

people have toward each other' (1998, p. 104). Consequently, they neglect the question of 'what would be a good way to live together' (2010, p. 337). To correct this, social egalitarians like Wolff argue that we need to pay closer attention to the ethos of a society. On this account, an egalitarian society is distinguished by the fact that its members share a commitment to an underlying set of egalitarian values, which influence the principles they adopt and inform their everyday practices and behaviour.

To see why egalitarians might have reasons to be concerned with the ethos of a society, we can perform the following thought experiment. Suppose that two similar societies simultaneously decide to institute an equal distribution of whatever you think should be distributed equally (resources, say, or welfare or capabilities). If equality is a purely distributive ideal, then both of these societies will be egalitarian to an identical extent, at least for the time being. Meanwhile, if equality is a social or relational ideal, then one society might still outperform the other. For instance, suppose that the members of the first society share a strong sense of community, such that they care both for and about one another. Because they are committed to one another, they are motivated by what Cohen calls 'communal reciprocity'. This means that they serve one another not because of what they can get in return, but because others want or need their service (Cohen, 2009, p. 39). Moreover, they also cherish the ideal of equality, such that egalitarian principles inform their everyday decisions (Cohen, 2008, p. 123). Consequently, they are willing to forgo economic and other gains for themselves, if doing so will benefit the least advantaged members of their society. By contrast, suppose that the members of the second society lack a strong sense of community, and do not really care for or about one another. Unlike the members of the first society, they are motivated mainly by market incentives, such as greed and fear, and are willing to serve one another only in exchange for whatever goods and services others are willing to pay in return. In the second society, people do not value co-operation for its own sake, and there is none of the social friendship that characterises the first society. Moreover, its members are eager to get as much as they can for themselves, even if their doing so is at the expense of everyone else.

Not only might the first society be more pleasant than the second, but it might also be more egalitarian, in at least two different ways. First, as we shall see in the first key debate, talented members of the first society, motivated by communal reciprocity and an egalitarian ethos, might be willing to exchange their socially productive skills for less than the maximum rate they could command at a competitive market. By contrast, talented members of the second society, motivated mainly by greed and fear, may demand comparatively higher wages for performing the same kind of work. Consequently, it may not be possible to sustain an egalitarian distribution over time in the second society, if its members are unwilling to make sacrifices for the sake of equality. Second, the relationships amongst the members of the first society may have an egalitarian quality that is absent in the second society. This may have the effect of reducing the likelihood that status hierarchies and oppressive relationships will develop. For instance, suppose that the members of the first society are determined to face one another as equals, because they are jointly committed to sustaining an egalitarian political community. It does not seem inconceivable to say that these members will be more attuned to the threat of hierarchy. Consequently, in their everyday lives they may be more likely to act in ways to avoid allowing inequalities of status from emerging or becoming entrenched. Similarly, if they are cognisant of the tendency of people to marginalise, stigmatise, misrecognise or exploit one another, it is likely that they will not only institute mechanisms and procedures to protect their most vulnerable members, but that they will also try to avoid contributing to oppression in their everyday lives.

Key debates

Is distributive equality an ideal that should be promoted?

As we have seen, distributive egalitarians object to the unequal distribution of something, such as welfare, resources or capabilities. Social egalitarians also object to the unequal distribution of these things, if such a distribution is likely to undermine a society of equals, for instance by supporting status hierarchies or oppression. This key debate will concentrate on two different objections that have been registered against equality as a distributive ideal. According to the first, distributive equality is not itself valuable. Rather, ensuring that everyone has enough, or improving the position of the least advantaged, are more important political goals. As we shall see, whilst distributive egalitarians must reject the principles of 'sufficiency' or 'priority', social egalitarians may be able to accommodate them. The second objection is that some forms of distributive inequality are desirable, since unequal shares incentivise valuable activities. As we shall see, whilst this objection poses a serious challenge to the ideal of distributive equality, one promising response to it derives from a social egalitarian perspective.

Let us start with the idea that distributive equality is not, as such, valuable. According to some political theorists, unequal shares can be preferable to equal shares, at least under some circumstances. To see why this might be the case, imagine a simple society, containing two people – A and B. Let us suppose that this society is radically unequal, since A has 100 units (of whatever) and B has only 10. Now also suppose that a distributive egalitarian arrives on the scene. Unsurprisingly, they condemn the current arrangement and propose to equalise the distribution. For some reason, the only policies that could achieve this outcome would leave both A and B with either 10 units each, or with 5 units each. Should this society adopt one of these policies, or stick to its current arrangements? Many people think that it would be absurd to change track, since the first alternative makes no one better off and makes A worse off, whilst the second makes both A and B worse off. However, from the vantage point of distributive equality, both of these distributions are preferable to the starting point. Moreover, distributive egalitarians do not have a reason to prefer one of the distributions to the other, since they both satisfy the demands of equality to the same extent.

Derek Parfit has labelled this the 'levelling down' objection (Parfit, 1998, 2000; see also Flew, 1981). From it, he draws the conclusion that we should reject views which say that distributive equality is the only goal to promote, or that its demands should always prevail over other considerations. Notice, however, that accepting the levelling down objection does not commit egalitarians to abandoning the goal of distributive equality, only to saying that it should be considered alongside other values. As such, it does not demonstrate that distributive equality is not valuable, only that it is not the only value.

Harry Frankfurt has suggested a stronger objection to distributive equality, which does imply that it is not, as such, valuable. On his account, distributive egalitarianism goes wrong because it is a comparative ideal. As he puts it: '[t]he fundamental error of egalitarianism lies in supposing that it is morally important whether one person has less than another regardless of how much either of them has' (Frankfurt, 1987, p. 34). Comparing how well people fare in relation to one another does not tell us anything about how well their lives are going in absolute terms, and this is what Frankfurt thinks that morality should be concerned with.

Instead of distributive equality, Frankfurt proposes that we endorse the 'doctrine of sufficiency'. According to this view, what is important 'is not that everyone should have the *same* but that each should have *enough*' (Frankfurt, 1987, p. 21). The intuitive appeal of this view is easy to see. For instance, recall our unequal two-person society. Many people cannot decide whether the inequality between A and B is itself wrong. However, they have much clearer intuitions if we tell them that B, but not A, is living in poverty. *That*, they say, would definitely be objectionable. This seems to tell us that the wrong of poverty is that the poor do not have enough, and not that the rich have more than the poor. In support of this, we might also note that although people often have strong intuitions about the wrong of poverty, it is less common to have strong intuitions about equal shares. For instance, consider inequalities *amongst* the wealthy. Typically, we do not regard these as particularly troubling (does it really matter that some investment bankers earn less than some movie stars?). Similarly, consider the duty to assist the needy, through charitable donations for example. Typically, we do not extend this duty to everyone with less than us. Instead, we tend to believe that we only have duties towards those who do not have enough.

Although the sufficiency principle has a strong intuitive appeal of its own, it still faces difficulties, since its proponents need to decide how much is enough, which means settling on a threshold that tells us when efforts to improve the position of B have been satisfied. Sufficiency theorists can adopt more or less demanding views about this. For example, as we saw, capability theorists like Nussbaum define the threshold by reference to a list of 'functionings'. Similarly, Anderson (2007) and Satz (2007) believe that people have enough when they are able to participate as equals in a democratic society. Frankfurt sets a different bar, and says that people have enough when they are 'content', such that having more money would not enable them to become significantly happier:

> A contented person regards having more money as *inessential* to his being satisfied with his life … His attention and interest are not vividly engaged by the benefits which would be available to him if he had more money. (Frankfurt, 1987, p. 39)

One difficulty with Frankfurt's solution is that some people could be content with too little. For example, the phenomenon of 'adaptive preferences', which we examined earlier, suggests that some people might be content with less than we think they should be. Another difficulty that all sufficiency theorists face is that their thresholds could be too demanding for some societies, if nearly everyone currently falls below it. In such societies, the sufficiency principle cannot tell us where scarce resources should be targeted. (For instance, would it be better to raise a small number of people above the threshold, or to make a minor improvement in everyone's situation without raising anyone above it?) A final worry is whether we should really be indifferent about inequality above the sufficiency threshold. For example, even if the inequalities between A and B might seem less urgent once B has crossed the threshold, they might disrupt the possibility of achieving a society of equals.

Instead of replacing distributive equality with the doctrine of sufficiency, some political theorists favour a third alternative, which says that what matters is improving the position of the worst-off. To motivate support for this view, imagine that your government proposes to 'regenerate' a historically deprived region, perhaps by subsidising local companies and encouraging business investment, or by knocking down slums and replacing them with modern housing. The aim of regeneration, let us stipulate, is to improve the conditions or the prospects of the least advantaged members of society. Despite having an egalitarian 'feel', these policies are unlikely to qualify as strictly egalitarian if they do not work towards eliminating the gap between the rich and the poor. They will also fail to satisfy the sufficiency principle, if the poor already have enough or if regeneration will not bring them above the threshold. If you nevertheless can imagine circumstances in which these policies are justified, then it might be because you favour the view that Parfit has labelled 'prioritarianism' (Parfit, 1998, 2000).

Prioritarianism is so called because it demands that we 'prioritise' the least advantaged members of society. Prioritarians endorse three claims: that benefits should be distributed according to where they can do the most good; that benefiting the worse off takes priority over benefiting the better off; and that benefiting the worse off matters more the less they have. Suppose that you accept the first claim, what can be said in support of the other two? Their attraction can be illustrated by considering a further thought experiment, in which you are responsible for deciding how to distribute the profits of a government scheme in our two-person society (perhaps mineral deposits were recently discovered beneath their territory). One option would be to split these evenly between A and B. However, assuming that A already has more than B, it is likely that the benefit which B derives from their (equal) share of the profits will outweigh the benefit that A derives. Moreover, not only might the benefit to B be greater, but 'on the moral scale' it might 'matter more' (Parfit, 2000, p. 24). Thus, you might decide to direct more of the profits towards B to maximise the value that they purchase, and the less well-off B is by comparison with A the more you might be inclined to allocate to them. Of course, real decisions are much more complex than this, since they involve larger population groups. One puzzle, which we examine in Box 8.6, has to do with what prioritarians should say when they are faced with the choice of benefiting a large group of moderately disadvantaged people or a smaller group of very disadvantaged people.

Because prioritarians are concerned to improve the position of the least advantaged members of society, they escape the levelling down objection. To see why this is so, recall the egalitarian's proposal to change the unequal distribution in our two-person society, where A had 100 and B had 10. As we saw, distributive egalitarians should favour moving towards an equal distribution, even if that leaves A and B with less than they started, for instance with 10 each or 5 each. Meanwhile, prioritarians believe that leaving A and B with 10 each is no improvement, since the position of B remains the same. Furthermore, and unlike

> ## BOX 8.6   WEIGHTED AND ABSOLUTE PRIORITY
>
> Imagine that you are a government minister, charged with the responsibility of choosing between two policy proposals. The first scheme is intended to improve the circumstances of the urban poor and is likely to improve the lives of a great many people in your society, many of whom are currently badly off. The second scheme is intended to improve the circumstances of the rural poor, who are currently even worse off than the urban poor. To complicate matters, officials working in your department have informed you that the second scheme is likely to bring relatively modest benefits to a small number of people, whilst the first scheme will bring greater benefits to a larger group of people. If you think that benefiting the worse off has absolute priority over benefiting the better off, then you should favour the second scheme, simply because the rural poor are worse off than the urban poor, and regardless of the considerations introduced by your officials. This option is favoured by supporters of the 'absolute' priority view, which says that 'when benefiting others, the worst-off individual (or individuals) is (or are) to be given absolute priority over the better off' (Crisp, 2003, p. 752). Meanwhile, you might favour the urban poor if you think that a large benefit can outweigh a small benefit, or if you think that benefiting more people can outweigh benefiting fewer people. Prioritarians who accept one or both of these possibilities favour a 'weighted' priority principle, which says that 'benefiting people matters more the worse off those people are, the more of those people there are, and the greater the benefits in question' (Crisp, 2003, p. 752).
>
> *Which version of the priority principle, if any, is preferable?*

egalitarians, they have grounds to condemn a policy that would leave A and B with 5 each, as it would worsen both of their positions beneath B's starting point. Instead, prioritarians will only favour policies that will have the effect of improving the position of the least well off member (who is currently B).

So far, we have seen that some political theorists believe that either sufficiency or priority is a more appropriate goal than distributive equality. A different reason for objecting to distributive equality is that it might make everyone worse off, since it discourages people from working hard and developing their talents. Although this argument is typically associated with the political right, it has also been defended by some left-wing political theorists, including Rawls. For instance, after noting the importance of 'economic efficiency' and 'the requirements of organisation and technology', Rawls suggests that 'inequalities in income and wealth, and differences in authority and degrees of responsibility' will seem acceptable to us *if* they 'make everyone better off in comparison with the benchmark of equality' (Rawls, 1999a, p. 131). The idea here is that some forms of distributive inequality, such as unequal wages, might encourage people to deploy their talents in socially productive ways, thereby benefiting everyone, including the least advantaged. Consequently, everyone – including the least advantaged themselves – should favour these inequalities, since they benefit us all.

This particular justification of inequality has come to be known as the incentives argument (Estlund, 1998; Williams, 1998; Cohen, 2001, 2008). G. A. Cohen, who criticises this argument, formulates it as follows: 'talented people will produce more than they otherwise would if, and only if, they are paid more than an ordinary wage, and some of the extra that they will then produce can be recruited on behalf of the worst off' (Cohen, 2008, p. 119). To illustrate this argument, consider a surgeon who is willing to perform surgery only on the condition that they receive an annual wage of €200,000, well in excess of the national average. This means that the members of their society face the choice of either acquiescing to the surgeon's demand or compromising the quality of medical care they receive. If surgeons are a scarce commodity, or if surgeons collectively make an analogous demand, then the latter option could result in a severe form of levelling down, making everyone worse off. Consequently, if they are to ensure the prospects of everyone, the members of this society might feel as if they have no choice but to accept the demands of the surgeon(s), along with the corresponding inequality.

Is it justifiable for the surgeon to hold their society to ransom in this way? Perhaps this is formulating things too strongly. For instance, suppose that the surgeon demands this wage because they would genuinely prefer to spend their time and energy writing poetry, even if doing so would only secure them an income of €20,000. For this person, working as a surgeon for, say, €150,000 would be less attractive a proposition than writing poetry for €20,000. If we believe that people should be allowed to select their own careers, then it might seem unfair to condemn the surgeon's behaviour. Nevertheless, egalitarians who emphasise the importance of an egalitarian ethos, such as Cohen, think that we do have grounds to criticise the surgeon's hard bargaining, if we think that an egalitarian society should be a genuine community, characterised by what Rawls calls the 'ties of civic friendship' (Rawls, 1999a, p. 470). On Cohen's account, part of what it is to experience such a community is being able to imagine ourselves justifying our preferred policies in a way that could be 'uttered by any member of society to any other member' (Cohen, 2008, p. 42). Although the poet-surgeon might be able to justify their demand for high wages in bland 'impersonal' terms ('incentives should be permitted to improve the quality of medical services') it will difficult for them to do so in 'interpersonal' terms – that is to say, on a face-to-face basis to the least advantaged themselves ("I will only save your lives if you pay me more'). What Cohen's response indicates is that if distributive egalitarians are to reject the incentives argument for inequality, they may have to accept at least part of the vision animating social egalitarianism.

Should equality be sensitive to responsibility?

In 1989, G. A. Cohen credited Ronald Dworkin with having 'performed for egalitarianism the considerable service of incorporating within it the most powerful idea in the arsenal of the anti-egalitarian right: the idea of choice and responsibility' (Cohen, 1989, p. 933). The position that Cohen was referring to subsequently came to be known as 'luck egalitarianism', a term coined by an influential critic Elizabeth Anderson (1999). In this key debate we will begin by examining some of the details of Dworkin's own theory, before looking at some of the criticisms that have been directed against both it and luck egalitarianism more generally.

Dworkin, as we have seen, thinks that the currency of equality is resources. For him, an initial distribution of resources qualifies as equal if it passes the 'envy test' (Dworkin, 2000, p. 67; 2011, pp. 356–8). Achieving this does not require that everyone have an identical bundle of resources, since people have different personalities and will prefer different resources to one another. Instead, an initial distribution of resources passes the envy test if no one prefers anyone else's bundle of resources to their own, and Dworkin illustrated this in a famous thought experiment discussed in Box 8.7. Dworkin also thought that an equal distribution ought to preserve ambition-sensitivity over time. Ambitions, as Dworkin

---

BOX 8.7 DWORKIN'S AUCTION

Dworkin asks us to imagine a shipwrecked group who find themselves on a previously uninhabited island (Dworkin, 2000, pp. 65–71). To allocate the various resources they discover, he proposes that they hold an auction, using clamshells as a currency. Each islander starts off with the same purchasing power as everyone else, and uses their clamshells to bid for their favoured resources. So, for instance, bidding for scarce or popular resources, such as delicious fruit trees or milking cows, uses up a considerable portion of an islander's quota of clamshells, whilst unpopular and plentiful resources are comparably cheaper. Since the islanders have different personalities, they will compete for different combinations of resources. After the auction is complete, some of the islanders might look at the bundles of their compatriots, and conclude that their bundle is less desirable than someone else's. If this happens, then the envy test has not been met, and the auction must be re-run. Now suppose that the auction has been repeated until the envy test has been satisfied – that is to say, until everyone prefers their own bundle of resources to anyone else's. According to Dworkin, the resulting distribution must qualify as equal, since everyone had an equal opportunity to bid for whatever resources they prefer.

Why is this distribution ambition-sensitive? Could an islander have grounds for objecting to the outcome of such a procedure?

uses the term, refer to a person's tastes, preferences, convictions and life plans. As such, they 'furnish ... reasons or motives for making one choice rather than another' (Dworkin, 2000, p. 322). Thus, a distribution is ambition-sensitive if it reflects people's voluntary choices about their goals, projects and preferences. Preserving ambition-sensitivity may mean permitting inequalities in the overall distribution of resources. For instance, in a Dworkinian society, Adrian might earn more than Bhikhu because Adrian chooses to work longer hours (perhaps Bhikhu prefers to spend time painting). Even though the distribution between the pair is uneven, it is ambition-sensitive.

In addition to ambition-sensitivity, Dworkin also thinks that an equal distribution of resources should also be endowment-insensitive, which means that it ought not be influenced by the underlying distribution of personal resources, such as natural talents and propensities. For instance, suppose that amongst the shipwrecked islanders discussed in Box 8.7 are some people who are blamelessly unable to emulate their more industrious compatriots, because their productive talents are limited by physical impairments. If this group fares worse than the others over time, because they use up their initial share of resources quickly and are unable to produce more, the resulting distribution would be highly endowment-sensitive, and thereby unequal by Dworkin's standards. As we saw earlier, Dworkin's solution to endowment-sensitivity is to implement compensation schemes for people equipped with lesser personal resources.

To determine how much compensation people who find themselves in this predicament are entitled to, Dworkin introduced another thought experiment – the hypothetical insurance market (Dworkin, 2000, pp. 77–109). Although the details of this are complex, the basic idea is simple. In ordinary life, people take out insurance policies to cover themselves and their families in the event of losses resulting from misfortune. Although lucky policy holders never need to make a claim, some unlucky ones do, and the money they receive comes partially from the contributions made by the lucky. Suppose that we could also hypothetically insure ourselves against being born with a disadvantage or impairment. Again, lucky people would not need to make any claims against their hypothetical insurance policy, but the unlucky would, and the money they receive would come partly from the contributions of the lucky. If we could purchase hypothetical insurance of this kind, it might be rational to sacrifice some of our initial resources to protect ourselves against some of the risks we anticipate. However, we would not sacrifice all of our initial resources for this purpose, since that would leave us unable to pursue our plans and projects. Dworkin thinks that the use of thought experiments such as this can deliver serviceable estimates of which hypothetical insurance packages 'the average member of the community [would] purchase' (2000, pp. 78–9). In turn, these estimates can form the basis of government policy. For instance, suppose that we can estimate which hypothetical insurance policies the average person would purchase to cover them in the event of being born blind. On Dworkin's account, this can help us to figure out the extent to which blind people in the real world should be compensated for their misfortune. Of course, in the real world compensation will not come from fellow purchasers of hypothetical insurance, but from taxation. However, the underlying mechanism of distribution – from the lucky to the unlucky – will remain the same.

Now it should be clear why Dworkin's view has been called 'luck egalitarian'. As Anderson summarises it, this view combines two ideas: 'that people should be compensated for undeserved misfortunes and that the compensation should come from only that part of others' good fortune that is undeserved' (Anderson, 1999, p. 290). In Dworkin's case, the central case of an undeserved misfortune is an unchosen deficiency in personal resources, such as a physical disability. In addition to this, someone might make lucky gains or unlucky losses during the course of their life. One of Dworkin's most important innovations was to notice that not all of these demand egalitarian correction. For instance, someone might gain or lose by 'accepting an isolated risk he or she should have anticipated and might have declined' (Dworkin, 2000, p. 73). Dworkin calls this 'option luck', and says that upholding ambition-sensitivity means that individuals themselves should pay its costs, or reap its rewards. Meanwhile, other gains or losses might be the result of what Dworkin calls 'brute luck'. To illustrate this distinction, Dworkin says that '[i]f I buy a stock on the exchange that rises, then my option luck is good' whilst 'if I am hit by a falling meteorite whose course could not have been predicted, then my bad luck is brute' (Dworkin, 2000, p. 73). He then goes on to acknowledge that in many cases 'we may be uncertain how to describe a particular piece of bad luck', giving the example of someone who develops cancer at least partially as a result of taking an unsuccessful gamble on heavy smoking (Dworkin, 2000, pp. 73–4). Some of the difficulties to which this distinction gives rise are discussed in Box 8.8. Regardless of them, Dworkin's underlying thought is a powerful one – namely that egalitarians should be concerned to ensure that people's lives are not worsened for reasons that they are not responsible for.

Luck egalitarianism has also been developed by distributive egalitarians who reject resourcism, such as Cohen, Arneson and Roemer. For example, Cohen argues that the purpose of egalitarianism is to 'eliminate involuntary disadvantage', by which he means 'disadvantage for which the sufferer cannot be held responsible' (Cohen, 2011, p. 13). Cohen has proposed two important modifications to Dworkin's theory. The first is that people with *unchosen* expensive tastes are entitled to compensation on egalitarian grounds, if they cannot reasonably be held responsible for having those preferences, and even if they identify with them. On Cohen's account, it is a mistake to hold people responsible for all of their preferences, since preferences are sometimes formed under circumstances beyond our control. The disagreement between Dworkin and Cohen can be illustrated by recalling Louis and his expensive tastes. As Dworkin interprets this case, compensating Louis would violate ambition-sensitivity, because Louis

BOX 8.8 BRUTE LUCK AND OPTION LUCK

Luck egalitarians disagree both about how to draw the line between brute luck and option luck, and about whether the distinction is significant. One view is that most inequalities are the result of option luck because people are largely responsible for what happens to them (Rakowski, 1991). For example, someone who fails to purchase health insurance when they had an opportunity to do so and who now faces exorbitant medical costs could be described as a victim of option luck (Dworkin, 2000, p. 74). Another view is that inequalities are mainly the result of brute luck and that people should not be held responsible for them (Lippert-Rasmussen, 2001; Barry, 2006, 2008). For example, the losses that someone suffers after choosing an occupation which became obsolete as a result of unexpected technological changes might be attributable to brute luck, even though their initial choice of occupation was a matter of option luck. A third 'all-luck' view is that the distinction between brute and option does not really matter all that much, since 'differential option luck should be considered as unjust as differential brute luck' (Segall, 2010, p. 47). For example, both of our victims have suffered bad luck, and whether their losses are properly attributed to brute or option luck might not tell us whether they should be held responsible for them.

Which view, if any, should luck egalitarians prefer?

identifies with his preferences, which are part of his personality. By contrast, compensating paraplegics upholds endowment-insensitivity, since disabled people suffer bad brute luck in the distribution of personal resources. Dworkin's version of luck egalitarianism therefore relies on his prior distinction between personality and preferences on the one hand, which are supposedly chosen, and personal resources on the other, which are supposedly unchosen (or part of our 'circumstances'). But if Dworkin has drawn the distinction between choice and circumstance in the wrong place, then his goal of an ambition-sensitive and endowment-insensitive distribution may not be the appropriate one for luck egalitarians to advocate. Instead, Cohen proposes 'relocating Dworkin's cut', insisting that the proper distinction to be drawn is between 'responsibility and bad luck' (Cohen, 2011, p. 20). Thus, if Louis is not responsible for having expensive tastes, and if instead we have grounds for saying that his preferences are a matter of brute luck, then luck egalitarians should favour compensating him for his misfortune.

Cohen's second modification to Dworkin's formulation of luck egalitarianism is that people should not be held responsible for their tastes being expensive, even when they are responsible for having those tastes in the first place. For example, suppose that someone positively values having a preference for listening to 'music of a sort difficult to obtain' (Dworkin, 2000, p. 82). It seems difficult to say that having that particular taste is a matter of bad luck for that person, since they identify with their preference and do not regret having it. However, and regardless of this, the fact that this preference is expensive to satisfy might not be something that the person should be held responsible for, as it was not something which they had any influence over and might be something they regret (Cohen, 2011, p. 25). Things would be different, of course, if they cultivated their preference for 'snobbish' reasons, such as having a preference for expensive tastes because they are expensive. However, some luck egalitarians believe that even in this case it would be unfair to penalise someone, if they regret the fact that they live in 'a social context in which it is valuable for one to satisfy snobbish preferences' (Lippert-Rasmussen, 2013, p. 449).

As should be clear, there are significant disagreements amongst luck egalitarians about what a responsibility-sensitive distribution would consist in. Meanwhile, some social egalitarian critics of luck egalitarianism have argued that the luck egalitarian project is fundamentally misguided, and that it could undermine the prospects of achieving a true society of equals (Wolff, 1998; Anderson, 1999; Scheffler, 2005). One reason for this is that luck egalitarianism often appears to be a very harsh or unforgiving doctrine, at least from the perspective of people who are identified as being responsible for their own misfortune. For instance, suppose that someone freely chooses to invest their life savings in a high-risk project, fully aware of the possibility that she may lose her money. Or consider someone who becomes disabled after freely choosing to participate in a high-risk activity. Luck egalitarians seem to be committed to holding these people responsible for their bad option luck. Consequently, applying their theory might mean leaving negligent victims dependent on the charitable generosity of others. In addition to the harsh treatment it metes out to victims of their own misfortunes, social egalitarians have also criticised luck egalitarianism for adopting a condescending or demeaning attitude towards victims of undeserved misfortunes. Such people, recall, are the intended beneficiaries of various compensation schemes envisaged by luck egalitarians. However, as discussed in Box 8.9, implementing these schemes may require the state to make intrusive and moralising evaluations of people's lives, in order to determine whether or not they are entitled to compensation.

Should equality be sensitive to difference?

As a political ideal, egalitarianism has traditionally been advanced in universal terms. Consider, for example, the various struggles for political and economic rights that have been fought by excluded, marginalised or oppressed groups, such as women, ethnic minorities, people with disabilities and LGBT people. Making progress toward a society of equals is often thought to require incorporating these groups on identical terms as everyone else, for instance by endowing their members with the same rights. However, as we saw in Chapter 2, some

BOX 8.9 LUCK EGALITARIANISM AND SOCIAL EQUALITY

Some social egalitarians have suggested that luck egalitarianism may be humiliating or insulting, because claiming luck egalitarian compensation could come at the cost of 'shameful revelation' (Wolff, 1998, pp. 113–14). Similarly, Elizabeth Anderson has argued that luck egalitarianism requires intrusive and stigmatising judgements about responsibility, and 'raises private disdain to the status of official recognised truth' (Anderson, 1999, p. 306). To illustrate this point, she imagines a 'state equality board' in a luck egalitarian society sending out the following letter:

To the disabled: Your defective native endowments or current disabilities, alas, make your life less worth living than the lives of normal people. To compensate for this misfortune, we, the able ones, will give you extra resources ... To the stupid and untalented: Unfortunately, other people don't value what little you have to offer in the system of production. Your talents are too meagre to command much market value. Because of the misfortune that you were born so poorly endowed with talents, we productive ones will make it up to you: we'll let you share in the bounty of what we have produced with our vastly superior and highly valued abilities. To the ugly and socially awkward: How sad that you are so repulsive to people around you that no one wants to be your friends or lifetime companion. We won't make it up to you by being your friend or your marriage partner – we have our own freedom of association to exercise – but you can console yourself in your miserable loneliness by consuming these material goods that we, the beautiful and charming ones, will provide. And who knows? Maybe you won't be such a loser in love once potential dates see how rich you are. (Anderson, 1999, p. 305)

Are these objections to luck egalitarianism convincing?

difference theorists have argued that equal treatment does not entail identical treatment, and equality sometimes requires special treatment for the members of disadvantaged or oppressed groups. In this key debate we will concentrate on the some of the controversies surrounding equality for women and cultural minorities, since in both cases egalitarians have adopted different views about whether equality requires (or opposes) differential treatment.

Let us begin with gender. In many societies, there are significant distributive inequalities between men and women. For example, in the UK men tend to earn more than women (Bradley, 2013, p. 102) and are more likely to occupy senior roles within public and private sector organisations (ONS, 2013). In politics, every democratic legislature contains more male representatives than female (Kenworthy and Malami, 1999). Moreover, in the developing world poverty more frequently affects women, and girls typically have fewer educational opportunities than boys (Nussbaum, 2000). In addition to these distributive inequalities, social egalitarians have also drawn attention to the persistence of patriarchy, which refers to men's domination of women. One way in which this is revealed is through the influence of traditional assumptions about masculinity and femininity, which continue to inform men and women's respective social statuses and roles. Furthermore, as we saw earlier, the ideal of a society of equals is undermined if women are exposed to greater risks of violence, if they are exploited in the workplace and in domestic settings, and if they are marginalised from major social institutions.

In many societies, progress towards gender equality has been achieved by implementing legislation requiring men and women to be treated in the same way, such as anti-discrimination laws to ensure women and men are paid at the same rates. However, feminists have pointed out that despite these, women continue to enjoy fewer effective opportunities than men, because of the persistence of social expectations about gender. For example, the expectation that women have a natural role as caregivers means that female employees and job-seekers often do not compete on a level playing field with men. A possible solution to this, discussed in Box 8.10, is to try to transform our social expectations of men and women's roles, for example by incentivising men to perform a greater share of domestic labour (Brighouse and Olin Wright, 2008; Gornick and Meyers, 2008). However, because biological differences cannot be changed in the same way as social categories, some egalitarians believe that equality might also require difference-sensitive policies to reflect interests and needs that are particular to women. For example, difference feminists like Carol Gilligan, Nancy Chodorow and Nel Noddings have argued that female employees ought to be granted more parental leave than male employees, because women are the ones who give birth. Meanwhile, some feminists are sceptical about such proposals. To see why, imagine a society in which there are already strong social expectations that women should act as primary caregivers (this should not be difficult!). In this society, granting women more leave than men might reinforce

BOX 8.10 EQUALITY AND A GENDERLESS SOCIETY?

According to Susan Okin, '[a] just future would be one without gender' (Okin, 1989, p. 171). Gender does not refer to the biological differences between men and women, but to 'the deeply entrenched social institutionalisation of sexual difference' (Okin, 1989, p. 6). In other words, gender is what society makes of the differences between men and women, shaping the allocation of roles, responsibilities and expectations. As we have seen, many feminists believe that our current understandings of gender work to frustrate women's equality. Thus, Okin has developed a vision of a society in which men and women perform the same social roles, distribute domestic labour without regard to biological differences, have equal opportunities to advance their careers, and are equally able to participate in politics and other activities.

Would a society without gender be a more equal one?

those expectations, pressuring individual women into taking on more than an equal share of domestic responsibilities. The cumulative effect of this might be that women have even fewer opportunities for accessing employment and career advancement, making them more dependent on male partners and reinforcing inequalities of power within the household (Okin, 1989, pp. 134–69).

Just as egalitarians adopt different views about whether gender equality requires identical or differential treatment, a similar disagreement has arisen concerning equality amongst cultural groups. One argument in favour of differential treatment has been suggested by proponents of the politics of recognition – examined in Box 8.4 – who identify equal recognition as an important component of a truly egalitarian social order. These theorists observe that culturally diverse societies often distribute recognition unequally, such as by designating dates associated with the majority religion as public holidays, or by officially recognising some but not all languages. According to Alan Patten, the unequal recognition of dominant and subaltern social groups is an important inequality, since it means that only some ways of life are symbolically affirmed, that only some cultural practices are accommodated, and that only some cultures are able to maintain and reproduce themselves over time (Patten, 2000, p. 196). Being part of a group that is not recognised might affect people in a variety of everyday activities. For example, schools might think that minority students who request alternative examination arrangements to accommodate their religious holidays are demanding too much, even though they unthinkingly do the same for students from the majority faith. Similarly, members of linguistic minorities may be unable to complete routine administrative tasks in their own language, even though this opportunity is extended to speakers of officially recognised languages. One way to accommodate cultural minorities is to exempt their members from particularly burdensome laws, and we discuss some of the issues to which this gives rise in Box 8.11.

Interestingly, Patten formulates his theory of equal recognition in distributive terms, arguing that since recognition is a valuable resource, it should be distributed in such a way that treats all with equal concern and respect. He believes that this means 'designing a public sphere that equally distributes identity-related institutional space and capacity' (Patten, 2000, p. 210). Iris Marion Young makes a similar claim, albeit framed in the language of social rather than distributive equality, and she argues that '[g]roups cannot be socially equal unless their specific experience, culture, and social contributions are publicly affirmed and recognised' (Young, 1990, p. 174). Implementing either of these theories might mean, for example, that the histories of indigenous peoples should be publicly recognised in the teaching of history, or that the value of a minority language should be publicly affirmed by promoting its use in official settings, such as legislatures and bureaucracies. The equal recognition of minority groups may also require allocating rights to groups to enable them to preserve and promote their particular identities, such as those we examined in Chapter 2.

BOX 8.11   RELIGIOUS EXEMPTIONS

A variety of religious minorities are currently exempted from some otherwise generally applicable laws. For example, Sikhs are sometimes exempted from the requirement to wear protective headgear on a motorcycle or a building site, and Muslims and Jews are sometimes exempted from humane slaughter regulations to allow them to consume *kosher* or *halal* meat. Like other forms of 'differential treatment', religious exemptions have attracted controversy, including amongst egalitarians. Some social egalitarians might favour them on the basis that they sustain equality of recognition or status. For instance, if a particular legal rule favours the majority group, even unwittingly, then equalising recognition may mean exempting a minority from that rule. Or the failure to accommodate the religious practices of a minority group might confer a second-class status on its members that needs to be corrected, especially if the religious practices of the majority are accommodated. Meanwhile, distributive egalitarians might also have grounds to favour religious exemptions. For instance, a law that has the effect of preventing Sikhs from riding motorbikes or working on building sites arguably leaves them with fewer opportunities for employment or welfare, or with fewer effective functionings, than other people. However, one 'luck egalitarian' response to this argument is to say that these inequalities are relevantly similar to expensive tastes, since they are the result of religious beliefs that are endorsed by their holders. On this view, the law does not really prevent Sikhs from riding motorcycles, because they could do so if they wanted.

Should egalitarians favour exempting religious minorities from generally applicable laws?

Egalitarian critics of the politics of recognition, such as Brian Barry and Susan Okin, have three important objections to the equal recognition argument. First, as we saw in Chapter 3, differential treatment of the kind advocated by multi-culturalists might undermine gender equality. Second, it might be patronising to affirm the value of minority cultural accomplishments, if this is done solely to improve the self-esteem of group members. For example, consider the teaching of literature or philosophy courses in schools and universities. On the one hand, as we saw in Chapter 6, excluding authors from marginalised social groups can be a damaging form of unequal recognition that social egalitarians should oppose. But on the other hand, including additional perspectives may paradoxically convey the impression that they are inferior, if they are included only for the sake of equalising recognition. Third, in some cases it might be incoherent to positively affirm the value of different cultural identities, since some cultures contain beliefs and values that are incompatible with one another (Barry, 2001a, pp. 270–1). For example, it is a core belief of many religious traditions that homosexuality is sinful, whilst other cultures celebrate the diversity of human sexuality. Regardless of the merits of either view, it seems unintelligible to require someone to positively affirm the value of each.

Future challenges

Egalitarians have traditionally campaigned for equality within their own societies. Recently, however, some have extended the reach of their theories by applying them globally. These authors begin from the observation that global inequalities 'dwarf those found within the domestic societies that are familiar to us' (Beitz, 2001, p. 95). For example, the World Bank has reported that the life expectancy of a child born in 2012 varies from 45 years in Sierra Leone to 83 years in France, Switzerland, Iceland, Italy and Japan. Similarly, the world is becoming increasingly unequal. For example, in 1900 the income of the average North American was eight times that of the average African, whilst by 2000 it was 18.5 times as much (Sutcliffe, 2007, p. 57).

We will conclude this chapter by examining a proposal for global egalitarianism, suggested by Simon Caney (2005, pp. 121–5). Caney defends a complex theory with a number of different prongs. For instance, he argues for a global version of the sufficiency principle, according to which each person has a human right to subsistence (we will return to this view in Chapter 10). He also favours a version of the priority principle, which says that benefiting people matters more the less well-off they are. More relevantly for the concerns addressed in this chapter, Caney also defends two explicitly egalitarian proposals. First, he argues that people are entitled to equal pay for equal work. As we have seen, this principle has informed the efforts of many domestic egalitarians, especially feminists. Although Caney acknowledges that pay inequalities reflecting different local living costs may be justified, his principle would clearly rule out the grossly exploitative wage-labour exchanges that currently characterise the global order. Second, and more demandingly, Caney also says that 'persons of different nationalities should enjoy equal opportunities [such that] no one should face worse opportunities because of their nationality' (Caney, 2005, p. 122). Interestingly, his argument in favour of this also supports his case for equal pay, and it appeals to the same considerations that motivate luck egalitarians:

> The logic underpinning equality of opportunity entails that it should be globalised. Consider a world in which people's basic rights are secured but in which people of different nations face radically unequal opportunities. This world does not include starvation but it does consign some to misery and poverty and others to great wealth for no reason other than that some are Namibian, say, and that others are American. It is difficult to see why such arbitrary facts about people should determine their prospects in life. (Caney, 2005, p. 123)

On this account, where one happens to be born is a matter of brute luck that has far-reaching consequences. For example, some people are born into societies beset by civil wars, famine or poverty, and others grow up in states with inadequate education systems or poor healthcare systems. If people should not have fewer opportunities because of their nationality, then equality requires eradicating these effects of brute luck.

Critics object that a global principle of equality of opportunity would be too demanding to realise (Moellendorf, 2002, p. 79). For example, ensuring that educational and healthcare resources are distributed equally, and that all people everywhere have effective protections against discrimination, will require massive investment in the world's poorest societies. This is likely to be unpopular for at least two reasons. First, some societies currently reject equality for women and minorities, and may therefore be reluctant to allow equality of opportunity to be introduced. Second, the members of wealthy societies might be unwilling to make the necessary sacrifices, if globalising equality of opportunity would compromise their existing living standards. Additionally, some political theorists think that the principle of global equality of opportunity sits awkwardly alongside the principle of popular self-determination. For example, Rawls believes that global egalitarianism compromises the respect that is owed to political communities as self-governing entities. To make this point, he suggests the following thought experiment:

> Two ... countries are at the same level of wealth and have the same size population. The first decides to industrialize and to increase its rate of (real) saving, while the second does not. Being content with things as they are, and preferring a more pastoral and leisurely society, the second reaffirms its social values. Some decades later, the first is twice as wealthy as the second. Assuming ... [that both societies are democratic], and able to make their own decisions, should the industrializing country be taxed to give funds to the second? (Rawls, 1999b, p. 117)

On the one hand, provided that both societies are democratic, we might say that the inequalities between them are the result of their choices, and are therefore not liable to luck egalitarian correction. On the other hand, individual members of each society might not have supported the policy adopted by their society, or might not have been born when it was adopted, and might do better under a strict egalitarian principle.

9

Justice

Introduction

Justice is about giving people what they are due, and theories of social or distributive justice aim to explain how the benefits and burdens of social life should be shared. Typically, this is done by specifying principles that tell us how things like wealth, goods, services, opportunities, liberties and rights should be allocated. Philosophers and lawyers also discuss retributive justice, which is concerned with the treatment of people who break laws and with the justification of punishment. However, in this chapter 'justice' is used to refer to distributive or social justice, and these two terms are used interchangeably. In the first half of the chapter we will compare three rival perspectives, summarised in Table 9.1, contrasting them with the egalitarian view already explored in Chapter 8.

The first theory we shall consider – utilitarianism – says that we improve or worsen social affairs as we increase or decrease the sum of individual well-being, which it refers to as utility. Moreover, it says that we should continually strive to maximise utility, so that when it comes to things like the distribution of property, or the design of taxation systems, or making decisions about how to allocate public funds, we should select whichever option will bring about this outcome. Radically, utilitarians also argue that every other political value – such as rights, freedom and equality – is subordinate to the principle that people ought to perform whatever actions will maximise utility.

Utilitarianism is the oldest of the doctrines we shall examine in this chapter, and it was developed in its classical form during the eighteenth and

Table 9.1 Summary of rival perspectives on justice

	Utilitarianism	Justice as fairness	Entitlement theory
Basic principle(s)	Maximise aggregate (or average) utility	Equal basic liberties; fair equality of opportunity; difference principle	Justice in transfer; justice in acquisition; justice in rectification
Distinctive value	Well-being	Fairness	Self-ownership
Site	All social life and the distribution of well-being	Basic structure of society and the distribution of social primary goods	Individual conduct and 'holdings'
Temporal orientation	Forward looking (consequentialist)	Mixed	Backward looking (historical)
Patterned or unpatterned	Patterned	Patterned	Unpatterned
Rights	Individual rights are subordinate to utility – to be recognised and protected when doing so maximises utility	Basic rights are protected by the first principle; some socio-economic rights likely to be ensured by the second principle	'Negative' rights are allocated an absolute priority ('side-constraints'); no socio-economic rights
Wealth and redistribution	Inequality of wealth is compatible with justice; attempts to redistribute wealth are permitted if doing so will increase overall utility	Fair equality of opportunity to be guaranteed; some wealth inequalities are permitted, but only if they benefit the least advantaged	Substantial wealth inequality is compatible with justice; attempts to redistribute wealth are forbidden
Liberty	Freedom has no independent value; but, a possible connection can be drawn between individual well-being and self-realisation (positive liberty)	Some negative liberties to be secured (e.g. the basic liberties); positive or republican liberty potentially secured	Some negative liberties to be secured (property rights, contractual rights etc.)

nineteenth centuries, in the writings of Jeremy Bentham, John Stuart Mill and Henry Sidgwick. Although contemporary utilitarians have refined the doctrine, mainly in order to bolster it against various criticisms, its core has remained consistent. Meanwhile, the second theory we shall consider – justice as fairness – appeared during the second half of the twentieth century, in John Rawls's *A Theory of Justice*. When he wrote this book, utilitarianism was the dominant approach in moral and political philosophy, and one of Rawls's major contributions was to dislodge it. In the course of doing so, he outlined a compelling and highly influential vision of a just society, in which each person is guaranteed as much freedom as possible, where there is genuine equality of opportunity, and where inequalities are permitted only when they benefit the least advantaged. Like some other liberal egalitarian political theorists, such as Ronald Dworkin, Rawls sought to reconcile the values of freedom and equality. For its supporters, the attraction of justice as fairness lies not only in the principles that Rawls defended, but also in the way in which they are presented as logical implications of a careful consideration of the demands of impartiality.

In his *Anarchy, State and Utopia*, libertarian philosopher Robert Nozick responded to Rawls's theory by developing a rival 'entitlement' theory of justice. The startling impact and enduring influence of Nozick's book is at least partly due to its provocative conclusions. Whilst Rawls and the utilitarians developed theories that would justify a more extensive welfare state than any liberal democracy has so far established, Nozick's entitlement theory instead points towards a minimal state, 'limited to the narrow functions of protection against force, theft, fraud, enforcement of contracts and so on' (Nozick, 1974, p. xi). On Nozick's view it is not the job of the state to redistribute wealth, to maximise well-being, or to ensure fair equality of opportunity. In these respects, his theory anticipated the rise of the New Right, and especially the radical 'rolling back' of the state that was pioneered by Ronald Reagan and Margaret Thatcher.

After setting out these rival perspectives and considering some of the objections that have been levelled against them, we will consider two general issues. The first of these has to do with the 'site' that principles of justice apply to. Whilst some political theorists say that principles of justice can be used to evaluate all human conduct – including the actions of governments, the design of laws and institutions, and the behaviour of individuals and voluntary associations – others think that they have a more limited domain of application. Thus, political theorists adopt more inclusive or exclusive views about the kinds of objects that should be regulated or evaluated by principles of justice. The second key debate concerns the 'scope' of principles of justice, which has become an especially pressing issue in recent years. Until recently, it was largely assumed that principles of justice had a domestic scope, and did not apply internationally. Under this view, if we had duties to distant strangers, they were humanitarian duties to alleviate poverty, and not duties of justice. By contrast, some cosmopolitan political theorists have recently appealed to each of our rival perspectives to extend our traditional theories of justice, arguing that justice has a global scope.

Justice is the central and defining concept for much contemporary political theory. We will conclude the chapter by examining some reasons to be sceptical about attaching such a high priority to it. As we shall see, whilst some political theorists have argued that justice needs to be complemented by other virtues, such as care or fraternity, others have launched a more provocative assault on what they believe to be an unhealthy moralism that is implicit in much writing about justice.

Rival perspectives

Utilitarianism

Utilitarians – such as Peter Singer, Shelly Kagan and Robert Goodin – believe that we ought to make the world as good as we can and that this is achieved by making the lives of people as good as possible. Stated like this, utilitarianism may seem quite trivial, since few people say that we ought to do less good than we can, or that the world is not made better by making the lives of people as good as possible. However, as we shall see, utilitarianism is far more controversial than it first appears. Here, we will begin by examining utilitarianism as a moral theory, focussing especially on what utilitarians mean by the term 'utility'. Then we will examine some of the difficulties faced by utilitarianism when it is presented as a theory of social justice.

A simple way to grasp what it means to maximise utility is to envisage utilitarianism as a three-stage decision procedure, in which you start by figuring out which options are available, estimate their likely outcomes, and select the course of action that yields the greatest utility. Strictly speaking, utilitarianism is not a decision procedure, but a theory that identifies utility-maximisation as the criterion of rightness. However, this kind of thought experiment is a helpful way to capture the utilitarian approach. For example, suppose you want to know what you ought to do, morally speaking, when your friend asks your opinion about their ugly shoes, and when only two options are available to you – to tell the truth or to lie. To estimate the outcome of both courses of action, you need to go through each individual, assign them a positive or negative utility score, and sum those scores together. Importantly, utilitarians believe that the best outcome is defined by the *total* amount of utility it contains, and not only by the gains and losses experienced by you and your friend. This captures the sense in which their doctrine is impartial and egalitarian, since everyone's utility counts, and counts equally. Take the option of telling your friend that their shoes are ugly. You might assign yourself a small positive score since telling the truth is difficult but will release you from a long-suffered burden, you might assign your friend a large negative score since discovering the ugly truth about their footwear will be painful for them, and you might assign each of your friend's workmates a small positive score as they will never have to witness the offending shoes again. After performing the same exercise for the other option, and being careful to count the utility of everyone, you will be in a position to select whichever option contains the largest sum of utility. According to utilitarians, whichever option has the largest utility score is the right one to choose.

Utilitarians are consequentialists, since they judge the rightness or the wrongness of an action according to its consequences. There are many different species of consequentialism, all of which hold that 'the right action in any given situation is the one that will produce the best overall outcome, as judged from an impersonal standpoint which gives equal weight to the interests of everyone' (Scheffler, 1988, p. 1). Utilitarianism is distinguished from other consequentialist theories because it equates the 'best overall outcome' with 'maximising utility'. Consequently, in order to grasp utilitarianism, we need to figure out what utility refers to. Earlier, I used the term 'well-being' as an approximation. However, the concept of well-being is slippery, and different theorists attach different meanings to it. Very generally, a person's well-being concerns what is good for them, or what makes their life worthwhile. Some utilitarians fill this out by saying that what is good for a person is pleasure, and what is bad for them is displeasure, or pain. Other utilitarians instead say that what is good for a person is the satisfaction of their desires, and what is bad for them is the frustration of their desires. Each of these views delivers a serviceable account of utilitarianism, but each has its difficulties, as we shall now see.

Let us start with the idea what is good for a person is the sensation of pleasure, a view known as hedonism. At first glance, hedonism might seem flawed because some unpleasant things contribute to our well-being, such as eating vegetables or going to the dentist. However, even though these things are temporarily unpleasant, the hedonist can still say that they are good for us, provided that consuming or doing them will increase our future pleasures. Notwithstanding this, hedonism faces at least three further difficulties that are less easily dealt with. First, some pleasurable sensations might not contribute to our well-being at all. For example, I might mistakenly take pleasure in something because I do not know the full facts, as when I experience a relationship as pleasurable even though my partner is cheating on me. Whilst the hedonist seems to be committed to saying that ignorance is bliss, it seems counter-intuitive to say that not knowing the truth is good for me. Second, some intensely pleasurable sensations might contribute less to my well-being than some less intensely pleasurable sensations. For example, suppose that I find reading poetry difficult, and enjoy it less than watching television. Even though television gives me more pleasure, we might still want to say that poetry makes a greater contribution to my well-being. Third, something might be good for a person without them experiencing it as pleasurable. For instance, it might be good for someone to be kind, honest or courageous, regardless of any pleasant sensations that may accompany these things. One way to decide whether hedonism is an attractive doctrine is to consider thought experiments such as the one discussed in Box 9.1.

The main alternative to hedonism instead equates well-being with the satisfaction of desires, or preferences. On this view, endorsed by many economists and political scientists, utilitarians should favour outcomes that satisfy people's desires and should disfavour outcomes that frustrate people's desires. Since we can desire things that are not pleasant, this approach can generate different results to hedonism. For example, suppose that your friend desires to be told the

BOX 9.1 WELL-BEING AND PLEASURE

Hedonists believe that well-being consists in nothing other than the sensation of pleasure. To test this theory, Robert Nozick suggested the following thought experiment:

> Suppose there were an experience machine that would give you any experience you desired. Superduper neuropsychologists could stimulate your brain so that you would think and feel you were writing a great novel, or making a friend, or reading an interesting book. All the time you would be floating in a tank, with electrodes attached to your brain. Should you plug into this machine for life, preprogramming your life's desires? (1974, p. 42)

According to Nozick, there is no reason for the hedonist not to plug into the machine, since it would maximise the amount of pleasure they would experience over the course of their lives. However, many people think that it would be a mistake to do so, and would not choose to live such a life.

Should a hedonist plug into Nozick's machine? What does this tell us about the doctrine of hedonism?

truth about their shoes, even if it is upsetting. On the desire-satisfaction view telling the truth would increase your friend's utility score, whilst on the hedonist view it would have the opposite result. An attraction of the desire-satisfaction view is that it avoids some of the pitfalls associated with hedonism. For example, it can respond to Nozick's 'experience machine' discussed in Box 9.1 by pointing out that a person who desires to do things themselves will not plug into it. Likewise, it can cope with cases like the cuckold, since even though they experience their relationship as pleasurable, the fact that their partner is cheating on them means that their desires have been frustrated. Additionally, defining well-being in terms of desire-satisfaction allows utilitarians to address public policy issues in a transparent and efficient way. For example, suppose that the government is deciding where to build a new airport, and three options are possible. The government can select the utility-maximising location by collating and aggregating each person's preference-ordering, adjusting the figures to take into account the strength of each person's preferences. (This is more difficult than it sounds, and many of the complexities are addressed by something called social choice theory.) Notwithstanding these attractions, the desire-satisfaction view also encounters difficulties, some of which are explored in Box 9.2.

For the moment, let us set aside the difficulty of defining well-being in order to consider utilitarianism as a theory of social justice. Utilitarians say that social institutions and public policies should be selected, designed and arranged so as to maximise overall utility. Thus, if a government is deciding whether to increase taxes to fund additional payments for the unemployed, it should first

BOX 9.2 WELL-BEING AND SATISFYING DESIRES

Some utilitarians equate well-being with the satisfaction of desires. However, satisfying a person's desires might not always contribute positively to their well-being, since people can be mistaken about what they desire, and because satisfying some desires might be bad for a person. For example, suppose that I desire to eat the meal in front of me, unaware that it is contaminated with poison. Satisfying this desire would most likely make a negative contribution to my well-being! Some philosophers explain away cases like these by saying that what I really desired was to eat a tasty meal, and not a tasty poisonous meal, and therefore that eating the poisoned dish did not satisfy my desires after all. However, other cases of mistaken preferences cannot be dealt with in the same way, such as those indicated by the phenomenon of 'adaptive preferences', discussed in Chapter 8. For example, satisfying the desire of the tamed housewife to please her domineering husband might do less for her well-being than ridding her of the desire in the first place. To address cases like these, some utilitarians instead say that we should only aim to maximise informed or rational desires, such as those which do not disappear after therapy (Brandt, 1979). However, this solution raises problems of its own, since it is difficult to know when a person's desires are rational, or rational enough. Moreover, even if a desire is irrational, satisfying it might still contribute to someone's well-being. For example, all things considered, it might be irrational for me to waste my time trying to prepare the perfect soufflé, or trying to construct a gigantic house of cards, but if I succeed and thereby satisfy my lifelong desire, I might conclude that this contributes positively to my overall well-being.

Does satisfying a person's desires always contribute positively to their well-being? Should utilitarians be committed to maximising the satisfaction of individual desires?

compare the likely outcome of this policy against every other feasible alternative (including, say, sticking to current arrangements, or adopting a policy of cutting both taxes and unemployment supports). As we have seen, the outcome of each alternative is arrived at by aggregating the various utility scores assigned to each person. Whichever definition of utility is adopted, it is likely that alterations to current arrangements will improve the position of some and worsen those of others, and whether these gains and losses are justified is determined solely by reference to their cumulative impact on overall utility. This approach to thinking about social justice is attractive for at least two reasons. First, it supplies an impartial perspective from which to judge the outcomes of different policy options, and can therefore be a powerful weapon against prejudice and bias. Second, it weighs the utility of each person equally, thereby ensuring that the impact of a policy on marginal social groups is taken into account. However, critics of utilitarianism have suggested three important objections to it as a theory of social justice.

First, because utilitarianism is committed to maximising overall utility, it might require unacceptable sacrifices for individuals. In some circumstances, making sacrifices for the sake of maximising utility seems perfectly rational. For instance, we often accept losses in one part of our lives for the sake of gains in others, such as if we work hard in the winter to afford a holiday in the summer. But utilitarians apply the same logic to society as a whole, accepting that losses for some are justified by gains for others. According to its critics, this means that utilitarianism is insufficiently appreciative of the importance of individual lives. For example, Thomas Nagel claims that '[t]o sacrifice one individual's happiness for another's is very different to sacrificing one gratification for another within a *single* life' (Nagel, 1970, p. 138). The objection here cannot be that utilitarians do not care about individual well-being, since they clearly do care about this. Rather, it is that utilitarians treat the utility of one person as interchangeable with the utility of another, and thus fail to appreciate the 'distinction between persons' (Rawls, 1999a, p. 163). For utilitarians, this is an attraction of their theory: it is because each person's utility feeds into their calculations on equal terms that no one counts for more than anyone else. However, critics worry that this could leave the well-being of one person vulnerable to counter-intuitive trade-offs. Thomas Scanlon has suggested a particularly gruesome example to illustrate this (Scanlon, 1998, p. 235). He imagines a worker trapped in the machinery of a television transmission station. If the worker is released, millions of viewers will be slightly disappointed, since their programme will be interrupted. Prolonging the misery of the worker could therefore be the utility-maximising strategy, if there are enough viewers whose gains compensate his losses.

Second, when applied to society, utilitarianism requires fine-grained comparisons of how proposed policies improve and worsen the lives of different people, and this may be implausible. In some cases, interpersonal comparisons of well-being are straightforward. For example, as prioritarians argue (see Chapter 8), a policy of feeding the hungry clearly improves the well-being of the malnourished to a greater extent than a policy of reducing ticket prices improves the well-being of theatre goers. Other comparisons, however, are more difficult. Whilst hedonists face the challenge of finding out how intensely people experience particular sensations, the desire-satisfaction view requires detailed information about people's preference-orderings. One solution, suggested by Robert Goodin (1995), is to adopt a rough-and-ready version of utilitarianism, which compares people according to the satisfaction of their interests in particular welfare goods, such as education, employment, life expectancy and so forth. Although this solves the comparison problem, it excludes potentially salient information.

Third, utilitarianism also seems to require that under certain circumstances we ought to be unjust. A famous illustration of this problem has been suggested by McCloskey (1957), who asks us to imagine a small town sheriff, who can prevent serious riots only by framing and executing an innocent man. Clearly, being executed is a loss for the innocent man. However, this loss could be offset in the overall utility calculation if enough lives are saved by preventing the riots. Perhaps a utilitarian might say that, all things considered, the sheriff should not execute the man, because if his dishonesty was publicised it might weaken respect for law and order, with even worse consequences than the rioting. However, as McCloskey notes, this is a possibility that can be extinguished from the example, if we say that the sheriff knows that he is likely to get away with executing the innocent man. If this were the case, then a utilitarian would seemingly be unable to resist saying the sheriff ought to act unjustly.

Justice as fairness

John Rawls developed his theory of justice as fairness in his *A Theory of Justice*, first published in 1971 and revised in 1999. As we saw in Chapter 1, the impact of Rawls's work on subsequent political theory is difficult to understate. In place of the principle of utility, Rawls defended two principles of justice, and we shall begin by exploring these. After this we will consider what has perhaps become the most influential feature of Rawls's approach, namely his innovative justification for these principles, which revived the idea of a social contract – a tradition developed in previous centuries by Locke, Rousseau and Kant.

Rawls's theory of justice as fairness describes a normative ideal to enable us to evaluate the 'basic structure' of society, by which Rawls means the major political, social and economic institutions. According to him (Rawls, 1996, p. 291), the basic structure should be designed to realise the following principles:

I. Each person has an equal right to a fully adequate scheme of equal basic liberties which is compatible with a similar scheme of liberties for all.
II. Social and economic inequalities are to satisfy two conditions. First, they must be attached to offices and positions open to all under conditions of fair equality of opportunity; and second, they must be to the greatest benefit of the least advantaged members of society.

By convention, the first principle is referred to as the equal basic liberties principle, and the second comprises both the fair equality of opportunity principle and the difference principle. These principles are ordered 'lexically', which means that the first principle has priority over the second, and the fair equality of opportunity principle has priority over the difference principle. Thus, although Rawls thinks that society should be arranged so that social and economic inequalities are to the greatest benefit to the least advantaged, he also thinks that improving the economic position of the least well-off must not compromise everyone's enjoyment of an adequate range of basic liberties. In effect, the prior principles override the subsequent ones, such that it would be unjust to deny the equal basic liberties to an individual or a social group even if doing so would encourage economic productivity.

By 'basic liberties', Rawls means the freedoms of thought and conscience, the freedom of association, the freedom to choose one's own occupation, and the rights and liberties covered by the rule of law, such as freedom from arbitrary arrest. In addition to these, he also lists a number of political liberties, such as the freedom to participate in representative democratic institutions, the freedoms of speech and the press, and the freedom of assembly. These liberties have a special significance because people need them if they are to develop and exercise their moral personality. Rawls's first principle requires that they should be maximised, subject only to an egalitarian constraint, which means that the only permissible grounds for sacrificing one person's freedom is to secure someone else's. Notice that although utilitarians might favour a similar bundle of basic liberties, their support for them is conditional on whether they turn out to maximise utility. By contrast, by attaching lexical priority to his first principle, Rawls guarantees the basic liberties regardless of their consequences.

When it comes to goods other than freedom, Rawls is not a strict egalitarian. For example, he thinks that it might be justified for some people to have more wealth than others, provided that this inequality maximises the position of the least advantaged members of society. This is an implication of the difference principle, which combines two ideas we examined in Chapter 8. First, it is a prioritarian principle, since it requires us to continually strive to improve the position of the least well-off. Second, it incorporates the incentives argument, because it says that inequalities are permissible if they encourage people to develop and exercise socially productive talents, thereby benefiting the least advantaged. Notice that the difference principle may rule out some utility-maximising consequences. For example, it is likely to forbid alterations to the basic structure that would improve the circumstances of the well-off and do nothing for the least well-off. Similarly, it says that it would be impermissible to expand opportunities for the middle classes if doing so had a negative effect upon the opportunities available to the socially disadvantaged.

The other part of Rawls's second principle – the fair equality of opportunity principle – is substantively egalitarian. We can see this by contrasting Rawls's favoured principle with a less demanding version. According to the less demanding view, the allocation of offices and positions should be determined strictly by talents. Although applying this principle would rule out nepotistic, sexist and racist hiring practices, it would not guarantee that everyone had an equal opportunity to access advantageous jobs, since a person's talents are shaped by their circumstances, including the educational opportunities made available to them as children. Thus, if society was regulated according to the less demanding principle, some people might have greater opportunities as a result of their schooling and upbringing. Rawls's stronger principle aims to guarantee that people with the same abilities and propensities have an equal prospect of success, regardless of their starting point or social circumstances, and this may require preventing individuals or social groups from accumulating too much wealth. Because this principle has priority over the difference principle, the effect of the two principles combined is to limit the scope for permissible inequalities of wealth and to require society to prioritise the interests of its least advantaged members.

As I mentioned earlier, probably the most influential feature of Rawls's *A Theory of Justice* is the argument he developed in support of these two principles, which involved an innovative reformulation of the idea of a social contract. Social contract theory envisages an agreement between people about the terms of social and political cooperation. In Rawls's case, this agreement concerns the principles of justice that are to regulate the basic structure of society. This agreement is reached in an imaginary choice situation, which the classical social contract theorists called the 'state of nature' and Rawls called the 'original position'. Thus, it is not an actual or historical agreement, but a hypothetical one made by fictional parties, reflecting what the theorist believes are the terms that rational people living in the real world would consent to, if they considered things properly and under appropriate circumstances. Although hypothetical consent is not real consent, the content of a hypothetical agreement still has force, provided that the circumstances under which the parties deliberate reflect considerations that we think are appropriate. Thus, there is a deep connection between this way of justifying regulatory principles and the ideal of democratic citizenship, since if we accept the constraints under which parties deliberate we will accept the principles they adopt, and if we organise our society according to those principles then social institutions will appear to us as if we have chosen them.

The original position is not intended to be taken literally. It is an 'expository device' that 'sums up the meaning' of our notions of fairness and 'helps us to extract their consequences' (Rawls, 1999a, p. 19). Rawls achieves this by stipulating that the deliberating parties should be hidden behind a 'veil of ignorance'. This means that 'no one knows his place in society, his class position or social status, nor does anyone know his fortune in the distribution of natural assets and abilities, his intelligence, strength and the like' (1999a, p. 11). Because they are shielded in this way, the parties do not know if they subscribe to any religious doctrines, or which activities give value or meaning to their lives, or what their special psychological propensities are, such as whether they are generous, kind, optimistic, anxious or fearful. Hiding parties behind a veil of ignorance requires participants to adopt an impartial perspective, preventing them from favouring principles because they will advantage them in light of their characteristics or circumstances. For example, if I do not know which religion I follow, if any, I have no reason to select principles on the grounds that they favour or disfavour particular doctrines. The effect of hiding the parties behind a veil of ignorance is that it forces them to concentrate on morally relevant considerations during their deliberations.

The parties are not completely empty vessels, however, and Rawls stipulates that they are familiar with the sciences of psychology, economics and sociology, such that they have an understanding of human nature and social institutions.

He also tells us that they have an interest in pursuing a life of their own, and that they know they will be committed to some conception of the good, even if they do not know which conception it will be. Furthermore, he describes them as rational, in the sense of having an interest in promoting their own good, and in the sense of knowing that they will be unwilling to make strongly altruistic sacrifices to benefit others. Finally, he equips them with two special pieces of knowledge about their society: that it is characterised by moderate scarcity and that it is a closed scheme of social co-operation, which means that there is no possibility of emigration. These ensure that the parties will take their task seriously, since they will have to live with whatever decisions are reached.

From these various assumptions, three important conclusions follow. First, each participant should want to maximise their share of 'primary goods'. Primary goods are a particular kind of resource, which are useful to people whatever style of life they lead, or whatever conception of the good they endorse. Some primary goods are like Dworkin's personal resources, which we examined in Chapter 8, and cannot be distributed by social institutions. Rawls labels these 'natural primary goods' and they include things like health, intelligence, vigour, imagination and natural talents. By contrast, 'social primary goods' resemble Dworkin's impersonal resources, as they can be distributed by social institutions, and they include things like income, wealth, opportunities, powers, rights, liberties and the social bases of self-respect. Second, in addition to seeking to maximise their share of social primary goods, the parties should be averse to taking risks. Since they are unsure about their own location in society, and since they know there is no possibility of leaving, they should prefer social arrangements that would be satisfactory even if their enemies were to decide which location they eventually end up in. Third, and as a consequence of the first two conclusions, the parties should apply the 'maximin' decision rule when selecting amongst the rival principles of justice. This rule says that we should maximise the minimum position when deciding under conditions of uncertainty. For example, suppose you must emigrate to one of two societies. Although you can choose which society you will end up in, you cannot control where you will end up in that society, and you do not even know how many people are well off or badly off in each place. The maximin rule instructs you to select whichever society has the better worst position. In some circumstances it would be irrational to apply this decision rule, since it would recommend that people should not cross roads because they might be hit by a car and that they should never get married as it might end in disaster (Harsanyi, 1975, p. 595). However, Rawls thinks that it makes sense for the risk-averse parties in the original position to accept the conservative implications of the maximin rule, because they are making a highly significant decision and cannot predict where they will end up in society.

On the basis of these conclusions, we can see why Rawls thinks that parties in the original position would reject utilitarianism and instead opt for his two principles of justice. Recall, parties in the original position lack information about

their talents and preferences, but they know that it would be rational to maximise their share of social primary goods. To apply the maximin rule, they will
need to rank all of the possible principles in terms of their worst anticipated outcomes, whereby the worst outcome refers to the social position that supplies its
occupier with the fewest primary goods. After they have done this, they should
select whichever set of principles delivers the best worst outcome (Rawls, 1999a,
pp. 130–8). Thus, suppose that society is arranged so as to maximise the total
sum of utility, or to maximise average utility. Under either of these principles,
the worst outcome could be very bad indeed, since utilitarians allow the gains
of some to offset the losses of others. To put this starkly, a slave society might
maximise total or average utility, provided that the gains of the slave-owners are
significant enough. Even if slavery were outlawed by some additional principle,
Rawls still thinks that parties in the original position should reject the principle
of utility, because it requires the least-well off to sacrifice their prospects for the
good of society. In doing so, not only does it ask too much of people, but it also
risks cultivating subservient dispositions amongst the socially or economically
disadvantaged.

Meanwhile, the parties in the original position would look favourably on
Rawls's own principles. In the case of the equal maximal liberty principle, the
participants know that they have an interest in pursuing their own conception
of the good. Thus, attaching lexical priority to the first principle makes sense,
since freedom is absolutely necessary to choosing, developing and pursuing a
plan of life. Similarly, they will support the fair equality of opportunity principle,
because they do not know which social group(s) they will belong to, and will
want to ensure that they have the best possible prospects for success even if they
are born into a socially unpopular group. Finally, they will support the difference
principle, because they do not know what talents they will be endowed with, and
will want to ensure that the position of the least advantaged is as good as possible
because they might end up being part of that group.

Thus, by invoking the thought experiment of the original position, Rawls
provides a compelling justification for his particular conception of justice.
Although the original position is a hypothetical setting, Rawls and his followers
believe that we should be morally interested in the results it delivers, since the
constraints imposed upon the deliberators are widely accepted as reasonable.

Justice as entitlement

At the centre of Nozick's entitlement theory of justice is the idea of rights, a topic
we shall consider in greater depth in Chapter 10. It is because Nozick attaches
such a high priority to rights that he rules out a more extensive state, such as a
Rawlsian or a utilitarian welfare state. Because 'rights' mean something quite
specific in the context of Nozick's theory, we will begin by picking out four

features of his conception. First, by rights Nozick means moral rights, which are a property of a moral system, and not legal rights, which are enumerated and enforced by legal systems. Moral rights are 'prior' to the state and political authority, and they constrain what people should do to one another, or what they are morally permitted to do to one another. Second, by rights Nozick does not mean what are sometimes called 'welfare' rights, which are rights that require other people or institutions to do things for us or to provide us with things. For example, a 'right to life' might be interpreted as a welfare right, if it means that other people have a duty to provide us with the necessities of life, such as food or medical treatment. Nozick does not disallow the possibility that one person can have a right that someone else do something for them, but for him such rights are always 'special rights', arising out of contracts that people voluntarily enter into. Third, and relatedly, by rights Nozick generally means rights to non-interference. If a 'right to life' is interpreted in this way, then it means that other people should refrain from acting in ways that jeopardise your life (such as assaulting you, or driving recklessly). Similarly, property rights can be interpreted in this way, if they are understood to mean that others should not interfere with your things (by stealing or destroying them, for example). Nozick captures this feature of rights by describing them as 'side-constraints', to indicate that rights limit what others may legitimately do. Fourth, Nozick maintains that rights are inviolable, which means that they cannot be overridden by other concerns, such as maximising utility or improving the position of the least well-off. Thus, for example, suppose Bert has a right to his boat, which you want to use to rescue a group of schoolchildren stranded on an island. By describing Bert's right as a side-constraint, Nozick intends to convey that the option of stealing his boat is blocked to you, morally speaking, even if doing so would be the utility-maximising course of action.

Nozick's view of rights strikes many people as severe. Its attraction, for Nozick, is that it takes Rawls's criticism of utilitarianism more seriously than Rawls's own theory of justice does. Recall that Rawls condemns utilitarianism for not respecting the 'distinction between persons', since it permits trade-offs between people in order to maximise utility. According to Nozick, the principle underlying Rawls's objection to utilitarianism is 'that individuals are ends and not merely means, that they may not be sacrificed or used for achieving the ends of others without their consent' (Nozick, 1974, pp. 30–1). But on Nozick's account, this principle also condemns Rawls's second principle of justice, which sanctions taxing the wealthy to improve the circumstances of the least well-off. On Nozick's account, only a theory that incorporates his conception of rights respects the principle that people ought not to use others as means for achieving their ends.

Rawls and Nozick therefore disagree about redistributive taxation, and this disagreement is connected to a deeper one about the idea of self-ownership. Nozick employs a strong interpretation of this concept, according to which 'each person is the morally rightful owner of his own person and powers, and, *consequently*

... each is free (morally speaking) to use those powers as he wishes, provided that he does not deploy them aggressively against others' (Cohen, 1995, p. 67). This conception commits Nozick to what Brian Barry has called an 'extreme anti-utilitarianism', since he believes that 'making someone only a little worse off and making someone a lot better off is *never* a reason for coercing someone to do something he would not otherwise do' (Barry, 1975, p. 335). Nozick illustrates the appeal of his view by discussing the example of 'the forcible redistribution of body parts' (Nozick, 1974, p. 206). As he points out, even if we knew that transferring non-vital organs from one person to another would improve overall utility, or benefit the least advantaged, most of us think that people should not be forced to sacrifice their body parts. Furthermore, we tend to stick to this belief even when the lives of others depend on transplants. We have strong intuitions about cases like these, Nozick thinks, because we are deeply committed to the idea that people own themselves, and have rights over themselves. As we explore in Box 9.3, Nozick also thinks that these strong intuitions rule out redistributive taxation, since taxation is relevantly like the forced transfer of body parts.

Meanwhile, self-ownership must play a different role in Rawls's theory. As we have seen, he rejects utilitarianism on the grounds that it fails to properly respect the integrity of the person and might compromise the social bases of self-respect, because it could lead to the least advantaged cultivating subservient dispositions. However, his anti-utilitarianism is less extreme than Nozick's, since he

---

BOX 9.3 SELF-OWNERSHIP AND REDISTRIBUTIVE TAXATION

Nozick believes that respect for the principle of self-ownership rules out redistributive taxation. He makes this claim in typically bold terms, suggesting that '[t]axation of earnings from labour is on a par with forced labour' (1974, p. 169). To see what he means by this, consider a hypothetical worker, who receives a wage in return for five days of labour. If the worker's income is taxed at a rate of 40%, then Nozick thinks that they effectively work two days for the government, and three days for themselves:

> Seizing the results of someone's labour is equivalent to seizing hours from him and directing him to carry out various activities. If people force you to do certain work, or unrewarded work, for a certain period of time, they decide what you are to do and what purposes your work is to serve apart from your decisions. This ... makes them a part-owner of you; it gives them a property right in you. (1974, p. 172)

Thus, according to Nozick, taxing workers violates their self-ownership, since it forces them to transfer something that belongs to them (their talents and labour) to someone else.

Is taxation on earnings on a par with forced labour?

holds that a 'well-ordered society' is a 'cooperative venture for mutual advantage' that should aim to 'advance the good of its members' (Rawls, 1999a, p. 4). Rawls also rejects the strict connection that Nozick draws between self-ownership and property rights. Rawls, recall, does not give the parties in the original position information about their talents, abilities and earnings capacity, since he holds that the distribution of these things is arbitrary from a moral point of view. As a consequence, people have a much weaker claim to the fruits of their efforts in a Rawlsian society. Thus, in Rawls's theory, people do not own their own talents in the strict sense that Nozick insists upon, and taxing high-income earners does not violate their self-ownership, provided that doing so does not threaten their integrity or self-respect.

Now we are in a position to explore the content of Nozick's own entitlement theory of justice, which he captures in the slogan: 'from each as they choose, to each as they are chosen' (Nozick, 1974, p. 160). This theory combines three ideas: that voluntary exchanges are justice preserving ('justice in transfer'); that people can appropriate goods which were previously unowned by mixing their labour with them, provided that doing so does not leave others worse off ('justice in acquisition'); and that unjust acquisitions and transfers should be corrected ('justice in rectification'). Let us examine each of these in turn.

On the face of things, the idea that voluntary exchanges are justice preserving seems innocuous. If I sell you my car, in which I originally held full and legitimate property rights, it now belongs to you and no injustice has arisen. But if you steal my car, or pay for it with forged banknotes, then an injustice has occurred, since the exchange was involuntary or fraudulent, and the car is not yours, morally speaking at least. Nozick uses this intuitively appealing idea to defend a far-reaching conclusion, which is that substantial inequalities of wealth can be just, provided they arise after a sequence of voluntary transfers. To illustrate this, he invented a now famous hypothetical example, featuring Wilt Chamberlain, a real-life and popular basketball player (Nozick, 1974, pp. 160–2). At the beginning of the story, we are asked to imagine that there is a just distribution of wealth (the nature of this distribution does not matter, only that you think it is just). Nozick supposes that Wilt has signed a contract with his team requiring that a portion of each admission ticket goes to him. As the season progresses, people enthusiastically pay their admission fees, in full knowledge of Wilt's arrangement, and by the end of the season Wilt is considerably wealthier than most other people. According to Nozick, no one has any legitimate grounds to object to Wilt's windfall. The fans, for example, freely chose to buy tickets, whilst those who stayed at home are no worse off than before. Even if the resulting inequality upsets your preferred distributive principle, Nozick thinks that you have no grounds to describe the new distribution as unjust.

On the basis of examples like this, Nozick concludes that it is a mistake to equate justice with the 'pattern' in which goods and resources are distributed, since patterned principles of justice cannot be 'continuously realized without continuous interference with people's lives' (Nozick, 1974, p. 163). A simple illustration of this is the practice of gift giving, because one person giving some of their resources to another will upset the pattern in which resources are distributed, leaving it out of kilter with whatever principle prescribed the initial distribution. Instead of a 'patterned' principle of justice, Nozick favours an historical one, which says that 'whatever arises from a just situation by just steps is itself just' (1974, p. 151). An important implication of this is that a radically unequal distribution of wealth could nevertheless be just. We need to be careful here, since Nozick's view is that inequality of wealth *can* be morally innocent, and not that all inequality of wealth is morally innocent. Indeed, his historical approach can condemn actual inequality, if we can demonstrate the current structure of property rights did not arise from a just situation by just steps. For example, suppose that you give me a pen, which you brought from a shop, whose owner bought it from a wholesaler. If the wholesaler stole it from the manufacturer, then everyone else has been passing on stolen goods. On Nozick's account, if any step in a chain of transfers is polluted by force, fraud, or theft, then the subsequent transfers are not legitimate, and the outcome is not just. Notice that this way of evaluating the justice of a distribution is indifferent to a person's needs, or to considerations of equality, fairness, or utility-maximising. However, as we shall see, it potentially has some significant implications when it comes to evaluating the justice of existing social arrangements.

Since some things are initially unowned, like natural resources, Nozick needs to explain how people can come to have entitlements over them. He addresses this with the principle of justice in acquisition. The question of initial acquisition is prior to the question about transfer, because without a legitimate initial acquisition there can be no legitimate transfers. For example, recall our pen, which was stolen from the manufacturer. If the manufacturer was the rightful owner of the pen, then they must have held full property rights in each of its component parts, including the resources used in its production, such as the oil from which its plastic casing was made. Even if the plastic was purchased from a supplier, someone must have initially acquired the oil as private property, in order for it to have been legitimately transferred. Following John Locke, Nozick thinks that people may rightfully appropriate unowned resources, under certain circumstances, by mixing their labour with them (Nozick, 1974, pp. 174–8). However, as we discuss in Box 9.4, he disagrees with Locke about the circumstances under which appropriation is permissible.

Nozick's final principle concerns the rectification of unjust acquisitions and transfers. Righting past wrongs is no small order, since by Nozick's standards the existing distribution of property has been heavily tainted by a legacy of injustice. For example, in many societies the current allocation of property reflects a history of violent conquest, including the expulsion of indigenous peoples from their

> ## BOX 9.4 APPROPRIATING UNOWNED RESOURCES
>
> According to 'Locke's proviso', people may legitimately appropriate unowned things only if they leave 'enough and as good' for others. So, for example, it is acceptable to appropriate a field or a well or a tree, even if that makes it impossible for anyone else to acquire those things for themselves, provided that adequate fields, wells and trees are left for others. Nozick believes that this constraint on legitimate acquisition is too stringent, since it says that appropriation is legitimate only if it does not worsen other people's opportunities to appropriate things. Potentially, this could mean that all appropriations are illegitimate, a point Nozick illustrates as follows:
>
>> Consider the first person Z for whom there is not enough and as good left to appropriate. The last person Y to appropriate left Z without his previous liberty to act on an object, and so worsened Z's situation. So Y's appropriation is not allowed under Locke's proviso. Therefore the next to last person X to appropriate left Y in a worse position, for X's act ended permissible appropriation. Therefore X's appropriation wasn't permissible. But then the appropriator two from last, W, ended permissible appropriation and so, since it worsened X's position, W's appropriation wasn't permissible. And so on back to the first person A to appropriate a permanent property right. (Nozick, 1974, p. 176)
>
> Consequently, Nozick reformulates the proviso, so that appropriation is legitimate only if it does not worsen other people's situation. The case in favour of this reformulation has two aspects. First, being unable to acquire something for yourself does not necessarily mean that you will be unable to use it. For example, one person's acquisition of the last remaining tree might leave you unable to appropriate a tree for yourself, but not unable to use wood, if timber can be purchased on an open market. Second, allowing people to appropriate things potentially benefits everyone, including those who have not appropriated anything themselves. For instance, according to Nozick, the institution of private property benefits everyone by incentivising efficiency, productivity, experimentation and risk-taking (Nozick, 1974, p. 177).
>
> *What restrictions should apply to the acquisition of resources?*

territories, the involuntary incorporation of previously independent regions, the appropriation of land from socially stigmatised groups, and innumerable other acts of force, fraud, theft and bribery. Moreover, by Nozick's account, there is a great deal of injustice still going on, since recipients of things like welfare payments, government grants, public education and public healthcare are benefiting from resources that rightfully belong to others (resources often obtained through income tax, which – recall – is on a par with forced labour).

Even if there was widespread agreement about which past and current injustices need rectifying, figuring out the appropriate compensation scheme is a task of baffling complexity. For example, it would require us to decide how much compensation the descendants of victims of past injustices are entitled to, and the extent to which people currently living should be held liable for injustices committed by their ancestors and their governments (Nozick, 1974, p. 152). Although Nozick only touches on these difficult issues, his solution is startling. After acknowledging that we lack much of the relevant historical information, he proposes that as 'a rough rule of thumb for rectifying injustices' we ought to 'organize society so as to maximize the position of whatever group ends up least well-off in the society' (Nozick, 1974, p. 231). The rationale for this is that the least-well off, taken as a group, are likely to contain descendants of historical victims, whilst the descendants of perpetrators are more likely to be found amongst the ranks of the wealthy. Surprisingly, not only will implementing this solution require an extensive state, at least in the short term, but it will also require institutionalising Rawls's difference principle, at least on a one-off basis.

Key debates

What do principles of justice apply to?

Some political theorists think that principles of justice are moral principles that should be applied generally, whilst others adopt a more limited view, for instance saying that they only apply to governments, or to the regulation of society's major institutions, or to the ways in which individuals behave, or their characters. These are disagreements about the 'site' of justice – that is to say, which objects are appropriately evaluated by principles of justice – and in this key debate we will compare how our rival perspectives address this issue. Utilitarians adopt the most expansive view, since they usually believe that the same moral principles apply to all social forms, including governments and voluntary associations, as well as the choices and actions of individuals. Nozick's libertarian view is much narrower, and it says that principles of justice apply only to the conduct of individuals and governments. As we have seen, this view implies that it is a mistake to use principles of justice to evaluate things like the distribution of wealth and opportunities. Rawls's view falls somewhere in between, and it identifies the basic structure of society as the site to which principles of justice apply. Although this view is more expansive than Nozick's, feminists and other egalitarians worry that it is too restrictive, and that it might undermine Rawls's own commitment to equality and fairness.

Let us start with the most expansive view, which is that the principle of utility applies across all social domains. This seems like a natural position for a utilitarian to adopt, since utilitarianism is a general standard of goodness or rightness. Indeed, it would be strange for a utilitarian to distinguish amongst the different settings in which moral principles might apply, because the consequences of maximising utility are equally valuable regardless of where it is done and who does it. Thus, just as governments should always act so as to maximise utility, so too should sports associations, families and individuals. An attraction of this approach is that it encourages us to think carefully about the impact of our everyday decisions on the well-being of others. However, it faces two different kinds of objection: it might be undesirable for individual people to always act as utilitarianism seemingly demands, and acting so as to maximise utility might be collectively self-defeating.

The first objection was suggested by Bernard Williams, who begins from the observation that acting so as to maximise overall utility may sometimes require people to set aside their own projects. For instance, even if I prefer to practise the clarinet, utilitarianism might demand that I concentrate my efforts on alleviating poverty. Williams's objection is not that utilitarianism disallows the pursuit of personal projects, since it does not. Rather, it is that utilitarianism requires us to treat our own projects as only 'one set of satisfactions' amongst others (Williams, 1973, p. 115). This is unreasonable, according to Williams, because some projects are central to defining what our lives are about. For example, people often iden- tify deeply with certain goals and projects that give shape and meaning to their lives, and in which they are 'deeply and extensively involved' (1973, p. 116). On Williams's account, insisting that a person be willing to set these 'ground projects' aside is 'in the most literal sense, an attack on [their] integrity' (1973, p. 117). In response to this, utilitarians insist that we should not bracket off people's projects from moral scrutiny (Railton, 1984, p. 147). Goodin makes this point in particularly forceful terms, giving the example of someone who protests against the closure of their wine club because they believe that it is connected to their sense of self. According to him, to say that someone 'cannot bear to contemplate abandoning these luxuries so that others may be given the necessities of life is to say that their capacity for moral agency was pretty meagre all along' (Goodin, 1995, p. 68). The underlying disagreement here is a deep one. On the one hand, Williams argues that utilitarians cannot appreciate what it is for a person to have goals and projects which they cannot imagine themselves without. He thinks that this is a serious shortcoming, since a life that lacks these commitments and attachments is an impoverished one. On the other hand, utilitarians argue that all of our commitments and attachments should feed into utilitarian calcula- tions, even if this sometimes requires sacrificing our own projects for the good of others. On their account, having commitments and attachments that prevent us from doing good is a moral failing, and we would be better off without them.

For the sake of argument, suppose that the utilitarian position is both plaus- ible and desirable. Now imagine a society composed of what Derek Parfit calls 'pure do-gooders' (Parfit, 1984, p. 27), who have internalised utilitarianism to the extent that they always do whatever they can to make outcomes as good as possible (in other words, they are untroubled about setting their 'ground projects' aside). At this point the second objection arises, since the efforts of pure do-gooders might be collectively self-defeating. One reason for this is that do-gooders will seldom act on particular kinds of desires, such as the 'desires that are involved in loving other people' or the 'desire to work well' (Parfit, 1984, p. 27). As a consequence, their society might contain less utility than one that contained fewer or no do-gooders. Another reason is that do-gooders might waste too much time calculating what utilitarianism demands, thereby preventing them from doing as much good as they would otherwise be able to do. Finally, a society of do-gooders might also fail to maximise utility for more mundane reasons, if they lack coordination mechanisms to ensure that their efforts bear fruit. For example, suppose that everyone is committed to improving the circumstances of the most impoverished members of society, but that they do so without organising their efforts. Perhaps some people donate money to homeless shelters, others volunteer in house building projects and others donate food and clothes. The uncoordinated efforts of these people might be less effective, from a utilitarian standpoint, than a single government scheme that could be applied regardless of the dispositions of citizens. According to some 'government house' utilitarians, examined in Box 9.5, this problem can be solved by restricting the site of utilitarian principles to governments, thereby releasing individuals from the responsibility to perform complex utility calculations.

BOX 9.5 GOVERNMENT HOUSE UTILITARIANISM

Some utilitarians, like Robert Goodin (1985), argue that the principle of utility should only apply to public policies, and that it should not be used to evaluate the behaviour of citizens or voluntary associations. Thus, in the design of things like taxation, social, education and foreign policies, governments should select policies that maximise utility. Meanwhile, in their everyday lives citizens are free to pursue their own self-interests. An attraction of this view is that it treats governments as co-operative agencies through which citizens achieve their goal of promoting utility. However, this view may be less attractive if maximising utility requires misleading or manipulating citizens, as can be seen in the following example (adapted from 'The West Wing', 2006). Suppose that a nuclear reactor is going into meltdown, and that the only way to prevent a catastrophic explosion is to release radioactive material into the atmosphere, which will increase the incidence of cancer among people in the immediate vicinity. The government knows two things. First, that more people will die as a result of the explosion than as a result of radiation poisoning. Second, that informing the local population about releasing radioactive material is likely to cause even more deaths in the ensuing chaos, as people desperately try to evacuate the area.

Should the government release the radioactive material? Should it inform the local population about its intentions?

Nozick's entitlement theory suggests that principles of justice apply to a much narrower site, because he rules out using principles of justice to criticise distributive patterns. What matters on this view is that rights are respected, and Nozickian rights require only that people refrain from interfering with others and their property. Critics often argue that Nozickian indifference about distributive patterns is unacceptably callous. For example, in a blistering review, Brian Barry accuses Nozick of:

> proposing to starve or humiliate ten percent or so of his fellow citizens ... by eliminating all transfer payments through the state, leaving the sick, the old, the disabled, the mothers with young children and no breadwinner, and so on, to the tender mercies of private charity, given at the whim and pleasure of the donors and on any terms that they choose to impose. (Barry, 1975, p. 332)

Libertarians cannot respond to this kind of objection by incorporating a minimum welfare threshold into their theory, since funding that baseline through taxation would violate rights. However, they do have two different replies available to them. First, they can point out that the members of a Nozickan society could freely choose to transfer their holdings amongst one another so as to achieve a particular distributive pattern. However, the long-term prospects of such a scheme are bleak. Maintaining the pattern would require everyone to gather and evaluate complex information, to ensure their actions do not disrupt their chosen pattern, and it would be impermissible (by Nozick's standards) to sanction those who refused to participate in the scheme. Second, they can distinguish between a just society and a good society. Nozickian justice rules out coercing the rich to transfer their wealth, but it does not prohibit them from doing so voluntarily, and in a good society people might voluntarily act upon philanthropic impulses. However, not only might uncoordinated charitable assistance be inadequate for the purposes of addressing large-scale deprivation, but charitable giving may also be demeaning and disempowering for recipients.

Rawls's view about the site of justice falls somewhere between the utilitarian and libertarian approaches. On his account, 'the primary subject of justice is the basic structure of society, or more exactly the way in which the major social institutions distribute fundamental rights and duties and determine the division of advantages from social cooperation' (Rawls, 1999a, p. 6). The basic structure refers to 'the arrangement of major social institutions into one scheme of cooperation' (1999a, p. 47). A Theory of Justice identifies the component parts of this structure as 'the political constitution and the principal economic and social arrangements' (1999a, p. 6), whilst Political Liberalism lists 'the constitution, the economic regime, the legal order and its specification of property and the like' (1996, p. 301). Rawls focuses on these institutions because they are maintained through coercion and because they profoundly influence our lives, shaping not only the opportunities available to us but also our 'aims, aspirations and character' (2001, p. 10).

Because he identifies the basic structure as the site of justice, there is a clear distinction between Rawls's view and the more expansive approach favoured by utilitarians, since he does not require that individual people, in their private lives, act in accordance with his preferred principles of justice. To be clear, Rawls does not intend to suggest that considerations of justice do not apply outside the basic structure, and he describes justice in the basic structure as only 'a special case of the problem of justice' (Rawls, 1999a, p. 7). However, he also warns us that '[t]he principles of justice for institutions must not be confused with the principles which apply to individuals and their actions in particular circumstances' (1999a, p. 47). This is because these are different subjects, in which different considerations apply, and which might lend themselves to different kinds of principles. Thus, it is not an implication of Rawls's theory that the difference principle, or the principle of fair equality of opportunity, should regulate the internal life of a voluntary association, such as a religious group or a sports club (1996, p. 283; 2001, p. 10). However, nor is it an implication of his view that considerations of justice do not apply at all within these institutions. Moreover, since the operation of these institutions is constrained in important ways by the basic structure itself, which includes the legal system, it would be a mistake to think of these institutions as beyond the reach of justice.

At the same time as being narrower than the one favoured by utilitarians, Rawls's view about the site of justice is wider than Nozick's. As we have seen, a central plank of Nozick's theory is that 'whatever arises from a just situation by just steps is itself just' (Nozick, 1974, p. 151). At least superficially, Rawls accepts this principle, but he insists on a far more demanding conception of a just situation. On Nozick's account, as we have seen, a situation is just provided that everyone is entitled to their holdings. If this is the case, then Nozick believes that any additional voluntary exchanges will have a justice-preserving quality, regardless of their consequences. Meanwhile, Rawls emphasises that transactions and exchanges must occur against just background conditions, which themselves may be undermined by the cumulative effects of otherwise fair exchanges (Rawls, 1996, pp. 265–9; 2001, pp. 52–5). For example, in an otherwise just society, fair equality of opportunity might become compromised over time, if some individuals or groups amass enough resources to enable them to purchase educational advantage for their children. Thus, on Rawls's account, if social cooperation is to proceed on fair terms, it will be essential to continually interfere so as to preserve justice in society's background conditions, and this is the role of the basic structure.

Some of Rawls's critics have argued that his view is too restrictive, and two variations of this objection are worth considering, both of which resurrect the old slogan that 'the personal is the political'. First, as we saw in Chapter 3, Susan Okin thinks that Rawls undermines the potential of his theory to secure gender justice because he does not apply his principles of justice to the internal life of families. In the course of developing this criticism, Okin identifies an 'internal paradox' in Rawls's theory (Okin, 1989, p. 108). On the one hand, Rawls treats 'the family in some form' as part of the basic structure, because of the crucial role it plays in the moral development of children, and because it reproduces society and its culture 'from one generation to the next' (Rawls, 2001, pp. 10, 162). On the other hand, Rawls also treats families as non-political institutions, comparing them to churches, universities, professional associations, unions and firms (Rawls, 2001, p. 164). These institutions, Rawls says, should not be required to regulate their internal affairs according to the principles of justice as fairness, even if in some respects those principles limit what they may do. The paradox, according to Okin, is that if the family is the place where a sense of justice is first developed in the young, then it needs to be internally just, but Rawls does not require this, since he treats the internal life of a family as falling outside the domain of his principles (Okin, 2005, p. 245). To resolve this paradox, Okin proposes a reinterpretation of Rawls's thought experiment of the original position, which is discussed in Box 9.6.

A second variation of this type of objection has been raised by G. A. Cohen (2008, 2011). Recall, as we saw in Chapter 8, Cohen objects to the 'incentives argument' for inequality, which says that wage inequalities are justified if they encourage talented people to produce more, and if those productive activities maximise the position of the least advantaged. Cohen emphasises that inequalities like these, which seem to be licensed by Rawls's difference principle, are not 'strictly

BOX 9.6   GENDER AND THE ORIGINAL POSITION

The parties in Rawls's original position are hidden from information about their tastes, talents and social position. However, Rawls does not stipulate that they should be unaware of their biological sex. Meanwhile, Okin argues that withholding this information from the parties would force them to take into account the positions of both sexes when selecting principles of justice, since they would not want to be disadvantaged as a result of their biological sex. Doing this, Okin thinks, would have far-reaching implications, revealing that '[g]ender, with its ascriptive designation of positions and expectations of behaviour in accordance with the inborn characteristic of sex, could no longer form a legitimate part of the social structure, whether inside or outside the family' (Okin, 1989, p. 103). For example, she thinks that the parties would opt for an interpretation of the fair equality of opportunity principle that would prohibit any linkage between biological sex and the social roles of mother, father, husband and wife. In other words, she believes that a properly constructed original position would reveal that making gender irrelevant is a precondition for achieving a just society.

What difference would it make to shield the parties in Rawls's original position from knowledge of their biological sex?

necessary to make the worst off better off' (Cohen, 2011, p. 246). Wage inequalities may *appear* to be necessary, if the talented present their demands as such, but this appearance is deceptive since they could voluntarily reduce their wage expectations. Indeed, if the talented fully accepted Rawls's difference principle, to the extent that they always acted in conformity with it in their personal economic decisions, then they would 'forbear from seizing the advantages that their bargaining power puts within their reach' (Cohen, 2011, p. 247). The lesson Cohen draws from this is that a society whose members are motivated by an 'egalitarian ethos' would be more just than one whose members acted on selfish grounds, even if the institutional structures of each society were identical. But this suggests that Rawlsian background justice is not the full story about justice, since the choices and actions of individuals also matter when we evaluate social arrangements. If this is correct, then it would be a mistake to say that principles of justice apply only to the basic structure. Instead, it would be better to follow the lead of the utilitarians, and accept that principles of justice also apply to individual choices and conduct.

How far do principles of justice extend?

One of the liveliest debates in recent political theory concerns the plausibility of cosmopolitan theories of justice. Cosmopolitanism signifies a number of different things in political theory. Etymologically, it is derived from an Ancient Greek word, combining *cosmos*, meaning the world or the universe, with *polites*, meaning a citizen. Taken literally, then, a cosmopolitan is a citizen of the world, and as we saw in Chapter 2, some people use the term to describe an advocate of a world state. Cosmopolitanism also denotes a particular kind of attitude or disposition, which involves being outward-looking and open to new influences, and which has been used to criticise the conception of culture deployed by multiculturalists, as we saw in Chapter 7. Here, I use cosmopolitanism to refer to a moral view about the scope of principles of justice. Someone is a cosmopolitan in this sense if they believe that principles of justice have a general and universal scope, applying to all people equally, and not only amongst the members of a particular community (Pogge, 2002, p. 169). Although this view is sometimes used to support the idea of a world state, the two forms of cosmopolitanism do not always accompany one another (Beitz, 1999, p. 287). In this key debate we explore the possibilities for configuring our three rival perspectives as cosmopolitan theories of justice.

Many utilitarians are also cosmopolitans (e.g. Singer, 1972; Goodin, 1995, pp. 161–9, 263–87; Unger, 1996). The best-known account of a cosmopolitan form of utilitarianism has been proposed by Peter Singer, who believes that we have utilitarian duties to assist the global poor, wherever they live, even if we have no personal relationships with them, and even if we are not responsible for their suffering. His argument for these duties is disarmingly simple. Suppose you see a child drowning in a shallow pond. Most people think that they have a duty to save the child, even if doing so carries a minor cost, such as muddying their clothes. The duty to alleviate distant poverty is relevantly similar, Singer argues, since there is great suffering in some parts of the world, which others are in a position to lessen, without exposing themselves to great costs. Thus, he concludes that we should assist those in poverty, either up to the point of sacrificing something of comparable moral significance, such as bringing ourselves or our dependents below the welfare level of the global poor, or up to the point of incurring 'morally significant' costs (Singer, 1972, p. 231). However it is formulated, Singer's duty of assistance requires the global rich to radically increase their contributions to poverty alleviation.

Singer's argument has been criticised in four different ways. First, some philosophers object to Singer's utilitarianism. For example, like other utilitarians, Singer does not distinguish between acts and omissions, and seems to imply that there is no morally relevant difference between walking past a drowning child and pushing a child into the pond. Moreover, like other utilitarian principles, Singer's duty of assistance seems to leave very little space for comparatively wealthy individuals to pursue their own goals and aspirations, since even on Singer's less onerous formulation of the principle they are expected to incur morally significant costs in the course of upholding their duties towards the global poor. Second, some philosophers think that the analogy between the pond case and global poverty fails (Cullity, 2004; Miller, 2007). The scale of poverty is far greater, and to make the analogy accurate we would need to imagine many different children drowning in the pond and many different passers-by surrounding them, some of whom who are better equipped to rescue the children than others. The two cases are also different because poverty relief is a long-term commitment, unlike saving a child, which is a one-off event. Furthermore, saving a drowning child is relatively straightforward, whilst contributing to efforts to alleviate poverty is more complex, since it requires us to discriminate amongst better and worse charities, and to anticipate the likely consequences of aid-giving efforts.

Third, some philosophers object to Singer's humanitarianism, complaining that his principle does not address underlying inequalities in power or the distribution of control over material resources. One possible problem of aid schemes is that they establish asymmetries amongst recipients and donors, who can 'turn off the taps' or use their advantageous bargaining position to attach unsavoury conditions to their aid. Concerns such as these prompt Brian Barry to say that we should think about our duties to the global poor in terms of ensuring that everyone gets what they are due, and not in Singer's terms of improving the well-being of the global poor:

> To talk about what I ought, as a matter of humanity, to do with mine makes no sense until we have established what is mine in the first place. If I have stolen what is rightly somebody else's property, or if I have borrowed from

him and refuse to repay the debt when it is due, and as a result he is destitute, it would be unbecoming on my part to dole out some part of the money that should belong to him, with various strings attached as to the way in which he should spend it, and then go around posing as a great humanitarian. That is, in my judgment, an exact description of the position in which the rich countries have currently placed themselves. (Barry, 2006a, p. 735)

If Barry is right, then implementing Singer's principle would not address the hypocrisy of wealthy nations, whose own wealth is at least partially derived from their exploitation of natural resources.

Fourth, some utilitarians reject Singer's conclusions on the grounds that poverty relief programmes may diminish overall utility. The objection is not that aid is too costly for donors, since their negative utility scores are counterbalanced by the positive utility scores of recipients. Rather, it is that aid might not bring about overall increases in utility. For example, according to Garrett Hardin (1996), humanitarian aid might encourage population growth in poor countries, thus leading to an overall increase in human suffering. If humanitarian relief does not solve poverty but instead creates more poor people and more suffering, then consistent utilitarians should oppose it. However, one reply to this objection questions the underlying assumption that aid causes population explosions, since economic development tends to decrease the rate of population growth and wealthy societies tend to combine higher life expectancies with lower birth rates.

Whilst most utilitarians are cosmopolitans, Rawls and his followers are divided. Although Rawls himself rejected it (Rawls, 1999b), others have argued that the underlying logic of his theory entails globalising his principles of justice (Richards, 1982; Scanlon, 1985; Pogge, 1989; Beitz, 1999; Tan, 2004). One argument for extending Rawlsian principles begins from the idea that no individual or group is morally entitled to the benefits of whatever natural resources – such as water, coal, oil or mineral supplies – happen to reside near or beneath their territories. In place of the current arbitrary distribution of these resources, Charles Beitz proposes adapting Rawls's original position so as to determine what a just global allocation would look like. He imagines the representatives of different societies, unaware of which society they represent, gathering together to 'agree on a resource redistribution principle that would give each society a fair chance to develop just political institutions and an economy capable of satisfying its members' basic needs' (Beitz, 1999, p. 141). This principle would not require that everyone everywhere have an equal share of natural resources, only that resource-rich countries share some of their good fortune with resource-poor countries. Nevertheless, Rawls himself rejected this principle, on the grounds that the distribution of natural resources is not as significant as Beitz thinks, since 'the crucial element in how a country fares is its political culture – its members' political and civic virtues' (Rawls, 1999b, p. 117). If Rawls is right, then Beitz's resource redistribution principle is unlikely to substantially improve the lives of the global least-advantaged.

Another argument for extending Rawlsian justice concerns the emergence of global economic interdependence, which has benefited some members of global society and disadvantaged others. For example, whilst globalisation has given professional elites access to new employment and leisure activities, and enabled firms to sell their goods in previously inaccessible markets, it has also dramatically worsened the labour conditions of the poorest members of the poorest societies. According to Beitz, the global economy now resembles a domestic one, in the sense that it 'constitutes a scheme of social cooperation' (Beitz, 1999, p. 54). Consequently, he argues that it should be regulated by principles of global justice (Beitz, 1999, pp. 131, 150). To determine what these principles should be, Beitz returns to Rawls's hypothetical device of an original position, and this time imagines one composed of representatives of individuals (not societies), hidden from all of the information that Rawls hides his parties from *and* who do not know where on the planet they live. According to Beitz, these parties would favour a global difference principle, since they would be especially concerned with the prospects of the least advantaged members of the poorest societies. Recall, the difference principle does not merely require that we improve the circumstances of the least well-off, but that we maximise their prospects, permitting inequalities only if they benefit the least advantaged themselves. Thus, implementing a global difference principle would require radical changes in the current global order, such as the creation of institutions to regulate trade and to promote the rapid development of poor societies.

Beitz's argument for a global difference principle has met with a mixed reception, and the debate surrounding it reflects some of the controversies we have already examined about the 'site' of distributive justice. On the one hand, supporters argue that since something like a global basic structure already exists, adjusting it to conform to the difference principle is an ambitious but feasible proposal (Tan, 2004). On the other hand, critics protest that global institutions do not constitute a basic structure in Rawls's sense of the term, since they do not constitute a cohesive system of social, economic and political institutions, and because they do not have the same kind of pervasive impact on our life chances. For example, Samuel Freeman concludes that a global difference principle would be 'doubly infirm' because there are no institutions capable of applying it and because there is no global legal system to which it could apply (Freeman, 2007, p. 444). Against this, cosmopolitans have two responses available to them. First, even if global institutions do not constitute a properly complete basic structure, they clearly do have an impact on people's prospects. For example, the operation of intellectual property rights and international lending practices both have a significant influence on people's lives, shaping the availability of medical resources and employment opportunities. Bringing these practices and institutions under the regulation of principles of justice might still be an improvement, even if the absence of a global legal structure frustrates the full realisation of the difference principle. Second, the absence of a global basic structure and an authority to regulate it might simply be an argument in favour of creating one – that is to say, creating and empowering institutions that are capable of implementing a global difference principle.

Rawls himself rejected the cosmopolitan extension of his theory because he thought it failed to respect the political autonomy of 'peoples', which was his term of art for societies or political communities (Rawls, 1999b, pp. 115–18). We saw one illustration of this in Chapter 8, in his argument against global equality of opportunity. Rawls's anti-cosmopolitanism is also reflected in his distinctive approach to international ethics, explored in Box 9.7. Unlike the cosmopolitans he denied that the problem of global justice was analogous to

---

BOX 9.7 RAWLS AND INTERNATIONAL ETHICS

In *The Law of Peoples* (1999b) Rawls tried to explain what justice demands of the foreign policy of a liberal society. To address this problem, he envisaged a two-stage hypothetical bargaining process, to deliver two distinctive sets of principles, each with their own scope. At the first stage, the bargaining parties are representatives of individual people, hidden behind a veil of ignorance, who agree to principles to regulate their own society. At the second stage, the bargaining parties are representatives of decent or liberal 'peoples', who are tasked with finding mutually acceptable principles to adjudicate conflicting claims in international society. These parties are also hidden behind a veil of ignorance, depriving them of information about the size of their population, their relative strength, the extent of their natural resources, and their level of economic development. After deliberating, Rawls thinks that these parties would agree to the following principles:

1. Peoples are free and independent, and their freedom and independence is to be respected by other peoples.
2. Peoples are to observe treaties and undertakings.
3. Peoples are equal and parties to the agreements that bind them.
4. Peoples are to observe a duty of non-intervention.
5. Peoples have the right of self-defence but no reason to instigate war for reasons other than self-defence.
6. Peoples are to honour human rights.
7. Peoples are to observe certain specified restrictions in the conduct of war.
8. Peoples have a duty to assist other peoples living under unfavourable conditions that prevent their having a just or decent political and social regime. (Rawls, 1999b, p. 37)

This list is strongly orientated towards securing and maintaining peace through mutual toleration, and it imposes only modest burdens on the global rich to improve the circumstances of the global poor.

Would the parties in Rawls's original position select the principles he identifies? Is this the right way to think about international ethics?

the problem of domestic justice, and instead of a global difference principle he proposed a more moderate 'duty of assistance', requiring wealthy societies to assist 'burdened' societies to establish and maintain just institutions of their own (1999b, pp. 105–13). As we have seen, Rawls believed that burdened societies are disadvantaged because they lack the necessary 'political and cultural traditions, the human capital and know-how and, often, the material and technological resources' (1999b, p. 106). Meeting the duty of assistance therefore requires equipping those societies with these things. Consequently, and unlike the global difference principle, Rawls's duty has a clearly defined target, and is not 'meant to apply continuously and without end' (1999b, p. 117). After it has been fulfilled, some societies are likely to be poorer than others, offering their members fewer prospects. On Rawls's account, provided that an adequate threshold is met, such inequalities are not unjust. As a result, and taken as a whole, Rawls's theory is far more permissive of international inequality than it is of domestic inequality. His overall position is that although we have duties of justice both to foreigners and compatriots, our duties to the latter are much stronger than our duties to the former, and the difference principle applies only within states.

Rawls's conclusions have proven to be extremely controversial. On the one hand, his cosmopolitan followers protest that permitting inequalities influenced by arbitrary factors like nationality conflicts with the arguments Rawls himself presented in A Theory of Justice. A related objection, examined in Box 9.8, is that the modesty of Rawls's duty of assistance is made plausible only by making the questionable assumption that less well-off societies are responsible for their own predicament. On the other hand, statist Rawlsians defend his two-tiered approach to global justice. For example, Michael Blake (2013) argues that it is consistent with Rawls's earlier work, since it emerges from the principle of respect for reasonable pluralism defended in Political Liberalism (1996), and which we examined in Chapter 3. More strongly, Thomas Nagel argues that Rawls concedes too much ground to the cosmopolitans, since he should have rejected all international principles of justice and instead accepted the less demanding principle that the duties of the global rich to the global poor consist only in 'basic humanitarian duties' (Nagel, 2005, p. 125). To support his position, Nagel argues that 'justice is something we owe through our shared institutions only to those with whom we stand in a strong political relation' (Nagel, 2005, p. 121). Nagel thinks that states are special because they are coercive and because they profoundly shape the prospects of their members, who jointly authorise them and consequently owe one another a duty of normative justification. Meanwhile, global institutions are not jointly authorised by citizens themselves and lack some of the properties Nagel associates with states. Consequently, he concludes that the members of international society do not owe one another a duty of normative justification and do not have obligations of justice towards one another.

BOX 9.8 GLOBAL POVERTY AND RESPONSIBILITY

According to Thomas Pogge, people in developed societies are collectively responsible for much of the poverty in the world today, since it is a product of a global institutional order that is 'shaped by the better-off and imposed on the worst-off' (Pogge, 2002, p. 199). Thus, in contrast to Rawls, he argues that 'the underfulfilment of human rights in the developing countries is not a homegrown problem, but one we greatly contribute to through the policies we pursue and the international order we impose' (Pogge, 2001, p. 22). For example, wealthy societies use their advantageous bargaining positions to secure favourable international trade regulations, and they subsidise their own industries whilst imposing tariffs on goods produced in poor countries (2002, p. 18). According to Pogge, the current global system is coercively imposed by wealthy societies, and only they are in a position to reform it. By refusing to do so, wealthy societies violate an important 'negative responsibility'. Thus, he concludes that members of wealthy societies have not only a positive responsibility to uphold Rawls's 'duty of assistance', but also 'a negative responsibility to stop imposing the existing global order and to prevent and mitigate the harms it continually causes for the world's poorest populations' (Pogge, 2001, p. 22).

What do Rawls and Pogge disagree about? Which theory is preferable?

Nozick's entitlement theory of justice may not appear to be a promising starting point for advocates of global justice, since he rules out redistributive taxation and patterned principles of justice. However, applying libertarian ideals to global society might have at least two far-reaching implications. First, applying the principle of rectification at the global level might require substantial transfers from former colonial powers, as well as other beneficiaries of historical rights violations. Second, and more radically, some left-libertarians have argued that libertarian justice requires an egalitarian form of global redistribution. We shall conclude by exploring one version of this argument.

Left-libertarians – such as Hillel Steiner, Michael Otsuka and Peter Vallentyne – agree with Nozick about the importance of self-ownership, and accept his principle of justice in transfer. However, they take a different view about the acquisition of natural resources, such as land, water, oil and minerals. As we saw in Box 9.4, Nozick thinks that individuals may appropriate unowned resources for themselves provided they do not violate his proviso. Meanwhile, left-libertarians believe that unappropriated resources are not unowned but are the equal property of everyone. Thus, if individuals or states appropriate more than their share, they should compensate those who they have taken that additional share from (i.e. everyone else) (Steiner, 1994, p. 268). One form this compensation might take is as a tax paid into a global fund, whose proceeds could then be distributed on an egalitarian basis, such as by funding a universal basic income scheme or one-off stakeholder payments (we examined both of these in Box 2.2). Another way to look at this proposal is to say that each land and resource owner owes, to each other person, 'an equal slice of the current site value of their property: that is, the gross value of that property *minus* the value of whatever labour-embodying improvements they and their predecessors may have made to it' (Steiner, 2005, p. 35). This might mean that people who own land should pay a rent on it, and their contributions to the global fund should reflect the value of their land and the resources above or below it.

Although the details of this scheme are complex, applying it globally would have significant implications for the distribution of wealth, because the members of resource-rich countries would pay into the fund and those from resource-poor ones would draw from it. In addition to benefiting the least well-off directly, Steiner points out that his scheme might establish three additional 'benign incentive structures' (Steiner, 2005, pp. 36–7). First, economic inequalities both within and between states would be radically reduced, thereby discouraging 'brain drain' in poor countries. Second, it might encourage compromises over previously intractable boundary disputes, because acquiring additional territory will become more costly. Third, it would discourage 'such odious practices as ethnic cleansing and forced expatriation, since their society's receipts from the [global] fund would thereby decline with their loss of those members' (2005, p. 37).

Future challenges

A striking feature of recent debates about inequality and poverty, whether domestic or global, is that many philosophers assume that addressing these problems requires a theory of justice. Perhaps more than anything else, this reflects the centrality of justice for contemporary political theory. In various ways, this assumption has recently been challenged by some communitarians, difference feminists and realists, who suggest that justice should be complemented or eclipsed by other virtues, such as fraternity, care or political order. To conclude this chapter we will explore these three related challenges.

The priority of justice was given its clearest expression by Rawls, who began his *A Theory of Justice* by declaring that:

> Justice is the first virtue of social institutions, as truth is of systems of thought. A theory however elegant or economical must be rejected or revised if it is untrue; likewise laws and institutions no matter how efficient and well-arranged must be reformed or abolished if they are unjust ... Being the first virtues of human activities, truth and justice are uncompromising. (Rawls, 1999a, pp. 3–4)

According to Rawls, people have an 'intuitive conviction of the primacy of justice', and this explains why utilitarianism strikes many people as misguided, since people are strongly committed to the idea that 'the rights secured by justice are not subject to political bargaining or the calculus of social interests' (1999a, p. 4). In his own theory he sought to honour these intuitive convictions by assigning 'lexical' priority to the first principle of justice, insisting that our basic rights and liberties must be secured before anything else. Nozick's description of rights as 'side-constraints' is similarly uncompromising, since he believes that a person's rights may not be violated even if doing so would not harm the rights-holder at stake and would benefit others greatly. Thus, even though the two authors favour different conceptions of justice, commending what the other condemns, both agree that justice is the primary virtue of politics.

Against Rawls and Nozick, communitarian political theorist Michael Sandel has argued that justice is a 'remedial' rather than a 'first' virtue (Sandel, 1998, p. 32). He makes this claim by arguing that justice could only have primacy for a particular kind of society, namely one 'where conditions are such that the resolution of conflicting claims among mutually disinterested parties is the most pressing social priority' (Sandel, 1998, p. 30). These conditions are what Rawls, following the eighteenth-century philosopher David Hume, called the 'circumstances of justice', and they capture the idea that we need principles of justice wherever there is a scarcity of resources and only limited levels of altruism (Rawls, 1999a, pp. 109–12). Although these seem like realistic assumptions to make, Sandel emphasises that they are assumptions. If we instead assume that society is characterised by circumstances of social generosity or enlarged affections, then we will be led to different conclusions about which virtues have primacy. Thus, Sandel concludes that 'justice is the first virtue of social institutions not absolutely, as truth is to theories, but only conditionally, as physical courage is to a war zone' (Sandel, 1998, p. 31).

Sandel's claim is stronger than simply saying that justice is appropriate only to certain circumstances, since he also wants to motivate support for two further claims: that fraternity may have priority over justice, and that emphasising justice could weaken fraternity. To make his case Sandel begins from examples of associations where the circumstances of justice do not obtain, such as families, tribes, neighbourhoods, universities, trade unions and political movements. In groups like these, 'the values and aims of participants coincide' (Sandel, 1998, p. 30), since although their members might compete over resources, or have different interests, they are united by a common identity or a shared purpose. Consequently, members are often moved by a 'spirit of generosity' that disinclines them from making demands about their 'fair share' or invoking '[i]ndividual rights and fair decision procedures' (Sandel, 1998, p. 33). If a political society were organised along similar lines, and its members were disposed to act benevolently, then Sandel thinks that it would not occur to them to make demands about justice, because fraternity would make doing so unnecessary.

Furthermore, imagine that a political community was arranged around the ideal of fraternity and its members had 'a sufficient measure of benevolence' (Sandel, 1998, p. 32). Sandel thinks that the primacy of justice could undermine this society, because justice is contagious and once people develop a sense of justice they begin to act upon it. Rawls makes the same claim, and regards it as a merit of this theory. However, Sandel emphasises that people who forcefully insist on their rights, or their fair share, will gradually bring about a 'reorientation of prevailing understandings and motivations' (Sandel, 1998, p. 35). Thus, even if the circumstances of a society once lent themselves to fraternity, too much talk of justice and rights will transform them.

Difference feminists, such as Carol Gilligan (1982) and Nel Noddings (1984), have suggested a different version of a similar objection. They start from the ideas that there are different ways of reasoning about morality, and that men and women tend to enter the moral domain 'through a different door' (Noddings, 1984, p. 3). From this, they draw the implication that the style of moral reasoning associated with justice is only one amongst others, and that a 'care perspective' is an equally legitimate approach to thinking about morality and its demands. The differences between an ethics of care and an ethics of justice are not easy to pin down. As Noddings and Gilligan describe it, an ethics of care focusses on the demands of human connectedness, stresses relationships and responsibilities, and conceives of morality in terms of empathy, nurturing and preserving ongoing relationships. They contrast this vision with an ethics of justice, which focusses on abstract rights and principles, stresses impartiality and independence, and conceives of morality in terms of universal rules. Noddings and Gilligan present these as two different 'moral voices', each of which has a distinctive way of orientating us towards the world and framing the demands of moral life.

To the extent that we allocate primacy to justice, we privilege its demands ahead of those of care. Proponents of care ethics think that this is a mistake, and encourage us to take caring more seriously as parts of a good life and a good society. On their account, caring is not only about wanting the best for others, but is about being enmeshed in ongoing relationships with them. When we care about others we react spontaneously to their needs, and the situation in which they find themselves presents itself to us with a vivid immediacy. Thus, a caring response to other people and their needs is less calculating than a just response, since it is not mediated through concepts like rights or equality or fairness. Seyla Benhabib (1986) captures this by saying that care requires us to relate to one another as 'concrete' others, whilst justice requires only that we see other people in 'generalised' terms. By this, she means that justice asks us to focus on the properties that we share in common, such as being rational or holding rights. Contrastingly, care demands that we view each person in light of their history, identity and situation, drawing attention to their individuality. This is because caring for someone involves a relationship with *them*, as a real person, whilst acting justly toward someone only requires moderating one's behaviour in accordance with certain norms.

An ethics of care has at least three attractions. First, it might be less conflictual than an ethics of justice, since care is less assertive and uncompromising and is orientated towards preserving webs of existing relationships. Like fraternity, care might be a virtuous disposition that societies should aim to cultivate amongst citizens and decision makers. Second, care ethics might improve how we understand particular social problems, such as poverty and social disadvantage. Whilst an ethics of justice addresses these issues abstractly, an ethics of care draws our attention to the subjective experiences of the disadvantaged themselves, and might thereby direct us towards different solutions or draw our attention to morally salient phenomena that would otherwise be obscure. Third, an ethics of care emphasises human interdependency, thereby complementing the ethics of justice in much the same way as social (or relational) theories of equality complement distributive conceptions (see Chapter 8). Thus, it might better equip us to understand and repair the complex social harms associated with hierarchy, oppression and misrecognition.

Both difference feminists and communitarians articulate an ideal of the good society in which justice lacks the primacy that Rawls and Nozick attribute to it. Meanwhile, a recent wave of 'realist' political theorists have launched a powerful attack on the 'political moralism' which they believe to be implicit in leading political theories. Much like the agonists we discussed in Chapter 3, realist political theorists – including Bernard Williams, Raymond Geuss, Jeremy Waldron and Glen Newey – worry about the exclusion of *politics* from political theory and object to what Geuss (2008, p. 9) calls an 'ethics-first' approach to political theory. This approach applies moral ideals directly to political problems and treats political theory as a branch of applied moral philosophy. According to realists, this underappreciates the autonomy of political life and is naive about the roles of self-interest, corruption, passions and partisanship in real politics. Realists insist that politics is much more complex and messy than it appears in the leading theories of justice, and that its relationship with ethics may be more complicated than these theories imply.

According to them, political life is ineradicably conflictual, and this is something that theorists of justice tend to gloss over too quickly. For example, Waldron (1999) criticises Rawls for neglecting the 'circumstances of politics', by which he means persistent disagreement amongst citizens about how political power should be exercised, about how political decisions should be made, about which freedoms should be guaranteed, about how wealth and resources should be distributed, and so forth. As we saw in Chapter 3, Rawls does have a theory about how we might reach an 'overlapping consensus' about some of these questions, but this is a highly idealised account, which cannot tell us what to do if such an agreement cannot be reached. Since this is highly likely, and since every political community needs to settle these issues, realists insist that the most basic problems for political theory have to do with 'the securing of order, protection, safety, trust, and the conditions of cooperation' (Williams, 2005, p. 3). This is because it is only after solving these problems that it becomes possible to address the other problems that political life throws up. Thus, they argue that justice cannot be the first virtue of *politics*, because there is no hope of attaining it without first securing political order and stability.

10

Rights

Introduction

Assertions of rights are a persistent and important feature of contemporary politics. Consider, for example, the various debates that have been triggered by claims concerning children's rights, animal rights and workers' rights. Or, think about the various controversies concerning how we should interpret the rights to free expression, to privacy, or to marry. Rights are claims with a special normative force, which Ronald Dworkin captured by comparing them to 'trumps' (Dworkin, 1984). By this, Dworkin did not mean that rights are absolute, only that they outweigh routine political considerations and themselves are only outweighed by considerations of special urgency. For example, consider situations in which upholding an individual right could jeopardise the pursuit of another goal, such as when the right to free expression is believed to jeopardise social peace. The metaphor of rights as trumps suggests that a society which values rights must place limits on how it is to pursue its various ambitions.

Rights-talk has deeply influenced the way in which we address social, economic, cultural and political problems within political communities. One reason for this is that the successful assertion of a right can have the effect of transforming how we understand an issue. For example, when politicians, charities, commentators and others discuss the problem of homelessness, it is sometimes suggested that people have a right to housing, and that people who lack stable access to adequate housing suffer a rights violation. In saying this, advocates of a right to housing urge us to refrain from seeing homelessness as an individual failing or as a regrettable misfortune. Instead, they ask us to think of housing as something to which we are all entitled, or that we have a claim to. Crucially, in saying that each of us has a right to housing, advocates also imply that someone else, such as the government, has a duty to vindicate that right.

In addition to profoundly shaping political discourse within states, rights-talk also plays a significant role in the international arena. In particular, human rights – which are rights that belong to all people by virtue of their humanity and do not depend on a person's membership in a particular society – are now an important feature of global politics. For example, consider the practice by which wealthy states make the provision of development aid conditional on the governments of recipient countries upholding the human rights of their citizens. Or, consider the disagreements surrounding whether one state is entitled to intervene in the affairs of another in order to prevent a human rights catastrophe. As these examples indicate, many of the most controversial issues in international politics involve difficult and contested claims about rights. Consequently, understanding and addressing these issues requires a clear understanding of what is meant when a right is asserted.

Critics of rights have complained about rights-inflation, by which they mean the tendency to advance more and more political claims using the language of rights. This might be a problem in two different senses: because upholding the various duties associated with an extensive set of rights might be very costly or demanding, and because an extensive set of rights might give rise to conflicts of rights. For example, consider the disagreements that arise when the defenders of controversial works of art appeal to a right to free expression and their opponents counter this with a right not to be mocked or demeaned. In cases such as these, different individuals or groups within society assert conflicting rights, and it may be impossible to find ways to simultaneously vindicate both claims.

As shall become clear, rights are complex and contested because the term 'right' has a number of different meanings. To start with, it is worth drawing an important preliminary distinction between legal and moral rights. Legal rights are the product of legal systems, and to say that an individual or a group holds such a right implies that they possess a claim, liberty, power or immunity that is recognised in domestic or international law. Holding a right in this sense means that it will be enforced by some authoritative and competent body, such as a state. By contrast, moral rights are not defined by legal systems and instead are said to be 'prior' to government. Moral rights are entitlements that exist independently of human institutions and are justified by moral systems. Some purported moral rights are recognised by some legal systems, such as the rights to religious freedom that are guaranteed under the American and French constitutions. However, some purported moral rights, including ones that are familiar staples of liberal and democratic political thought, are not recognised by all legal systems. For example, if there is a moral right to free expression, then legal systems that prohibit particular classes of speech, such as blasphemous speech, fail to uphold that right. Thus, states that prosecute individuals for blasphemy arguably violate the moral rights of their citizens despite respecting their legal rights.

This chapter will begin by discussing the structure of rights, using Wesley Hohfeld's landmark analysis of legal rights as a starting point. On his account, rights in the strictest sense correlate to duties, so that if I have a right to something then someone else owes a duty to me. We shall then go on to examine two rival perspectives, summarised in Table 10.1. These explain the relationship between rights and duties in different ways. Whilst interest theorists say that rights-holders are beneficiaries of other people's duties, choice theorists say that rights give us the power to waive or require the performance of other people's duties. They also disagree about the function of rights, which according to the interest theory are to protect interests, and according to the choice theory are to protect freedoms. In the second half of the chapter we will take up some pressing contemporary controversies concerning human rights and group rights. First, we shall explore the nature, function and scope of human rights, comparing some different views about what it is that human rights are supposed to do and asking whether welfare rights should count as human rights. Second, we will examine two different critiques that call into doubt both the existence and the morality of rights and human rights. Third, we will examine the idea of group rights, exploring disagreements about which groups qualify for them and about the kinds of goods they should secure. Finally, we will also examine a recurrent criticism of both rights and human rights, which is that they are a 'Eurocentric' ideal.

Table 10.1 Summary of rival perspectives on rights

	Interest	Choice
Function of rights	Protect interests	Demarcate domains and protect freedoms
Rights-holders are...	Beneficiaries of duties	Small-scale sovereigns over other people's duties
Qualification for holding rights	Sufficiently weighty interests	Capable of making choices and exercising Hohfeldian 'powers'
Possible rights	Extensive – include alienable and inalienable rights	Limited – no inalienable rights
Possible rights-holders	Mentally competent adults; children; cognitively impaired humans; comatose humans; non-human animals; future and past generations; groups	Mentally competent adults; some groups
Human rights	All widely recognised human rights are compatible with the interest theory	Some widely recognised human rights are incompatible with the choice theory

The structure of rights

Contemporary discussions about rights have been profoundly influenced by Hohfeld's analysis of legal rights, contained in his *Fundamental Legal Conceptions* (1919). Hohfeld distinguished between four kinds of legal incident that have each attracted the label 'right' – claims, liberties, powers and immunities. Although Hohfeld believed that only claims were rights in the strict sense, other scholars have argued that many rights combine multiple Hohfeldian incidents. Thus, after setting out each of Hohfeld's categories individually, we will take a closer look at the idea of a property right, which conceivably incorporates all four incidents.

Claims are held against other people or institutions, and always correlate to a duty, or a series of duties. For example, suppose that X and Y have entered into a contract, whereby Y has agreed to pay a sum of money to X. As a result, X has a claim (to be paid) and Y has a duty (to pay). Many claim-rights are more complex than this because the duty that correlates to the right may apply to more than one person. For example, if X has a right not to be tortured then everyone else has a duty to refrain from torturing X. As these two examples indicate, a claim might require others to refrain from particular actions, to perform particular actions, or to do both of these things. For example, a right not to be physically assaulted implies that everyone else has a 'negative' duty to refrain from assaulting me, whilst a right to medical assistance in the event of accidental injury implies that some person or institution has a 'positive' duty to provide me with such assistance. Typically, if a right requires others to refrain from actions then those (negative) duties will usually apply to everyone else, whilst if a right requires others to perform particular actions then those (positive) duties will typically fall on a specified individual or institution. For example, a right to a particular public or welfare service would typically be held against a government and in saying that X has a right to healthcare we generally mean that X's government has a duty to provide X with healthcare services. Sometimes, a right might imply both positive and negative duties. For example, a right not to be tortured might be understood to mean that everyone has a 'negative' duty not to torture me and that the state has a 'positive' duty to prevent my being tortured by others.

In addition to claims, sometimes we use the term 'right' to describe 'liberties' or 'privileges' or 'permissions'. If X has a liberty to do P, then X does not have a duty to refrain from doing P, which means that no one else has a claim-right against X to not do P. For example, I am at liberty to juggle tennis rackets in my back garden this evening because I have no duty not to do so. Importantly, X could be at liberty to do P without having a right in the 'strict sense' to do P, which is to say, without anyone else having a duty to assist X in doing P or to refrain from preventing X from doing P. For example, suppose that my liberty to juggle is not accompanied by a claim-right to juggle. This would mean that no one else has a duty to support my efforts or to refrain from undermining them, and that my liberty would be undisturbed even if my neighbour insisted on shouting absurdities over our fence in an attempt to frustrate my efforts. Thus, having a liberty to do something neither assumes or guarantees that a person is able to do that thing – liberties describe whatever options are not disallowed by a set of rules and not whatever options are possible, and are negative freedoms in the sense we discussed in Chapter 7.

Some liberties are dispersed throughout society and apply to all (or most) members. For example, citizens of liberal democracies mostly have the liberty to dress as they please or to participate in religious congregations of their choosing. Liberties of this form are mostly signified by the silence of the laws, since people are usually at liberty to do whatever is not legally prohibited. Meanwhile, some liberties are held only by particular people or by those who occupy particular roles. In these cases, the liberty-holder has a 'privilege' since they are exempted from a generally applicable rule. For example, as we saw in Chapter 8, Sikhs (but not others) may ride motorcycles without crash helmets in the UK. Put in Hohfeldian terms, Sikhs have no duty not to ride a motorcycle without a crash helmet whilst everyone else does have such a duty, and therefore Sikhs have a privilege that everyone else lacks. Similarly, law enforcement officials are often exempted from road traffic laws when it is operationally necessary. In Hohfeldian terms, this means that under certain circumstances a police officer has no duty not to drive beyond the legally recognised speed limit, whilst everyone else does have such a duty.

Are liberties rights? On the one hand, it seems natural to describe some privileges or exemptions as rights, as when we say that Sikhs have a right to ride a motorcycle without a crash helmet, or that police officers have a right to drive faster than the speed limit would ordinarily permit. On the other hand, many liberties are insignificant and it would not occur to us to describe them using the language of rights, such as my liberty to juggle tennis rackets. Meanwhile, some liberties may take the form of rights because they are accompanied by claims. For example, the right to free expression is often understood to mean both that people have a liberty (to speak freely within the confines of the law) and a claim (such that other people have a negative duty to refrain from impeding or censoring their speech).

Let us now move onto Hohfeld's third category – 'powers'. A power entitles someone to change existing legal relations. Thus, to have a power means that at least one other person (or perhaps everyone) is liable to having their claims, duties or liberties altered by my actions. For example, suppose that an employer is entitled to direct an employee to perform a new task. This is a power, since the rules governing the relationship between the employer and the employee enable the former to alter the situation of the latter. Powers are correlated with liabilities rather than duties, since they expose other people to having their legal position altered. Bearing a liability is not always unpleasant. For example, gift-giving is a practice in which one party exercises a power that hopefully benefits another.

As with liberties, sometimes it seems to make sense to describe powers as rights. For example, consider someone who is writing a will (Jones, 1994, p. 22). Being able to write a will is a power – since it entitles a person to decide how their property should be disposed of after their death – that seems to be describable as a right. Indeed, imagine a legal system that did not recognise wills as having legal force and treats them as mere wishes. In this society it would be true to say that people are at liberty to write wills, since no one would have a duty not to do so, but we would also want to say that people in this society lacked a right to make wills, since other people would be free to ignore their requests. By implication, if other people are not free to ignore wills, as is usually the case, then it seems to make sense to say that people have a right to make wills.

Just as liberties describe the spaces where people are unburdened by other people's claims, Hohfeld's fourth category – immunities – describe a form of protection against other people's powers. To have an immunity is to be protected against, or not liable to, someone else's power. For example, recall our employee who was liable to having their duties altered by their employer. Suppose that the task they were asked to perform was a dangerous one, prohibited by workplace safety regulations. Such regulations shield employees from the power of their employers, and as such are immunities. Constitutional rules can also perform a similar role for citizens. For instance, suppose that a constitution grants the legislature the power to make laws, and thereby makes citizens ordinarily liable to having their situation altered by the actions of their legislators. However, suppose also that the constitution constrains the power of the legislature to ensure that citizens remain free to associate with one another. This would grant citizens an immunity since the legislature would lack the power to pass laws that would jeopardise the ability of people to freely associate. As this and the previous example illustrate, we are prone to describing immunities as rights, as when we say that a constitution guarantees free association rights or when we say that workplace safety provisions protect the rights of workers.

Like liberties, immunities are defined negatively. Recall, a person has a liberty to do something provided that no other person (or institution) has a claim-right that they not do that thing. Thus, I have a liberty to attempt to juggle tennis rackets since I have no duty not to attempt to do so. Similarly, a person has an immunity in some respect provided that they are not under some other person's (or institution's) power in that respect. However, in another sense, immunities are more like claim-rights, since they are both 'passive' (Lyons, 1970). When X has an immunity or a claim, they are able to regulate or limit the actions of others (so that, for example, Y cannot make X do something). Meanwhile, both liberties and powers are 'active', because they concern what we can do – when X has a liberty or a power, then X is entitled to do something.

So far we have looked at each of the Hohfeldian incidents separately. However, as we noted earlier, many interesting rights seem to combine more than one incident. Indeed, according to one scholar, most rights are 'complex molecular rights' that are 'made up of multiple Hohfeldian incidents' (Wenar, 2005, p. 234). For example, property rights seem to combine claims, liberties, powers and immunities. To see this, imagine that X owns a car. Usually, we would interpret this to mean each of the following things. First, that everyone else has a duty to refrain from using the car without X's permission. Second, that X is free – within the confines of the law – to drive, paint or destroy the car. Third, that X may waive their property rights, for example by allowing others to drive the car, or that X may transfer their property rights, for example by selling or giving away their car. Fourth, that no one else is entitled to waive or transfer X's property rights, for example by selling it on X's behalf. Each of these implications corresponds to Hohfeld's respective incidents.

Rival perspectives

The interest (or benefit) theory

Recall Hohfeld's suggestion that rights in the 'strict sense' are correlated with duties. This means that my having a right to something implies that someone else (or everyone else, or some institution) stands under a positive or negative duty toward me. This can make it seem as if rights are simply a convenient (and perhaps assertive) way of expressing the idea that people and governments have duties. Thus, my having a right to be paid appears to be another way of saying that my employer has a duty to pay me for the work I have done. Or, my having a right to healthcare appears to be another way of saying that my government has a duty to provide me with adequate medical services. If we think of rights in this way, then rights-holders are 'beneficiaries' of other people's duties, and rights themselves are essentially the 'benefits' that accrue (or would accrue) when people, or institutions, uphold their duties.

Contemporary proponents of the interest, or benefit, theory of rights – such as Joel Feinberg, Joseph Raz, Neil MacCormick and Matthew Kramer – think that this captures an important truth about the nature and function of rights. For them, rights are benefits that advance the interests of a rights-holder, and someone can be said to hold a right by virtue of the fact that someone else, or some institution, has a duty to perform some act (or omission) that benefits them. As MacCormick puts it, 'the essential feature of rules which confer rights is that they have as their specific aim the protection or advancement of individual interests or goods' (MacCormick, 1977, p. 192). An attraction of this theory is that it potentially explains why rights are justified, since it enables an advocate of a particular right to appeal to the interests that it secures. Thus, for example, interest theorists can argue that a child has a right to food because their interest in nourishment is sufficiently important as to put other people under a positive duty to provide them with food. Furthermore, connecting rights to interests also helps interest theorists to discriminate amongst stronger and weaker rights claims. For example, compare a right not to be tortured with a right to play sports. No doubt people have interests in both of these things, but our interests in the former are far more fundamental and basic than the latter.

One proponent of the interest theory, Raz, formalises this account of the justification of rights as follows: X has a right 'if and only if X can have rights, and other things being equal, an aspect of X's well-being (his interest) is a sufficient reason for holding some other person(s) to be under a duty' (Raz, 1986, p. 166). In describing the justification of rights in this way, Raz makes a modest modification to Hohfeld's schema. For Hohfeld, recall, a claim-right is correlated with a duty, so that to say that X has a claim-right is also to say that Y has a corresponding duty. Meanwhile, for Raz, a right is a reason for, or a grounds for, a duty. In other words, for Raz but not for Hohfeld, Y has a duty *because* X has a right. In turn, on Raz's account, X has a right because X's interest in something is of sufficient import to place Y under a duty. This means that my right not to be tortured does not merely correlate with your duty not to torture me. Rather, my interest in not being tortured is a sufficient reason to place you (and everyone else) under a duty not to torture me.

Because it says that, in principle at least, rights may be allocated to anything with sufficiently weighty interests, the interest theory is compatible with a generous view about what kinds of beings are entitled to hold rights. Consequently, interest theorists have no difficulties in ascribing rights to children and to the cognitively impaired, which – as we shall see in the following section – cannot be said of the theory's major rival. More controversially, it also potentially sanctions rights for non-human animals, for future and past generations, and even for the environment. For example, some animals might have an interest in the introduction of less cruel farming practices, past generations might have an interest in being represented positively in the school curriculum, and the environment might have an interest in decelerating the rate of deforestation. If these interests are sufficiently weighty to put others under a duty, then it looks as if the interest theorist has grounds for concluding that each of them generates a right.

Unsurprisingly, critics worry that the interest theory is too capacious about the ascription of rights. To evaluate this objection, and to see how interest theorists have addressed it, let us look more closely at the case of animal rights, such as those which aim to protect animals against various forms of mistreatment. Disputes about such rights proceed at two distinct levels. On the one hand, as we explore in Box 10.1, political theorists disagree about whether animals have the right kind of moral standing and the appropriate capabilities to hold rights. On the other hand, as we shall now explore, they also disagree about whether animals relate to their own interests in the right kind of way for interest theorists to ascribe rights to them (see McCloskey, 1965; Feinberg, 1984). Recall, interest theorists say that rights are justified when protecting or advancing the interests of a rights-holder is a sufficient reason for assigning positive and negative duties

BOX 10.1 ANIMAL RIGHTS AND MORAL RIGHTS

If they are to qualify for rights, then animals must have a comparable moral standing to human beings. To accept this does not require saying that humans and animals share an identical moral status, only that both are part of the same moral community in which rights apply. Some philosophers deny this. For example, according to Roger Scruton 'a creature with rights is duty-bound to respect the rights of others' (1998, p. 58). Since it would be absurd to say that a fox, for example, is 'duty-bound to respect the right to life of the chicken' (1998, p. 58), Scruton concludes that animals cannot have rights. A different reason for excluding animals from the constituency of rights-holders is that they cannot vindicate or enforce their rights, for example by pursuing legal remedies against rights-violators. As we shall see, some political theorists think that a right 'is something which can be exercised, earned, enjoyed, or given, which can be claimed, demanded, asserted, insisted on, secured, waived, or surrendered' (White, 1984, p. 90). Since animals cannot do many of these things, some political theorists believe that it is inappropriate to ascribe rights to them.

Must rights-holders be duty-bearers? Must rights-holders be capable of exercising, claiming or asserting their rights?

to others. Although animals certainly have interests in a general sense, they might not have a 'stake' in the satisfaction of their interests, if they do not have aims and desires in the same way that human beings do. Further, if animals do not really have a 'stake' in the kinds of things that animal rights are said to protect, then it seems difficult to see why those rights would be justified in the first place. For example, sceptics about animal rights say that although animals have an interest in being fed, since being fed contributes to their well-being, this is similar to the way in which plants have an interest in having access to water and sunlight, and motor engines have an interest in being well-oiled. Meanwhile, human beings relate to their interests in a different kind of way, because of the way in which the satisfaction of their desires matters to them. Against the sceptic, proponents of animal rights argue that some animals, like humans, have aims and desires and really do have a stake in their own well-being. For example, David DeGrazia argues that animals have 'pleasant and unpleasant feelings' and are capable of engaging in goal-directed behaviour 'to do something in response to those feelings' (DeGrazia, 1996, p. 136), whilst Tom Regan similarly argues that some animals have 'beliefs and desires ... feelings of pleasure and pain ... the ability to initiate action in pursuit of their desires and goals' (Regan, 1983, p. 243). Notice that neither of these philosophers says that animals are capable of complex reasoning. Rather, their point is that animals, like human beings, have sufficient capacities for us to conclude that they have appetites, urges, purposes and goals. If they are correct, then it seems reasonable to conclude that animals have a stake in the satisfaction of their interests, and that their interests are of the appropriate kind to justify rights and duties.

In addition to disagreeing about what kinds of creatures are capable of bearing rights, interest theorists also disagree about what kinds of interests are weighty enough to deserve the protection of rights. For example, with respect to human beings, nearly everyone agrees that our interest in not being assaulted qualifies, but they disagree about whether our interests in education or healthcare are sufficiently weighty to justify imposing positive duties on others to pay for these services. Finally, another difficulty confronted by proponents of the interest theory concerns rights that do not seem to confer benefits upon or serve the interests of rights-holders. For example, the right to declare an election result confers only a trivial benefit upon whichever official is allocated this right, and it seems strange to say that having this right serves their interests, as the interest theory seemingly does.

The choice (or will) theory

The major rival to the interest theory of rights is the choice (or will) theory, which has been defended by H. L. A. Hart, Carl Wellman and Hillel Steiner. According to this view, the essential feature of a right is that it endows the rights-holder with the ability (or the power) to control the performance of duties. As Hart puts it, the 'individual who has the right is a small scale sovereign to whom the duty is owed' (Hart, 1982, p. 183). What he means by this is that a person can be said to have a right if and only if they are entitled to choose whether or not to release another person from a duty that is owed to them. Importantly, this theory of rights makes no reference to the interests that rights potentially protect or advance. Rather, it says that rights secure for their holders a kind of dominion over a designated sphere.

To see what this might mean, let us consider two examples. First, suppose that X is owed a sum of money by Y, as a result of some contractual arrangement between the pair. As we have already seen, this means that X has a claim and Y has a duty. According to choice theorists, the most important feature of this relationship is that X can choose whether or not to require Y to uphold their duty. For instance, X might demand payment immediately, or they might allow Y more time to pay off their debt, or they might even choose to release Y from their obligation. Whatever course of events transpires, X (and only X) has control over Y's duties, and it is because X has this ability to choose that it makes sense to describe them as holding a right. Second, suppose that X holds property rights over L (a field, say). Again, this right corresponds to a series of duties, in this case negative duties that apply to everyone else, requiring them to refrain from entering L. What makes X's right a right, according to the choice theorist, is that X has the power to waive the corresponding duties. For instance, suppose that Y is walking across L. On the one hand, if X has invited Y as a guest, then X has (in effect) released Y from their duty not to enter L. On the other hand, if X has not invited Y onto L or otherwise waived their duty, then X (in effect) makes Y a trespasser.

Like the interest theory, the choice theory contains a general explanation about the function of rights. On this view, it is the 'job' of rights to 'demarcate domains' within which people are free (Steiner, 1998, p. 238). Thus, on this view, rights allocate freedom, since people (or groups) are free to do as they please within the spheres that are marked out by their rights. Steiner captures this by saying that rights 'reserve parts of the world to their owners' discretion and imply that, within those domains, such changes (or continuities) in the state of that world as these owners wish must not be obstructed by others' (Steiner, 1998, p. 238). This can be illustrated by recalling our example of X, who owned a car. As we noted earlier, it is a general truism of rights that if X holds property rights over their car then they are free to dispose of it as they please, for instance by painting or destroying it, or selling it or giving it away. What the choice theory draws atten-tion to is that as a result of having rights vested in their car, it becomes a 'domain' that is reserved for X's discretion, who stands over it as 'a small scale sovereign'.

The choice theory delivers fewer rights to fewer rights-holders than the interest theory. Because it says that rights equip their holders with Hohfeldian powers, which are powers to create or waive duties held by other parties, the choice theory restricts rights to creatures that are capable of making choices (MacCormick, 1982, pp. 154–66). As discussed in Box 10.2, this is controversial, as it seems to rule out allocating rights to 'foetuses, minors, the comatose, the mentally disabled ... the dead ... members of future generations ... [and] members of virtually all other known species' (Steiner, 1998, p. 259). Furthermore, the choice theory also rules out some potentially significant rights, including so-called 'inalienable' rights, which are rights that no one, including the rights-holder, can waive. Some political theorists believe that insisting that all rights can be waived by rights-holders is normatively unattractive. For example, suppose that workers are said to have a right to a minimum wage or to a holiday with pay. If the state empowers individual workers to release their employers from their correspond-ing duties, then this might have the effect of driving down the pay and conditions of workers in general, since they might find themselves having to compete against others who are willing to accept less than the law requires. Furthermore, as we shall see in the first key debate below, the choice theory's inability to account for inalienable rights poses special difficulties when it comes to human rights.

Because it insists that all rights must be alienable, the choice theory also implies that criminal law grants ordinary citizens far fewer rights than we might expect (Steiner, 1998, p. 251). To see why this might be the case, consider laws that prohibit murder. Standardly, it is said that such laws confer rights against being murdered. These rights take the form of claims that correlate to two duties: a negative duty (held by everyone) to refrain from murdering and a positive duty (held by the state, or its agencies) to protect people against being murdered.

BOX 10.2 RIGHTS AND THE CAPACITY TO CHOOSE

According to its critics, the extent to which the choice theory narrows the constituency of rights-holders makes it sound 'outlandish' (Kramer, 1998, p. 69) and renders it 'at variance with ordinary understanding' (Wenar, 2005, p. 240). Meanwhile, proponents of the choice theory have employed two strategies to soften the force of this objection. The first is to argue that people can have duties without those duties corresponding to rights (Hart, 1984; Steiner, 1998, pp. 259–62). For example, each of us might have a duty not to mistreat animals or to exploit comatose hospital patients, even if neither animals nor hospital patients hold rights to that effect. The second strategy is instead to say that 'representatives' are entitled to exercise rights on behalf of their holders (Hart, 1982, p. 184). For example, parents might exercise rights on behalf of their children and animal welfare charities might exercise rights on behalf of animals. This second strategy raises two different kinds of difficulty. On the one hand, allocating the power to exercise rights to a representative seems to come at the cost of 'suppressing' the central thesis of the choice theory of rights, which is that 'a rightholder is sovereign over the duty of another' (Wenar, 2005, p. 240). On the other hand, since the represented party (by definition) is incapable of making decisions, these representatives must be more like trustees than delegates. But as we saw in Chapter 4, it can be difficult to ensure that trustees are genuinely accountable to those they represent.

Must rights-holders be able to make choices?

Interest theorists can explain these rights and their corresponding duties without difficulty, since each person's interest in not being murdered is a weighty one. Meanwhile, choice theorists cannot accept that a law against murder endows people with a right to not be murdered, if the putative rights-holders are not equipped with the legal ability to release their fellow citizens or their government from their corresponding duties. Since this is typically not the case, choice theorists seem to be committed to believing that a law against murder does not confer a right to not be murdered (Kramer, 1998, p. 71). Indeed, criminal codes rarely empower people to release others from their duties. For instance, victims cannot usually 'consent' to being physically assaulted, unless that 'assault' is part of the expected course of a sports event or medical procedure.

For many of its critics, it is a real shortcoming of the choice theory that it disallows the possibility of saying that some rights cannot be waived by their holders (MacCormick, 1977). Meanwhile, choice theorist Steiner has suggested an intriguing way to respond to this objection (Steiner, 1998, pp. 248–56). On his account, the rights that we associate with the criminal law are not vested in their victims but in government officials, who are at discretion to waive the corresponding duties. For example, suppose you are the victim of a robbery. On Steiner's account, it is not your rights but those of a government official that have been violated, since they (and only they) can decide whether or not to waive the duties of the robber. They might do so, for example, as a result of plea bargaining, or by the 'granting of clemency, pardons, reprieves, paroles, and immunities from prosecution' (Steiner, 1998, p. 251). An attraction of Steiner's account is that it is consistent with the widely shared intuitions that robbery, assault and murder violate rights. However, it comes at two significant costs. First, it seems counter-intuitive to attribute rights to officials rather than victims. Second, attributing discretionary powers to officials means that we cannot describe those same officials as being 'under an obligation to take enforcement action' (Kearns, 1975, p. 478). This might be particularly concerning, since exercising discretion over criminal matters seems more likely to qualify as a failing of a legal system, rather than a necessary condition for the presence of rights.

Notwithstanding these shortcomings, the choice theory has a significant advantage over the interest theory, which is that it supplies a more convincing explanation of promises and contracts that benefit third parties. Steiner suggests the following example to illustrate this point:

> Suppose you and I conclude a contract which imposes a duty on you to make a payment to my brother: he is the third party beneficiary of our agreement. According to the Will [or Choice] Theory, I am the only right-holder involved in this arrangement. I can demand your compliance or, alternatively, waive it and thereby extinguish your duty ... According to the Interest Theory, however, not only am I definitely a beneficiary but also my brother, as another beneficiary, is also a right-holder in respect of your duty. True, he has no control over that duty. But that is irrelevant in determining his right-holder status, so far as the Interest Theory is concerned. (Steiner, 1998, p. 284; see also Hart, 1982, p. 187)

Both the interest and the choice theorist can agree that Steiner (the 'I' in this example) has a right that his brother be paid, either because doing so benefits Steiner or because Steiner controls the correlative duty. However, they disagree about whether Steiner's brother has a right to be paid. On the one hand, being paid clearly benefits Steiner's brother, so it might make sense to describe him as holding an interest theory right (Lyons, 1969, pp. 180–82). On the other hand, Steiner's brother is not entitled to control your performance of the correlative duty, so it does not make sense to describe him as holding a choice theory right. According to the choice theorist, the problem with accepting that Steiner's brother has an interest theory right is that it raises the 'danger of a proliferation of right-holders' (Steiner, 1998, p. 284). For example, suppose that Steiner's brother proposes to use his anticipated payment to purchase a car, and that the seller of this car also proposes to gift their profits to their son. On the interest theory, since the car seller and their son will also benefit from Steiner's brother being paid, then they too seem to have a right that you pay him, which seems strange since they – like Steiner's brother – were not parties to the original contract.

Key debates

What is a human right?

Human rights are rights that are said to be possessed by all human beings, regardless of their citizenship or nationality, or their religion or race. There is widespread agreement that these rights have a special force or significance. For example, Tom Campbell describes them as 'overriding' since 'they take precedence over all other considerations, including other rights' (Campbell, 2006, p. 34). In a similar fashion, Maurice Cranston says that '[a] human right is something of which no one may be deprived without a grave affront to justice' (Cranston, 1973, p. 68). In this key debate we will examine four related questions about human rights. First, what is it that distinguishes a human right from other kinds of rights? Second, what is the function or the purpose of a human right? Third, what kinds of rights, if any, qualify as human rights? Fourth, against whom are human rights held?

Let us begin with the first question. The idea of a human right came to prominence in the years following the Second World War, and especially after the publication of the Universal Declaration of Human Rights, adopted by the General Assembly of the United Nations in 1948. This document listed several universal and binding rights and called on all states to recognise and uphold them. Some of the most significant rights it enumerated included a right to a fair trial (Articles, 6, 7, 10 & 11); rights to hold property and to marry (Articles 16 & 17); the freedoms of conscience, thought, expression and association (Articles 18, 19 & 20); the right to participate in politics (Article 21); as well as rights against slavery, arbitrary arrest, torture and degrading punishments (Articles 4, 5 & 9). These are sometimes described as first-generation human rights and they generally correlate with negative duties. Additionally, it also listed some rights that correlated to positive duties, such as a right to an education (Article 26) and a right to a standard of living adequate for health and well-being (Article 25). These are sometimes described as second-generation or socio-economic human rights and they were expanded upon by subsequent human rights documents, such as the International Covenant on Economic, Social and Cultural Rights (1966). As we shall see later, these second-generation human rights have been especially controversial.

In contrast to the rights we hold as members of a particular political community – which are sometimes described as citizenship rights – human rights are universal, since they apply to all people and not just to the members of one society or another. Some scholars capture this feature of human rights by referring to Hart's distinction between 'general rights' and 'special rights' (Hart, 1984, pp. 84–8; see Jones, 1994, p. 81; Caney, 2005, p. 64). A person has a 'special right' when there is some special feature of that person that gives rise to a right, such as their occupying a particular role or having entered into a particular agreement.

Rights that we hold by virtue of being a member of a political community, which we would lack if we were not members of that community, such as the right to stand for a particular political office or the right to reside on a particular territory, are therefore special rights. Meanwhile, 'general rights' do not presuppose that the right-holder has entered into a particular transaction or relationship. Human rights are therefore 'general rights' in this sense, since all persons have them.

The function of human rights is contested in at least two different ways. First, interest and choice theorists endorse rival explanations about what it is that human rights do. For choice theorists, human rights protect personal autonomy by allocating discretionary powers to rights-holders over the performance of duties. Thus, for example, if X has a human right to privacy (Article 12) or to a holiday with pay (Article 24) then X (and only X) is entitled to waive the corresponding duties. Meanwhile, interest theorists say that the purpose of human rights is to protect basic or fundamental interests that all people have. Thus, for example, to say that people have a human right against arbitrary detention (Article 9) or degrading treatment (Article 5) is to say that each of us has an interest in these things that is sufficiently weighty so as to place other people – or states, or international institutions – under a set of corresponding duties. Both theories encounter different kinds of difficulty when it comes to explaining human rights. For the choice theory, the main difficulty concerns the fact that at least some human rights are said to be 'inalienable'. For example, the right against slavery (Article 4) is standardly understood to mean both that no one else may enslave you *and* that you may not sell yourself into slavery. As we have seen, a right that cannot be waived is incoherent according to the choice theory, since it would deny the putative right-holder the power to control the corresponding duty. Meanwhile, although the interest theory can explain 'inalienable' human rights, it encounters a different difficulty concerning their universality. For interest theorists, human rights must protect certain fundamental and basic interests that all people share in common, simply by virtue of being human. However, as we shall see in the 'future challenges' section of the chapter, there is considerable disagreement both within and across different cultures about what interests are truly human and should qualify for the protection of human rights.

The second way in which the function of human rights is contested concerns their political role, and at least three different purposes have been attributed to them. The first connects human rights to political legitimacy (Rawls, 1999b; Pogge, 2002; Buchanan, 2004). On this account, human rights are 'necessary conditions for any system of social cooperation' (Rawls, 1999b, p. 68) and any society that regularly violates them lacks legitimacy. One controversial implication of this, discussed in Box 10.3, is that rights-violating states might legitimately be vulnerable to external interference, including military intervention. A second purpose attributed to human rights is that they provide a common standard to evaluate the behaviour of states and other powerful actors (Beitz,

BOX 10.3   HUMAN RIGHTS AND LEGITIMACY

According to Rawls, political communities that violate human rights lack legitimacy and may permissibly be subject to external interference. There are at least two important objections to this understanding of the political role that human rights play. First, it requires limiting which rights qualify as human rights so as to avoid sanctioning a proliferation of interventions. For instance, Rawls's own specification runs as follows:

> Among the human rights are the right to life (to the means of subsistence and security); to liberty (to freedom from slavery, serfdom, and forced occupation, and to a sufficient measure of liberty of conscience to ensure freedom of religion and thought); to property (personal property); and to formal equality as expressed by the rules of natural justice (that is, that similar cases be treated similarly). (Rawls, 1999b, p. 65)

Noticeably, this list excludes many of the 'standard' human rights, such as the freedoms of expression and association, the right to participate in democratic politics, and nearly all of the socio-economic rights (with the exception of a right to the 'means of subsistence'). As a result, some critics have concluded that Rawls's list of human rights is excessively parsimonious (Caney, 2005, p. 84). Second, this approach to human rights also neglects some important functions that they perform (Griffin, 2008, p. 24). For example, the language of human rights often empowers domestic opposition movements to criticise their government. Similarly, international agencies such as Amnesty International and Human Rights Watch often draw attention to human rights shortcomings in order to encourage domestic political reform or to protest against the treatment of minorities.

What is the purpose of human rights? Should a theorist's view about the purpose of human rights influence the list of human rights they endorse?

2001). This view draws attention to the ways in which the language of human rights can empower individuals and groups to protest against abuses, enabling people to pursue legal remedies against their states or to shame rights-violating states into conformity with human rights norms. The capacity of 'naming and shaming' to shape the behaviour of states is considerable, and 'there is now scarcely a nation on earth which is not sensitive to or embarrassed by the charge that it is guilty of rights violations' (Waldron, 1987, p. 155). The third view about the purpose of human rights instead treats them as goals or aspirations, or as what are sometimes called 'manifesto rights' (Feinberg, 1973, p. 67). To describe a human right as such is to say that all states should aspire to uphold it, even if they are incapable of currently doing so, and this way of thinking about human rights is often applied to second-generation or socio-economic rights. However, as discussed in Box 10.4, many political theorists are sceptical about whether manifesto rights qualify as human rights.

BOX 10.4 HUMAN RIGHTS AND WELFARE RIGHTS

Article 25.1 of the Universal Declaration of Human Rights says that everyone has a 'right to a standard of living adequate for the health and well-being of himself and of his family, including food, clothing, housing and medical care and necessary social services, and the right to security in the event of unemployment, sickness, disability, widowhood, old age or other lack of livelihood in circumstances beyond his control'. This is a welfare right, and many states are currently incapable of upholding it, or could not do so without jeopardising other essential functions. Thus, some lawyers and political theorists believe that we should treat welfare rights like these as manifesto rights – as goals or aspirations to which international society should aim. Against them, other political theorists believe that this obscures the sense in which human rights are said to be *rights*. On their view, human rights must be enforceable claims. Sometimes this point is made in order to distinguish supposedly genuine and enforceable first-generation human rights from supposedly hypothetical and impractical second-generation rights (Cranston, 1962, p. 37). However, many advocates of second-generation human rights have also objected to treating human rights as mere goals or aspirations, instead arguing that human rights are a kind of baseline that express a minimal threshold beneath which all should be prevented from falling (e.g. Nickel, 1987; Cohen, 2004). According to these authors, human rights do include welfare rights, but they do not embody 'great aspirations and exalted ideals'. Rather, they set the 'lower limits on tolerable human conduct' (Shue, 1996, p. xi).

Should welfare rights qualify as human rights?

As we have seen, the view one endorses about the role of human rights will be connected to how extensive one thinks the list of human rights should be, and therefore to our third question about what kinds of rights should qualify as human rights. With the notable exception of Rawls, there is widespread consensus amongst contemporary political theorists about nearly all of the first-generation human rights. More fiercely debated are the second-generation or socio-economic human rights (Beetham, 1999). Sometimes scepticism about these rights is motivated by a concern about feasibility, since vindicating them could be prohibitively expensive. However, as a reason for discriminating amongst first- and second-generation rights this seems to be misleading, since first-generation rights are also expensive to fulfil (Shue, 1996). A different concern is that they 'inflate' the concept of a human right too far, since they are less significant, or less fundamental, than 'real' or first-generation human rights. However, this also seems unlikely, since the enjoyment of at least some socio-economic rights (such as rights to clean water, food, clothing, shelter and healthcare) is a necessary condition for the enjoyment of other rights (Shue, 1996, pp. 22–7).

Political theorists have applied both direct and indirect strategies for defending an extensive list of human rights that includes socio-economic rights or rights to democracy. The direct strategy appeals to the fundamental interests or needs that all people share in common (Jones, 1999, pp. 61–2; Buchanan, 2004, p. 66; Miller, 2007, pp. 178–85). Since it seems plausible to say that each of us has an interest in being healthy, in avoiding starvation and disease, and in influencing decisions that concern us, then interest theorists seem to have ample grounds for concluding that people have at least some socio-economic and democratic rights. Meanwhile, the indirect strategy says that socio-economic and democratic rights are justified because they guarantee the worth of the other human rights (Shue, 1996). For instance, Andrew Kuper has argued that protecting civil liberties, such as free expression rights, will require upholding a right to democratic government, because only in a democracy can expressive liberties be secure (Kuper, 2000, pp. 663–4; see also Rawls, 1999b, p. 79). However, against the indirect strategy, some critics have argued that people might still be able to exercise many of their most basic rights even without a right to participate in democratic politics or a right to food and shelter (Nickel, 1987, pp. 103–4; Caney, 2005, p. 120).

The final issue we shall consider concerns how the duties that correspond to human rights should be allocated, which seems to be especially pressing in the case of socio-economic rights (Griffin, 2008, p. 109). Indeed, Onora O'Neill suggests that this is the central challenge for human rights advocates, because if it is not 'clear where claims should be lodged, appeals to supposed universal rights to goods or services ... are mainly rhetoric' (O'Neill, 1996, p. 132). One answer to this problem is to say that each individual has a duty to ensure that every other individual's socio-economic claims are met. This could be achieved, for example, by requiring people living in wealthy states to dedicate part of their income to the alleviation of global poverty and hunger. However, unless the actions of individuals were adequately coordinated, this solution may be inefficient and individuals may become overwhelmed. An alternative answer is to emphasise the role of political institutions in vindicating socio-economic rights (Jones, 1999, pp. 68–9). Thus, one leading theorist argues that '[w]e should conceive human rights primarily as claims on coercive social institutions and secondarily as claims against those who uphold such institutions' (Pogge, 2002, pp. 44–5). This second view treats human rights as claims against political institutions, towards which individuals have positive duties to play their part in creating and supporting (Caney, 2005, p. 121).

Are rights morally justified?

There is a long tradition of rights-scepticism in political theory, according to which there are no good reasons for accepting the existence of moral rights (see Waldron, 1987). For instance, in the eighteenth century Jeremy Bentham famously described them as 'rhetorical nonsense – nonsense upon stilts' (Bentham, 1987, p. 53), a view endorsed more recently by communitarian Alasdair MacIntyre:

The best reason for asserting so bluntly that there are no such rights is indeed of precisely the same type as the best reason we possess for asserting that there are no witches and the best reason which we possess for asserting that there are no unicorns: every attempt to give good reasons for believing that there are such rights has failed. (MacIntyre, 1985, p. 69)

MacIntyre's claim is not that there are no legal rights, since that would clearly be false. Rather, his scepticism, like Bentham's, concerns moral rights. But does it make sense to compare moral rights to witches and unicorns? One significant difference is that witches and unicorns are purported to be physical entities, whilst moral rights are purported to be moral entities. Consequently, the criteria that we use to ascertain the existence of either kind of thing are likely to be different (Mandle, 2006, p. 60). In the case of witches and unicorns, scepticism about their existence follows from the current state of our scientific knowledge. In short, their existence is incompatible with how we understand the physical universe to work. Meanwhile, moral rights are said to be part of the moral universe, and to assert a moral right is to say that people have particular entitlements by virtue of certain moral principles. On the one hand, this means that moral rights are likely to be controversial, since all moral claims are controversial. On the other hand, as Jones notes, 'there is no reason why moral rights should be any *more* morally controversial than any other element of morality' (1994, p. 91). Thus, scepticism about the existence of moral rights depends either on scepticism about morality in general, or on the claim that morality – properly understood – does not contain any rights.

Even if one accepts that moral rights exist, one might be sceptical about human rights, since there is considerable disagreement about their foundations. As we have seen, moral rights are justified by moral principles, and if there is no agreement about the principles that justify human rights then we might have grounds for scepticism about them. One of the difficulties here is pluralism, which we discussed in Chapter 3, and which has haunted human rights doctrines since their inception, as can be seen in Box 10.5. Contemporary critics of human rights have also argued that using international institutions to advance human rights amounts to a form of cultural imperialism, since they reflect specifically Western values. During the future challenges section of this chapter, we will consider some of the ways in which contemporary political theorists have recently sought to rescue the doctrine of human rights from this kind of objection.

A different kind of objection to moral rights concerns their morality rather than their existence. An early critic of rights-based political moralities was nineteenth-century economist and philosopher Karl Marx (2000), who associated rights with separation, disagreement and conflict. On his account, a political morality that conceived of people as rights-bearers – asserting and enforcing their various claims against one another – was incompatible with a truly human society. As we saw in Chapter 9, communitarian political theorist Michael Sandel

BOX 10.5   HUMAN RIGHTS AND PLURALISM

Human rights are said to have universal application, and therefore apply to people who disagree deeply about morality, religion and politics. Moreover, they make similar demands on societies that otherwise share very little in common, for instance in terms of their histories, traditions, practices, institutions and cultures. One long-standing challenge that human rights pose is whether they can be justified to everyone to whom they are said to apply. For example, in their 'Statement on Human Rights', issued in 1947, the American Anthropological Association asked whether the proposed Universal Declaration of Human Rights could really be applicable to all human beings, without it being 'a statement of rights conceived only in terms of the values prevalent in the countries of Western Europe and America?' (American Anthropological Association, 1947, p. 539). The members of the association had two related worries. First, they interpreted human rights against a backdrop of European colonialism, in which powerful nations had sought to 'civilise' others by imposing their own traditions and institutions. Second, they believed that 'standards and values are relative to the culture from which they derive' (American Anthropological Association, 1947, p. 542). If this is true, then judgements about right and wrong are relative to particular cultures and worldviews, and 'what is held to be a human right in one society may be regarded as anti-social by another people' (American Anthropological Association, 1947, p. 542).

Can there be truly universal human rights? Are these compatible with respect for cultural diversity?

(1998) has recently voiced a similar concern about the corrosive effects of rights, and proponents of care ethics have likewise objected to the tendency of rights-talk to displace other significant ethical concerns. In the case of human rights, a similar objection has also been developed by proponents of the 'Asian Values' thesis, who argue that some of the distinctive traits and values of traditional societies could be jeopardised by the spread of human rights. For example, Bilahari Kausikan – a government official from Singapore – has suggested that 'many East and Southeast Asians tend to look askance at the starkly individualistic ethos of the West in which authority tends to be seen as oppressive and rights are an individual's "trump" over the state' (Kausikan, 1993, p. 36).

In different ways, these critics object to the morality of rights, associating them with an unattractive form of individualism that threatens communal cohesion, stability and relationships. Advocates of rights have responded to these criticisms in two different ways. On the one hand, some have argued that many rights are actually compatible with community, and that some rights can help to support communal activities (Raz, 1986, pp. 251–5). For example, a right to freely associate can enable communities to practise their own distinctive traditions, shielding them from the disapproval of others. On the other hand, others have argued that even if rights do jeopardise some communal or traditional ways of life, this might not be a decisive reason to reject them, if the things that rights protect are themselves valuable.

Are there any group rights?

Group rights are held by groups rather than individuals. Probably the best-known example of a group right is the right to self-determination, which is attributed to 'peoples' in both the International Covenant on Civil and Political Rights (1966) and the International Covenant on Economic, Social and Cultural Rights (1966). The understanding of this right has legal and moral implications for the question of secession, as discussed in Box 10.6.

BOX 10.6 SELF-DETERMINATION AND THE RIGHT TO SECEDE

Secession occurs when a group creates a new state on territory that was previously part of another state. A group can have a (moral) right to secede in two senses. First, a constitution might incorporate an exit clause, for example by permitting a group to secede after a referendum to that effect. Second, a group might have a unilateral right to secede. If a group has such a right, then it must be justified by appealing to a theory of secession, and political theorists have defended two such theories. According to 'primary right' theories, groups may rightfully secede either because they have the appropriate identity or because their members desire it. Some nationalists, for example, believe that national groups have a right to self-determination, because they are nations (Margalit and Raz, 1990; Miller, 1995, 2007). However, even if we accept that nations have self-determination rights, it does not settle the question about which groups are entitled to secede, since the definition of a nation is widely contested (compare, for example, Smith, 1986; Anderson, 1991; Miller, 1995; Yack, 2012). A different version of the primary right theory says that any group, and not only nations, is entitled to secede, provided that enough of its members would like to do so (Philpott, 1995). This argument connects the justification of secession to democratic principles. A difficulty it faces concerns identifying which people are entitled to participate in the decision about whether to secede, since the drawing of boundaries is likely to effect the end result. The other kind of theory that might justify unilateral secession is the 'just cause' or 'remedial right only' theory. This view says that secession is justified if and only if a group has been the victim of an injustice (Buchanan, 2004). For instance, if a state has persistently violated the basic rights of a minority group, or if it has failed to uphold agreements that it made with them, or if it acquired the territory at stake unjustly, then the minority may be entitled to leave the current political formation and create its own state. Because this theory places stricter conditions on the right to secede than primary right theories, it allocates secession rights to fewer groups.

Under what conditions, if any, does a group have a right to secede?

Other group rights have been sought by cultural and linguistic minorities within existing states. For example, as we saw in Chapters 1 and 6, groups have sought rights to ensure that their language is the dominant one within a particular territory, to guarantee that their way of life be accorded public recognition or support, to various forms of political autonomy, and to enable them to preserve their own traditions and to resist assimilation into majority society. According to one scholar, the beneficiaries of such rights include 'the Scots and Welsh in the United Kingdom; the Catalans and Basques in Spain; the Flemish in Belgium; the Québécois in Canada; the Puerto Ricans in the United States; the Corsicans in France; the German minority in South Tyrol in Italy; the Swedes in Finland; and the French and Italian minorities in Switzerland' (Kymlicka, 2007, p. 177).

What makes these various rights group rights is that they are held by the groups themselves. This point can be confusing, since many minority rights are held by individuals rather than groups. For example, as we saw in Chapter 1, multiculturalists and difference theorists sometimes argue for 'group differentiated' rights, such as exemptions from generally applicable laws (Young, 1990; Kymlicka, 1995). These rights are held and exercised by individuals, who are entitled to them because of their membership in some particular group, and they are not group rights in the strict sense that we shall use the term here. The relationship between individual rights and group rights is further complicated by the latter's relationship with human rights. On the one hand, minority rights are sometimes presented as an integral component of human rights, as in UNESCO's (2001) 'Universal Declaration on Cultural Diversity':

> The defence of cultural diversity is an ethical imperative inseparable from respect for human dignity. It implies a commitment to human rights and fundamental freedoms, in particular the rights belonging to minorities and those of indigenous peoples. Cultural rights are an integral part of human rights, which are universal, indivisible and independent.

On the other hand, however, group rights have faced a mixed reaction amongst proponents of human rights, as we explore in Box 10.7.

The first theoretical puzzle raised by group rights concerns the conditions that a group must satisfy to qualify for them. As we have seen, choice theorists believe that rights-holders must be capable of making choices about how to exercise their powers. Thus, they believe that groups must be capable of agency if they are to bear rights. Some proponents of the choice theory are sceptical about this possibility. For instance, Wellman concludes that there are 'no irreducible moral group rights because no group as such possesses the agency required to be a moral right holder' (Wellman, 1995, p. 176). Meanwhile, others have suggested that at least some groups are capable of at least some forms of agency, and consequently that it might be possible to ascribe choice theory rights to them

BOX 10.7 GROUP RIGHTS AND HUMAN RIGHTS

Will Kymlicka has observed that for much of the twentieth century, minority group rights and human rights were widely believed to be in opposition to one another (Kymlicka, 2007, pp. 27–60). Indeed, the Universal Declaration of Human Rights made no reference to minority rights because its authors believed that universal and individual human rights offered sufficient protections to the members of minority cultures. For them, group rights as such were either unnecessary or dangerous and divisive. This sceptical attitude had softened by 1966, and Article 27 of the International Covenant on Civil and Political Rights insisted that the members of ethnic, religious and linguistic minorities should 'not be denied the right, in community with the other members of their group, to enjoy their own culture, to profess and practice their own religion, or to use their own language'. Noticeably, however, Article 27 did not grant any rights to groups themselves, instead emphasising that individual members of minority groups should not be subject to discrimination on the basis of their cultural, religious or linguistic identity. Meanwhile, in recent years human rights have been interpreted as group rights in the stricter sense. For example, the Declaration on the Rights of Indigenous Peoples, adopted by the General Assembly of the UN in 2007, asserted that indigenous peoples have a right to 'self-determination' (Article 3), a right to 'establish and control their educational systems' (Article 14), a right to 'own, use, develop and control the lands, territories and resources that they possess by reason of traditional ownership or other traditional occupation or use' (Article 26) and a right 'to maintain, control, protect and develop their cultural heritage, traditional knowledge and traditional cultural expressions' (Article 31).

Can group rights be human rights?

(Preda, 2012). However, even these more generous accounts must restrict group rights to those groups that are capable of agency in a meaningful sense, and this is likely to mean that only groups that already possess an institutional framework will be in a position to hold rights. One implication of this is that some indigenous peoples, for example, will not qualify for group rights on the choice theory.

Meanwhile, interest theorists are not committed to the idea that rights-holders must be capable of agency. Instead, they say that if groups have rights then they must have interests that ground duties. Although this may be a more promising starting point for proponents of group rights, it raises a difficult question about what it is for a group to have interests. One demanding view says that the interests which justify group rights must belong to the group itself, and not simply to the individuals who compose that group (May, 1987; McDonald, 1991). Meanwhile, others discard this approach as mysterious and instead say that the interests of a group are simply the shared interests of its members (Raz, 1986; Green, 1991). The most promising version of this argument has been suggested by Raz, who thinks that a group is entitled to rights if the aggregated interests of its members are sufficiently weighty to ground duties (Raz, 1986, pp. 207–10). For example, suppose that the individual members of an indigenous group each have an interest in controlling a given territory, so as to allow them to continue with their traditional hunting practices. Considered in isolation, these interests are unlikely to be sufficiently weighty to justify placing non-members under a corresponding negative duty to refrain from using that land, especially if those non-members have conflicting place-related interests. But, tallying up the individual interests of each group member might be enough to ground a group right. Although this approach is promising, it has two implications that many find normatively unattractive. First, smaller groups will have less forceful cases for rights than larger groups. Second, the rights to which a group is entitled may change over time, since the content and weight of shared interests are 'highly vulnerable to changes in membership' (Newman, 2004, p. 134). For example, if some of the members of our indigenous group were to assimilate into majority society, the group itself could cease to hold rights to control its territory.

As I have developed it so far, there is nothing in this theory of group rights to suggest that groups must have a particular character in order to hold rights. For example, at least in principle, the aggregated interests of a group of pedestrians might be sufficiently weighty to ground a group right to the maintenance of walkways (Jones, 2008). However, some political theorists have sought to restrict group rights to groups of a particular kind. For example, Marlies Galenkamp (1993) has argued that only constitutive communities, such as those celebrated by communitarians (see Chapter 2), are entitled to group rights. This view is broadly consistent with the practice of group rights, since most of the groups that have claimed such rights are constitutive communities. However, it is not obvious why having this kind of character is a necessary condition for holding group rights, unless one believes that only such groups have the required moral standing to be rights-holders.

The second theoretical puzzle raised by group rights has to do with what kinds of goods they secure. One view, suggested by Raz (1986), says that group rights are rights to 'public goods', which are a particular kind of good with the properties of being non-excludable and non-rival. This means that the goods secured by group rights must be ones that are available to every member of the group and ones for which any member's use of the good in question will not diminish it for any other. Consequently, according to this view, groups cannot have rights to things like scarce resources, but they can have rights to things like self-determination, since all members can enjoy this good without compromising any other member's enjoyment.

A difficulty with this view is that it struggles to explain why the rights in question should be held by groups and not individuals. For example, Raz believes that the 'right to know' could be a group right. On his account, disclosing how and why particular political decisions were reached is a public good, and therefore the possible object of a group right, since each member of the public can share in this knowledge without thereby disadvantaging anyone else's access to the same information (Raz, 1986, p. 209). However, even if this is true, the good at stake is enjoyed on an individual basis – that is to say, by people separately and not jointly. This is also the case for many other public goods, such as clean air and the containment of infectious diseases. Moreover, in those cases it seems to make more sense to say that it is individuals, and not groups, who have rights to the goods in question (Réaume, 1988, p. 9). So why, then, should it be groups and not individuals who have a 'right to know', or a right to self-determination? As we have seen, Raz's answer to this is to say that groups are the most appropriate rights-holder if individual interests (counted singly) are not weighty enough. But this is unsatisfying because it implies that the goods secured by group rights could also be secured by individual rights, and that the difference between the two has only to do with the contrasting 'weights' of the interests that underlie them.

Some political theorists reject this approach because they believe that there must be something distinctive about the goods secured by group rights, which they capture by describing the goods at stake as being 'communal' (Waldron, 1993, pp. 339–69), 'common' (Marmor, 2001), 'irreducibly social' (Taylor, 1995, p. 137) or 'participatory' (Réaume, 1988, 1994). According to these accounts, the goods secured by group rights involve essentially social activities that cannot be enjoyed by persons in isolation. For example, Denise Réaume thinks that group rights are rights to things like being part of a thriving linguistic community or continuing a traditional way of life. For these, at least part of 'the good *is* the participation' (Réaume, 1988, p. 10), and in this sense they resemble the enjoyment of friendship (Réaume, 1988, p. 12) and convivial dinner parties (Waldron, 1993, pp. 355–6). Réaume labels the goods secured by group rights participatory goods, since they can only be enjoyed if others participate in their production and consumption. Moreover, she argues that participatory goods, unlike many public goods, 'cannot be the object of an individual right' because they 'inherently involve collective activity as part of their value' (1988, p. 13). Thus, she concludes that these goods can only be secured by group rights.

What might a right to a participatory good entail? In some cases, upholding a cluster of individual rights, such as those listed in Article 27, might be enough to ensure that people can continue to enjoy their language or culture. However, as we saw in Chapter 7, stronger rights might be required if a vulnerable community is to be protected against the pressures of assimilation. For example, it might be necessary to require schools, bureaucracies and businesses to use the language at stake, or to restrict non-members from purchasing property on the territory occupied by an indigenous group. Réaume herself generally formulates group rights as claims held against outsiders, such as a negative duty of non-interference or a positive duty to provide subsidies. However, the continued survival of a participatory good might also require imposing burdensome duties on members, so that others can continue to enjoy participation. For example, members of linguistic minorities might be duty-bound to continue using their ancestral language, or dissenting members of indigenous groups might be duty-bound to conform to traditional practices. At least when pushed to its extremes, this seems to be an unattractive consequence of a theory of group rights. Thus, Réaume gives two reasons to resist the conclusion that securing participatory goods justifies disciplining 'wayward' members. First, because doing so would 'constitute a serious infringement on the autonomy of those against whom the right is asserted' (Réaume, 1988, p. 17). Second, because it would 'require the compulsion of that which cannot be compelled, namely willing participation' (Réaume, 1988, p. 13). The outcome of her view is that the substantive justification of group rights will depend upon carefully balancing the competing interests of individuals and groups.

Future challenges

In this chapter we have seen that interest and choice theories of rights supply rival explanations about the function of rights, and that this disagreement has important implications for how we think about the nature, scope and possibility of animal, human and group rights, amongst other things. In contemporary politics, it is the doctrine of human rights that continues to attract the fiercest controversies. As we have seen, one reason for this is that critics charge human rights with being 'fundamentally Eurocentric' (Mutua, 2002, p. 11). According to this view, promoting human rights amounts to cultural imperialism because their content reflects values and concerns that are peculiarly Western. Since it is certainly true that the Universal Declaration of Human Rights – and rights-discourse in general – is a product of European and North American political and intellectual culture (Griffin, 2008, p. 133), an ongoing challenge for proponents of human rights is to find ways to address this criticism.

In support of the thesis that human rights have a universal application, it might be argued that their Western origins do not limit their scope, because moral ideas that originate in one part of the world can still be adopted elsewhere. Against this, critics of human rights sometimes advance a stronger thesis, which is that the values underlying human rights are specific to a particular worldview or value tradition. For example, both critics and proponents of rights often connect them to an eighteenth-century European intellectual movement known as the Enlightenment, which sought to replace religious revelation with reason as the proper basis for ethics and political morality. According to critics, this implies that human rights are intelligible only within a particular worldview, which emerged in one part of the world at one time in history, and that they cannot be justified outside of this framework. However, this stronger thesis arguably relies on an exaggeration, since the ideas that animate human rights are not all that unique. For instance, Amartya Sen has pointed out that the kinds of values which nourish human rights can be found across a wide variety of religious and cultural traditions, including Islam, Buddhism and Confucianism (Sen, 1999, pp. 234–40).

If the ideas and values that underlie human rights are widely dispersed and can be found in a variety of different value traditions and political ideologies, it might be possible to support their universal application by appealing to some of the ideas associated with political liberalism, which we examined in Chapter 3. Indeed, according to some human rights theorists, we should aspire to reach an international 'overlapping consensus' about the content of human rights (Donnelly, 2003, p. 40; see also Cohen, 2004). A distinctive feature of this approach is that it drops the requirement that human rights should be defended by appealing to a single cluster of foundational values – such as a particular interpretation of the relationships between morality, freedom and reason – and instead says that we should aim to get an international agreement about the content of the rights themselves. According to this view, provided adherents of different cultural and ideological traditions endorse the same list of human rights, it does not matter if they disagree about the underlying values. Different people from different traditions might support human rights for different moral reasons, using arguments and ideas drawn from their own distinctive worldviews.

This strategy for justifying human rights is similar to the one adopted by the Human Rights Commission, which was responsible for drafting the original Universal Declaration of Human Rights. That commission contained permanent representatives from a variety of different states and was led in its work by Eleanor Roosevelt along with philosophers from China (Peng Chun Chang) and Lebanon (Charles Malik). It was assisted by a Committee on the Theoretical Bases of Human Rights, which was established by UNESCO (the UN's Educational, Scientific and Cultural Organisation). According to an account of their deliberations, the work of this committee revealed that 'the principles underlying the draft Declaration were present in many cultural and religious traditions, though not always expressed in the terms of rights' (Glendon, 2001, p. 76). However, although there was widespread consensus about what kinds of things should qualify for the protection of human rights, this was not matched by any substantive consensus about the foundation or ultimate justification of human rights, as was revealed by Jacques Maritain, a French philosopher, in the following anecdote:

It is related that at one of the meetings of a UNESCO National Commission where human rights were being discussed, someone expressed astonishment that certain champions of violently opposed ideologies had agreed on a list of those rights. 'Yes', they said, 'we agree about the rights but on condition that no one asks us why'. (Maritain, 2007, p. 148)

Thus, the 'overlapping consensus' strategy was already implicit in the approach adopted by the United Nations in the aftermath of the Second World War. For them, and perhaps for us too, agreement about the content of human rights had a much higher priority than agreement about the moral foundations of human rights.

According to contemporary proponents of the overlapping consensus approach, the list of rights that could attract support from the major traditions is extensive, and would not differ much from existing formulations of human rights. What is essential, on their view, is that people from different parts of the world accept human rights voluntarily – that is to say, they endorse them as genuine moral commitments and not only for strategic reasons, for instance because powerful states threaten to impose sanctions if they refuse to do so. This is important both because reaching a genuine overlapping consensus about human rights would defeat the objection that they are fundamentally Eurocentric, and because human rights must be internalised by people if they are to perform their various functions. Furthermore, if people from different cultural and religious backgrounds are able to ground their support for human rights within their own traditions and values, it is likely to make their support for those rights stronger and more durable, since they will recognise them as their own. For example, according to Abdullahi Ahmed An-Na'im '[t]o be committed to carrying out human rights standards, people must hold these standards as emanating from their worldview and values' (1992, p. 431). Thus, an overlapping consensus approach could facilitate the dispersal and internalisation of human rights norms amongst adherents of non-Western intellectual, cultural, ethical and religious traditions.

11

Conclusion

Introduction

As we have seen throughout this book, contemporary political theorists use theories in different ways and for different purposes. Sometimes they use theories critically, to draw attention to particular forms of oppression or injustice that might otherwise be invisible, or to reveal the shortcomings or limitations of our current social practices and ways of doing things. At other times they use theories more constructively, to propose principles that we ought to use to govern our collective lives, or to identify the different ways in which we might understand basic political values. Behind these different uses lurk some substantive disagreements, both about what political theory ought to be and about how we ought to do it. In this short conclusion we will explore some of these disagreements, initially by examining the idea that political theory has recently experienced an 'ontological turn', and then by contrasting some different accounts of what political theory and political theorists should aspire to. Throughout, I will emphasise some of the objections that have been raised against 'mainstream' approaches to political theory, and consider some of different ways in which proponents of these approaches might respond.

At the turn of the millennium, Steven White identified a 'curious commonality' amongst some different strands of political theory. According to him, a recent generation of political theorists were exhibiting a 'growing propensity to interrogate more carefully those "entities" presupposed by our typical ways of seeing and doing in the modern world' (White, 2000, p. 4). He labelled this the 'ontological turn'. Ontology is that branch of philosophy concerned with 'being', and ontological inquiries have to do with finding out what things exist, in what sense they exist, and what it is that distinguishes one thing from another. For example, determining the existence of the German language, the property of roundness and the number 20 are all ontological issues, as is figuring out whether these are the same kinds of thing, or whether and how they are distinguished from one another. However, the political theorists whom White had in mind employ the term ontology in a distinctive and narrower sense, to refer to human subjects and their relations. For these theorists, an ontology consists in 'a set of fundamental understandings about the relations of humans to themselves, to others, and to the world' (Connolly, 1987, p. 9). Or, as a similar definition has it, an ontology consists in 'an implicit or explicit interpretation of the fundamental conditions of life in the social and political world, the kinds of things that exist there, and the range of possibilities that it bears' (Markell, 2003, p. 195). Thus, the 'entities' that White thinks are now being interrogated more carefully are people themselves, and the 'ontological turn' he identifies consists in 'the emergence of new rules for the game of reflecting upon the most basic conceptualizations of self, other, and world, as well as for how such reflections in turn structure ethical-political thought' (White, 2000, p. 6). In other words, White's ontological turn amounts to a renewed engagement by political theorists with fundamental questions about what human beings are and about the world they inhabit.

Liberal ontology and its critics

White believes that this constitutes a 'turn' because the dominant mode of political theory – liberalism – has 'generally ignored or suppressed ontological reflection' (White, 2000, p. 7). Certainly, and as we have seen throughout this book, many recent liberal political theorists seem to have been determined to avoid controversial speculations about human nature. For example, consider Isaiah Berlin's criticism of the 'positive' conceptions of freedom, which we examined in Chapter 7. Berlin's scepticism about these conceptions was motivated by, amongst other things, his belief that they were unavoidably bound up with dubious claims about autonomy, rationality and authenticity – in other words, with claims about what human beings are really like. For Berlin, such ideas were potentially dangerous since they could be employed to license authoritarian interventions. By contrast, he thought that 'negative' conceptions of freedom were preferable because they were less reliant upon controversial philosophical theses. Similarly, consider John Rawls's theory of political liberalism, which we examined in Chapter 3. This theory purposefully avoids taking a view about the human subject and 'deliberately stays on the surface, philosophically speaking' (Rawls, 1996, p. 230). These parts of Rawls's work were animated by an acknowledgement that people will inevitably and permanently disagree about ethical and religious questions, and consequently about human nature too. From this, he drew the conclusion that basic political principles ought to be based on uncontroversial assumptions which can support an 'overlapping consensus' amongst adherents of different comprehensive doctrines.

Thus, if we take the statements of liberal political theorists at face value, then many of the proponents of liberalism profess to disavow ontological speculation, in some cases seeking to exclude it entirely from the domain of political theory. Nevertheless, on occasions at least, some liberals seem to have been willing to endorse substantive commitments about what human beings are really like. For example, consider Berlin's account of how negative liberty should be distributed. Here, he argues that freedom ought to be restricted for the sake of justice, and justifies this by claiming that 'respect for the principles of justice' is 'as basic in men as the desire for liberty' (Berlin, 2002, p. 215). Likewise, he describes justified constraints on freedom as being grounded 'deeply in the nature of men as they have developed through history' and emanating from a sense of 'part of what we mean by a normal human being' (Berlin, 2002, p. 210). Another example of a substantive ontological commitment that can seemingly be found in the writings of some liberal political theorists is the description of human beings as rational choosers and self-interest maximisers. This conception is often employed within the disciplines of economics and political science, and it also informs Rawls's A Theory of Justice, which we examined in Chapter 9. Scholars often justify employing this conception of the person by presenting it as a useful construct or fiction for modelling human behaviour or for grounding principles of justice. However, their critics argue that because the assumptions underlying this depiction of the human subject are contestable, the conclusions that theorists derive from it are unstable.

It is in this sceptical vein that White objects to mainstream liberals for having 'tacitly' affirmed an impoverished conception of the person, which he labels the 'Teflon self' (White, 2000, pp. 7–8). Much like Sandel's 'unencumbered self', which we examined in Chapter 2, White's 'Teflon self' is intended to capture the idea that some liberal political theorists seem to employ a conception of the person who lacks 'sticky' attachments and is 'disengaged' (2000, p. 8). To illustrate this, he suggests that some liberals neglect the extent to which people are entangled with their languages, and instead conceive of language in purely instrumental terms. White follows the German philosopher Heidegger in characterising this as an unrealistic 'figuration' of what human beings are really like, because it leaves us with the impression that although 'we always "have" language; it never "has" us' (2000, p. 9). White believes that these shortcomings of the liberal conception of the human subject are significant, since liberals cannot altogether evade ontological questions. For one thing, contemporary theories of liberalism insist that people owe one another some form of respect and that a just society will embody something like a norm of equal respect. But according to White, filling out what this means will inevitably implicate a theorist in a richer ontology than many liberals are willing to admit.

As we saw in Chapter 2, White was not the first political theorist to criticise mainstream liberals for smuggling apparently unrealistic assumptions about human beings into their theories. For example, during the 1980s the communitarian political theorist Alasdair MacIntyre attributed to Rawls the view that 'a society is composed of individuals, each with his or her own interest, who then have to come together and formulate common rules of life' (MacIntyre, 1985, p. 250). This is an ontological view, which puts the individual before society, and says that an individual's interests are prior to, and independent of, their social ties and memberships. Since Rawls assumes that people will inevitably disagree about the purposes of human life, the effect of this ontological commitment – according to MacIntyre – is to exclude the possibility of a community whose members are bound by a shared understanding of the good, in which their individual projects and goals are defined by reference to their shared goals and bonds. At around the same time and in a similar spirit, Michael Sandel also argued that liberal individualism was self-defeating, since by teaching 'respect for the distance of self and ends' it effectively puts 'the self beyond the reach of politics' (Sandel, 1998, p. 183). Consequently, on Sandel's reading, because liberalism treats the human self as a 'premise of politics rather than its precarious achievement', it is unable to appreciate 'the pathos of politics' and obscures the 'inspiring possibilities' of collective forms of political activity and life (1998, p. 183).

A related line of criticism also issued from feminist political theorists during this period. For example, Alison Jaggar charged liberal political theory with 'political solipsism, the assumption that human individuals are essentially self-sufficient entities' (1983, p. 40). However, maintaining the ontological assumption that people are self-sufficient is impossible, according to Jaggar, once 'one takes into account the facts of human biology, especially reproductive biology' (1983, pp. 40–1). More generally, she also points out that liberals have tended to neglect the extent to which human characteristics, needs, interests, desires and capacities are shaped by other people and by social contexts. One consequence of this, according to Valerie Bryson, is that liberal political theorists are prone to ignoring 'the emotion, nurturing, co-operation and mutual support that are an essential basis for human society, and that have historically been central to women's lives' (Bryson, 2003, p. 156).

Thus, some of liberalism's critics believe that its main ontological failing is not that it eschews ontological speculation, but rather that it employs a minimal and individualistic conception of the person that leaves too much out. For them, because liberalism relies on an unrealistic ontology, it neglects important normative possibilities and ends up delivering impoverished normative judgements.

Arguably, however, at least some of these criticisms rely on a misunderstanding of contemporary theories of liberalism, and especially of Rawls's work. For example, in *Political Liberalism*, and in direct opposition to MacIntyre's construal of his thought, Rawls insisted that '[w]e have no prior identity before being in society' (Rawls, 1996, p. 41). By this, he meant that people's characters, self-understandings, conceptions of the good and moral beliefs are 'first acquired' in their 'social world' (1996, p. 41). Indeed, it is because we are socially formed that it is so important to get our principles of justice right, since these principles will shape the institutions that define us. Similarly, although it is true that Rawls invoked an unrealistic figuration of the person in his original position (an 'unencumbered' or a 'Teflon' self), the purpose of that thought experiment was not to describe a foundational ontology – a theory about what human beings are really like – but was instead to model and draw out some of our deepest intuitions about justice. Thus, Rawls characterises Sandel's interpretation of his theory as 'an illusion caused by not seeing the original position as a device of representation' (Rawls, 1999d, p. 402). Finally, something similar also applies to the objection that Rawls and his followers envisage the human subject as self-sufficient. Again, although the hypothetical parties in the original position might be describable as such, Rawls himself clearly rejected the view that self-sufficiency was something that actual human beings should, or even could, aspire to. This becomes clear when we consider his account of self-respect, which he thought was perhaps the most important primary good. On the one hand, a self-sufficient person might be able to secure some of what Rawls thinks we need in order to be self-respecting, such as having a sense that one's life has a meaning and being confident in one's abilities to plan and carry out various projects and goals. On the other hand, Rawls also thought that self-respect had social bases or a relational dimension, which he captured by saying that 'unless our endeavours are appreciated by our associates it will be impossible for us to maintain the conviction that they are worthwhile' (Rawls, 1999a, p. 387).

A different reason for objecting to liberalism's minimalist ontology is that it restricts the range of questions that are deemed to be 'political'. For example, Nathan Widder describes Rawls's political thought as 'superficial' because 'its image of politics [is] one of already established constituencies with divergent interests competing over the distribution of goods in a public institutional setting, where the primary concern is to ensure neutrality and fairness in procedures' (Widder, 2012, p. 7). Though Widder acknowledges the importance of this domain of politics, he also suggests that it is only one domain amongst others, and that liberalism neglects these other arenas of political life. As we saw in Chapters 8 and 9, something very similar has also been suggested in some recent feminist writings, which emphasise the narrow scope of liberal political thought and the tendency of liberals to ignore cultural forms of oppression and inequalities within the family.

Poststructuralist political theorists have been the most forceful advocates of the idea that liberal conceptions of politics – and therefore liberal approaches to political theory – are unduly limiting. For example, consider the different theories of representation that we explored in Chapter 4. Many liberal political theorists associate good representation with the accurate depiction of beliefs or identities. Thus, a representative legislature should be composed of accountable politicians, who effectively articulate the views and interests of their constituents. Meanwhile, poststructuralists like Michael Saward criticise this conception for treating people's political identities and preferences as givens, as if they already exist prior to the act of representation. On his account, the error of the liberal view is that it misses the creative dimension of representation itself, in which new identities and constituencies are called into existence. This is an ontological critique, since it invites us to reconsider the basic categories that make up political life and democratic representation, such as constituents, interests, identities and representatives.

The seeming narrowness of the liberal vision of politics has also been called into question by the emergence of poststructuralist theories of power. For example, as we saw in Chapter 6, Michel Foucault argues that power is not just about repression, or about getting others to do things. Rather, it is a relation that constitutes human subjects and social orders. Within his framework, ideologies, ways of being and human subjectivities are all products of the multiple and complex operations of power. From this vantage point, Foucault criticises liberal ontology for its assumption that individuals could be sovereign over themselves – authors of their own lives who select their plans and projects with a free hand. Instead, he insists that who we are and what we think are shaped by the particular regimes of truth we inhabit. Although this ontological critique undercuts the ideal of freedom as it is typically understood within the confines of liberalism, Foucault and his followers believe that it carries within itself a different kind of emancipatory potential. In particular, they emphasise that unmasking covert forms of domination can unsettle our self-understandings, make the familiar seem strange, and open up new avenues for political critique. For example, as we saw in Chapter 6, Foucault's critique of the emergence of a disciplinary society draws various phenomena into view that would otherwise be difficult to perceive, such as the ways in which modern subjects feel the watchful eye of authority looking over them and actively participate in their own self-surveillance.

Foucault's radical theories of power and the human subject have attracted a mixed reaction amongst political theorists. On the one hand, some of his critics believe that his ontological critique reaches too far, since it seems to repudiate the possibility of establishing or asserting an underlying truth about what human beings are (Taylor, 1985, pp. 152–84). According to this kind of reading, Foucault is ultimately a kind of nihilist, and the effect of his work is to undermine the possibility of adopting an independent standpoint from which to criticise contemporary social and political practices. On the other hand, more sympathetic readers of Foucault believe that an engagement with his ideas can teach us the valuable lesson that the human subject as we recognise it now is 'an essentially ambiguous achievement of modernity' (Connolly, 1985, p. 374). According to this view, Foucault's ontology can help us to see that things like insanity, criminality and perversity are not natural or timeless categories, but are instead produced by the same operations of power from which we too are constituted. Thus, Foucault's genealogical investigations bring out the contingency of our contemporary discourses about mental illness, sexuality and crime. Such insights are valuable, since they may prompt us 'to reconsider the politics of containment that now governs institutional orientations to otherness' (Connolly, 1985, p. 374).

Alternative ontologies and alternatives to ontology

According to White, we ought to draw two conclusions from these various critiques of the liberal ontology: first, that 'all fundamental conceptualizations of self, other, and world are contestable'; and second, that 'such conceptualizations are nevertheless necessary or unavoidable for an adequately reflective ethical and political life' (White, 2000, p. 8). In turn, these conclusions rule out two different ways in which we might conceive of the relationship between ontology and political theory. First, they rule out deriving moral and political principles directly from highly confident judgements about human nature and about how the world is, since doing so fails to acknowledge the contestability of all ontological views. Second, they also rule out the possibility of doing political theory without ontology, as White believed that Rawls had sought to do, because in the end such approaches do not really eschew ontology but instead only conceal their own controversial assumptions behind a veneer of neutrality.

By White's account, then, political theorists must not abandon ontological speculation, because doing so would leave them unable to structure their priorities. But at the same time, although all ontologies are contestable and ought to be contested, White resists the conclusion that ontological affirmations should be regarded as nothing more than blunt assertions about how the world appears from a particular perspective. Instead, he advises political theorists to proceed cautiously from an awareness of the partiality and incompleteness of their ontological assumptions, to acknowledge that all ontological views are ultimately mysterious, and to recognise that any particular affirmation they endorse will be fraught with uncertainty. White labels the theories that embody the kind of modesty he favours 'weak ontologies'. These are not 'thin' or minimalist, in the sense that White had characterised liberal ontology, and instead they have a 'satisfying' richness (White, 2000, p. 76). Part of their richness derives from their recognition of 'certain existential realities', and this allows them to portray the human subject as a 'stickier subject' than does the liberal figuration of a 'Teflon' or 'unencumbered' self. For example, instead of thinking of the modern subject as someone who freely chooses their ends, weak ontologies acknowledge that people are entangled with languages and are always already attached to 'backgrounds' or 'sources', which animate their lives and can evoke a sense of awe or reverence. Similarly, they acknowledge the consciousness that people have of their own mortality as well as their capacity for novelty and newness, characteristics that White labels finitude and natality respectively.

To illustrate how a weak ontology might be employed by a political theorist, White refers to William Connolly, whose work we examined in Chapter 3. Connolly's political theory exemplifies White's preferred approach because it is based on 'an interpretation of being [an ontology] that is not provisional or thin, but rather deeply affirmed and rich, yet ultimately contestable' (White, 2000, p. 114). An example of Connolly's affirmative, rich yet contestable ontology can be found in his analysis of the 'constitutive relation' between identity and difference:

> An identity is established in relation to a series of differences that have become socially recognized. These differences are essential to its being. If they did not coexist as differences, it would not exist in its distinctness and solidity. Entrenched in this indispensable relation is a second set of tendencies, themselves in need of exploration, to congeal established identities into fixed forms, thought and lived as if their structure expressed the true order of things. When these pressures prevail, the maintenance of one identity (or field of identities) involves the conversion of some differences into otherness, into evil, or one of its numerous surrogates. Identity requires difference in order to be, and it converts difference into otherness in order to secure its own self-certainty. (Connolly, 1992, p. 64)

Here, Connolly starts from the ontological thesis that identity and difference have a 'constitutive' and 'indispensable' relation. By this, he means that a subject's identity cannot be defined in isolation, but must be defined by reference to what it is not. For example, ethnic and religious identities are defined by their relations to other ethnic and religious identities, and one identity cannot be defined without reference to the other. Then, he proceeds to acknowledge that this interplay of identity and difference has an ambiguous and sometimes unpredictable dimension. On the one hand, there are 'tendencies' and 'pressures' to 'congeal identities into fixed forms', so that an identity can 'secure its own self-certainty'. If this happens, then differences will be converted into 'otherness', and the identities against which we define ourselves will appear to us as 'evil' or as 'one of its numerous surrogates'. On the other hand, Connolly also describes this process of converting differences into otherness as a 'tendency' and not as an inevitably. Thus, as White summarises Connolly's view, it is not 'our ontological destiny' to go with 'the flow of these pressures', and the fixing of identities can be resisted (White, 2003, p. 214).

Not only is Connolly's ontology richer and more ambiguous than the liberal conceptions of the person we explored earlier, but White also thinks that it can help us to address some pressing normative issues in contemporary political life. For example, consider Connolly's preferred theory of agonism, which we examined in Chapter 3. According to this view, an important aim of democratic politics is to convert antagonistic hostility into agonistic respect. Equipped with Connolly's ontological account of the interplay of identity and difference, we are better able to appreciate some of the challenges that this may pose and how they might be overcome. For example, the desire to secure their identities may encourage religious believers to fix their identities in opposition to others, and to police the identities of their co-religionists, prompting them to adopt a less open or welcoming attitude towards other religious views and followers of different faiths. At the same time, however, a mere awareness that identity and difference have an indispensable relation may also counter this tendency, since we will come to recognise that 'the imperious demand for security' is 'somewhat suspicious' and that 'conforming to these pressures puts one deeply at odds with the character of being' (White, 2003, p. 215). Thus, Connolly's ontology can be invoked as a reason to resist the pressures that push us towards otherness and antagonism, and can therefore play a positive role in securing agonistic respect.

A deep engagement with ontology and its relation to politics has also been a distinctive characteristic of contemporary French philosophy. For example, during the 1960s Gilles Deleuze embarked on developing a distinctive ontology that can be usefully contrasted with Connolly's. Deleuze was critical of the tendency to privilege identity over difference, and instead proposed a highly intricate 'philosophy of difference', developed initially in his *Difference and Repetition* (2004). Here, Deleuze cast doubt on the idea that identity is established through difference, and instead insisted that 'all identities are only simulated, produced as an optical "effect" by the more profound game of difference and repetition' (Deleuze, 2004, p. xvii). Deleuze's theories of difference and repetition have complex philosophical roots, which we cannot explore here. For present purposes, however, it is worth emphasising how far-reaching his scepticism about identity was. For example, in *A Thousand Plateaus*, a work he co-authored with his long-standing colleague Félix Guttari, they expressed a desire '[t]o reach, not the point where one no longer says I, but the point where it is no longer of any importance whether one says I' (Deleuze and Guttari, 2013, pp. 1–2). Deleuze's project of putting identity in its proper place has implications for political theory, because it calls into doubt those theories which privilege identity and its cognate categories, including not only authenticity but also otherness. Thus, from this perspective, even theories like Connolly's – which emphasise responsive engagement and oppose the policing or fixing of identities – are dubious, since they retain the idea that identity is a central or foundational category of being.

Whilst Deleuze criticised the content of prevailing ontological assumptions, another radical French philosopher – Jacques Rancière – recommended that political theorists abstain altogether from ontology (Ieven, 2009). Rancière criticises the idea that political principles ought to be traced back to ontological principles, such as White's 'certain existential realities' or Connolly's 'constitutive' and 'indispensable' relation of identity and difference. Moreover, he associates the recent turn to ontology with the 'dissolution of politics' (Rancière, 2011, p. 12). For him, it is a mistake to appeal to an account of the human subject to justify political principles or forms of political activity, because it is by way of politics that political subjects emerge. Moreover, grounding political projects on ontological assumptions is dangerous, since it distracts attention away from the specifics of any particular political moment or struggle.

Rancière employs his defiantly anti-ontological stance to support a distinctive view of politics, as well as a disruptive and polemical account of political activity. On his account, subjects do not engage in political struggles because of their identity. Rather, they do so because they are 'in between two or more identities' (Deranty, 2003, p. 8). On the one hand, they inhabit a world that is basically unequal, and which is marked by hierarchy and domination. As such, they have one identity that is defined by the structures that regulate social life, which Rancière gives the name la police. On the other hand, there is also a logic of la politique, in which subjects are constituted democratically, as equals, and which also supplies them with another identity. For Rancière, it is the contradiction between these two identities that makes it possible for people to be political subjects. It also opens up a space where the two identities can be mediated, which Rancière calls le politique. Here, 'the underlying equality operating within social inequality is verified pragmatically in struggles and demands of equality' (Deranty, 2003, p. 6). Thus, politics – or le politique – consists in attempts to disrupt la police. Characteristically, these disruptions take the form of polemics, in which the oppressed make themselves and their demands visible through speech and action, and in so doing reshape the political order.

Rancière's theory of politics is anti-ontological because it rejects the image of a political subject lying behind – and motivating – political activity. We can see this more clearly by considering the opposing view. According to this, when the suffragettes demanded votes for women, they were articulating a moral demand (for equality) based on an ontological foundation (that women are as rational as men and have interests in being treated with equal dignity). As such, the politics of the suffragettes was motivated by their affirmation of a particular ontology. Similarly, Marxists affirm a particular ontology (that the class struggle is the basic substance of social life) which allows them to explain how politics itself operates (that different classes with different interests come into conflict over the organisation of society). Meanwhile, Rancière proposes an alternative image, which removes the idea that there is an ontological reality or truth hiding somewhere behind politics. For him, it is not that the class struggle is behind the political. Rather, the class struggle is the political. Turning things around in this way has two important implications. First, by Rancière's account, political subjects 'do not exist prior to the declaration of [a] wrong' (Rancière, 1999, p. 39), and it is through political activity that political subjects are created. Thus, he thinks that the proletariat had no real existence prior to the revelation of 'the wrong that its name exposes' (1999, p. 39). Second, political subjects can claim identities in a flexible and creative way, as when someone claims 'to be a proletarian without being a worker, or conversely to be a poet without being a bourgeois' (Deranty, 2003, p. 8).

The purposes of political theory

Underlying some of these disagreements about ontology are some further disagreements about what it is that political theorists should be doing. As we have seen, many normative political theorists believe that good political theory will do two things. First, it will help us to comprehend our basic moral commitments, allowing us to identify normative principles that are consistent with those commitments. Second, it will also help us to understand the various logical relations between our different moral judgements, thereby allowing us to better comprehend some of the apparent tensions between different values, such as freedom, equality and justice. Within this framework, the overall goal of the political theorist is to discover, clarify, justify and criticise moral and political principles – such as principles to regulate the major institutions of a well-ordered or just society. In turn, the test for such principles is whether they are consistent with our moral intuitions, or our considered moral judgements. For example, Rawls's test of 'reflective equilibrium', which we explored in Chapter 1, says that we ought to reject normative theories and principles which contradict our considered judgements. Thus, if a theory lends support to oppressive institutions, or to policies that would conflict with our deeply help beliefs, then it should be modified or abandoned. By contrast, normative theories and principles that are consistent with our considered judgements are, for that reason, preferable.

Meanwhile, other political theorists think of themselves as engaged in a different kind of critical project, which pays closer attention to the contradictions and tensions implicit in our current social practices and ways of doing things. For example, consider Foucault's belief that his genealogical investigations could help to identify the limits to our current ways of thinking (Foucault, 1984, pp. 32–50, 1986, 1996). This self-understanding makes it clear that his project is very different to Rawls's. Ultimately, Foucault hopes to reveal that our ideologies, concepts and categories are the contingent products of a particular history and particular relations of power. In doing so, he unsettles and problematises the same considered judgements to which Rawls gave a privileged status.

Critical approaches to political theory – including those inspired by Foucault, Deleuze and Rancière – often appear to be essentially negative. Indeed, this impression is sometimes reinforced by their proponents, who tend to be sceptical about the idea of progress and who expressly renounce normative approaches to political theory, such as those in which the theorist sets out to defend a particular vision of a just or good society. Nevertheless, many of these theorists believe that their work has a positive and transformative dimension. For example, Foucault believed that carefully charting out the different ways in which power makes us into subjects can help individuals and groups to mount projects of resistance, in which people refashion themselves and 'refuse what we are' (Foucault, 1982, p. 785). As we saw in Chapter 6, this idea has recently been extended by the feminist political theorist Judith Butler, who developed a controversial performative theory of resistance. Similarly, Deleuze and Guttari also emphasised the need for 'resistance to the present' (Deleuze and Guttari, 1994, p. 108), which in their case was to be achieved through the creation of new vocabularies and concepts that make it possible to transform our current ways of thinking and doing. They believed that conceptual innovation could serve a radical purpose, since creating new concepts could vividly reveal how strange, remarkable and contingent the familiar really is. Nevertheless, they did not intend their concepts to entirely replace our current ones, or those which are utilised by mainstream political theorists. As one commentator summarises their work, '[t]he particular concepts they propose ... are not meant as substitutes for existing concepts of justice, rights, democracy, or freedom, but they only serve the pragmatic goal of philosophy to the extent that they assist in bringing about another justice, new rights, or novel forms of democracy and freedom' (Patton, 2006, p. 137).

Although it may seem as if practitioners of these different approaches to political theory might profitably learn from one another, in practice there is relatively little dialogue between the two traditions, and when it occurs it is too often superficial and fraught with misunderstandings. One likely explanation for this is the forbidding character of the terminology that each side uses, which can make it difficult to translate insights from one approach into the other. Another explanation is perhaps more basic, and more difficult to overcome. Whilst normative political theorists might welcome the transformative projects of resistance celebrated by their more critical colleagues, they will do so only if the means and ends of those projects are themselves normatively justified. Meanwhile, critical political theorists emphasise that transformation has an open-ended and unpredictable aspect, and they insist that philosophical critique must be immanent, in the sense that it ought to proceed from the internal logic of a domain rather than by reference to external standards. As a result, the two approaches will often tend to undermine one another. For normative theorists, unless critical approaches are guided by normative principles, which themselves can be independently justified, they risk being pointless and perhaps even dangerous. But critical approaches to political theory explicitly problematise the basis on which such normative judgements might be made.

It would be a mistake, though, to conclude that normative and critical approaches to political theory can only proceed on separate paths, or that one approach can be celebrated only at the cost of diminishing the other, or that nothing of value has made it across the divide. Whilst constructive dialogue between practitioners of each approach is admittedly rare, the most significant insights and developments from either side inevitably make it onto the radar of the other. For example, just as critical political theorists now inhabit an intellectual universe that has been profoundly shaped by Rawls's work, so too do the concepts employed by normative political theorists bear the imprint of Foucault's influence.

Bibliography

Abizadeh, A. (2008) 'Democratic Theory and Border Coercion: No Right to Unilaterally Control Your Own Borders', *Political Theory*, 36, 37–65.

Ackerly, B. (2005) 'Is Liberalism the Only Way Toward Democracy? Confucianism and Democracy', *Political Theory*, 33, 547–57.

Ackerman, B. (1991) *We the People 1: Foundations* (Cambridge, MA: Harvard University Press).

Alcoff, L. (1990) 'Feminist Politics and Foucault: The Limits to a Collaboration', in A. Dallery & C. Scott (eds.), *Crises in Continental Philosophy* (Albany, NY: SUNY Press).

Alcoff, L. (1991) 'The Problem of Speaking for Others', *Cultural Critique*, 20, 5–32.

American Anthropological Association (1947) 'Statement on Human Rights', *American Anthropologist*, 49, 539–43.

Anderson, B. (1991) *Imagined Communities: Reflections on the Origin and Spread of Nationalism*, Second edition (London: Verso).

Anderson, E. (1999) 'What is the Point of Equality?', *Ethics*, 109, 287–337.

Anderson, E. (2007) 'Fair Opportunity in Education: A Democracy Equality Perspective', *Ethics*, 117, 595–622.

Anderson, E. (2010) *The Imperative of Integration* (Princeton, NJ: Princeton University Press).

Ankersmit, F. (2002) *Political Representation* (Stanford, CA: Stanford University Press).

An-Na'im, A. (ed.) (1992) 'Conclusion', in A. An-Na'im (ed.), *Human Rights in Cross-Cultural Perspectives: A Quest for Consensus* (Philadelphia, PA: University of Pennsylvania Press).

Appiah, K. (2005) *The Ethics of Identity* (Princeton, NJ: Princeton University Press).

Archibugi, D. (2008) *The Global Commonwealth of Citizens: Toward Cosmopolitan Democracy* (Princeton, NJ: Princeton University Press).

Arendt, H. (2004) *The Origins of Totalitarianism* (New York: Shocken Books).

Aristotle (1996) '*The Politics*' and '*The Constitution of Athens*', trans. J. Barnes (Cambridge: Cambridge University Press).

Arneil, B. (2006) *Diverse Communities: The Problem with Social Capital* (Cambridge: Cambridge University Press).

Arneson, R. (1989) 'Equality and Equal Opportunity for Welfare', *Philosophical Studies*, 56, 77–93.

Arneson, R. (1999) 'Equal Opportunity for Welfare Defended and Recanted', *Journal of Political Philosophy*, 7, 488–97.

Arneson, R. (2006) 'Justice After Rawls', in J. Dryzek, B. Honig & A. Phillips (eds.), *The Oxford Handbook of Political Theory* (Oxford: Oxford University Press), 45–64.

Arneson, R. (2013) 'Egalitarianism', in E. Zalta (ed.), *The Stanford Encyclopedia of Philosophy*. Available at: http://plato.stanford.edu/archives/sum2013/entries/egalitarianism/

Bachrach, P. & M. Baratz (1962) 'Two Faces of Power', *American Political Science Review*, 56, 941–52.

Bachrach, P. & M. Baratz (1963) 'Decisions and Nondecisions: An Analytical Framework', *American Political Science Review*, 57, 641–51.

Bachrach, P. & M. Baratz (1970) *Power and Poverty: Theory and Practice* (Oxford: Oxford University Press).

Baiocchi, G. (2005) *Militants as Citizens: The Politics of Participatory Democracy in Porto Alegre* (Stanford, CA: Stanford University Press).

Ball, T. (1992) 'New Faces of Power', in T. Wartenberg (ed.), *Rethinking Power* (Albany, NY: SUNY Press), 14–31.

Barber, B. (1984) *Strong Democracy: Participatory Politics for a New Age* (Berkeley, CA: University of California Press).

Barry, B. (1975) 'Review Article: Anarchy, State and Utopia (Robert Nozick)', *Political Theory*, 3, 331–6.

Barry, B. (1981) 'Do Neighbors Make Good Fences?: Political Theory and the Territorial Imperative', *Political Theory*, 9, 293–301.

Barry, B. (1991) *Democracy and Power: Essays in Political Theory* (Oxford: Clarendon Press).

Barry, B. (2001a) *Culture and Equality: An Egalitarian Critique of Multiculturalism* (Cambridge: Polity).

Barry, B. (2001b) 'The Muddles of Multiculturalism', *New Left Review*, 8, 49–71.

Barry, B. (2006a) 'Humanity and Justice in Global Perspective', in R. Goodin & P. Pettit (eds.), *Contemporary Political Philosophy: An Anthology*, Second edition (London: Blackwell Publishing), 721–36.

Barry, N. (2006b) 'Defending Luck Egalitarianism', *Journal of Applied Philosophy*, 23, 89–107.

Barry, N. (2008) 'Reassessing Luck Egalitarianism', *Journal of Politics*, 70, 136–50.

Bartky, S. (1990) *Femininity and Domination: Studies in the Phenomenology of Oppression* (London: Routledge).

Beetham, D. (1999) *Democracy and Human Rights* (Cambridge: Polity).

Beitz, C. (1999) *Political Theory and International Relations* (Princeton, NJ: Princeton University Press).

Beitz, C. (2001) 'Human Rights as a Common Concern', *American Political Science Review*, 95, 269–82.

Benhabib, S. (1986) *Critique, Norm and Utopia* (New York: Columbia University Press).

Benhabib, S. (1992) *Situating the Self: Gender, Community and Postmodernism in Contemporary Ethics* (Cambridge: Polity).

Benhabib, S. (1995) 'Subjectivity, Historiography, and Politics', in L. Nicholson (ed.), *Feminist Contentions: A Philosophical Exchange* (Abingdon: Routledge), 107–26.

Benhabib, S. (1996) 'Toward a Deliberative Model of Democratic Legitimacy', in S. Benhabib (ed.), *Democracy and Difference* (Princeton, NJ: Princeton University Press).

Bentham, J. (1987) 'Anarchical Fallacies', in J. Waldron (ed.), *Nonsense upon Stilts: Bentham, Burke and Marx on the Rights of Man* (London: Methuen), 46–76.

Berlin, I. (2002) *Liberty*, ed. H. Hardy (Oxford: Oxford University Press).

Bertram, C. (2012) 'Rousseau's Legacy in Two Conceptions of the General Will: Democratic and Transcendent', *The Review of Politics*, 74, 403–20.

Bhabha, H. (1994) *The Location of Culture* (Abingdon: Routledge).

Bingham Powell, G. (2004) 'The Chain of Responsiveness', *Journal of Democracy*, 15, 91–105.

Birch, A. (2001) *The Concepts and Theories of Modern Democracy* (London: Routledge).

Blake, M. (2013) *Justice and Foreign Policy* (Oxford: Oxford University Press).

Bohman, J. (1996) *Public Deliberation: Pluralism, Complexity and Democracy* (Cambridge, MA: MIT Press).

Bradley, H. (2013) *Gender* (Cambridge: Polity).

Brandt, R. (1979) *A Theory of the Right and the Good* (Oxford: Oxford University Press).

Brennan, G. (2001) 'Collective Coherence?', *International Review of Law and Economics*, 21, 197–211.

Brighouse, H. & E. Olin Wright (2008) 'In Defence of Strong Gender Egalitarianism', *Politics and Society*, 36, 360–72.

Brito Viera, M. & D. Runciman (2008) *Representation* (Cambridge: Polity).

Brown, W. (2006) *Regulating Aversion: Tolerance in an Age of Empire and Identity* (Princeton, NJ: Princeton University Press).

Bryson, V. (2003) *Feminist Political Theory: An Introduction*, Second edition (Basingstoke: Palgrave Macmillan).

Buchanan, A. (2004) *Justice, Legitimacy and Self-Determination: Moral Foundations for International Law* (Oxford: Oxford University Press).

Buckler, S. (2002) 'Normative Theory', in D. Marsh and G. Stoker (eds.), *Theory and Methods in Political Science*, Second edition (Basingstoke: Palgrave Macmillan), 172–94.

Burke, E. (1996) 'Speech at the Conclusion of the Poll, 3 November 1774', in W. M. Elofson & J. A. Woods (eds.), *The Writings and Speeches of Edmund Burke: Volume III* (Oxford: Clarendon), 63–70.

Butler, J. (1990) *Gender Trouble* (Abingdon: Routledge).

Callan, E. (1997) *Creating Citizens: Political Education and Liberal Democracy* (Oxford: Oxford University Press).

Campbell, T. (2006) *Justice*, Third edition (Basingstoke: Palgrave Macmillan).

Caney, S. (2005) *Justice Beyond Borders: A Global Political Theory* (Oxford: Oxford University Press).

Caney, S. (2006) 'Global Justice: From Theory to Practice', *Globalizations*, 3, 121–37.

Canovan, M. (1996) *Nationhood and Political Theory* (Cheltenham: Edward Elgar).

Canovan, M. (2000) 'Patriotism is Not Enough', *British Journal of Political Science*, 30, 413–32.

Carens, J. (1987) 'Aliens and Citizens: The Case for Open Borders', *Review of Politics*, 49, 251–73.

Carens, J. (1992) 'Migration and Morality: A Liberal Egalitarian Perspective', in B. Barry & R. Goodin (eds.), *Free Movement: Ethical Issues in the Transnational Movement of People and Money* (Hemel Hempstead: Harvester Wheatseaf).

Carens, J. (2013) *The Ethics of Immigration* (Oxford: Oxford University Press).

Carter, S. (1987) 'Evolutionism, Creationism, and Treating Religion as a Hobby', *Duke Law Journal*, 977–96.

Chakrabarty, D. (2007) *Provincializing Europe: Postcolonial Thought and Historical Difference* (Princeton, NJ: Princeton University Press).

Chambers, S. (2003) 'Deliberative Democratic Theory', *Annual Review of Political Science*, 6, 307–26.

Chatterjee, P. (2013) 'Lineages of Political Society', in M. Freeden & A. Vincent (eds.), *Comparative Political Thought: Theorizing Practices* (Abingdon: Routledge).

Christman, J. (1991) 'Liberalism and Individual Positive Freedom', *Ethics*, 101, 343–59.

Cohen, G. A. (1995) *Self-Ownership, Freedom and Equality* (Cambridge: Cambridge University Press).

Cohen, G. A. (2008) *Rescuing Justice and Equality* (Cambridge, MA: Harvard University Press).

Cohen, G. A. (2009) *Why Not Socialism?* (Princeton, NJ: Princeton University Press).

Cohen, G. A. (2011) *On the Currency of Egalitarian Justice, and Other Essays in Political Philosophy*, ed. M. Otsuka (Princeton, NJ: Princeton University Press).

Cohen, J. (1989) 'Deliberation and Democratic Legitimacy', in A. Hamlin & P. Pettit (eds.), *The Good Polity* (Oxford: Blackwell).

Cohen, J. (1996) 'Procedure and Substance in Deliberative Democracy', in S. Benhabib (ed.), *Democracy and Difference* (Princeton, NJ: Princeton University Press).

Cohen, J. (2001) 'Taking People as They Are?', *Philosophy and Public Affairs*, 30, 363–86.

Cohen, J. (2004) 'Minimalism About Human Rights: The Most We Can Hope For?', *Journal of Political Philosophy*, 12, 190–213.

Cohen, J. & J. Rogers (2003) 'Power and Reason', in A. Fung and E. O. Wright (eds.), *Deepening Democracy: Experiments in Empowered Participatory Governance* (London: Verso), 237–55.

Connolly, W. (1985) 'Connolly, Foucault and Truth', *Political Theory*, 13, 365–76.

Connolly, W. (1987) *Politics and Ambiguity* (London: University of Wisconsin Press).

Connolly, W. (1992) *Identity/Difference: Democratic Negotiations of Political Paradox* (Ithaca, NY: Cornell University Press).

Connolly, W. (1993) *The Terms of Political Discourse* (Princeton, NJ: Princeton University Press).

Connolly, W. (2002) *Identity/Difference: Democratic Negotiations of Political Paradox*, Expanded edition (London: University of Minnesota Press).

Connolly, W. (2005) *Pluralism* (Durham and London: Duke University Press).

Cranston, M. (1962) *Human Rights Today* (London: Ampersand).

Cranston, M. (1973) *What are Human Rights?* (London: Bodley Head).

Crenson, M. (1971) *The Un-Politics of Air Pollution: A Study of Non-Decisionmaking in the Cities* (Baltimore, MD: John Hopkins Press).

Crick, B. (1962) *In Defence of Politics* (Harmondsworth: Penguin).

Crisp, R. (2003) 'Equality, Priority, and Compassion', *Ethics*, 113, 745–63.

Cullity, G. (2004) *The Moral Demands of Affluence* (Oxford: Oxford University Press).

Cunningham, F. (2002) *Theories of Democracy: A Critical Introduction* (London: Routledge).

Dahl, R. (1957) 'The Concept of Power', *Behavioural Science*, 2, 201–15.

Dahl, R. (1958) 'A Critique of the Ruling Elite Model', *American Political Science Review*, 52, 463–9.

Dahl, R. (1961a) *Who Governs? Democracy and Power in an American City* (New Haven, CT: Yale University Press).

Dahl, R. (1961b) 'The Behavioral Approach in Political Science: Epitaph for a Monument to a Successful Protest', *American Political Science Review*, 55, 763–72.

Dahl, R. (1970) *Modern Political Analysis*, Second edition (Englewood Cliffs, NJ: Prentice Hall).

Dahl, R. (1989) *Democracy and its Critics* (New Haven, CT: Yale University Press).

Dallmayr, F. (ed.) (1999) *Border Crossings: Toward a Comparative Political Theory* (Lanham, MD: Lexington Books).

Dallmayr, F. (2004) 'Beyond Monologue: For a Comparative Political Theory', *Perspectives on Politics*, 2, 249–57.

DeGrazia, D. (1996) *Taking Animals Seriously: Mental Life and Moral Status* (Cambridge: Cambridge University Press).

Deleuze, G. (2004) *Difference and Repetition*, trans. P. Patton (London: Continuum).

Deleuze, G. & F. Guttari (1994) *What is Philosophy?*, trans. H. Tomlinson and G. Burchell (New York: Columbia University Press).

Deleuze, G. & F. Guttari (2013) *A Thousand Plateaus: Capitalism and Schizophrenia*, trans. B. Massumi (London: Bloomsbury).

Deranty, J.-P. (2003) 'Rancière and Contemporary Political Ontology', *Theory and Event*, 6/4, 1–38.

Deveaux, M. (1999) 'Agonism and Pluralism', *Philosophy and Social Criticism*, 25, 1–22.

Deveaux, M. (2005) 'A Deliberative Approach to Conflicts of Culture', in A. Eisenberg & J. Spinner-Halev (eds.), *Minorities Within Minorities: Equality, Rights and Diversity* (Cambridge: Cambridge University Press).

Disch, L. (2011) 'Toward a Mobilization Conception of Democratic Representation', *American Political Science Review*, 105, 100–14.

Donnelly, J. (2003) *Universal Human Rights in Theory and Practice*, Third edition (Ithaca, NY: Cornell University Press).

Dowding, K. (1991) *Rational Choice and Political Power* (London: Edward Elgar).

Downs, A. (1957) *An Economic Theory of Democracy* (New York: Harper and Row).

Dryzek, J. (2000) *Deliberative Democracy and Beyond: Liberals, Critics, Contestations* (Oxford: Oxford University Press).

Dryzek, J. (2006) *Deliberative Global Politics: Discourse and Democracy in a Divided World* (Cambridge: Polity Press).

Dryzek, J. (2010) *Foundations and Frontiers of Deliberative Governance* (Oxford: Oxford University Press).

Dummett, M. (2001) *On Immigration and Refugees* (New York: Routledge).

Dummett, M. (2004) 'Immigration', *Res Publica*, 10, 115–22.

Dworkin, G. (1989) 'The Concept of Autonomy', in J. Christman (ed.), *The Inner Citadel: Essays on Individual Autonomy* (Oxford: Oxford University Press), 54–62.

Dworkin, R. (1984) 'Rights as Trumps', in J. Waldron (ed.), *Theories of Rights* (Oxford, Oxford University Press), 153–67.

Dworkin, R. (2000) *Sovereign Virtue* (Cambridge, MA: Harvard University Press).

Dworkin, R. (2011) *Justice for Hedgehogs* (Cambridge, MA: Harvard University Press).

Elster, J. (1983) *Sour Grapes: Studies in the Subversion of Rationality* (Cambridge: Cambridge University Press).

Elster, J. (1986) 'The Market and the Forum', in J. Elster & A. Hylland (eds.), *Foundations of Social Choice Theory* (Cambridge: Cambridge University Press), 103–32.

Elster, J. (1999) 'Accountability in Athenian Politics', in A. Przeworski, S. Stokes & B. Manin (eds.), *Democracy, Accountability and Representation* (Cambridge: Cambridge University Press), 253–78.

Estlund, D. (1998) 'Liberalism, Equality and Fraternity in Cohen's Critique of Rawls', *Journal of Political Philosophy*, 6, 99–112.

Falk, R. & A. Strauss (2001) 'Toward Global Parliament', *Foreign Affairs*, 80, 212–20.

Fearon, J. (1999) 'Electoral Accountability and the Control of Politicians: Selecting Good Types versus Sanctioning Poor Performance', in A. Przeworski, S. Stokes & B. Mannin (eds.), *Democracy, Accountability, and Representation* (Cambridge: Cambridge University Press).

Feinberg, J. (1973) *Social Philosophy* (Englewood Cliffs, NJ: Prentice-Hall).

Feinberg, J. (1984) *Harm to Others: The Moral Limits of Criminal Law, Volume 1* (Oxford: Oxford University Press).

Fishkin, J. (1991) *Democracy and Deliberation: New Directions for Democratic Reforms* (New Haven, CT: Yale University Press).

Fishkin, J. (1995) *The Voice of the People: Public Opinion and Democracy* (New Haven, CT: Yale University Press).

Fishkin, J. (2009) *When the People Speak: Deliberative Democracy and Public Consultation* (Oxford: Oxford University Press).

Flew, A. (1981) *The Politics of Procrustes: Contradictions of Enforced Equality* (London: Temple Smith).

Foucault, M. (1980) *Power/Knowledge: Selected Interviews and Other Writings, 1972–77*, ed. C. Gordon (New York: Pantheon).

Foucault, M. (1982) 'The Subject and Power', *Critical Inquiry*, 8, 777–95.

Foucault, M. (1984) 'Space, Knowledge and Power', in P. Rabinow (ed.), *The Foucault Reader* (London: Penguin).

Foucault, M. (1986) 'Kant on Enlightenment and Revolution', *Economy and Society*, 15, 88–96.

Foucault, M. (1987) 'The Ethic of Care for the Self as a Practice of Freedom: An Interview with Michel Foucault on January 20, 1984, conducted by R. Fornet-Betancourt, H. Becker & A. Gomez-Müller, translated by J. D. Gauthier', *Philosophy and Social Criticism*, 12, 112–31.

Foucault, M. (1991) *Discipline and Punish: The Birth of the Prison*, trans. A. Sheridan (London: Penguin).

Foucault, M. (1996) 'What is Critique?', in J. Schmidt (ed.), *What is Enlightenment?* (Los Angeles, CA: University of California Press).

Foucault, M. (1998) *The Will to Knowledge: The History of Sexuality 1*, trans. R. Hurley (London: Penguin).

Foucault, M. (2004) *Society Must Be Defended: Lectures at the Collège de France 1975–6*, trans. D. Macey (London: Penguin).

Frankfurt, H. (1987) 'Equality as a Moral Ideal', *Ethics*, 98, 21–43.

Fraser, N. (1989) *Unruly Practices: Power, Gender and Discourse in Contemporary Critical Theory* (Cambridge: Cambridge University Press).

Fraser, N. (1997) *Justice Interruptus: Critical Reflections on the 'Postsocialist' Condition* (London: Routledge).

Fraser, N. (2008) *Adding Insult to Injury* (London: Verso).

Freeman, S. (2007) *Rawls* (London: Routledge).

Fricker, M. (2007) *Epistemic Injustice* (Oxford: Oxford University Press).

Galenkamp, M. (1993) *Individualism and Collectivism: The Concept of Collective Rights* (Rotterdam: Rotterdamse Filosofische Studies).

Gallie, W. (1956) 'Essentially Contested Concepts', *Proceedings of the Aristotelian Society*, 56, 167–98.

Galston, W. (1988) 'Liberal Virtues', *American Political Science Review*, 82, 1277–89.

Galston, W. (1991) *Liberal Principles: Goods, Virtues and Diversity in the Liberal State* (Cambridge: Cambridge University Press).

Galston, W. (2002) *Liberal Pluralism: The Implications of Value Pluralism for Political Theory and Practice* (Cambridge: Cambridge University Press).

Galtung, J. (2000) 'Alternative Models for Global Democracy', in B. Holden (ed.), *Global Democracy* (London: Routledge), 143–61.

Garland, D. (1990) *Punishment and Modern Society: A Study in Social Theory* (Oxford: Oxford University Press).

Garsten, B. (2009) 'Representative Government and Popular Sovereignty', in I. Shapiro, S. Stokes, E. Wood & A. Kirshner (eds.), *Political Representation* (Cambridge: Cambridge University Press), 90–110.

Gaventa, J. (1980) *Power and Powerlessness: Quiescence and Rebellion in an Appalachian Valley* (Oxford: Clarendon Press).

Gay, C. (2002) 'Spirals of Trust?', *American Journal of Political Science*, 4, 717–32.

Geuss, R. (2008) *Philosophy and Real Politics* (Princeton, NJ: Princeton University Press).

Gilligan, C. (1982) *In a Different Voice: Psychological Theory and Women's Development* (Cambridge, MA: Harvard University Press).

Glendon, M. A. (2001) *A World Made New: Eleanor Roosevelt and the Universal Declaration of Human Rights* (New York: Random House).

Goodin, R. (1995) *Utilitarianism as a Public Philosophy* (Cambridge: Cambridge University Press).

Goodin, R. (2003) *Reflective Democracy* (Oxford: Oxford University Press).

Goodin, R. (2004) 'Representing Diversity', *British Journal of Political Science*, 34, 453–68.

Goodin, R. (2006) 'Liberal Multiculturalism: Protective and Polyglot', *Political Theory*, 34, 289–303.

Goodin, R. (2008) *Innovating Democracy: Democratic Theory and Practice After the Deliberative Turn* (Oxford: Oxford University Press).

Goodin, R. (2010) 'Global Democracy: In the Beginning', *International Theory*, 2, 175–209.

Gornick, J. & M. Meyers (2008) 'Creating Gender Egalitarian Societies: An Agenda for Reform', *Politics and Society*, 36, 313–49.

Gould, C. (1981) 'Socialism and Democracy', *Praxis International*, 1, 49–63.

Gould, C. (1988) *Rethinking Democracy* (Cambridge: Cambridge University Press).

Gray, J. (1977) 'On the Contestability of Social and Political Concepts', *Political Theory*, 5, XX.

Gray, J. (1993) *Post-Liberalism: Studies in Political Thought* (London: Routledge).

Gray, J. (2000) *Two Faces of Liberalism* (Cambridge: Polity).

Green, L. (1991) 'Two Views of Collective Rights', *Canadian Journal of Law and Jurisprudence*, 4, 315–27.

Green, L. (1994) 'Internal Minorities and their Rights', in J. Baker (ed.), *Group Rights* (Toronto: Toronto University Press), 100–117.

Griffin, J. (2008) *On Human Rights* (Oxford: Oxford University Press).

Guinier, L. (1994) *The Tyranny of the Majority: Fundamental Fairness in Representative Democracy* (New York: Free Press).

Gutmann, A. & D. Thompson (1996) *Democracy and Disagreement* (Cambridge, MA: Harvard University Press).

Gutmann, A. & D. Thompson (2004) *Why Deliberative Democracy?* (Princeton, NJ: Princeton University Press).

Gutmann, A. (1995) 'Civic Education and Social Diversity', *Ethics*, 105, 557–79.

Gutmann, A. (2007) 'Democracy', in R. Goodin, P. Pettit & T. Pogge (eds.), *A Companion to Contemporary Political Philosophy*, Second edition (Oxford: Blackwell Publishing), 521–31.

Habermas, J. (1976) *Legitimation Crisis* (London: Heinemann).

Habermas, J. (1990) *The Philosophical Discourse of Modernity* (Cambridge, MA: MIT Press).

Habermas, J. (1996) *Between Facts and Norms: Contributions to a Discourse Theory of Law and Democracy*, trans. W. Rehg (Cambridge: Polity).

Habermas, J. (1998) *The Inclusion of the Other: Studies in Political Theory* (Cambridge: Polity).

Habermas, J. (2006) *The Divided West* (Cambridge: Polity).

Hall, C. (2007) 'Recognizing the Passion in Deliberative Democracy: Toward a More Democratic Theory of Deliberative Democracy', *Hypatia: A Journal of Feminist Philosophy*, 22/4, 81–95.

Hampshire, S. (1965) *Thought and Action* (London: Chatto and Windus).

Hardin, G. (1996) 'Lifeboat Ethics: The Case Against Helping the Poor', in W. Aiken & H. La Follette (eds.), *World Hunger and Morality*, Second edition (Englewood Cliffs, NJ: Prentice Hall), 5–15.

Harsanyi, J. (1975) 'Can the Maximin Principle Serve as a Basis for Morality? A Critique of John Rawls's Theory', *American Political Science Review*, 69, 594–606.

Hart, H. L. A. (1961) *The Concept of Law* (Oxford: Clarendon Press).

Hart, H. L. A. (1982) *Essays on Bentham* (Oxford: Clarendon Press).

Hart, H. L. A. (1984) 'Are There any Natural Rights?', in J. Waldron (ed.), *Theories of Rights* (Oxford: Oxford University Press), 77–90.

Hartstock, N. (1990) 'Foucault on Power: A Theory for Women?', in L. Nicholson (ed.), *Feminism/Postmodernism* (London: Routledge), 157–75.

Hay, C. (2002) *Political Analysis: A Critical Introduction* (Basingstoke: Palgrave Macmillan).

Hearn, J. (2011) *Theorizing Power* (Basingstoke: Palgrave Macmillan).

Held, D. & D. Archibugi (1995) *Cosmopolitan Democracy: An Agenda for a New World Order* (Cambridge: Polity).

Held, D. & M. Koenig-Archibugi (2003) *Taming Globalization* (Cambridge: Polity Press).

Held, D. (1995) *Democracy and the Global Order: From the Modern State to Cosmopolitan Governance* (Cambridge: Polity).

Held, D. (2006) *Models of Democracy*, Third edition (Stanford, CA: Stanford University Press).

Held, D. (2010) *Cosmopolitanism: Ideals and Realities* (Cambridge: Polity Press).

Hilmer, J. (2010) 'The State of Participatory Democratic Theory', *New Political Science*, 32, 43–63.

Hindess, B. (1996) *Discourses of Power: From Hobbes to Foucault* (Oxford: Blackwell Publishing).

Hohfeld, W. (1919) *Fundamental Legal Conceptions as Applied in Judicial Reasoning and Other Legal Essays* (New Haven, CT: Yale University Press).

Holmes, S. (1988) 'Gag Rules or the Politics of Omission', in J. Elster & R. Slagstad (eds.), *Constitutionalism and Democracy* (Cambridge: Cambridge University Press).

Honig, B. (1993) *Political Theory and the Displacement of Politics* (Ithaca, NY: Cornell University Press).

Honneth, A. (1995) *The Struggle For Recognition* (Cambridge: Polity).

Honneth, A. (2007) *Disrespect: The Normative Foundations of Critical Theory* (Cambridge: Polity).

Horton, J. (2010) 'Realism, Liberal Moralism and a Political Theory of Modus Vivendi', *European Journal of Political Theory*, 9, 431–48.

Horton, J. (2011) 'Modus Vivendi and Religious Conflict', in M. Mookherjee (ed.), *Democracy, Religious Pluralism and the Liberal Dilemma of Accommodation* (Dordrecht: Springer), 121–36.

Hunter, F. (1953) *Community Power Structure: A Study of Decision Makers* (Chapel Hill, NC: University of North Carolina Press).

Hyland, E. (1995) *Democratic Theory: The Philosophical Foundations* (Manchester: Manchester University Press).

Ieven, B. (2009) 'Heteroreductives – Rancière's Disagreement with Ontology', *Parallax*, 15, 50–62.

Ingram, A. (1996) 'Constitutional Patriotism', *Philosophy and Social Criticism*, 22, 1–18.

Jaggar, A. (1983) *Feminist Politics and Human Nature* (Lanham, MD: Rowman and Littlefield).

Jones, C. (1999) *Global Justice* (Oxford: Oxford University Press).

Jones, P. (1994) *Rights* (Basingstoke: Palgrave Macmillan).

Jones, P. (2008) 'Group Rights', in E. Zalta (ed.), *The Stanford Encyclopedia of Philosophy*. Available at: http://plato.stanford.edu/archives/spr2014/entries/rights-group/

Joppke, C. & S. Lukes (eds.) (1999) *Multicultural Questions* (Oxford: Oxford University Press).

Kateb, G. (1981) 'The Moral Distinctiveness of Representative Democracy', *Ethics*, 91, 357–74.

Kaufman, A. (1968) 'Participatory Democracy: Ten Years On', *La Table Ronde*, 251–2, 216–28.

Kausikan, B. (1993) 'Asia's Different Standard', *Foreign Policy*, 92, 24–41.

Kearns, T. (1975) 'Rights, Beneficiaries and Normative Systems', *Archiv fur Rechts und Sozialphilosophie*, 61, 465–83.

Kelly, J. (2012) *Framing Democracy: A Behavioral Approach to Democratic Theory* (Princeton, NJ: Princeton University Press).

Kenworthy, L. & M. Malami (1999) 'Gender Inequality in Political Representation: A Worldwide Comparative Analysis', *Social Forces*, 78, 235–68.

Keohane, R. & J. Nye (2003) 'Redefining Accountability for Global Governance', in M. Kahler & D. Lake (eds.), *Governance in a Global Economy: Political Authority in Transition* (Princeton, NJ: Princeton University Press), 386–411.

Klausen, J. (2009) *The Cartoons That Shook the World* (New Haven, CT: Yale University Press).

Korsgaard, C. (1996) *The Sources of Normativity* (Cambridge: Cambridge University Press).

Kramer, M. (1998) 'Rights Without Trimmings', in M. Kramer, N. Simmons & H. Steiner (eds.), *A Debate Over Rights* (Oxford: Oxford University Press).

Kraus, P. (2008) *A Union of Diversity: Language, Identity and Polity-Building in Europe* (Cambridge: Cambridge University Press).

Krause, S. (2008) *Civil Passions: Moral Sentiment and Democratic Deliberation* (Princeton, NJ: Princeton University Press).

Kukathas, C. (1995) 'Are There Any Cultural Rights?', *Political Theory*, 20, 105–39.

Kukathas, C. (1997) 'Cultural Toleration', in I. Shapiro & W. Kymlicka (eds.), *NOMOS XXXIX: Ethnicity and Group Rights* (New York: New York University Press), 69–104.

Kukathas, C. (2003) *The Liberal Archipelago: A Theory of Diversity and Freedom* (Oxford: Oxford University Press).

Kukathas, C. (2005) 'The Case for Open Immigration', in A. Cohen & C. Wellman (eds.), *Contemporary Debates in Applied Ethics* (Malden, MA: Blackwell Publishing), 207–20.

Kuper, A. (2000) 'Rawlsian Global Justice: Beyond The Law of Peoples to a Cosmopolitan Law of Persons', *Political Theory*, 28, 640–74.

Kuper, A. (2004) *Democracy Beyond Borders: Justice and Representation in Global Institutions* (Oxford: Oxford University Press).

Kuran, T. (1998) 'Insincere Deliberation and Democratic Failure', *Critical Review*, 14, 529–44.

Kymlicka, W. & W. Norman (1994) 'Return of the Citizen', *Ethics*, 104, 352–81.

Kymlicka, W. (1989a) *Liberalism, Community and Culture* (Oxford: Oxford University Press).

Kymlicka, W. (1989b) 'Liberal Individualism and Liberal Neutrality', *Ethics*, 99, 883–905.

Kymlicka, W. (1995) *Multicultural Citizenship: A Liberal Theory of Minority Rights* (Oxford: Oxford University Press).

Kymlicka, W. (2001) *Politics in the Vernacular: Nationalism, Multiculturalism and Citizenship* (Oxford: Oxford University Press).

Kymlicka, W. (2007) *Multicultural Odysseys: Negotiating the New International Politics of Diversity* (Oxford: Oxford University Press).

Laborde, C. (2008) *Critical Republicanism: The Hijab Controversy and Political Philosophy* (Oxford: Oxford University Press).

Laborde, C. (2010) 'Republicanism and Global Justice: A Sketch', *European Journal of Political Theory*, 9, 48–69.

Laclau, E. & C. Mouffe (2001) *Hegemony and Socialist Strategy: Towards a Radical Democratic Politics*, Second edition (London: Verso).

Lacroix, J. (2002) 'For a European Constitutional Patriotism', *Political Studies*, 50, 944–58.

Landman, T. (2005) 'The Political Science of Human Rights', *British Journal of Political Science*, 35, 549–72.

Larmore, C. (1990) 'Political Liberalism', *Political Theory*, 18, 339–60.

Laslett, P. (ed.) (1956) *Philosophy, Politics and Society* (Oxford: Blackwell).

Lassman, P. (2011) *Pluralism* (Cambridge: Polity).

Levy, J. (2007) 'Contextualism, Constitutionalism, and Modus Vivendi Approaches', in A. Laden & D. Owen (eds.), *Multiculturalism and Political Theory* (Cambridge: Cambridge University Press).

Lewis, P., G. Simons & C. Fennig (eds.) (2014) *Ethnologue: Languages of the World*, Seventeenth edition (Dallas, TX: SIL International). Available at: http://www. ethnologue.com (accessed 17 July 2014).

Linklater, A. (1998) *The Transformation of Political Community: Ethical Foundations of the Post-Westphalian Order* (Cambridge: Polity).

Lippert-Rasmussen, K. (2001) 'Egalitarianism, Option Luck, and Responsibility', *Ethics*, 111, 548–79.

Lippert-Rasmussen, K. (2013) 'Offensive Preferences, Snobbish Tastes, and Egalitarian Justice', *Journal of Social Philosophy*, 44, 439–58.

List, C. & P. Pettit (2002) 'Aggregating Sets of Judgments: An Impossibility Result', *Economics and Philosophy*, 18, 89–110.

List, C. & P. Pettit (2004) 'Aggregating Sets of Judgments: Two Impossibility Results Compared', *Synthese*, 140, 207–35.

List, C. & P. Pettit (2011) *Group Agency: The Possibility, Design, and Status of Corporate Agents* (Oxford: Oxford University Press).

Locke, J. (1988) *Two Treatises of Government* (Cambridge: Cambridge University Press).

Lovett, F. & P. Pettit (2009) 'Neorepublicanism: A Normative and Institutional Research Program', *Annual Review of Political Science*, 12, 11–29.

Lovett, F. (2001) 'Domination: A Preliminary Analysis', *The Monist*, 84, 98–112.

Lovett, F. (2010) *A General Theory of Domination and Justice* (Oxford: Oxford University Press).

Lukes, S. (2005) *Power: A Radical View*, Second edition (Basingstoke: Palgrave Macmillan).

Lyons, D. (1969) 'Rights, Claimants, and Beneficiaries', *American Philosophical Quarterly*, 6, 173–85.

Lyons, D. (1970) 'The Correlativity of Rights and Duties', *Nous*, 4, 45–57.

MacCallum, G. (1967) 'Negative and Positive Freedom', *Philosophical Review*, 76, 312–34.

MacCormick, N. (1977). 'Rights in Legislation', in P. M. S. Hacker & J. Raz (eds.), *Law, Morality and Society: Essays in Honour of HLA Hart* (Oxford: Clarendon Press), 189–209.

MacCormick, N. (1982) *Legal Right and Social Democracy: Essays in Legal and Political Philosophy* (Oxford: Clarendon Press).

Macedo, S. (1990) *Liberal Virtues: Citizenship, Virtue, and Community in Liberal Constitutionalism* (Oxford: Clarendon Press).

Macedo, S. (1995) 'Liberal Civic Education and Religious Fundamentalism: The Case of God v. John Rawls?', *Ethics*, 105, 468–96.

MacIntyre, A. (1985) *After Virtue*, Second edition (London: Duckworth).

Mackie, G. (2009) 'Schumpeter's Leadership Democracy', *Political Theory*, 37, 128–53.

Macpherson, C. B. (1973) *Democratic Theory* (Oxford: Clarendon Press).

Macpherson, C. B. (1977) *The Life and Times of Liberal Democracy* (Oxford: Oxford University Press).

Majone, G. (1994) 'Independence versus Accountability? Non-Majoritarian Institutions and Democratic Governance in Europe', *European Yearbook of Comparative Government and Public Administration*, 1, 117–40.

Mandle, J. (2006) *Global Justice* (Cambridge: Polity).

Manin, B. (1987) 'On Legitimacy and Political Deliberation', trans. E. Stein & J. Mansbridge, *Political Theory*, 15, 338–68.

Manin, B. (1997) *The Principles of Representative Government* (Cambridge: Cambridge University Press).

Manin, B., A. Przeworski & S. Stokes (1999) *Democracy, Accountability and Representation* (Cambridge: Cambridge University Press).

Mansbridge, J. (1999) 'Should Blacks Represent Blacks and Women Represent Women? A Contingent "Yes"', *Journal of Politics*, 61, 628–57.

Mansbridge, J. (2003) 'Rethinking Representation', *American Political Science Review*, 97, 515–28.

Mansbridge, J. (2009) 'A "Selection Model" of Political Representation', *Journal of Political Philosophy*, 17, 369–98.

Mansbridge, J., J. Bohman, S. Chambers, D. Estlund, A. Føllesdal, A. Fung, C. Lafont, B. Manin & J. L. Martí (2010) 'The Place of Self-Interest and the Role of Power in Deliberative Democracy', *Journal of Political Philosophy*, 18, 64–100.

March, A. (2009) 'What is Comparative Political Theory', *The Review of Politics*, 71, 531–65.

Margalit, A. & J. Raz (1990) 'National Self-determination', *Journal of Philosophy*, 87, 439–61.

Margalit, A. & M. Halbertal (1994) 'Liberalism and the Right to Culture', *Social Research*, 61, 529–48.

Maritain, J. (2007) 'Inaugural Address to the Second International Conference of UNESCO', in J. Witte Jr & F. Alexander (eds.), *The Teachings of Modern Roman Catholicism: On Law, Politics and Human Nature* (New York: Columbia University Press), 148–9.

Markell, P. (2003) *Bound by Recognition* (Princeton, NJ: Princeton University Press).

Marmor, A. (2001) 'Do We have a Right to Common Goods?', *Canadian Journal of Law and Jurisprudence*, 14, 213–25.

Marshall, T. H. (1992) *Citizenship and Social Class* (London: Pluto).

Martin, J. (2009) 'Poststructuralism, Civil Society and Radical Democracy', in A. Little & M. Lloyd (eds), *The Politics of Radical Democracy* (Edinburgh: Edinburgh University Press), 92–111.

Marx, K. (2000) 'On the Jewish Question', in D. McLellan (ed.), *Karl Marx: Selected Writings* (Oxford: Oxford University Press), 46–70.

Mason, A. (2000) *Community, Solidarity and Belonging* (Cambridge: Cambridge University Press).

May, L. (1987) *The Morality of Groups: Collective Responsibility, Group-Based Harm, and Corporate Rights* (Notre Dame: University of Notre Dame Press).

McCloskey, H. J. (1957) 'An Examination of Restricted Utilitarianism', *Philosophical Review*, 37, 307–25.

McCloskey, H. J. (1965) 'A Critique of the Ideals of Liberty', *Mind*, 74, 483–508.

McCrone, D. & J. Kuklinski (1979) 'The Delegate Theory of Representation', *American Journal of Political Science*, 23, 278–300.

McDonald, M. (1991) 'Should Communities have Rights? Reflections on Liberal Individualism', *Canadian Journal of Law and Jurisprudence*, 4, 217–37.

Mehta, U. S. (1999) *Liberalism and Empire: A Study in Nineteenth-Century British Liberal Thought* (Chicago, IL: University of Chicago Press).

Mill, J. (1992) 'Government', in T. Ball (ed.), *James Mill: Political Writings* (Cambridge: Cambridge University Press), 1–42.

Mill, J.-S. (1993) 'Considerations on Representative Government', in J. M. Dent (ed.), *Utilitarianism, On Liberty, Considerations on Representative Government* (London: Everyman), 188–428.

Miller, D. (1995) *On Nationality* (Oxford: Oxford University Press).

Miller, D. (1999) *Principles of Social Justice* (Cambridge, MA: Harvard University Press).

Miller, D. (2005) 'Immigration: the Case for Limits', in A. Cohen & C. Wellman (eds.), *Contemporary Debates in Applied Ethics* (Oxford: Blackwell), 193–206.

Miller, D. (2007) *National Responsibility and Global Justice* (Oxford: Oxford University Press).

Miller, D. (2008) 'Immigrants, Nations, and Citizenship', *Journal of Political Philosophy*, 16, 371–90.

Miller, D. (2010) 'Why Immigration Controls Are Not Coercive: A Reply to Arash Abizadeh', *Political Theory*, 38, 111–20.

Miller, D. (2013) *Justice for Earthlings: Essays in Political Philosophy* (Cambridge: Cambridge University Press).

Mills, C. W. (1959) *The Causes of World War Three* (London: Secker & Walburg).

Mills, C. W. (2000) *The Power Elite* (Oxford: Oxford University Press).

Moellendorf, D. (2002) *Cosmopolitan Justice* (Boulder, CO: Westview Press).

Montanaro, L. (2012) 'The Democratic Legitimacy of Self-Appointed Representatives', *The Journal of Politics*, 74, 1094–107.

Morrell, M. (2010) *Empathy and Democracy: Feeling, Thinking and Deliberation* (University Park, PA: Pennsylvania State University Press).

Morriss, P. (2002) *Power: A Philosophical Analysis*, Second edition (Manchester: Manchester University Press).

Morriss, P. (2006) 'Steven Lukes on the Concept of Power', *Political Studies Review*, 4, 124–35.

Mouffe, C. (1996) 'Democracy, Power and the "Political"', in S. Benhabib (ed.), *Democracy and Difference* (Princeton, NJ: Princeton University Press).

Mouffe, C. (2000) *The Democratic Paradox* (London: Verso).

Mouffe, C. (2005) *On the Political* (Abingdon: Routledge).

Mulhall, S & A. Swift (1996) *Liberals and Communitarians* (Oxford: Blackwell Publishing).

Müller, J.-W. (2007) *Constitutional Patriotism* (Princeton, NJ: Princeton University Press).

Mutua, M. (2002) *Human Rights: A Political and Cultural Critique* (Philadelphia: University of Pennsylvania Press).

Nagel, T. (1970) *The Possibility of Altruism* (Princeton, NJ: Princeton University Press).

Nagel, T. (2005) 'The Problem of Global Justice', *Philosophy and Public Affairs*, 33, 113–47.

Newman, D. (2004) 'Collective Interests and Collective Rights', *American Journal of Jursiprudence*, 49, 127–64.

Nickel, J. (1987) *Making Sense of Human Rights: Philosophical Reflections on the Universal Declaration of Human Rights* (Berkeley, CA: University of California Press).

Niemeyer, S. (2004) 'Deliberation in the Wilderness: Displacing Symbolic Politics', *Environmental Politics*, 13, 347–72.

Noddings, N. (1984) *Caring: A Feminine Approach to Ethics and Moral Education* (Berkeley, CA: University of California Press).

Norman, W. (2006) *Negotiating Nationalism: Nation-Building, Federalism, and Secession in the Multinational State* (Oxford: Oxford University Press).

Nozick, R. (1974) *Anarchy, State and Utopia* (Oxford: Blackwell).

Nussbaum, M. (1990) 'Aristotelian Social Democracy', in R. Douglas, G. Mara & H. Richardson (eds.), *Liberalism and the Good* (New York: Routledge).

Nussbaum, M. (1992) 'Human Functioning and Social Justice: In Defence of Aristotelian Essentialism', *Political Theory*, 20, 202–46.

Nussbaum, M. (1999) *Sex and Social Justice* (Oxford: Oxford University Press).

Nussbaum, M. (2000) *Women and Human Development* (Cambridge: Cambridge University Press).

Nussbaum, M. (2003) 'Rawls and Feminism', in S. Freeman (ed.), *The Cambridge Companion to Rawls* (Cambridge: Cambridge University Press).

Nussbaum, M. (2011) *Creating Capabilities: The Human Development Approach* (Cambridge, MA: Harvard University Press).

Nussbaum, M. (2012) *Philosophical Interventions: Reviews 1986–2011* (Oxford: Oxford University Press).

O'Neill, O. (1996) *Towards Justice and Virtue: A Constructive Account of Practical Reasoning* (Cambridge: Cambridge University Press).

Oldfield, A. (1990) *Citizenship and Community: Civic Republicanism and the Modern World* (London: Routledge).

Okin, S. (1989) *Justice, Gender and the Family* (New York: Basic Books).

Okin, S. (1994) 'Political Liberalism, Justice, and Gender', *Ethics*, 105, 23–43.

Okin, S. (1998) 'Feminism and Multiculturalism: Some Tensions', *Ethics*, 108, 661–84.

Okin, S. (2005) 'Forty acres and a mule' for women: Rawls and feminism', *Politics Philosophy Economics*, 4, 233–48.

ONS (2013) *Full Report – Women in the Labour Market* (London: Office for National Statistics). Available at: http://www.ons.gov.uk/ons/dcp171776_328352.pdf (accessed 17 July 2014).

Parekh, B. (2000) *Rethinking Multiculturalism: Cultural Diversity and Political Theory* (Basingstoke: Palgrave Macmillan).

Parekh, B. (2008) *A New Politics of Identity: Political Principles for an Interdependent World* (Basingstoke: Palgrave Macmillan).

Parel, A. & R. Ketih (eds.) (1992) *Comparative Political Philosophy: Studies under the Upas Tree* (New Delhi and Newbury Park: Sage Publications).

Parfit, D. (1984) *Reasons and Persons* (Oxford: Oxford University Press).

Parfit, D. (1998) 'Equality and Priority', in A. Mason (ed.), *Ideals of Equality* (Oxford: Blackwell Publishing), 1–20.

Parfit, D. (2000) 'Equality or Priority?', in M. Clayton & A. Williams (eds.), *The Ideal of Equality* (London: Palgrave Macmillan), 81–126.

Parkinson, J. & J. Mansbridge (2009) *Deliberative Systems: Deliberative Democracy at the Large Scale* (Cambridge: Cambridge University Press).

Parkinson, J. (2006) *Deliberating in the Real World: Problems of Legitimacy in Deliberative Democracy* (Oxford: Oxford University Press).

Parry, G. (1969) *Political Elites* (London: Allen and Unwin).

Pateman, C. (1970) *Participation and Democracy Theory* (Cambridge: Cambridge University Press).

Pateman, C. (1985) *The Problem of Political Obligation: A Critique of Liberal Theory* (Berkeley, CA: University of California Press).

Pateman, C. (2012) 'Participatory Democracy Revisited', *Perspectives on Politics*, 10, 7–19.

Patten, A. (1996) 'The Republican Critique of Liberalism', *British Journal of Political Science*, 26, 25–44.

Patten, A. (2000) 'Equality of Recognition and the Liberal Theory of Citizenship', in C. McKinnon & I. Hampsher-Monk (eds.), *The Demands of Citizenship* (London: Continuum).

Patton, P. (2006) 'After the Linguistic Turn: Post-Structuralist and Liberal Pragmatist Political Theory', in J. Dryzek, B. Honig & A. Phillips (eds.), *The Oxford Handbook of Political Theory* (Oxford: Oxford University Press), 125–41.

Perry, M. (1988) *Morality, Politics and Law* (Oxford: Oxford University Press).

Pettit, P. (1996) 'Freedom as Anti-Power', *Ethics*, 106, 576–604.

Pettit, P. (1997) *Republicanism: A Theory of Freedom and Government* (Oxford: Oxford University Press).

Pettit, P. (2001) 'Deliberative Democracy and the Discursive Dilemma', *Philosophical Issues* (supplement to *Nous*), 11, 268–99.

Pettit, P. (2002) 'Keeping Republican Freedom Simple: On a Difference with Quentin Skinner', *Political Theory*, 30, 339–56.

Pettit, P. (2006) 'Depoliticizing democracy', in S. Besson & J. L. Martí (eds.), *Deliberative Democracy and Its Discontents* (Aldershot: Ashgate).

Pettit, P. (2009) 'Varieties of Public Representation', in I. Shapiro, S. Stokes, E. Wood & A. Kirshner (eds.), *Political Representation* (Cambridge: Cambridge University Press), 61–89.

Pettit, P. (2010) 'A Republican Law of Peoples', *European Journal of Political Theory*, 9, 70–94.

Pettit, P. (2012) *On The People's Terms: A Republican Theory and Model of Democracy* (Cambridge: Cambridge University Press).

Phillips, A. (1995) *The Politics of Presence* (Oxford: Oxford University Press).

Phillips, A. (1998) *Feminism and Politics* (Oxford: Oxford University Press).

Philp, M. (2009) 'Delimiting Political Accountability', *Political Studies*, 57, 28-53.

Philpott, D. (1995) 'A Defense of Self-Determination', *Ethics*, 105, 352-85.

Pitkin, H. (1967) *The Concept of Representation* (Berkeley, CA: University of California Press).

Plamenatz, J. (1938) *Consent, Freedom and Political Obligation* (Oxford: Oxford University Press).

Plotke, D. (1997) 'Representation is Democracy', *Constellations*, 4, 19-34.

Pogge, T. (1989) *Realizing Rawls* (Ithaca, NY: Cornell University Press).

Pogge, T. (2001) 'Priorities of Global Justice', *Metaphilosophy*, 32, 6-24.

Pogge, T. (2002) *World Poverty and Human Rights: Cosmopolitan Responsibilities and Reforms* (Cambridge: Polity).

Polsby, N. (1963) *Community Power and Political Theory* (New Haven, CT: Yale University Press).

Posner, R. (2003) *Law, Pragmatism and Democracy* (Cambridge, MA: Harvard University Press).

Preda, A. (2012) 'Group rights and group agency', *Journal of Moral Philosophy*, 9, 229-54.

Putnam, R. (2000) *Bowling Alone: The Collapse and Revival of American Community* (New York: Simon & Schuster).

Railton, P. (1984) 'Alienation, Consequentialism, and the Demands of Morality', *Philosophy and Public Affairs*, 13, 134-71.

Rakowski, E. (1991) *Equal Justice* (Oxford: Oxford University Press).

Rancière, J. (1999) *Disagreement: Politics and Philosophy*, trans. J. Rose (London: University of Minnesota Press).

Rancière, J. (2009) *Hatred of Democracy*, trans. S. Corcoran (London: Verso).

Rancière, J. (2011) 'The Thinking of Dissensus: Politics and Aesthetics', in P. Bowman & R. Stamp (eds.), *Reading Rancière* (London: Continuum).

Rawls, J. (1996) *Political Liberalism* (New York: Columbia University Press).

Rawls, J. (1999a) *A Theory of Justice: Revised Edition* (Cambridge, MA: Harvard University Press).

Rawls, J. (1999b) *The Law of Peoples* (Cambridge, MA: Harvard University Press).

Rawls, J. (1999c) 'The Moral Basis of Political Liberalism', *Journal of Philosophy*, 96, 599-625.

Rawls, J. (1999d) *Collected Papers* (Cambridge, MA: Harvard University Press).

Rawls, J. (2001) *Justice as Fairness: A Restatement* (Cambridge, MA: Harvard University Press).

Raz, J. (1986) *The Morality of Freedom* (Oxford: Clarendon Press).

Réaume, D. (1988) 'Individuals, Groups, and Rights to Public Goods', *University of Toronto Law Review*, 38, 1-27.

Réaume, D. (1994) 'The Group Right to Linguistic Security: Whose Right, What Duties?', in J. Baker (ed.), *Group Rights* (Toronto: Toronto University Press), 118-41.

Regan, T. (1983) *The Case for Animal Rights* (London: Routledge).

Rehfeld, A. (2005) *The Concept of Constituency: Political Representation, Democratic Legitimacy and Institutional Design* (Cambridge: Cambridge University Press).

Rehfeld, A. (2006) 'Towards a General Theory of Representation', *Journal of Politics*, 68, 1-21.

Rehfeld, A. (2009) 'Representation Rethought: On Trustees, Delegates, and Gyroscopes in the Study of Political Representation and Democracy', *American Political Science Review*, 103, 214–30.

Richards, D. (1982) 'International Distributive Justice', in J. R. Pennock & J. W. Chapman (eds.), *Ethics, Economics and the Law: NOMOS XXIV* (New York: New York University Press).

Roemer, J. (1996) *Theories of Distributive Justice* (Cambridge, MA: Harvard University Press).

Russell, B. (1938) *Power: A New Social Analysis* (London: Allen & Unwin).

Said, E. (1979) *Orientalism* (New York: Random House).

Sandel, M. (1984) 'The Procedural Republic and the Unencumbered Self', *Political Theory*, 12, 81–96.

Sandel, M. (1996) *Democracy's Discontent: America in Search of a Public Philosophy* (Cambridge, MA: Harvard University Press).

Sandel, M. (1998) *Liberalism and the Limits of Justice*, Second edition (Cambridge: Cambridge University Press).

Sanders, L. (1999) 'Against Deliberation', *Political Theory*, 25, 347–76.

Santos, Boaventura de Sousa (2006) 'Participatory Budgeting in Porto Alegre: Towards a Redistributive Democracy', in Boaventura de Sousa Santos (ed.), *Democratizing Democracy: Beyond the Liberal Democratic Canon* (New York: Verso).

Sapiro, V. (1981) 'When are Interests Interesting? The Problem of Political Representation of Women', *American Political Science Review*, 75, 701–16.

Satz, D. (2007) 'Equality, Adequacy and Education for Citizenship', *Ethics*, 117, 623–48.

Saward, M. (2006a) 'The Representative Claim', *Contemporary Political Theory*, 5, 297–318.

Saward, M. (2006b) 'Democracy and Citizenship: Expanding Domains', in J. Dryzek, B. Honig & A. Phillips (eds.), *The Oxford Handbook of Political Theory* (Oxford: Oxford University Press), 400–422.

Saward, M. (2006c) 'Representation', in A. Dobson & R. Eckersley (eds.), *Political Theory and the Ecological Challenge* (Cambridge: Cambridge University Press), 183–99.

Saward, M. (2009) 'Authorisation and Authenticity: Representation and the Unelected', *Journal of Political Philosophy*, 17, 1–22.

Saward, M. (2010) *The Representative Claim* (Oxford: Oxford University Press).

Scanlon, T. (1985) 'Rawls's Theory of Justice', in N. Daniels (ed.), *Reading Rawls: Critical Studies of A Theory of Justice* (Oxford: Blackwell).

Scanlon, T. (1998) *What We Owe to Each Other* (Cambridge, MA: Harvard University Press).

Schattschneider, E. E. (1960) *The Semi-Sovereign People: A Realist's View of Democracy in America* (New York: Holt, Rhinehart & Winston).

Scheffler, S. (ed.) (1988) *Consequentialism and Its Critics* (Oxford: Oxford University Press).

Scheffler, S. (2003) 'What is Egalitarianism?', *Philosophy and Public Affairs*, 31, 5–39.

Scheffler, S. (2005) 'Choice, Circumstance and the Value of Equality', *Politics, Philosophy and Economics*, 4, 5–28.

Scheffler, S. (2010) *Equality and Tradition* (Oxford: Oxford University Press).

Schumpeter, J. (1956) *Capitalism, Socialism and Democracy* (London: Unwin).

Scott, J. (1992) *Domination and the Arts of Resistance* (New Haven, CT: Yale University Press).

Scruton, R. (1998) *Animal Rights and Wrongs* (London: Demos).

Segall, S. (2010) *Health, Luck and Justice* (Princeton, NJ: Princeton University Press).

Sen, A. (1980) 'Equality of What?', in S. McMurrin (ed.), *Tanner Lectures on Human Values Volume 1* (Cambridge: Cambridge University Press).

Sen, A. (1987) *The Standard of Living* (Cambridge: Cambridge University Press).

Sen, A. (1992) *Inequality Reexamined* (Oxford: Oxford University Press).

Sen, A. (1999) *Development as Freedom* (New York: Knopf).

Sen, A. (2009) *The Idea of Justice* (Cambridge, MA: Harvard University Press).

Shapiro, I. (1999) *Democratic Justice* (London: Yale University Press).

Shapiro, I. (2003a) *The State of Democratic Theory* (Princeton, NJ: Princeton University Press).

Shapiro, I. (2003b) *The Moral Foundations of Politics* (New Haven, CT: Yale University Press).

Sheridan, A. (1997) *Michel Foucault: The Will to Truth* (Abingdon: Routledge).

Shue, H. (1996) *Basic Rights: Subsistence, Affluence and US Foreign Policy*, Second edition (Princeton, NJ: Princeton University Press).

Singer, P. (1972) 'Famine, Affluence and Morality', *Philosophy and Public Affairs*, 1, 229–43.

Skinner, Q. (ed.) (1985) *The Return of Grand Theory in the Human Sciences* (Cambridge: Cambridge University Press).

Skinner, Q. (1998) *Liberty Before Liberalism* (Cambridge: Cambridge University Press).

Skinner, Q. (2002) 'A Third Concept of Liberty', *Proceedings of the British Academy*, 117, 237–68.

Skinner, Q. (2005) 'Hobbes on Representation', *European Journal of Philosophy*, 13, 155–84.

Skinner, Q. (2008) 'Freedom as the Absence of Arbitrary Power', in C. Laborde & J. Maynor (eds.), *Republicanism and Political Theory* (Oxford: Blackwell Publishing).

Smith, A. (1986) *The Ethnic Origins of Nations* (Oxford: Blackwell Publishers).

Smith, G. (2009) *Democratic Innovations: Designing Institutions for Citizenship Participation* (Cambridge: Cambridge University Press).

Spivak, G. (1988) 'Can the Subaltern Speak?', in C. Nelson & L. Grossberg (eds.), *Marxism and the Interpretation of Culture* (Urbana, IL: University of Illinois Press), 271–313.

Squires, J. (2008) 'The Constitutive Representation of Gender: Extra Parliamentary Re-Presentations of Gender Representations', *Representation*, 44, 187–204.

Steiner, H. (1975) 'Individual liberty', *Proceedings of the Aristotelian Society*, 75, 33–50.

Steiner, H. (1994) *An Essay on Rights* (Oxford: Blackwell).

Steiner, H. (1998) 'Working Rights', in M. Kramer, N. Simmons & H. Steiner (eds.), *A Debate Over Rights* (Oxford: Oxford University Press).

Steiner, H. (2005) 'Territorial Justice and Global Redistribution', in G. Brock & H. Brighouse (eds.), *The Political Philosophy of Cosmopolitanism* (Cambridge: Cambridge University Press).

Stilz, A. (2009) *Liberal Loyalty: Freedom, Obligation and the State* (Princeton, NJ: Princeton University Press).

Sunstein, C. (2002) 'The Law of Group Polarization', *Journal of Political Philosophy*, 10, 175–95.

Sutcliffe, B. (2007) 'The Unequalled and Unequal Twentieth Century', in D. Held & A. Kaya (eds.), *Global Inequality* (Cambridge: Polity), 50–72.

Swain, C. (1993) *Black Faces, Black Interests: The Representation of African Americans in Congress* (Cambridge, MA: Harvard University Press).

Swift, A. & S. White (2008) 'Political Theory, Social Science and Real Politics', in D. Leopold & M. Stears (eds.), *Political Theory: Methods and Approaches* (Oxford: Oxford University Press), 49–69.

Talisse, R. (2007) *A Pragmatist Philosophy of Democracy* (London: Routledge).

Tan, K.-C. (2004) *Justice Without Borders* (Cambridge: Cambridge University Press).

Taylor, C. (1985) *Philosophy and the Human Sciences: Philosophical Papers 2* (Cambridge: Cambridge University Press).

Taylor, C. (1994) 'The Politics of Recognition', in A. Gutmann (ed.), *Multiculturalism and the Politics of Recognition* (Princeton, NJ: Princeton University Press).

Taylor, C. (1995) *Philosophical Arguments* (Cambridge, MA: Harvard University Press).

Taylor, C. (1996) 'Why Democracy Needs Patriotism', in J. Cohen (ed.), *For Love of Country* (Boston, MA: Beacon Press).

The West Wing (2006) 'Episode 144: Duck and Cover', Television programme, *NBC*, January 22.

Tilly, C. (1991) 'Domination, Resistance, Compliance … Discourse', *Sociological Forum*, 6, 593–602.

Tomasi, J. (1995) 'Kymlicka, Liberalism and Respect for Cultural Minorities', *Ethics*, 105, 580–603.

Trouillot, M.-R. (1995) *Silencing the Past: Power and the Production of History* (Boston, MA: Beacon Press).

Unger, P. (1996) *Living High and Letting Die: Our Illusion of Innocence* (Oxford: Oxford University Press).

Urbinati, N. & M. Warren (2008) 'The Concept of Representation in Political Theory', *Annual Review of Political Science*, 11, 387–412.

Urbinati, N. (2006) *Representative Democracy: Principles and Genealogy* (London: University of Chicago Press).

Van Parijs, P. (2004) 'Basic Income: A Simple and Powerful Idea for the Twenty-First Century', *Politics and Society*, 32, 7–38.

Van Parijs, P. (2011) *Linguistic Justice for Europe and for the World* (Oxford: Oxford University Press).

Waldron, J. (1987) 'Nonsense upon Stilts: A Reply', in J. Waldron (ed.), *Nonsense Upon Stilts: Bentham, Burke and Marx on the Rights of Man* (London: Meuthen), 151–209.

Waldron, J. (1991) 'Homelessness and the Issue of Freedom', *UCLA Law Review*, 39, 295–324.

Waldron, J. (1993) *Liberal Rights: Collected Papers 1981-1991* (Cambridge: Cambridge University Press).

Waldron, J. (1995) 'Minority Cultures and the Cosmopolitan Alternative', in W. Kymlicka (ed.), *The Rights of Minority Cultures* (Oxford: Oxford University Press).

Waldron, J. (1999) *Law and Disagreement* (Oxford: Oxford University Press).

Waldron, J. (2000) 'What is Cosmopolitan', *Journal of Political Philosophy*, 8, 227–43.

Walzer, M. (1983) *Spheres of Justice* (New York: Basic Books).

Walzer, M. (1997) *On Toleration* (New Haven, CT: Yale University Press).

Walzer, M. (2004) *Politics and Passion: Toward a More Egalitarian Liberalism* (New Haven, CT: Yale University Press).

Warren, M. (1996) 'What Should We Expect From More Democracy? Radically Democratic Responses to Politics', *Political Theory*, 24, 241–70.

Warren, M. (2007) 'Institutionalizing Deliberative Democracy', in S. Rosenberg (ed.), *Can the People Govern? Deliberation, Participation, and Democracy* (Basingstoke: Palgrave Macmillan), 272–88.

Weale, A. (2007) *Democracy*, Second edition (Basingstoke: Palgrave Macmillan).

Weber, M. (1978) *Economy and Society*, ed. G. Roth & C. Wittich (Berkeley, CA: University of California Press).

Weldon, T. D. (1953) *The Vocabulary of Politics* (London: Penguin).

Wellman, C. (1995) *Real Rights* (Oxford: Oxford University Press).

Wenar, L. (2005) 'The Nature of Rights', *Philosophy and Public Affairs*, 33, 223–53.

White, A. (1984) *Rights* (Oxford: Clarendon Press).

White, S. K. (2000) *Sustaining Affirmation: The Strengths of Weak Ontology in Political Theory* (Princeton, NJ: Princeton University Press).

White, S. K. (2003) 'After Critique: Affirming Subjectivity in Contemporary Political Theory', *European Journal of Political Theory*, 2, 209–26.

Widder, N. (2012) *Political Theory After Deleuze* (London: Continuum).

Williams, A. (1998) 'Incentives, Inequality, and Publicity', *Philosophy and Public Affairs*, 27, 225–47.

Williams, B. (1962) 'The Idea of Equality', in P. Laslett & W. G. Runciman (eds.), *Philosophy, Politics and Society*, Second series (Oxford: Blackwell), 110–31.

Williams, B. (1973) 'A Critique of Utilitarianism', in J. J. C. Smart & B. Williams (ed.), *Utilitarianism: For and Against* (Cambridge: Cambridge University Press), 77–150.

Williams, B. (2005) *In the Beginning was the Deed: Realism and Moralism in Political Argument*, ed. Geoffrey Hawthorn (Princeton, NJ: Princeton University Press).

Williams, M. (1998) *Voice, Trust and Memory: Marginalised Groups and the Failings of Liberal Representation* (Princeton, NJ: Princeton University Press).

Wolff, J. (1998) 'Fairness, Respect and the Egalitarian Ethos', *Philosophy and Public Affairs*, 27, 97–122.

Wolff, J. (2010) 'Fairness, Respect and the Egalitarian Ethos Revisited', *The Journal of Ethics*, 14, 335–50.

Wolfinger, R. E. (1960) 'Reputation and Reality in the Study of "Community Power"', *American Sociological Review*, 25, 636–44.

Wollheim, R. (1962) 'A Paradox in the Theory of Democracy', in P. Laslett & W. G. Runciman (eds.), *Philosophy Politics and Society*, Second series (Oxford: Blackwell), 71–87.

Yack, B. (2002) 'Multiculturalism and the Political Theorists', *European Journal of Political Theory*, 1, 107–19.

Yack, B. (2012) *Nationalism and the Moral Psychology of Community* (Chicago, IL: University of Chicago Press).

Young, I. (1989) 'Polity and Group Difference: A Critique of the Ideal of Universal Citizenship', *Ethics*, 99, 250–74.

Young, I. (1990) *Justice and the Politics of Difference* (Princeton, NJ: Princeton University Press).

Young, I. (1996) 'Communication and the Other: Beyond Deliberative Democracy', in S. Benhabib (ed.), *Democracy and Difference* (Princeton, NJ: Princeton University Press).

Young, I. (1997) 'Deferring Group Representation', in I. Shapiro & W. Kymlicka (eds.), *NOMOS XXXIX: Ethnicity and Group Rights* (New York: New York University Press), 349–76.

Young, I. (2000) *Inclusion and Democracy* (Oxford: Oxford University Press).

Young, I. (2010) *Responsibility for Justice* (Oxford: Oxford University Press).

Index

Lightning Source UK Ltd.
Milton Keynes UK
UKHW020441040722
405334UK00006B/287